Migration Impacts of Trade and Foreign Investment

Series on Development and International Migration in Mexico, Central America, and the Caribbean Basin

Sergio Díaz-Briquets and Sidney Weintraub,
Series Editors

Volume I
*Determinants of Emigration from Mexico,
Central America, and the Caribbean*

Volume II
*Regional and Sectoral Development in Mexico
as Alternatives to Migration*

Volume III
*Migration Impacts of Trade and Foreign Investment:
Mexico and Caribbean Basin Countries*

FORTHCOMING

Volume IV
*International Migration, Remittances,
and Small Business Development in Mexico
and Caribbean Basin Countries*

Volume V
*Small Country Development and International Labor Flows:
Experiences in Central America and the Caribbean,*
edited by Anthony P. Maingot

Volume VI
Receiving Country Policies and Migration Flows

Migration Impacts of Trade and Foreign Investment

Mexico and Caribbean Basin Countries

EDITED BY

Sergio Díaz-Briquets and Sidney Weintraub

Westview Press

BOULDER • SAN FRANCISCO • OXFORD

Series on Development and International Migration in Mexico, Central America, and the Caribbean Basin

Copyright © 1991 by Westview Press, Inc.

Published in 1991 in the United States of America by Westview Press, Inc., 5500 Central Avenue, Boulder, Colorado 80301, and in the United Kingdom by Westview Press, 36 Lonsdale Road, Summertown, Oxford OX2 7EW

Library of Congress Cataloging-in-Publication Data
Migration impacts of trade and foreign investment : Mexico and
  Caribbean basin countries / edited by Sergio Díaz-Briquets and
Sidney Weintraub.
     p. cm.— (Series on development and international migration
in Mexico, Central America, and the Caribbean Basin ; 3)
  Includes bibliographical references.
  ISBN 0-8133-8339-0
  1. Foreign trade and employment—Caribbean Area. 2. Foreign trade
and employment—Mexico. 3. Investments, Foreign, and employment—
Caribbean Area. 4. Investments, Foreign, and employment—Mexico.
5. Caribbean Area—Commercial policy. 6. Mexico—Commercial policy.
7. Exports—Caribbean Area. 8. Exports—Mexico. I. Díaz-Briquets,
Sergio. II. Weintraub, Sidney, 1922–   . III. Series.
HD5710.75.C27M54 1991
304.8′09729—dc20   91–8057
                                                                     CIP

Printed and bound in the United States of America

The paper used in this publication meets the requirements of the American National Standard for Permanence of Paper for Printed Library Materials Z39.48-1984.

10   9   8   7   6   5   4   3   2   1

Contents

Series Preface

The Immigration Reform and Control Act of 1986 (IRCA) was a manifestation of widespread public concern over the volume of undocumented immigration into the United States. The principal innovation of this legislation—the provision to impose penalties on employers who knowingly hire undocumented immigrants—was a response to this concern.

This effort at restriction was tempered in IRCA by other provisions permitting the legalization of two types of undocumented immigrants—those who had resided in the United States since January 1, 1982; and what were called special agricultural workers (SAWs), persons who had worked in perishable crop agriculture for at least 90 days during specified periods from 1983 to 1986. Approximately 3.1 million persons sought legalization (what is popularly referred to as amnesty) under these two provisions. The breakdown was roughly 1.8 million under the regular program and 1.3 million as SAWs. Mexicans made up 75 percent of the combined legalization requests.

Two elements—punishment and exoneration—were essential ingredients of the compromise that made possible the passage of IRCA, but they also had the effect of working at cross purposes, at least temporarily. For a time, many persons who might have crossed the border without papers took the opportunity to regularize their status and thus enter legally. In our research we discovered many non-farmers who had not earlier considered temporary migration but who obtained papers as SAWs to enter the United States. Officials of the U.S. Immigration and Naturalization Service (INS) asserted that there was widespread fraud under the SAWs program for applicants from Mexico and elsewhere. We verified from the Mexican side of the border that, indeed, there was fraud, but our evidence does not permit making an estimate of its magnitude. The two provisions together did not slow immigration but instead permitted some switching from undocumented to documented border crossing. During the period that legalization applications could be submitted, therefore, data showing a decline in unauthorized border crossings (apprehensions) were deceptive.

In due course, however, undocumented immigration began to pick up again, and apprehension data and other evidence now indicate that it is at a level similar to that before enactment of IRCA. There is ample proof of the production of fraudulent documents permitting immigrants to show employers that they are "legally" in the United States. It is probably impossible to end this entrepreneurial document production short of instituting a foolproof identity card, assuming the word "foolproof" is an accurate characterization of technology. The idea of Americans having to show an identity card when seeking employment has not been accepted.

It is an overstatement to say definitively that IRCA has failed to accomplish its main task, to staunch the flow of undocumented immigrants by means of penalties on employers, but that is the initial conclusion one must reach. Its failure means that the available options for reducing the inflow of undocumented immigrants—assuming this is still the U.S. goal—are reduced by the one option that was earlier considered the most promising.

An identity card is not acceptable. A high fence, patrolled by armed guards keeping persons without papers from entering the United States, would be unacceptably obtrusive and also alter the relationship with Mexico. It would be anomalous to forcefully close the border to people at the same time the United States and Mexico are planning to open the border to the free flow of goods and services.

There thus remains only one feasible option—short of leaving bad enough alone and letting those who wish to come do so—and that is to foster the economic development of those countries that send the bulk of undocumented migrants to the United States. If punishment is not the solution, then perhaps development is.

We did not know development was really the only option when this research project was started. However, IRCA had a little-noticed provision that established the Commission for the Study of International Migration and Cooperative Economic Development with the following mandate:

> The Commission, in consultation with the governments of Mexico and other sending countries in the Western Hemisphere, shall examine the conditions in Mexico and such other sending countries which contribute to unauthorized migration to the United States and [shall explore] mutually beneficial, reciprocal trade and investment programs to alleviate such conditions.

THE RESEARCH PROGRAM

The research program of the Commission focused on two broad themes: why people emigrate from their own countries to enter clandestinely into the United States, and what cooperative development measures are most appropriate to reduce the economic incentive to emigrate. More emphasis in the research was placed on the second of these two issues, particularly job creation in migrant-sending countries, because there was already ample scholarly literature on the motives for emigration. These motives are not solely economic, but evidence from years of research demonstrates clearly that the economic dominates.

We have culled the research supported by the Commission to sort out those essays that we think make valuable contributions to the literature on the relationship between development and migration. The authors of the essays are experts in this field from migrant-sending countries, Europe, and the United States. The essays selected are organized into six volumes, each dealing with a specific aspect of the development theme; each volume is therefore self-contained. In our judgment, the six volumes together make the most original contribution that exists to date on the development-migration relationship. We are gratified that Westview Press reached a similar conclusion and wished to publish the series.

Both editors were involved in the research program of the Commission: Sergio Díaz-Briquets as research director and Sidney Weintraub as senior research adviser. Our motive in bringing out the series is to provide scholars with a base of research from which they can delve further into the development-migration nexus.

As the listing of the series shows, one volume (Volume II) deals exclusively with Mexico, and three others (Volumes I, III, and IV) with Mexico and with other countries in Central America and the Caribbean. For the sake of convenience, we use the phrase Caribbean Basin to refer to the collectivity of countries in this region. The emphasis on Mexico is warranted by the evidence that Mexicans constitute about 70 percent of the unauthorized immigrants in the United States. Volume V deals with Central America and the Caribbean, and the final volume (Volume VI) with U.S. policies relating to development in and emigration from Mexico and other countries of the Caribbean Basin. Although we take responsibility as senior editors for all the volumes, the editor for Volume V is Anthony P. Maingot. The final volume contains the executive summary of the report of the Commission submitted to the Congress and the president.

The essays deal mostly with migrant-sending countries in the Western Hemisphere because that was the Commission's mandate and because the bulk of undocumented immigrants into the United States come from Mexico and other countries of the Caribbean Basin. However, the Western Hemisphere emphasis is not exclusive, and several comparative essays on receiving-country policies in Europe are included in Volume VI.

KEY OVERALL FINDINGS

Although research conclusions in the specific areas are discussed in each volume, some overall findings merit emphasis. The most important is the one already stated: that no viable alternative to economic development seems to exist that would significantly reduce undocumented immigration into the United States. It is hardly original to state that as a country becomes better developed, the economic pressure to emigrate is likely to be reduced. Historically, the development thesis has been demonstrated, particularly in Western Europe where countries of emigration became lands of immigration. Western Europe is now coping with its own undocumented, or unwanted, immigrants. Ireland, which has not enjoyed as much sustained growth as other countries in Western Europe, is still a country from which people emigrate. We observed, over time, that domestic economic well-being in European countries overcame the strength of networks in perpetuating outward migration.

Skeptics (including us) acknowledged the need for development, but they argued that it took too long to be relevant for dealing with current problems of undocumented immigration or, indeed, with anticipated migration movements over the next several decades. We do not know what income differential stimulates undocumented migration; nor do we know how much narrowing of this differential is necessary to deter emigration. We do know, however, that the difference between $1,900 and $19,000 a year—which are the respective 1990 per capita incomes in Mexico and the United States—is a stimulant to emigration. Completely closing this gap, even under wondrous estimates of Mexican economic growth, is apt to take more than 100 years. This is not the kind of assessment a policy maker likes to hear.

Yet, it is to this advice that our research leads. Sherlock Holmes was fond of saying that if all explanations but one to a conundrum must be discarded, then that one must contain the answer. This is the conclusion we reach. If emigration cannot be curtailed by other means, then the remaining viable option must be exploited; and it really does not matter if policy makers and legislators with a short-term outlook grumble at this conclusion.

The saving grace is that incomes do not have to be identical to act as a deterrent to clandestine migration. There is a natural desire of most persons to remain at home, which can be reinforced if economic hope is offered to would-be migrants and their children. We suspect, based on the research contained in the series, that absolute income differentials may matter less in the migrate-stay calculus than the direction of economic hope (that is, whether economic conditions at home are improving or deteriorating). We are not referring here to improved economic conditions for one year or two, but sustained over a decade or so.

The importance of sustaining economic growth over some unquantifiable time period must be emphasized. What we found in study after study was that a short-term increase in income, over one or two years, leads to increased emigration. We came across no study that contradicted this finding. The reason, presumably, is that a modest increase in income makes it possible for people to afford the trip. If, as in the Mexican case, income per person increases by, say, 3 percent after inflation, this adds only $57 to the annual income of the average Mexican. Even this overstates the case; the "average" Mexican, some 50 percent of the population, earns much less than $1,000 a year. An increase in income of $57 or less is not enough to deter the economic incentive to emigrate. But adding 3 percent a year, compounded over 10 or 20 years, might make a difference.

The conclusion that it requires continued economic growth to have a meaningful influence on curtailing emigration has as its corollary that the "cooperative" U.S. policy contained in the Commission's mandate must also be sustained. Although development is essentially an internal responsibility, and Mexico and other countries in the region are taking many needed steps to restructure their economies, the external environment plays a decisive role. This is not the place for a detailed discussion of U.S. economic policy except to note that if sustained economic growth is required in sending countries to reduce emigration pressures, then U.S. measures that frustrate this growth (particularly trade protectionism but also U.S. macroeconomic policy that slows U.S. growth or pushes up the interest rate that sending countries must pay on their foreign debt) will stimulate undocumented immigration. If the current push toward free trade between Mexico and the United States serves to augment the growth of income and employment in Mexico, it will also have a long-term effect of curtailing emigration pressure. Free trade between the United States and other countries of the region is a less immediate prospect, but it too may eventually help to stimulate the growth of income and employment of these nations.

One other overall conclusion that emerges from the research is that the economic development process as it has been pursued, certainly in the period since World War II, has stimulated internal migration. In country after country, the rural-urban population relationship has shifted in favor of the urban part of the ratio. Cities have burgeoned as the relative role of agriculture has diminished. Manufacturing and services have grown in importance compared with agriculture. This is the normal pattern of development, as witness the historical experience of Europe and the United States. Habits of migration have thus become commonplace in sending countries in the Western Hemisphere, as elsewhere. Although it is more traumatic to pick up stakes and leave one's own country than to shift within the country, the difference is a matter of degree. Once networks, or ethnic diasporas, have been established in the United States, as they generally have for migrant-sending countries in the Western Hemisphere, even the difference of degree between internal and external migration diminishes. Thus, the number of undocumented immigrants to the United States should not be expected to diminish for the foreseeable future; and this fact increases the importance of sustained economic growth to keep people home.

The relative importance of Mexico as a sending country may decline in coming decades because its economic prospects are more auspicious than those of other countries in the region, particularly in Central America. In addition, migrant networks in the United States have now been established for Central American countries.

Populations in the migrant-sending countries are quite young, and none of these countries is creating enough jobs to satisfy all persons entering the labor force. This situation, once more, points to the primacy of economic growth as the necessary deterrent to emigration.

We have been struck in our investigations by how extensively people in the world are on the move. Our studies concentrated on the movement of people in the Western Hemisphere to the United States, but there are large migrations within Africa and Asia, and into Western Europe from the east (the former Communist countries) and the south (such as from North Africa into France and Italy). It is easier—not easy, but easier—to control immigration into Western Europe than it is into the United States, to which migrants can come across a large land border with Mexico. Yet the West Europeans are not having much success either in dealing with their immigration problem. As with the United States, the key to control is development in the sending countries. We are dealing, in other words, with a global phenomenon. The subject presents itself as a migration issue, but at its core it is a development matter.

WHAT COMES NEXT

The proper approach to development must differ from country to country—even apart from the conceptual or ideological model that is used. Mexico is a large, populous country in which there is scope for regional differentiation. This approach is not available to any meaningful extent for other countries in the Caribbean Basin. Mexico has a substantial industrial structure on which to base export-led growth, as it is now doing. The industrial structure is more modest in Central America and hardly exists in much of the Caribbean.

Overall findings of the type set forth in this preface can take a policy maker only so far. Understanding the link between development and migration, and then making policy to influence both phenomena, requires intimate knowledge of conditions in sub-regions and in each country. This is provided in the six volumes in this series.

Our objectives in bringing out these volumes are twofold: to augment understanding of the development-migration relationship based on the extensive research that was carried out; and, much more importantly in the long run, to stimulate further scholarly research about this theme.

Sergio Díaz-Briquets
Sidney Weintraub

Introduction

Sergio Díaz-Briquets
and Sidney Weintraub

The premise of the chapters in this volume is that, over time, emigration pressures can be reduced only by sustained economic growth—and this, in turn, requires higher levels of investment and exports. However, it was demonstrated in the first volume of this series that the relationship between development and emigration is complex. Economic development is destabilizing and, in its initial stages, facilitates rather than deters population mobility. Only with the passage of time, as income levels and working conditions rise appreciably and expectations for a better future set in, will the pressure to emigrate decline.

The United States, for a variety of reasons mostly unrelated to emigration, has long encouraged direct foreign investment. Although the United States has a number of import restrictions affecting developing country exports, the general thrust of U.S. policy has been to encourage imports of manufactured goods from these nations. Limits on textile and apparel imports are an example of restrictions, although tariff preferences for developing country exports in general show U.S. openness. On the whole, the United States is much more open than other industrial countries to imports of manufactured goods from developing countries.

Trade and industrial policy is directly linked to migration in some instances. The Mexican Border Industrialization Program (BIP) was instituted to provide jobs for what was expected to be a large number of *braceros* returning from the United States in the mid-1960s. Favorable U.S. treatment of imports from plants established under BIP reinforced the purpose of the Mexican policy. When President Ronald Reagan proposed an increase in trade preferences to beneficiary nations under the Caribbean Basin Initiative (CBI), he cited the dampening of emigration pressures as one objective.

This volume examines the elusive relationship between investment and trade on the one hand and emigration on the other, focusing on selected aspects of the theme as they relate to Mexico and other Caribbean Basin countries. All the chapters in this volume were completed before Presidents Carlos Salinas de Gortari and George Bush announced their intention to enter into free-trade talks. President Bush's "Enterprise for the Americas"—contemplating debt reduction, increased investment, and eventual free trade from "Anchorage to Tierra del Fuego "—came after these chapters were written. However, many of the recommendations in these chapters address the same issues as those addressed by the proposals of the two presidents.

The first chapter, by Gregory K. Schoepfle and Jorge F. Pérez-López, provides an overview of export assembly operations that have sprung up in Mexico and the Caribbean Basin. The first of these programs was the Mexican BIP cited earlier, which led to the establishment of what are now about 1,500 *maquiladoras*—as these assembly plants are known in Mexico—mostly along Mexico's northern border. Other countries later took steps to encourage the establishment of free-trade zones and to attract foreign investment.

Growth of export assembly operations was facilitated by several U.S. tariff provisions. Among the most significant of these is the Generalized System of Preferences (GSP), which extends duty-free import treatment to several thousand items imported from approximately 140 countries. Mexico is one of the major beneficiaries of GSP. Under items 9802.00.60 and 9802.00.80 (formerly tariff items 806.30 and 807.00) of the harmonized U.S. tariff system, which have been in effect since 1963, U.S. import duties are levied only on the value added abroad of products made with U.S. components. Once again, Mexico is a major beneficiary of this global program, as are many other countries in the Caribbean Basin. The Caribbean Basin Economic Recovery Act (CBERA), better known as the CBI, was first approved in 1983 and then extended in 1990. It provides for nonreciprocal, duty-free treatment for selected imports from most Central American and Caribbean countries (in this case, excluding Mexico).

Schoepfle and Pérez-López demonstrate how important export assembly operations have become to the economies of Mexico and other Caribbean Basin nations. The growth of assembly operations has been especially significant because it took place when these countries were confronting grave domestic economic difficulties. In Mexico the *maquiladoras* now provide more than 450,000 jobs and generate $3 billion in value added. In the Dominican Republic, assembly operations are the source of half of all manufacturing jobs. Export assembly operations also lead indirectly to the creation of many jobs in firms that supply them with needed goods and services.

Schoepfle and Pérez-López point out that, despite their indirect job creation, export assembly operations have a shortcoming: They function largely as enclaves with limited linkages to national economies. Their potential to become more fully integrated into the mainstream economy is much greater in Mexico, which has a relatively sophisticated industrial base, than in the much smaller and industrially more backward Caribbean and Central American countries.

The chapter concludes with an assessment of controversies surrounding the impact that offshore export assembly operations have on U.S. competitiveness and employment. The authors believe that "movement offshore of certain labor-intensive operations . . . may be fairly small as a percentage of total employment in those industries." However, they also cite a study by the U.S. International Trade Commission that found that decisions by U.S. firms to produce offshore were based largely on the existence there of a low-wage and trainable work force and adequate infrastructure.

Stephen Lande and Nellis Crigler consider policy options to increase exports from Mexico and Caribbean Basin countries to the United States in order to increase employment and improve living conditions in these nations. In addition to analyzing trade relations between these countries and the United States, Lande and Crigler stress the importance of multilateral programs, such as those of the European Community and the General Agreement on Tariffs and Trade (GATT). Lande and Crigler continually remind the reader that trade initiatives are weakened by pressure groups with narrow interests. They cite U.S. sugar policy as a particularly flagrant example of trade policy that aids domestic growers at the expense of the consumer and of many Caribbean Basin countries that the United States presumably wishes to benefit with its preferential trade programs. They suggest ways to partially overcome special interest protectionism affecting exports of Mexico and other Caribbean Basin countries.

Stuart K. Tucker assesses the employment potential of trade expansion in Caribbean Basin countries. He puts into perspective the accomplishments of U.S. trade preference programs (such as that reviewed by Schoepfle and Pérez-López for export assembly products) and the economic benefit that could result if they were enhanced along the lines recommended by Lande and Crigler. He concludes, however, that even under the best circumstances, export expansion cannot generate sufficient employment opportunities in most countries in the region for currently unemployed persons and new entrants into the labor force. Prospects for sufficient employment creation are more promising in some countries such as Costa Rica and the Dominican Republic, but only if recent growth in manufactured exports is sustained.

Tucker concludes that over the medium term, "the countries of Central America and the Caribbean should not rely upon export-led growth only within the manufacturing sector [but that] a large majority of new employment . . . must be generated by agricultural exports and by production (manufacturing as well as agricultural) for domestic consumption." This requires a broad-based development strategy geared to the employment needs of the region in which foreign assistance continues to play a crucial role. It also calls for the elimination of U.S. trade barriers for those goods that the region can produce competitively.

With the purpose of promoting investment in Puerto Rico, Section 936 of the U.S. Internal Revenue Code exempts from taxation revenues generated by certain U.S. corporations operating there. Section 936 is challenged from time to time as providing businesses with an unwarranted tax loophole (resulting in the loss of about $15 billion in uncollected revenue in the late 1980s), especially during times of fiscal austerity. Puerto Rico now allows a portion of 936 funds to be invested in selected Caribbean countries as a complement to the CBI and as part of Puerto Rico's twin-plant program with other countries in the region. The rationale for broadening the program was that Section 936 funds could satisfy a substantial share of Caribbean Basin investment needs and, at the same time, support the development of Puerto Rico.

The broadening has not generated the expected investment because of the reluctance of private entrepreneurs to allocate substantial sums to the Caribbean Basin. One proposal for overcoming this reluctance is to permit the Puerto Rican Government Development Bank (by law it must receive 15 percent of 936 funds) to invest some of its 936 deposits in development projects in Caribbean Basin countries. However, even if this proposal was to be implemented, it is doubtful that sizeable investments would flow to Caribbean Basin countries. Many potential beneficiary countries could not host 936 projects because current guidelines call for targeting investments to export operations, which are not plentiful in many of the small economies of the region. Section 936 investments are intended for short- and medium-term programs and are therefore not suitable for infrastructure development.

Ramón Daubón proposes that the emphasis of 936 on lending exclusively to export operations be changed to encourage lending to small businesses producing for local and regional markets. Because the risk of failure is great for small local producers, Daubón suggests that a special fund be created whose loans would be guaranteed by Puerto Rico's Government Development Bank, the U.S. Overseas Private Investment Corporation (OPIC), the U.S. Agency for International Development (USAID), and the depositors themselves. Daubón feels that the promotion of small businesses with domestic and regional trade linkages will encourage regional development. An important premise of Daubón's analysis is that strengthening regional entrepreneurship will discourage emigration. His reasoning is that broadly based economies will provide much local employment and promote self-sustaining development.

Susan M. Kramer examines incentives and impediments encountered by investors in the Caribbean Basin. She conducted extensive interviews with representatives of U.S. firms doing business in the Dominican

Republic and Jamaica. She found that trade incentives provided by the United States (CBI, for example) and host country investment incentives, together with the availability of an inexpensive labor supply, are the main reasons why the firms examined had invested in these two countries. An added incentive in Jamaica is the availability of government-sponsored worker training programs.

The main impediments identified by Kramer were related to inadequate infrastructure and to frustrating procedures that interfere with the conduct of business. In both countries, but particularly in the Dominican Republic, the erratic electricity supply is a major problem. Another disincentive was the lack of spread industries—those providing products to the export assembly plants, and others buying the output of these plants—and the inability of most foreign firms to purchase replacement parts locally. Investors in Jamaica also must contend with smugglers concealing drugs in bona fide export shipments. Kramer concludes that the investment climate in these two countries could be improved considerably by "the development or extension of labor training programs, streamlining of customs and governmental procedures, and improvements in utilities provision—specifically for electricity generation."

The next three chapters focus on Mexico, examining various aspects of how that country's trade opening is related to its industrial and export performance in recent years. María de Lourdes de la Fuente Deschamps examines trends in the sectoral composition of exports and compares employment performance in industries producing for export and for domestic consumption. Using data from sample enterprises included in the Monthly Industrial Survey of the National Institute of Statistics, she compares how export firms fared in relation to nonexporting firms during two periods, January–June 1985 and January 1987–March 1989. The first period antedates the most aggressive export promotion policies, while the second reflects a post-opening period. Deschamps also presents the results of a series of statistical models built around four scenarios of global economic performance and the degree of Mexican protectionism in order to evaluate the likely long-run effects of the liberalized trade regime.

Deschamps finds that in the post-opening period overall production indicators, number of workers, and number of hours worked increased more significantly in exporting than in nonexporting firms. She found, however, that real wage growth rates were similar, most likely because export growth was made possible by the use of existing but idle productive capacity. She found that "the opening of trade has favored investment and creation of jobs in the export sector of the economy relative to the nonexport sector . . . At the same time, production processes have become more capital intensive during the period studied, with a concurrent improvement in labor productivity." Export performance, in general, was highly sensitive to policy measures (the exchange rate and level of protection); under policies designed to promote exports, Deschamps concludes that Mexico's export growth can be continued. However, export outcomes will vary from industry to industry.

Based on her econometric models, Deschamps concludes that "the industries with the highest probabilities of exporting are, in general, those that have high imports of intermediate and capital goods, a high flow of direct foreign investment, favorable relative prices and moderately low effective protection."

Alejandro Ibarra-Yunez and Chandler Stolp examine many of the same issues addressed by Deschamps, but with a different methodology. They focused more on the extent to which exports contribute to employment generation. Their findings generally concur with Deschamps's conclusions, but Ibarra-Yunez and Stolp draw attention to the issue of market substitution. Their contention is that if the employment growth associated with exports results from a reallocation of resources from domestic production, then the employment gains are less significant than suggested by employment trends in export industries alone.

Ibarra-Yunez and Stolp note that the surge in Mexican exports in the 1980s involved goods with high capital-to-labor ratios—a conclusion similar to that of Deschamps. They argue that this development might not be consistent with Mexico's labor-absorption needs unless capital acts as a complement rather than as a substitute for labor. The findings of the study suggest that the complementary role of capital is indeed being enhanced as the trade opening deepens. The findings are consistent with Deschamps conclusion that the growth of exports served to cushion the impact of the domestic crisis in production and employment as idle capacity was mobilized to produce for external markets. Ibarra-Yunez and Stolp stress that if Mexico is to take full advantage of market substitution, external markets must remain accessible and investment funds be readily available. These two conditions can be met if negotiations for a U.S.-Mexico free-trade agreement succeed. The authors also view the upgrading of Mexico's labor force as imperative if Mexico is to take full advantage of a more competitive global environment.

Kurt Unger examines how U.S. transnational corporations accommodated to the economic crisis and to Mexico's trade opening. His research deals with the manner in which manufactured goods are exported, whether through intra-firm or nonrelated party transactions. Unger's study reveals that Mexico's most modern and dynamic exports take place mostly through intra-firm transactions under which related firms (a parent and a wholly or partially owned subsidiary, for example, or from a contracted captive) sell to each other.

Unger's analysis, based on trade statistics and interviews with executives of transnational corporations, indicates that U.S. transnational corporations play a big role in Mexican trade, accounting for more than 40 percent of manufactured exports. U.S. firms in Mexico are concentrated in new-modern industries (this is a classification set forth by the United Nations Industrial Development Organization), while Mexican exporters dominate traditional and resource-based industries. Unger cautions that future high export rates may not be sustainable unless new investments are forthcoming to expand plant capacity.

Unger is pessimistic about the prospects for new investment because "decisions [by transnational corporations] to build Mexican plants are not based solely on the nation's competitive advantage [but] . . . on very complex motivations." Unger argues that transnational corporations decide how much and where to produce based on global strategies about how to serve regional markets and how best to use existing capacities.

Although it is too soon to reach conclusions about Unger's prediction, the pace of foreign investment in Mexico appears to have quickened. In addition, the prospect of a free-trade agreement with the United States will almost certainly lead to a further increase in investments by transnational corporations in Mexico.

The impact of economic crisis on the industrial restructuring of Mexico is assessed by Carlos Alba Vega and Bryan Roberts, who use data from industrial surveys conducted at various times in the state of Jalisco, especially the city of Guadalajara. Guadalajara is Mexico's second most populous city and one of the most important industrial centers of the country. It fared relatively well during the hard times of the 1980s, as firms re-oriented production from internal to external markets, and as some firms reduced production costs through informal subcontracting (i.e., hiring small producers in the informal market to obtain inputs into their own production). These developments, the rise in exports and the increasing informalization of production, led to polarization of the labor market. Employment opportunities for professionals and skilled workers became more abundant in the medium-to-large export firms, but scarcer in smaller firms catering to domestic needs.

Subcontracting by large to small firms is an important feature of industrial production in Guadalajara, and there is no evidence that such subcontracting increased between 1981 and 1989. Small firm employment has been reduced by competition from imports coming into Mexico since the trade opening. Labor rotation in these firms is high and rising, due perhaps to low real wages and the attraction of migrating to Mexico's border region or to the United States. Whereas in the 1970s informal employment "served to help households 'make it' in the city, permitting mobility to stable formal sector jobs and generating incomes that allowed families to educate their children . . . (in the 1980s) informal employment is more likely to lead to the reproduction of poverty and marginality."

Alba Vega and Roberts draw an important lesson from Guadalajara's experience: Although export promotion was accompanied by employment creation, it tended to accentuate labor market fragmentation and to weaken the small and informal labor shops that historically served to train new job entrants and provide the means for families to educate children—and, thus, future generations of skilled workers may not be forthcoming. This pool of skilled workers had always been important to the region's industrial growth, enabling Guadalajara to weather economic crises. But as small producers failed and real incomes declined, young workers were forced to seek jobs requiring low skills and forego training opportunities. This outcome points to the need for policy measures to revitalize the small- and medium-scale production sector.

William Glade, in the last chapter, examines the employment consequences of privatizing state-owned firms, one of the most politically volatile elements of Mexico's economic restructuring. His conclusions, based on the review of conflicting data from official Mexican sources and of the experiences of other Latin American countries, are not definitive. Disentangling what effects privatization has on employment trends is difficult because many other variables are simultaneously involved.

Glade believes that over the long term, privatization should lead to greater employment. As inefficient and costly state-owned enterprises are privatized, the economy will become more responsive to market forces. This should result in a more efficient allocation of investment and, hence, in faster growth and increased employment. Over the short and medium terms, however, privatization could have the opposite effect as redundant workers are let go and unprofitable plants are shut down.

The chapters in this volume tend to affirm the conclusion that although increases in direct foreign investment and exports are essential to Mexican and Caribbean Basin growth and to the long-term reduction of undocumented migration, these strategies are not sufficient by themselves to achieve either goal. The export-led growth policy that practically all of these countries is pursuing must be complemented by efforts to develop their internal markets.

Key to the success of these policies is the restructuring of economic institutions, including stifling bureaucracies, to make these countries more attractive to foreign and domestic investors. Mexico, Costa Rica, and other countries are well on their way toward this goal. In most countries, such changes are difficult to carry out in the face of opposition from powerful economic and political vested interests.

It is in the long-term interest of the United States to complement the programs of these countries by removing trade barriers, even when such action is opposed by the domestic pressure groups in the United States. A North American (United States/Canada/Mexico) free-trade arrangement, and potentially a free-trade agreement including all countries in the Western hemisphere (proposed by President Bush), augur well for the elimination of trade barriers. Achieving the desired outcome is not at all certain, nor will benefits flow in equal proportions to all countries. In any event—even if countries do meet their current economic growth objectives—emigration pressures will persist for many years to come.

1

Employment Implications of Export Assembly Operations in Mexico and the Caribbean Basin

Gregory K. Schoepfle
and Jorge F. Pérez-López

I. INTRODUCTION

Often lacking the necessary infrastructure for industrialization, but having abundant labor resources, some developing economies have recently adopted new development strategies. Such strategies aim to attract investment in export-oriented assembly operations that promote domestic employment opportunities, foreign exchange earnings and local development.

One institutional arrangement that has become increasingly popular in promoting assembly operations is the "export processing zone." Developing countries have established export processing zones (EPZs) as special enclaves to attract foreign investment through various incentives such as the waiver of import tariffs, tax holidays, subsidized rental of industrial shelters and other infrastructure, etc. In many cases, these assembly operations have become a dynamic source of employment generation in these countries.

The expansion of EPZs in developing countries, however, may not necessarily be the *sine qua non* for industrialization. Firms operating in these zones often are not integrated into the domestic economy and, in many cases, are precluded from selling their output in the host country's domestic market. This separation of domestic and export markets raises questions as to whether the full benefits of these investments are being realized and how long their benefits will continue. While assembly operations may provide immediate employment for large pools of unemployed workers, they often replace jobs that previously had added more value and earned more foreign exchange in primary-commodity export production (e.g., sugar). In many cases, new entrants (especially young women) have been attracted into the labor force; this may have important social implications.

On the other hand, the expansion of EPZs in developing countries is seen by many as a positive vehicle to foster industrialization, develop a work ethic, and develop potential backward linkages that encourage economic growth.

This paper focuses on export-oriented assembly operations in Mexico and the Caribbean Basin, preferred locations for assembly facilities of U.S. manufacturers. First, export-oriented assembly facilities in Mexico and the Caribbean Basin are described briefly. Next, trends in U.S. imports from Mexico and the Caribbean Basin are examined with special emphasis on products assembled from U.S.-origin components. Then, the employment implications of export-oriented assembly operations on both host country employment and U.S. employment are discussed. The paper closes with some general observations about the growth in offshore assembly operations that export products containing U.S. components to the U.S. market.

II. EXPORT-ORIENTED ASSEMBLY OPERATIONS IN MEXICO AND THE CARIBBEAN BASIN

By far, the largest concentration of export-oriented assembly operations in Mexico and the Caribbean Basin take place in export processing zones. EPZs are enclaves within a national customs territory into which foreign capital goods, components, and materials can be brought duty-free. Host governments generally grant fiscal and other incentives to companies that locate in these enclaves. Imported components and materials are processed within EPZs—typically they are assembled into a finished product—and then exported. Customs duties are not assessed on the imported components *unless* the final goods into which they are assembled enter the national customs territory of the host country.[1] The basic factors underlying EPZs (duty-free importation of equipment and materials, incentives to attract investors) are also present in other forms of export-oriented facilities that are not necessarily located in an enclave industrial park, special economic zone or customs in-bond territory.

Mexico

Established in 1965, the Mexican *maquiladoras*, or in-bond assembly plants, are among the oldest and most developed assembly operations in the Caribbean region. Initially, Mexico established a special customs regime for operations located in a 20-kilometer strip along the Mexico-United States border. Plants established in this area could import in-bond (i.e., without paying duty) foreign-made components or metal products to be assembled or further processed in Mexico and then exported. Similarly, imported machinery, equipment, raw materials, replacement parts, tools and accessories used by these plants in production for export were also subject to temporary duty-free entry.

Since 1972, the restriction that *maquiladoras* locate in the border region has been relaxed, and such operations have been allowed to locate anywhere in Mexico, subject to government approval. Despite the special incentives granted to companies that settle in the interior of the country, investors have continued to show a strong preference for settling in the border zone.[2] In 1987, the latest year for which official data have been published, 926 *maquiladoras* (82 percent of a total of 1,125 plants) that employed 251,400 workers (about 82 percent of all workers employed by *maquila-*

doras) were located in the border area.[3] Although *maquiladoras* operating during 1987 produced a wide variety of products from a broad cross section of industries, the greatest number of *maquiladoras* were involved in the assembly of electronics products (248 plants or 22 percent of the total number of plants) and textiles and apparel products (168 plants or about 15 percent).[4]

Caribbean Basin

In most Caribbean Basin countries, EPZs and other export-oriented facilities were initially established in urban areas, near an international port and/or airport. Such location ensured that a transportation infrastructure was already in place to permit the importation of materials for assembly and the export of the finished goods. As in the Mexican case, certain Caribbean Basin countries have begun recently to encourage the establishment of assembly operations in less developed and rural regions, but this policy has had limited success to date.

In 1986, the following Caribbean Basin nations reportedly had either EPZs or some other form of legal regime that supported export-oriented facilities: Antigua and Barbuda, the Bahamas, Barbados, Belize, Costa Rica, Dominica, the Dominican Republic, El Salvador, Grenada, Guatemala, Haiti, Honduras, Jamaica, Montserrat, the Netherlands Antilles, Nicaragua, Panama, Puerto Rico, St. Christopher-Nevis, St. Lucia, St. Vincent, and Trinidad and Tobago. With the exception of those located in the Bahamas, the Netherlands Antilles, Panama, and Trinidad and Tobago—which provided warehousing or banking facilities or engaged in oil refining—export-oriented facilities in the Caribbean Basin consisted primarily of assembly plants.

Some of the leading assembly locations in the Caribbean Basin include those in the following countries.

Dominican Republic. Assembly operations in the Dominican Republic are located in EPZs. The first EPZ, located at La Romana, began operations in 1969. Similar zones began operations in San Pedro de Macoris in 1973, Santiago in 1974, and Puerto Plata in 1983. Five other EPZs, several of them located in the interior of the country, began operations in 1986 or 1987 at Bani, La Romana II, San Cristobal, La Vega and San Isidro. During 1988, six new EPZs were opened and more than a dozen additional locations were under active development.[5]

According to the National Council of Industrial Free Zones, there were 187 assembly plants operating in nine Dominican EPZs in 1987. Much of the growth in the number of assembly plants has occurred since 1982, when only 88 plants were in operation.[6] The vast majority of the plants are now engaged in apparel assembly for the U.S. market; other significant assembly operations include footwear and electronics products. Two of the new zones that opened in 1988 have attracted precision tooling, data entry, computer graphics and other service operations.[7]

Haiti. While export-oriented assembly operations in Haiti began in 1960, it is only after 1973 that they became economically significant. Two industrial parks were created as the result of the growth of assembly plants in Port-au-Prince in the late 1970s; however, many export-oriented assembly firms are located outside the industrial parks. Most of the assembly plants are located near the airport in Port-au-Prince.[8]

In 1966, there were 13 assembly firms operating in Haiti; by 1981, the latest year for which data are available, the number of assembly firms had grown to 154.[9] Assembly firms located in Haiti produce a narrow range of products: apparel, electronics, sporting goods (especially baseballs and softballs) and toys.[10]

Costa Rica. Since 1972, Costa Rica has granted special tariff treatment to industries (also called *maquiladoras*) engaged in the production or assembly of nontraditional exports. Although there are no restrictions on where such plants may locate, all of the *maquiladoras* have located in the area around San Jose. In 1981, legislation was passed that authorized the establishment of EPZs in the oceanport cities of Moin (on the Atlantic) and Puntarenas (on the Pacific) and in the interior of the country in Cartago.[11]

In 1984, there were 78 *maquiladora* plants operating in Costa Rica: 56 were engaged in the assembly of apparel, five in electronic products, four in metal products and 13 in other products.[12]

Jamaica. In 1971, Jamaica led the Caribbean countries in assembled product exports, with about 25 assembly plants in operation.[13] The Kingston Export Free Zone, first established in 1976 as a warehousing and transshipment facility, was converted into an EPZ in 1982. Most of the 17 enterprises operating in the Kingston zone in 1984 were assembly-type operations; eight produced apparel products.[14] A second EPZ at Montego Bay began operations in 1984 and a third at Spanish Port is under construction.

El Salvador. Legislation authorizing EPZs in El Salvador was enacted in 1974. The next year, an EPZ was established at San Bartolo, approximately ten kilometers from the capital city of San Salvador. During the period 1977–78, 14 firms were operating in the San Bartolo EPZ; however, by 1980, only four plants remained in operation. Additional investments made in the early 1980s brought the number of plants up to eight in 1984; assembly operations are primarily in the apparel and electronics industries.[15]

Honduras. Established in 1976, the one EPZ in Honduras is located at the Caribbean port city of Puerto Cortes. As of April 1989, there were 26 plants (up from 24 in 1986) operating in this EPZ. These plants were engaged in the assembly of apparel (ten plants), broomsticks and mops (five), furniture (two), baseballs (one), plastics (one), seafood processing (one), and the distribution of finished imports (six). Plans have been made for developing five new EPZs.[16]

Barbados. Since 1969, Barbados has granted fiscal incentives to Barbadian firms exporting outside the CARICOM (Caribbean Community) area. In 1973, Barbados increased these incentives and began to promote industrial estates as a way to attract enclave enterprises; grants for new factories were also offered. Assembly facilities are situated primarily in industrial parks, administered by the Industrial Development Corporation, located throughout the nation.[17]

In 1985, there were 23 enclave enterprises operating in industrial estates: 13 assembled electronic, electrical and precision instruments; five assembled apparel and leather goods; and five were engaged in data processing activities. The Barbadian Government has targeted electronics, medical supplies, high quality apparel and data processing as the main focus of future enclave activities.[18]

Reliance on Assembled Product Exports

For Mexico and certain Caribbean Basin nations, products assembled from U.S. components for export to the U.S. market represent a major portion of *all* products exported to the United States. Further, the U.S. market is the primary destination of these countries' exports. Based on the importance of assembled products in total exports to the United States over the 1983–87 period, these countries can be grouped in three assembly export-reliance classes: high, medium and low.

Countries that are highly reliant on assembly exports (about two-thirds or more of their exports to the United States) include Antigua, Montserrat, St. Lucia and Haiti; however, the significance of assembly exports to the United States has been declining sharply for Montserrat and St. Lucia.

Countries that have a medium reliance on assembly exports (between one-third and two-thirds of their exports to the United States) include the Dominican Republic, St. Christopher-Nevis, Barbados, and St. Vincent and the Grenadines. Mexico would also fit into this category. While the significance of assembly exports to the United States has declined sharply for Barbados as well as St. Vincent and the Grenadines, it has grown rapidly for the Dominican Republic.

Countries that have a low reliance on export assembly (less than one-third of their exports to the United States) include Belize, Jamaica, Grenada, Costa Rica, El Salvador and Honduras. El Salvador has shown a decline in the reliance on these assembly exports to the United States while Belize and Jamaica—and recently Grenada—have shown an increasing reliance on assembly exports to the United States.

Within this low-reliance group, a subgroup of countries with a negligible reliance on export assembly (about one-tenth of their exports to the

United States) can be identified: Guyana, Guatemala and Panama. Guatemala appears to be the only country in this group where assembly exports to the United States are growing rapidly.

Finally, at present, the export of assembled products of U.S. components to the U.S. market does not appear to be important for the following Caribbean countries: Dominica, Turks and Caicos Islands, Bahamas, Netherlands Antilles-Aruba, Nicaragua, Cayman Islands, British Virgin Islands and Suriname.

III. TRENDS IN U.S. IMPORTS FROM MEXICO AND THE CARIBBEAN BASIN

Special U.S. Tariff Provisions for Products Assembled Abroad Using U.S.-Made Components

Two items (formerly known as items 806.30 and 807.00, now items 9802.00.60 and 9802.00.80 under the new Harmonized System nomenclature introduced on 1 January, 1989) in the Tariff Schedules of the United States (TSUS) provide for the assessment of import duties only on the value of work done abroad when U.S.-origin materials or components are sent to a foreign country for further work or assembly and are then returned to the United States. Item 807.00 of the TSUS, in effect since 1963, is by far the more important of the two provisions. It provides for duty-free treatment of U.S.-made components used in the assembly of products for the U.S. market. The other provision, item 806.30, applies only to the treatment of nonprecious metals that are sent abroad for processing and then imported for further processing in the United States. In recent years, item 807.00 imports have accounted for over 99 percent of U.S. imports under these two provisions.[19] In what follows, U.S. imports under item 807.00 will be used as a measure of offshore assembly activities.

While U.S. imports under TSUS 807.00 do provide a rough measure of the rapid growth of offshore assembly for the U.S. market, they tend to understate the dynamic nature of this phenomenon. These do not include *all* exports from processing zones or other assembly facilities (e.g., items exported to countries other than the United States or items produced and then exported to the United States under other available tariff provisions).[20]

Special U.S. Trade Preference Programs for Certain Items Imported from Mexico and the Caribbean Basin

In addition to the special tariff provision for items assembled abroad from U.S. components, the United States has several tariff preference programs for U.S. imports from developing countries. These programs offer even greater trade preferences (duty-free entry) for certain assembled products if sufficient backward linkages have been developed for local value-added to meet rule-of-origin requirements. One program, the U.S. Generalized System of Preferences (GSP), is available to Mexico and almost all of the nations of the Caribbean Basin. Another, the Caribbean Basin Initiative (CBI), is available only to some of the nations in the Caribbean Basin.[21] In addition, the United States has granted special access to the U.S. market for textile and apparel imports from Mexico and certain Caribbean Basin countries that use fabrics made and cut in the United States.

GSP. The U.S. GSP program extends duty-free treatment to approximately 3,000 tariff line items imported directly from 140 designated beneficiary countries. Certain import-sensitive textile and apparel, leather, glass, electronic, watch and steel products are statutorily excluded from the program. In order to receive GSP benefits, eligible items must meet rule-of-origin requirements (35 percent value-added in the beneficiary country), must not exceed certain competitive-need limitations (an absolute dollar-value level or specific percentage limit), and must not be subject to discretionary product/country exclusions (discretionary graduation).[22]

Mexico has been one of the top five GSP beneficiary countries since the inception of the program in 1975. However, Mexico has recently faced an increasing number of product exclusions as the result two factors: of exceeding competitive-need limits and being subject to discretionary graduation.[23] On the other hand, the nations of the Caribbean Basin, none of which are major GSP beneficiaries, have had only a few products excluded (e.g., sugar and analgesics) as the result of exceeding competitive-need limitations. In any case, the GSP program offers the opportunity for complete duty elimination on eligible products assembled in EPZs if the rules and limitations mentioned above are met.

CBI. The Caribbean Basin Economic Recovery Act (CBERA), often referred to as the Caribbean Basin Initiative (CBI), was signed into law by the President on 5 August, 1983. The centerpiece of the act was the provision for unilateral and nonreciprocal duty-free treatment for a wide range of U.S. imports from the Caribbean region for 12 years, beginning 1 January, 1984. At the end of 1987, 22 countries had been designated as beneficiaries under the CBERA. To be eligible for duty-free treatment under this program, articles must meet rule-of-origin requirements (35 percent value-added in beneficiary countries, of which 15 percent can be from the United States or Puerto Rico). In addition, most textile, apparel, leather goods and petroleum products are excluded.

In many respects, the tariff preferences under the CBI program are similar to those available under the GSP program. However, the CBERA provisions cover virtually all items eligible for GSP as well as many other products. The rule-of-origin test is also more liberal under the CBI program than under the GSP program. Moreover, there are no provisions for country/product graduation under the CBERA; that is, under the CBERA, U.S. market access is assured for eligible products.

During the first four years of the CBI program, the major beneficiaries (in terms of duty-free entry of items eligible for CBI but not GSP) have been the larger and more economically diversified countries in the Central Caribbean (the DominicanRepublic and Jamaica) and Central America (Costa Rica, Guatemala and Honduras). However, some of the smaller Eastern Caribbean island nations (e.g., Barbados, St. Christopher-Nevis, and St. Lucia) have begun to reap some benefits from the program as well.[24]

Special Textile Agreements. Recently, the United States has negotiated special textile and apparel arrangements with Mexico ("special regime," effective 1 January, 1988) and a few Caribbean countries ("special access program," announced February 1986).[25] These arrangements permit expanded U.S. textile and apparel quotas for operations that use fabric formed and cut in the United States; items produced under these conditions enter the United States under special provisions contained in item 807.00. While it is still too early to evaluate their effects, these arrangements are certain to stimulate Mexican and Caribbean assembly of apparel items made from U.S.-formed and -cut fabrics.[26]

U.S. Imports from Mexico and the Caribbean Basin

Total Value. Tables 1 and 2 present the value of U.S. imports from Mexico and the Caribbean Basin nations by major two-digit Standard Industrial Classification (SIC)-based commodity group in 1983 and 1987. Data are provided for total imports and those subject to duty, as well as for the portion that entered under available U.S. tariff preference programs (GSP, CBI or item 807.00) and the average rate of duty paid.

In 1987, U.S. imports from Mexico amounted to $19.8 billion or 4.9 percent of total U.S. merchandise imports from all countries, while U.S. imports from the Caribbean Basin countries amounted to $6.2 billion or 1.5 percent of total U.S. merchandise imports.

Commodity Composition. Over the period 1983–87, the industrial structure of U.S. imports from Mexico and the Caribbean Basin has changed dramatically. In the case of Mexico, crude and refined petroleum accounted for 56 percent of U.S. imports subject to duty from Mexico in 1983; by 1987, this share had fallen to 23 percent. In addition to petroleum, substantial declines have occurred in U.S. imports of metallic ores and tobacco manufactures from Mexico. On the other hand, substantial increases have been experienced in transportation equipment, electrical machinery, nonelectrical machinery, furniture and fixtures, rubber and miscellaneous plastics products.

In the case of the Caribbean Basin countries, crude and refined petroleum accounted for 72 percent of the value of U.S. imports subject to duty from the Caribbean Basin in 1983 (coming almost entirely from the Bahamas, Netherlands Antilles-Aruba, and Trinidad and Tobago); by 1987, this share had fallen to 35 percent. At the same time that Caribbean petroleum exports to the United States have fallen, apparel exports (primarily from the Dominican Republic, Costa Rica, Jamaica and Haiti) have risen dramatically, with the share of total U.S. apparel imports from the Caribbean Basin increasing from six percent in 1983 to 28 percent in 1987. The other major industrial group that has exhibited strong growth is miscellaneous manufactures (especially jewelry, toys and sporting goods). This change in the commodity structure of U.S. imports from the Caribbean Basin countries has resulted in a greater share entering the U.S. duty-free; however, the remaining dutiable amount has seen the average tariff rate increase from 1.3 percent in 1983 to 6.1 percent in 1987.

MFN Duty-Free. From 1983 to 1987, the share of U.S. imports from Mexico and the Caribbean Basin not subject to duty—i.e., duty-free on a most favored nation (MFN) basis—rose, especially for the Caribbean Basin nations. The MFN duty-free share of total U.S. imports from the Caribbean Basin increased from 23 percent in 1983 to 35 percent in 1987; for Mexico, the increase was less dramatic, from 14 to 17 percent. In the case of the Caribbean Basin, this reflects the continued importance of certain MFN duty-free primary product exports to the United States (e.g., bananas, coffee, bauxite). However, for the most part, this increase in the share of MFN duty-free trade has been the result of a greater number of U.S. import categories becoming MFN duty-free (or experiencing duty rate reductions). This is the result of staged tariff reductions agreed to in the Tokyo Round of multilateral trade negotiations. In general, these tariff reductions have reduced the margin of preference afforded to beneficiary countries under the GSP and CBI preference programs.[27]

Duty-Free under GSP and CBI. Of the U.S. imports from Mexico and the Caribbean Basin that are subject to duty, an increasing number have qualified for duty-free entry under special tariff preference programs for developing countries. During the period 1983–87, the share of U.S. imports subject to duty from Mexico that entered duty-free under GSP increased from five to 11 percent. In 1983, nine percent of U.S. imports subject to duty from the Caribbean Basin entered duty-free under the GSP program; by 1987, this share had tripled, due in part to additional benefits afforded by the introduction of the CBI program, beginning in 1984.

Assembled Products. From 1983 to 1987, the proportion of U.S. imports from Mexico and the Caribbean Basin entered under item 807.00 also expanded rapidly. By 1987, 49 percent (compared to 26 percent in 1983) of U.S. imports subject to duty from Mexico entered under item 807.00; in both years, the *dutiable* share of the item 807.00 entries (value-added in

TABLE 1

TOTAL U.S. IMPORTS AND THOSE SUBJECT TO DUTY FROM MEXICO BY 2-DIGIT SIC-BASED PRODUCT GROUP, 1983 AND 1987
(CUSTOMS VALUE IN MILLIONS OF DOLLARS; SHARE IN PERCENTAGE)

SIC-Based Product Group	Value of Imports				Share of Subject to Duty Entered under				Dutiable Share of Item 807		Average Tariff Rate	
	Total		Subject to Duty		GSP		Item 807					
	1983	1987	1983	1987	1983	1987	1983	1987	1983	1987	1983	1987
01—Agricultural Products	864.4	1,067.5	543.4	603.3	2.5	7.2					9.1	12.9
02—Livestock	140.0	253.3	138.8	250.9		0					1.5	1.6
08—Forestry Products	3.1	3.0	11.0	17.7	24.2	75.2					2.4	1.3
09—Fishery Products	408.1	459.1	8.8	3.6	50.2	52.5					3.8	2.5
10—Metallic Ores	40.9	10.2										
12—Coal and Lignite	0	1.0										
13—Crude Petroleum	7,900.0	3,500.8	7,520.7	3,500.8	53.0	25.4					0.3	0.4
14—Nonmetallic Minerals	123.9	157.7	44.2	28.3							3.8	5.6
20—Food and Kindred Products	283.8	608.8	231.8	531.3	36.1	25.7					14.5	10.6
21—Tobacco Manufactures	35.9	4.4	35.9	4.4	14.6	99.2					11.9	8.8
22—Textile Mill Products	48.9	80.5	28.9	70.2	7.3	6.5	3.7	2.1	80.9	45.9	12.9	10.7
23—Apparel	190.7	494.0	190.7	494.0	0.9	2.5	88.7	81.2	25.0	26.8	22.4	18.7
24—Lumber & Wood Products	105.0	163.2	99.7	138.3	34.3	55.4	0.1	1.5	35.8	32.8	3.2	2.6
25—Furniture & Fixtures	93.0	323.6	93.0	323.6	32.6	34.4	62.5	60.3	81.6	72.9	3.7	3.2
26—Paper & Allied Products	114.3	275.6	109.5	234.6	11.6	34.5	87.7	60.6	17.3	19.0	5.6	5.0
27—Printing & Publishing	13.6	17.5	1.9	4.5	88.9	54.8		37.5		52.7	3.2	3.6
28—Chemicals & Allied Products	298.5	382.7	154.1	230.7	71.5	63.8	0	0	71.6	16.9	7.0	6.8
29—Petroleum Refining	623.9	293.2	475.7	208.2	0	0.1					0.4	0.6
30—Rubber & Misc Plastics	59.9	225.9	59.5	224.0	56.7	51.4	40.1	41.3	23.2	41.1	17.2	7.5
31—Leather & Leather Products	77.0	151.1	77.0	127.0	12.2	21.8	50.3	33.1	18.7	31.4	8.4	8.9
32—Stone, Clay, Glass Products	199.7	450.9	148.0	299.0	52.7	64.8	6.1	8.3	84.1	81.8	14.1	13.0
33—Primary Metal Products	744.2	955.7	409.3	653.2	11.1	21.2	26.2	31.5	31.7	34.6	4.0	3.8
34—Fabricated Metal Products	177.7	335.5	173.8	314.3	24.5	32.6	40.0	42.5	30.6	24.5	4.5	4.4

35—Nonelectrical Machinery	357.8	1,066.8	325.8	675.1	16.0	15.5	72.6	51.3	46.4	41.6	4.6	3.2
36—Electrical Machinery	2,221.3	4,185.6	2,220.8	3,871.3	3.1	3.9	92.9	92.0	50.5	49.3	5.6	4.7
37—Transportation Equipment	713.8	2,814.3	709.9	2,805.4	3.2	1.1	85.6	89.6	64.5	58.4	3.6	2.7
38—Instruments	143.9	335.5	143.8	325.9	8.5	11.6	88.5	82.0	30.9	30.4	5.4	5.1
39—Miscellaneous Manufactures	134.6	236.9	126.9	235.5	21.9	51.9	62.3	33.4	44.6	44.1	10.6	7.0
91—Scrap and Waste	35.0	67.6	17.3	14.6	7.7	40.3	0.1	0.1	19.9	77.7	1.1	2.3
92—Used Merchandise	0.2	2.6	0.1	2.6	5.0	14.3	.	83.3	.	16.6	2.9	2.5
98—U.S. Goods Returned	267.1	569.6	1.0	0.7	.	.	.	.	18.3	.	0	0
99—Miscellaneous Commodities	198.7	271.9	147.3	181.6	0.1	0.8	0	0.1	35.9	35.9	0.5	0.1
TOTAL, ALL PRODUCTS	16,618.9	19,765.8	14,248.9	16,374.6	5.1	10.5	25.9	48.9	48.8	49.2	2.2	3.7

Note: . = zero and 0 = less than $500,000 or 0.05 percent. Data have been adjusted to remove MFN duty-free items from reported GSP or item 807.00 entries.

Source: Computed from official statistics of the U.S. Department of Commerce.

TABLE 2

TOTAL U.S. IMPORTS AND THOSE SUBJECT TO DUTY FROM THE CARIBBEAN BASIN COUNTRIES BY 2-DIGIT SIC-BASED PRODUCT GROUP, 1983 AND 1987 (CUSTOMS VALUE IN MILLIONS OF DOLLARS; SHARE IN PERCENTAGE)

SIC-Based Product Group	Value of Imports				Share of Subject to Duty Entered under				Dutiable Share of Item 807		Average Tariff Rate	
	Total		Subject to Duty		GSP or CBI		Item 807					
	1983	1987	1983	1987	1983	1987	1983	1987	1983	1987	1983	1987
01—Agricultural Products	1,051.9	1,297.1	70.4	139.2	45.2	82.0	.	.	.	.	10.6	10.4
02—Livestock	5.7	3.6	1.6	1.8	91.3	97.9	.	.	.	.	4.0	6.0
08—Forestry Products	2.9	5.6	0.2	0.3		71.2	.	.	.	.	3.7	3.7
09—Fishery Products	229.4	339.2	4.9	20.6	40.2	92.2	.	.	.	.	1.5	0.4
10—Metallic Ores	135.5	138.9	3.7	0.9	43.7		.	.	.	.	3.9	.
13—Crude Petroleum	1,000.0	525.6	1,000.0	525.6			.	.	.	.	0.3	0.6
14—Nonmetallic Minerals	20.3	17.0	10.6	0.4	96.2	96.4	.	.	.	.	1.5	4.5
20—Food and Kindred Products	698.9	415.2	661.3	370.0	44.8	90.8	.	.	.	.	1.4	3.1
21—Tobacco Manufactures	67.7	37.9	67.7	37.9	51.5	86.7	.	.	.	.	9.9	7.9
22—Textile Mill Products	18.3	42.9	13.0	39.3	9.6	3.2	27.6	31.8	14.1	21.3	15.1	10.8
23—Apparel	393.9	1,124.0	393.9	1,124.0	1.4	1.0	92.0	77.7	31.2	32.6	24.0	19.6
24—Lumber & Wood Products	18.9	38.9	11.7	21.5	69.4	94.8	.	.	.	.	3.3	4.7
25—Furniture & Fixtures	5.1	17.6	5.1	17.6	96.3	96.2	.	.	.	.	6.9	3.6
26—Paper & Allied Products	14.0	16.9	13.7	16.7	99.0	95.5	0.5	0.4	47.2	56.0	6.3	4.6
27—Printing & Publishing	1.1	3.1	0.3	0.6	53.5	72.4	.	.	.	.	3.8	4.7
28—Chemicals & Allied Products	302.9	303.4	79.0	188.7	71.1	83.0	.	.	.	.	7.3	8.5
29—Petroleum Refining	4,063.5	890.7	3,998.4	852.1	0	0.1	.	.	.	.	0.4	0.8
30—Rubber & Misc Plastics	14.3	30.7	14.3	30.7	39.5	55.2	54.9	39.4	37.4	32.4	12.8	12.7
31—Leather & Leather Products	79.2	100.1	79.2	95.2	57.5	63.8	16.1	12.9	37.1	33.1	9.7	10.1
32—Stone, Clay, Glass Products	7.8	16.6	6.3	8.9	87.0	90.9	1.1		28.6		10.2	11.0
33—Primary Metal Products	178.1	193.9	23.5	36.7	19.6	60.3	11.3	19.8	28.6	26.8	2.3	3.0
34—Fabricated Metal Products	7.1	24.8	7.0	15.8	86.9	81.1	0.9	10.4	59.9	39.1	5.0	5.3
35—Nonelectrical Machinery	19.5	18.4	18.1	8.7	11.6	16.0	78.4	53.8	38.0	28.2	4.6	4.1

36—Electrical Machinery	345.1	214.0	345.1	212.0	11.8	53.4	85.5	41.2	29.3	31.9	5.1	5.0
37—Transportation Equipment	1.4	3.0	0.9	2.7	91.7	77.6	.	3.0	.	82.6	3.4	2.8
38—Instruments	18.6	16.2	18.6	16.1	49.6	49.7	1.8	29.1	34.3	14.5	4.8	6.6
39—Miscellaneous Manufactures	84.5	195.8	72.8	185.9	17.5	54.5	70.6	41.2	31.5	12.1	5.9	5.1
91—Scrap and Waste	12.2	32.1	4.3	2.7	42.8	80.8	.	.	.	.	1.6	2.0
92—Used Merchandise	0.1	0.1	0.1	0.1	.	.	.	.	.	.	3.7	2.6
98—U.S. Goods Returned	192.2	89.1	1.4	0.5	.	5.0	.	.	.	.	0	0
99—Miscellaneous Commodities	15.7	25.8	12.1	23.7	.	0	.	.	.	.	22.7	1.8
TOTAL, ALL PRODUCTS	9,006.0	6,178.1	6,939.0	3,996.7	8.9	26.9	10.8	27.3	30.7	30.8	1.3	6.1

Note: . = zero and 0 = less than $500,000 or 0.05 percent. Data have been adjusted to remove MFN duty-free items from reported GSP, CBI or item 807.00 entries.

Source: Computed from official statistics of the U.S. Department of Commerce.

Mexico) was 49 percent. In the case of the Caribbean Basin nations, 27 percent of U.S. imports subject to duty in 1987 (compared to 11 percent in 1983) entered under item 807.00; in both years, the *dutiable* share of the item 807.00 entries (value-added in the Caribbean) was 31 percent.

Tables 3 and 4 present the total value of U.S. imports entered under item 807.00 from Mexico and the Caribbean Basin nations in 1983, 1985 and 1987; leading two-digit SIC-based product groups are also presented. Table 5 shows the total value of item 807.00 entries from each of the individual 27 Caribbean Basin countries over the same period.

During 1983–87, U.S. imports from Mexico under item 807.00 grew at an average annual rate of 21.4 percent (compared to an overall average annual increase of 4.4 percent). Similarly, item 807.00 imports from the Caribbean Basin over this period outperformed overall U.S. imports from the same region, increasing at an average annual rate of 9.9 percent, compared to a 9.0 average annual decline in overall imports.

In the case of Mexico (Table 3), U.S. imports under item 807.00 have been concentrated in electrical machinery and transportation equipment; together, these two groups have accounted for about three-quarters of the total value of item 807.00 imports from that country since 1983. Apparel imports have been a distant third, accounting for five percent of the total value of assembled products of U.S. materials from Mexico between 1983 and 1987.

Not only are item 807.00 entries from Mexico concentrated in a few product categories, but they often constitute the majority of total exports to the United States in those categories. For example, item 807.00 entries accounted for 90 percent of all U.S. transportation equipment imports from Mexico subject to duty in 1987, 92 percent of all electrical machinery imports, 81 percent of all apparel imports, and 82 percent of all instruments imports. In some cases, the share of a product category entered under item 807.00 has fallen as more value has been added in Mexico and products have qualified for duty-free entry under GSP (for example, paper, leather and miscellaneous manufactures products).

In the case of the Caribbean Basin (Table 4), U.S. imports under item 807.00 have also been concentrated in a few product categories. In 1987, 80 percent (up from 48 percent in 1983) of the value of all item 807.00 entries from the Caribbean Basin came from apparel products and represented 78 percent (down from 92 percent in 1983) of all apparel imports from the Caribbean Basin. The other major categories of item 807.00 entries in 1987 were electrical machinery and miscellaneous manufactures.

Over the period 1983–87, three import product groups from the Caribbean Basin—rubber and miscellaneous plastics, electrical machinery and miscellaneous manufactures—have shown a significant decline in the share of their products entered under item 807.00, as larger amounts qualified for duty-free entry under either GSP or CBI.

TABLE 3

U.S. IMPORTS UNDER ITEM 807.00 FROM MEXICO, TOTAL AND LEADING SIC-BASED COMMODITY GROUPS: 1983, 1985 AND 1987
(CUSTOMS VALUE IN THOUSANDS OF DOLLARS; SHARE IN PERCENTAGE)

SIC-Based Product Group	1983 Imports Under Item 807 Value	1983 Imports Under Item 807 Share	1983 Share of imports subject to duty	1983 Share value-added in 807 items	1985 Imports Under Item 807 Value	1985 Imports Under Item 807 Share	1985 Share of imports subject to duty	1985 Share value-added in 807 items	1987 Imports Under Item 807 Value	1987 Imports Under Item 807 Share	1987 Share of imports subject to duty	1987 Share value-added in 807 items
Mexico, total	3,686,564	100	25.9	48.8	5,522,571	100	33.2	47.1	8,013,136	100	48.9	49.2
36—Electrical Mach	2,063,560	56	92.9	50.5	2,658,910	48	85.5	48.9	3,562,824	44	92.0	49.3
37—Transportation Eq	607,440	16	85.6	64.5	1,367,915	25	89.9	54.5	2,513,752	31	89.6	58.4
23—Apparel	169,150	5	88.7	25.0	274,602	5	87.6	26.3	401,241	5	81.2	26.8
35—Machinery	236,396	6	72.6	46.4	404,897	7	71.4	43.4	346,164	4	51.3	41.6
38—Instruments	127,256	3	88.5	30.9	182,366	3	83.1	26.8	267,246	3	82.0	30.4
33—Primary Metals	107,128	3	26.2	31.7	120,342	2	35.3	32.2	205,562	3	31.5	34.6
25—Furniture	58,174	2	62.5	81.6	104,373	2	62.3	83.3	195,289	2	60.3	72.9
26—Paper	96,068	3	87.7	17.3	114,348	2	72.6	18.9	152,040	2	60.6	19.0
34—Fabricated Metals	69,479	2	40.0	30.6	106,268	2	44.6	42.1	133,681	2	42.5	24.5
30—Rubber & Plastics	23,880	1	40.1	23.2	46,551	1	33.0	18.9	92,420	1	41.3	41.1
39—Misc Manufactures	79,111	2	62.3	44.6	65,349	1	40.6	42.1	78,634	1	33.4	44.1
31—Leather	38,760	1	50.3	18.7	58,883	1	57.8	26.0	42,089	1	33.1	31.4
32—Stone & Glass	8,976	0	6.1	84.1	13,727	0	5.7	85.4	24,692	0	8.3	81.8
24—Lumber & Wood	82	0	0.1	35.8	597	0	0.6	30.3	2,045	0	1.5	32.8
22—Textiles	1,071	0	3.7	80.9	3,120	0	11.7	55.9	1,484	0	2.1	45.9

Source: Compiled from official statistics of the U.S. Department of Commerce.

TABLE 4

U.S. IMPORTS UNDER ITEM 807.00 FROM THE CARIBBEAN BASIN COUNTRIES, TOTAL AND LEADING SIC-BASED COMMODITY GROUPS: 1983, 1985 AND 1987 (CUSTOMS VALUE IN THOUSANDS OF DOLLARS; SHARE IN PERCENTAGE)

SIC-Based Product Group	1983				1985				1987			
	Imports Under Item 807		Share of imports subject to duty	Share value-added in 807 items	Imports Under Item 807		Share of imports subject to duty	Share value-added in 807 items	Imports Under Item 807		Share of imports subject to duty	Share value-added in 807 items
	Value	Share			Value	Share			Value	Share		
Caribbean Basin, total	750,513	100	10.8	30.7	783,085	100	16.9	30.4	1,093,030	100	27.3	30.8
23—Apparel	362,418	48	92.0	31.2	551,024	70	85.5	31.7	873,721	80	77.7	32.6
36—Electrical Mach	295,110	39	85.5	29.3	123,620	16	35.1	24.8	87,392	8	41.2	31.9
39—Misc Manufactures	51,409	7	70.6	31.5	63,424	8	47.5	26.3	76,659	7	41.2	12.1
22—Textiles	3,583	0	27.6	14.1	6,112	1	34.6	13.1	12,510	1	31.8	21.3
31—Leather	12,725	2	16.1	37.1	8,371	1	10.9	44.6	12,236	1	12.9	33.1
30—Rubber & Plastics	7,852	1	54.9	37.4	7,637	1	51.3	40.6	12,084	1	39.4	32.4
33—Primary Metals	2,669	0	11.3	28.6	8,064	1	20.0	25.1	7,245	1	19.8	26.8
35—Machinery	14,205	2	78.4	38.0	12,787	2	62.6	41.6	4,704	0	53.8	28.2
38—Instruments	340	0	1.8	34.3	165	0	1.4	19.6	4,678	0	29.1	14.5
34—Fabricated Metals	62	0	0.9	59.9	492	0	3.5	38.7	1,655	0	10.4	39.1
26—Paper	73	0	0.5	47.2	709	0	3.8	23.9	67	0	0.4	56.0
32—Stone & Glass	68	0	1.1	28.6	95	0	0.7	5.1	—	—	.	.

Source: Compiled from official statistics of the U.S. Department of Commerce.

Value-Added in Assembled Products. The U.S.-content value of item 807.00 imports from Mexico and the Caribbean is substantially greater than that from most other countries. This is not surprising, since many of the items produced by Mexico and Caribbean Basin countries for export involve labor-intensive assembly of materials imported from the United States. Hence, the value-added to the export product consists mainly of the labor costs of assembly.

During 1983–87, about 49 percent of the total value of item 807.00 imports from Mexico represented the value-added in Mexico. This overall figure conceals some variation across different industrial categories, however. For example, Mexico added over 70 percent of the total value of 807.00 items in furniture and in stone, clay and glass products. These items consisted mainly of furniture for use in motor vehicles and ceramic water closets, both items on which Mexico had been graduated from GSP duty-free benefits. Similarly, the increase in Mexican value-added in rubber and plastics products (from 23 percent in 1983 to 41 percent in 1987) can be explained, in part, by the graduation of certain laminated plastics products from GSP duty-free benefits as they were entered under item 807.00 provisions.

In the case of the Caribbean Basin countries, approximately 31 percent of the total value of 807.00 imports was added locally. Significant declines in value-added occurred in two product categories: miscellaneous manufactures (from 32 percent in 1983 to 12 percent in 1987) and instruments (from 34 percent in 1983 to 15 percent in 1987). Again, the shifts in value-added can be explained, in part, by the availability of duty-free entry under the CBI or GSP programs, since nearly all items in these product groups met the 35 percent rule-of-origin requirement of those programs. In the case of miscellaneous manufactures, most sporting goods and toys qualified for duty-free entry under CBI or GSP, primarily leaving jewelry of precious metals (three to four percent value-added) and softballs (23 percent value-added) as the major items entered under item 807.00. Similarly, a restructuring of the composition of 807.00 precision instrument imports from the Caribbean Basin is evident over this period, as more labor-intensive assembly of gauges, medical instruments and clock mechanisms gained importance within assembly exports, while other instrument exports were able to use the benefits of the CBI and GSP.

Leading Assembler Nations in the Caribbean Basin. Since 1983, the top five assembler nations in the Caribbean Basin have accounted for nearly 90 percent of all item 807.00 imports from that region (Table 5). In 1983, Haiti led the Caribbean with $197 million in exports to the United States under item 807.00, followed by the Dominican Republic (with $161 million), Barbados (with $155 million), and El Salvador and Costa Rica (each with $79 million). By 1985, the Dominican Republic (with $247 million) had taken the lead from Haiti (at $221 million), and Jamaica (with $41 million) had

TABLE 5

U.S. IMPORTS UNDER ITEM 807.00 FROM THE CARIBBEAN BASIN: 1983, 1985 AND 1987
(CUSTOMS VALUE IN THOUSANDS OF DOLLARS; SHARE IN PERCENTAGE)

Country	1983 Imports Under Item 807 Value	1983 Share	1983 Share of imports subject to duty	1983 Share value-added in 807 items	1985 Imports Under Item 807 Value	1985 Share	1985 Share of imports subject to duty	1985 Share value-added in 807 items	1987 Imports Under Item 807 Value	1987 Share	1987 Share of imports subject to duty	1987 Share value-added in 807 items
Caribbean Basin, total	750,513	100.0	10.8	30.7	783,085	100.0	16.9	30.4	1,093,030	100.0	27.3	30.8
Dominican Republic	160,958	21.4	33.8	30.7	246,796	31.5	39.8	28.4	428,068	39.2	53.1	31.3
Haiti	197,406	26.3	67.5	29.4	221,138	28.2	62.5	32.5	231,222	21.2	63.0	29.4
Costa Rica	78,800	10.5	42.7	23.0	98,439	12.6	39.2	28.1	145,600	13.3	36.1	33.1
Jamaica	15,495	2.1	24.2	44.9	41,482	5.3	31.2	29.7	115,820	10.6	44.5	26.3
Honduras	25,859	3.4	18.1	31.1	29,415	3.8	26.4	29.3	43,014	3.9	33.4	31.1
Guatemala	1,357	0.2	0.8	38.1	9,367	1.2	6.6	39.2	31,291	2.9	17.8	34.9
El Salvador	78,901	10.5	58.3	43.0	22,571	2.9	18.3	22.2	29,959	2.7	34.3	21.8
Barbados	154,885	20.6	78.6	28.0	69,218	8.8	35.2	36.7	17,252	1.6	34.5	50.5
Belize	6,398	0.9	31.8	27.3	14,383	1.8	39.2	27.8	14,262	1.3	42.6	28.3
St. Chris-Nev-Ang	8,571	1.1	48.6	28.2	6,219	0.8	39.7	25.2	10,164	0.9	44.1	36.0
St. Lucia	3,555	0.5	80.1	30.1	7,884	1.0	72.2	30.0	10,032	0.9	59.2	30.6
Antigua	5,794	0.8	70.8	20.9	5,763	0.7	54.5	25.7	5,180	0.5	70.5	30.4
St. Vincent & Gren	3,496	0.5	87.5	50.7	3,563	0.5	47.6	49.9	3,199	0.3	39.0	44.2
Panama	1,851	0.2	1.7	29.9	3,776	0.5	3.5	27.5	2,484	0.2	2.5	31.3
Guyana	3,623	0.5	19.3	42.8	426	0.1	9.3	29.8	2,366	0.2	25.8	41.9
Montserrat	787	0.1	93.7	32.0	1,387	0.2	61.9	22.3	1,237	0.1	64.4	33.4
Grenada	5	0.0	40.4	55.9	204	0.0	25.2	28.7	1,059	0.1	50.1	30.3
Trinidad & Tobago	41	0.0	0.0	62.1	—				477	0.0	0.1	66.3
Dominica	171	0.0	77.5	33.7	114	.	0.9	19.1	222	0.0	2.4	1.2
Turks & Caicos	—	.			—	.			76	0.0	16.6	28.9
Bahamas	240	0.0	0.0	31.1	415	0.0	0.1	11.6	34	0.0	0.0	55.5

Neth Antilles-Aruba	2,319	0.3	0.1	48.0	502	0.1	0.1	36.1	12	0.0	0.0	23.8
Nicaragua	—	.	.	.	11	0.0	0.1	13.6	—	.	.	.
Cayman Islands	—	.	.	.	8	0.0	0.5	24.8	—	.	.	.
British Virgin Is	3	0.0	0.5	44.8	4	0.0	0.0	15.2	—	.	.	.
Suriname	—	.	.	.	—	.	.	.	—	.	.	.

Note: — or . = zero and 0 = less than $500 or 0.05 percent.

Source: Compiled from official statistics of the U.S. Department of Commerce.

moved into the top five, replacing El Salvador (at $23 million). By 1987, Honduras had replaced Barbados in the top five which were led by the same top three as in 1985 (the Dominican Republic, Haiti and Costa Rica) plus Jamaica. The changes in the leading Caribbean Basin assembler countries is due, in part, to the type of product assembled.

Leading Assembled Products from the Caribbean Basin. Assembled apparel and electrical machinery products dominate U.S. imports from the Caribbean Basin, accounting for nearly 90 percent of total 807.00 entries from that region. The relative importance of these two categories of assembled products has changed dramatically since 1983.

As total U.S. imports of electrical machinery from the Caribbean Basin fell from $345.1 million in 1983 to $214.0 million in 1987, so too did those from the Caribbean Basin under item 807.00 (from $295.1 million to $87.4 million). In part, this reflected some changes in world demand patterns, as well as a restructuring of global production and sourcing patterns by multinational enterprises. However, over this same period, total U.S. imports of electrical machinery from Mexico grew from $2.2 billion in 1983 to $4.2 billion in 1987, and those under item 807.00 rose from $2.1 billion to $3.4 billion.

Over the 1983–87 period, five countries (the Dominican Republic, Haiti, El Salvador, Costa Rica and Barbados) provided approximately 97 percent of all 807.00 electrical machinery items from the Caribbean (Table 6). Imported products from the Caribbean Basin in this product category consist primarily of electronic components and accessories (e.g., semiconductors and capacitors), electrical lighting, wiring and switching equipment. The substantial decline in 807.00 electrical machinery imports from the Caribbean Basin was the result of large declines in imports of these items from Barbados (where they fell from 80 percent of all U.S. 807.00 imports from Barbados to just 19 percent) and El Salvador (where they fell from 92 percent to 43 percent of all U.S. 807.00 imports from El Salvador). In part, this overall decline reflects the fact that a smaller share of all U.S. electrical machinery imports is now entered under the 807.00 provisions because these items can qualify for duty-free entry under the CBI. Only in the case of the Dominican Republic was there a rise in 807.00 U.S. electrical machinery imports over the 1983–87 period, mostly in items with too little value-added to qualify for duty-free entry under CBI. By 1987, electrical machinery assembly was second to apparel assembly in all the major Caribbean Basin assembler countries.

Caribbean Basin apparel exports to the United States exploded during 1983–87, rising from $393.9 million in 1983 to $1.1 billion in 1987. Most of this surge was led by apparel assembled, in part, from U.S. materials. U.S. 807.00 apparel imports from the Caribbean Basin grew from $362.4 million in 1983 to $873.7 million in 1987 (with over two-thirds U.S.-content value). Over this same period, total U.S. apparel imports from Mexico

TABLE 6

U.S. IMPORTS OF ELECTRICAL MACHINERY (SIC 36) UNDER ITEM 807.00 FROM THE CARIBBEAN BASIN, TOTAL AND LEADING COUNTRY SUPPLIERS: 1983, 1985 AND 1987 (CUSTOMS VALUE IN THOUSANDS OF DOLLARS; SHARE IN PERCENTAGE)

Country	1983				1985				1987			
	Imports Under Item 807		807.00 % of ElecMach imports sub to duty	Share value-added in 807.00 ElecMach	Imports Under Item 807		807.00 % of ElecMach imports sub to duty	Share value-added in 807.00 ElecMach	Imports Under Item 807		807.00 % of ElecMach imports sub to duty	Share value-added in 807.00 ElecMach
	ElecMach Value	% all 807.00			ElecMach Value	% all 807.00			ElecMach Value	% all 807.00		
Caribbean Basin, total	295,110	39	85.5	29.3	123,620	16	35.1	24.8	87,392	8	41.2	31.9
Dominican Republic	11,816	7	73.7	25.2	15,392	6	68.5	17.1	37,741	9	67.6	31.9
Haiti	62,281	32	90.5	27.0	47,973	22	58.7	29.4	24,333	11	38.8	30.3
El Salvador	72,589	92	98.3	44.2	13,688	61	23.4	17.9	12,768	43	48.8	15.1
Costa Rica	14,990	19	79.6	20.4	11,042	11	42.4	28.2	6,775	5	30.9	41.7
Barbados	124,366	80	80.4	22.6	32,722	47	22.7	22.6	3,268	19	14.5	75.1
Montserrat	763	97	98.3	32.2	883	64	76.2	22.4	678	55	73.9	39.8
St Chris-Nev-Ang	3,672	43	80.9	32.5	392	6	5.6	29.5	669	7	6.4	73.3
St Vincent & Grenadines	1,985	57	100.0	46.1	273	8	72.4	39.6	518	16	100.0	44.7
St Lucia	753	21	53.2	27.4	320	4	14.7	39.9	511	5	18.1	31.0
Antigua	—	—	.	.	279	5	47.7	42.2	73	1	21.1	37.0
Panama	—	—	.	.	—	—	.	.	26	1	3.1	5.9
Trinidad & Tobago	41	100	8.2	62.1	—	—	.	.	15	3	3.3	45.7
Guyana	—	—	.	.	—	—	.	.	11	0	87.7	30.3
Neth Antilles—Aruba	969	42	56.7	45.0	103	21	9.4	76.4	2	17	0.6	23.4
Bahamas	240	100	77.6	31.1	341	82	92.8	6.1	—	—	.	.

Note: — or . = zero and 0 = less than $500 or 0.05 percent.

Source: Compiled from official statistics of the U.S. Department of Commerce.

grew from $190.7 million to $494.0 million, and those under item 807.00 rose from $169.2 million to $401.2 million (with about three-quarters U.S.-content value). By 1987, slightly over three-quarters of all 807.00 apparel imports from the world were provided by the top five supplier countries: Mexico, the Dominican Republic, Costa Rica, Haiti and Jamaica; however, total 807.00 apparel imports accounted for only 6.5 percent of all U.S. apparel imports.

In the Caribbean Basin, the top five supplier countries of 807.00 apparel products have accounted for between 85–88 percent of all these products exported to the United States from 1983–87 (see Table 7). Barbados, the fourth-largest Caribbean supplier of assembled apparel products to the U.S. market in 1983 dropped to ninth position in 1987, while some other countries (e.g., Jamaica, Guatemala, El Salvador, St. Lucia and Grenada) became larger suppliers. Over the 1983–87 period, Barbados and St. Vincent led other Basin suppliers in the share of value-added in assembled apparel (between 40 and 50 percent).

Miscellaneous manufactured products (primarily jewelry, toys and sporting goods) were the third largest category of assembled products exported to the United States from the Caribbean Basin from 1983–87. While the value of 807.00 entries of these items increased moderately over this period, value-added fell dramatically. Nearly all 807.00 miscellaneous manufactures imports from the Caribbean Basin were supplied by the top five supplier countries (Haiti, the Dominican Republic, Honduras, Jamaica and Costa Rica); Haiti and the Dominican Republic have accounted for nearly 90 percent of these items since 1983 (Table 8).

IV. IMPLICATIONS FOR EMPLOYMENT

Impact of Assembly Operations on Host Country Employment

One of the primary reasons that developing countries promote the establishment of assembly facilities—and offer incentives to enterprises that locate in their countries—is to create and expand employment in their manufacturing sectors and to provide jobs for the large number of new entrants into the labor force. Although data on employment created by assembly operations are sparse, fragmentary information suggests that these countries have been successful on this score.

Assembly operations in developing countries tend to employ primarily unskilled or semi-skilled production workers. Employment opportunities in managerial functions—such as production planning, marketing, etc.—are very limited, as many of these functions are carried out abroad by parent companies. Although local talent is hired for mid-level management and engineering positions, key managerial posts are often filled with foreign nationals from the parent company.[28]

Workers in assembly operations in Mexico and the Caribbean Basin are primarily women, especially young women (in the 16–25 age group). Reasons for this high proportion of young women range from their alleged better manual dexterity, which makes them more efficient in assembly tasks, to charges of their greater vulnerability to exploitation.[29] The very high participation of women in assembly operations holds for other nations as well; of an estimated 1.3 million workers in EPZs in developing nations in the mid-1980s, about 1 million (77 percent) were females.[30]

Table 9 presents estimates of employment in EPZs and other offshore manufacturing facilities in Mexico and selected Caribbean Basin nations in 1975 and 1986.[31] Also included in Table 9 are official statistics on employment in the manufacturing sector of those countries for around 1975 and 1986. According to the estimates in Table 9, EPZs and offshore manufacturing facilities in Mexico and the Caribbean Basin employed, at a minimum, 134,000 workers in 1975; by 1986, the total had risen to nearly 360,000. While these employment levels appear small when compared with the aggregate economically active population in the region, estimated at over 41 million in 1985,[32] they are significant for some countries. For example:

Mexico. The 250,000 workers employed by *maquiladoras* in 1986 represented only one percent of the economically active population, but about 11 percent of manufacturing employment;[33] *maquiladoras* accounted for about 26 percent of manufacturing employment in the six border states.[34]

According to a 1979 survey, women constituted 77 percent of total employment in *maquiladoras*; 62 percent of the women workers were in the 15–24 age group.[35] Since 1982, the share of females in the workforce of *maquiladoras* has been declining. In 1987, the most recent year for which official data are available, 66 percent of production workers of *maquiladoras* were females.[36]

Haiti. The 20,000 direct jobs associated with assembly industries in the early 1970s accounted for about one-fourth of the total labor force in manufacturing and construction.[37] According to data in Table 9, assembly employment accounted for about 20 percent of manufacturing employment in 1975; in 1986, there were 43,000 jobs associated with assembly operations, compared with employment in the manufacturing sector of 122,000 in 1983. Around 1979, women comprised 75 percent of the labor force in assembly plants.[38]

Dominican Republic. Assembly operations provided about five percent of manufacturing employment in 1975 and over 20 percent in 1986. According to other sources, assembly operations employed 6.3 percent of total urban wage earners in 1985,[39] and provided about 22 percent of the country's manufacturing employment.[40] In 1985, females comprised 68 percent of workers in EPZs.[41]

TABLE 7

U.S. IMPORTS OF APPAREL (SIC 23) UNDER ITEM 807.00 FROM THE CARIBBEAN BASIN, TOTAL AND LEADING COUNTRY SUPPLIERS: 1983, 1985 AND 1987 (CUSTOMS VALUE IN THOUSANDS OF DOLLARS; SHARE IN PERCENTAGE)

Country	1983 Imports Under Item 807 Apparel Value	% all 807.00	807.00 % of Apparel imports sub to duty	Share value-added in 807.00 Apparel	1985 Imports Under Item 807 Apparel Value	% all 807.00	807.00 % of Apparel imports sub to duty	Share value-added in 807.00 Apparel	1987 Imports Under Item 807 Apparel Value	% all 807.00	807.00 % of Apparel imports sub to duty	Share value-added in 807.00 Apparel
Caribbean Basin, total	362,418	48	92.0	31.2	551,024	70	85.5	31.7	873,721	80	77.7	32.6
Dominican Republic	137,300	85	94.4	32.7	205,304	83	89.4	32.0	350,631	82	88.2	34.0
Haiti	76,930	39	91.5	28.5	114,626	52	87.1	32.1	139,557	60	87.4	32.6
Costa Rica	60,128	76	97.2	23.4	84,641	86	88.9	28.4	136,849	94	76.1	32.9
Jamaica	12,823	83	98.9	45.5	39,422	95	72.6	29.4	103,363	89	60.2	27.1
Honduras	20,014	78	98.1	31.3	23,485	80	90.5	29.4	39,284	91	93.7	30.9
Guatemala	1,357	100	39.2	38.1	8,716	93	71.5	40.1	30,366	97	73.3	35.4
El Salvador	5,628	7	51.3	27.9	8,883	39	60.8	28.9	17,189	57	60.7	26.8
Belize	6,398	100	99.7	27.3	14,319	100	99.6	27.7	14,261	100	99.7	28.3
Barbados	21,273	14	99.5	47.2	24,753	36	99.1	47.4	9,414	55	96.6	43.3
St. Lucia	2,660	75	94.2	29.5	7,519	95	89.4	29.5	9,384	94	70.4	30.5
St Chris-Nev-Ang	4,899	57	99.9	24.9	5,753	92	97.4	24.5	9,268	91	98.0	33.0
Antigua	5,794	100	100.0	20.9	5,468	95	88.7	24.7	5,107	99	97.1	30.4
St. Vincent & Grenadines	1,511	43	100.0	56.8	3,289	92	99.8	50.7	2,678	84	96.4	44.2
Panama	1,851	100	24.1	29.9	3,744	99	23.7	27.3	2,457	99	5.6	31.6
Guyana	3,622	100	99.2	42.8	426	100	83.4	29.8	2,356	100	96.7	41.9
Grenada	1	20	10.2	47.9	204	100	92.2	28.7	1,059	100	78.5	30.3
Trinidad & Tobago	—	—	.	.	—	—	.	.	462	97	57.5	66.9
Bahamas	—	—	.	.	—	—	.	.	34	100	15.8	55.5

Montserrat	23	3	41.8	24.4	252	18	87.2	22.1	—
Neth Antilles-Aruba	31	1	10.9	25.3	141	28	66.9	29.0	—
Dominica	171	100	100.0	33.7	66	58	35.9	29.7	—
Cayman Islands	—	—	.	.	8	100	100.0	24.8	—
British Virgin Is	3	100	76.1	44.8	4	100	66.9	15.2	—

Note: — or . = zero and 0 = less than $500 or 0.05 percent.

Source: Compiled from official statistics of the U.S. Department of Commerce.

TABLE 8

U.S. IMPORTS OF MISCELLANEOUS MANUFACTURES (SIC 39) UNDER ITEM 807.00 FROM THE CARIBBEAN BASIN, TOTAL AND LEADING COUNTRY SUPPLIERS: 1983, 1985 AND 1987 (CUSTOMS VALUE IN THOUSANDS OF DOLLARS; SHARE IN PERCENTAGE)

Country	1983				1985				1987			
	Imports Under Item 807		807.00 % of MiscMfg imports sub to duty	Share value-added in 807.00 MiscMfg	Imports Under Item 807		807.00 % of MiscMfg imports sub to duty	Share value-added in 807.00 MiscMfg	Imports Under Item 807		807.00 % of MiscMfg imports sub to duty	Share value-added in 807.00 MiscMfg
	MiscMfg Value	% all 807.00			MiscMfg Value	% all 807.00			MiscMfg Value	% all 807.00		
Caribbean Basin, total	51,409	7	70.6	31.5	63,424	8	47.5	26.3	76,659	7	41.2	12.1
Haiti	38,263	19	75.1	33.8	36,971	17	57.3	37.5	38,046	16	53.0	17.8
Dominican Republic	6,210	4	51.5	16.1	19,586	8	40.8	4.6	32,641	8	37.9	2.7
Honduras	5,842	22	99.9	30.2	5,676	19	98.3	27.1	3,716	9	70.8	33.0
Jamaica	341	2	48.5	31.7	725	2	37.8	37.6	1,013	1	47.6	30.7
Costa Rica	129	0	13.2	76.1	383	0	9.7	12.6	1,012	1	10.7	6.6
Dominica	—	—	.	.	48	42	15.1	4.7	222	100	13.3	1.2
Montserrat	—	—	.	.	—	—	.	.	10	1	26.1	84.7
Panama	—	—	.	.	32	1	1.8	47.0	—	—	.	.

Note: — or . = zero and 0 = less than $500 or 0.05 percent.

Source: Compiled from official statistics of the U.S. Department of Commerce.

With the opening of six new EPZs since March 1988, total direct employment in the zones has soared from 60,000 workers to approximately 90,000 workers in March 1989, supporting an additional 24,000 indirect jobs. EPZ direct and indirect jobs now account for over eight percent of national employment and over half of all manufacturing jobs.[42]

Barbados. In 1975 and 1986, assembly operations provided over 20 percent and 60 percent, respectively, of manufacturing employment. Around 1984, women constituted 94 percent of the workforce in assembly operations.[43]

Costa Rica. In 1986, assembly operations accounted for about nine percent of manufacturing employment. According to another source, at the end of 1984, *maquiladora* operations employed approximately ten percent of employment in the industrial sector, and 82 percent of these workers were females.[44]

TABLE 9

EMPLOYMENT IN EPZs AND OTHER OFFSHORE MANUFACTURING FACILITIES IN MEXICO AND THE CARIBBEAN BASIN, 1975 AND 1986

Country	EPZ and Other Offshore Manufacturing		Total Manufacturing		EPZ and Other Offshore Share of Total (percent)	
	1975	1986	1975	1986	1975	1986
Barbados	3,000	6,865	13,800(d)	11,000	22	62
Montserrat	NA	220	250	533(c)	—	41
Haiti	25,000	43,000	122,300	121,690	20	35
Dominican Republic	6,500	36,000	122,131	144,420(a)	5	25
Mexico	84,308	250,000	1,576,000(e)	2,371,000	5	11
Costa Rica	NA	8,600	78,426(d)	100,000	—	9
Jamaica	6,100	8,000	73,900	115,300	8	7
El Salvador	6,143	2,079	49,490	48,960(b)	12	4
Honduras	NA	2,586	98,300(d)	128,600(f)	—	2
Belize	NA	200	NA	NA	—	—
Dominica	NA	200	NA	NA	—	—
St. Lucia	3,500	NA	NA	NA	—	—
St. Vincent	NA	844	NA	NA	—	—

(a) 1984	(b) 1985	(c) 1983	
(d) 1976	(e) 1977	(f) 1981	NA = not available

Sources: Employment in EPZs and other manufacturing facilities: International Labour Organisation and United Nations Centre on Transnational Corporations, *Economic and Social Effects of Multinational Enterprises in Export Processing Zones* (Geneva, 1988), p. 163. Employment in manufacturing: International Labour Office, *Year Book of Labour Statistics 1986* and earlier issues.

Honduras. In 1986, the existing EPZ employed 2,792 workers, only about two percent of total manufacturing employment. By April 1989, this total has grown to 3,878 workers, of which 72 percent are females.[45]

Another way to assess the impact of assembly operations on employment is by focusing on the share of new jobs they have created. This is particularly critical for Mexico and the Caribbean region, as the labor force in these nations has grown more rapidly than the sluggish industrial sectors have been able to absorb.[46] For Mexico, it has been estimated that since their establishment, *maquiladoras* have been responsible for about 20 percent of new manufacturing employment in that nation;[47] for the Dominican Republic, the corresponding share is over 30 percent.[48]

Assembly operations also generate indirect employment from the purchase of local inputs (backward linkages) and from local expenditures by assembly workers (multiplier effects). While the indirect employment impacts of assembly operations are more limited than those of other forms of investment—assembly operations receive most of their inputs from abroad and generally export most of their output—they are nevertheless significant. For example, in the Dominican Republic, it has been estimated that the 30,737 workers employed in assembly operations in 1984 supported an additional 5,777 workers (19 percent) supplying components, raw materials, parts and machinery.[49] A conservative estimate is that the number of jobs created in the local economy as the result of expenditures by assembly workers is at least of the same order of magnitude as the direct employment attributed to assembly operations.[50]

Impact of Offshore Assembly Operations on U.S. Competitiveness and Employment

U.S. Competitiveness. Since the early 1960s, U.S. industrial production has become more globally oriented. Led first by the larger multinational corporations and then by smaller companies, U.S. firms have responded to increased foreign competition and the desire to maintain and expand both domestic and world markets by restructuring their organizational practices, outsourcing certain services and labor-intensive assembly processes, and introducing new labor-saving production technologies. In particular, many of the more labor-intensive phases of production were moved to low-wage regions, initially within the United States—the South and sun belt states—and later to developing nations in Asia and Latin America.

During the early 1980s, the U.S. dollar appreciated significantly against other major currencies. This made U.S. exports less competitive and the outsourcing of more costly assembly phases of a production process to lower cost regions outside the United States much more attractive (especially to Mexico, as the peso was devalued against the U.S. dollar several times). This trend toward global sourcing by U.S. manufacturers has not been unique; Japanese and European manufacturers have followed similar patterns of outsourcing, industrial restructuring, and adoption of additional measures to increase international competitiveness.[51]

In addition, the institutional arrangement of EPZs is not unique to developing countries. The United States has established Foreign Trade Zones (FTZs), secured areas under U.S. Customs Service supervision that are physically located in the United States, but are legally outside the customs territory of the United States. Merchandise may enter the zone for storage, exhibition or manufacture; U.S. import duties are assessed only on the value of the foreign merchandise that leaves the zone and enters into the U.S. customs territory. For the most part, manufacturing activities in the FTZ are concentrated in the motor vehicles industry.[52]

The rapid worldwide expansion of export processing and foreign trade zones over the past two decades in both developed and developing countries not only reflects adjustment to competitive challenges, but also to the worldwide restructuring of manufacturing production. While the relative importance of the manufacturing sector in most developed countries has declined and the importance of the services sector has increased over this period, the manufacturing sector has become more important for the developing countries, providing more foreign exchange and employment than more traditional, but declining, economic sectors. To some extent, EPZs, FTZs and other assembly or processing zones have facilitated this move toward more global production sharing. In addition, more countries are now able to produce—and provide on a competitive basis—manufactured products.

U.S. Employment. A variety of studies have been conducted to examine the effects of offshore assembly operations on U.S. employment. In particular, several recent studies, summarized and reviewed elsewhere,[53] have estimated the U.S. employment effects of repealing provisions like items 806.30 and 807.00 that tend to encourage offshore processing and assembly. Studies by supporters of outsourcing usually point to the large number of jobs supported by component production and supporting services. Other studies have developed counterfactual scenarios of what might happen if these provisions were repealed; most of these studies weigh the potential loss of component production jobs against the potential gain in assembly jobs.

For example, a study by the U.S. International Trade Commission (USITC)[54] estimated a range of possible employment changes in the directly affected industries if items 806.30 and 807.00 were repealed. According to this study, an upper limit of up to 205,000 U.S. employment opportunities might be gained (about two percent of total employment in the directly affected industries) if all 806.30 and 807.00 imports were completely replaced by similar domestically produced goods, while a lower limit of up to 60,000 U.S. employment opportunities might be lost (less than one percent of total directly affected employment) if all 806.30 and 807.00 imports were completely replaced by other imports that did not incorporate U.S. components. It is very unlikely, of course, that either extreme would occur in the event of repeal.

Other types of studies (e.g., partial equilibrium economic models) that take into account consumers' and producers' reactions to the price increases of imports that would result from the repeal of 806.30 and 807.00 tariff preferences have also been used. Based on this approach, the USITC has estimated a more likely—and narrower—employment impact range. In this scenario an upper limit of up to 18,000 job opportunities might be gained if the reduction in 806.30 and 807.00 imports were replaced by domestically produced goods, while a lower limit of up to 16,000 job opportunities might be lost if the reduction were replaced by other imports. If the replacement were divided according to U.S.-foreign market share, the net effect might result in a gain up to 10,000 job opportunities. Other studies[55] have produced estimates that also fall within this narrower range.

When indirect effects are taken into account, studies[56] suggest that there might be a small short-run effect on U.S. employment if items 806.30 and 807.00 were repealed. That is, the number of domestic jobs involved in the *production* of components and services, transport, etc., in support of offshore assembly operations might slightly outweigh the number of jobs related to the *assembly* of those components.

While the estimated employment effects of the repeal of items 806.30 and 807.00 on employment in directly affected industries are fairly small (as a percentage of total employment in the directly affected industries), their industrial distribution is uneven. Over three-quarters of the employment impact would be concentrated in the machinery (including motor vehicles, electrical and electronic products), textiles and apparel, and footwear sectors. This suggests that special attention might need to be given to possible worker adjustment problems in these sectors if a repeal occurred.

These studies also indicate that items 806.30 and 807.00 might not be decisive factors in a firm's decision to move some of its operations offshore. Further, surveys have shown that some offshore assembly operations would continue even if item 807.00 were repealed. In terms of supporting U.S. component production and employment, offshore assembly operations in Mexico and the Caribbean Basin—with their high usage of U.S.-made components—appear to be less detrimental to U.S. employment than those located elsewhere.

The use of U.S. components by offshore assembler nations has a positive effect on U.S. exports to those nations. While the duty-free portion of item 807.00 imports (U.S. components) represents an underestimate of

U.S.-made merchandise contained in all U.S. imports, it can be viewed as a rough measure of U.S. exports that are generated in support of offshore assembly operations. Even with this limitation, U.S. materials and components incorporated into items that reentered the United States under the 807.00 provision (i.e., the U.S.-content value of item 807.00 imports) rose from three percent of total U.S. exports in 1983 to five percent in 1987. For Mexico and some Caribbean Basin nations, this share is substantially higher; for example, in 1987, 28 percent of U.S. exports to Mexico were used in support of production sharing, as were 37 percent of U.S. exports to Haiti, 26 percent of U.S. exports to the Dominican Republic, 17 percent of U.S. exports each to Belize and Costa Rica, and 15 percent of U.S. exports to Jamaica.

V. CONCLUDING OBSERVATIONS

At a time of depressed primary commodity prices, sluggish economic growth, high unemployment, and serious balance of payments difficulties, assembly operations have provided some welcomed relief to the economies of many developing nations. These export-oriented assembly operations have generated badly needed foreign exchange and provided expanded employment opportunities.

Mexico and nations of the Caribbean Basin are the leading assemblers of U.S. components for the U.S. market. In the 1980s, export assembly operations have been, by far, one of the most dynamic sectors of these nations. From 1983–87, U.S. imports of assembled products from Mexico grew at an average annual rate of 21 percent, compared to a rate of four percent for all U.S. imports from Mexico; for the Caribbean Basin, the average annual increase in assembled imports was nearly ten percent, compared to a nine percent average annual decline in overall U.S. imports. Assembled products were significant in the overall exports of several countries in the region. In 1986, for example, exports of assembled goods (domestic value-added only) accounted for 40 percent of Haiti's total exports, 19 percent of Mexico's and 13 percent of the Dominican Republic's. In some instances, assembled product exports have displaced certain traditional commodity exports as major sources of foreign exchange.

Assembly operations have been a dynamic source of employment opportunities in Mexico and the Caribbean Basin. These operations have created about 20 percent of the new manufacturing jobs in Mexico and about 30 percent of those in the Dominican Republic. In 1986, assembly operations accounted for about 62 percent of total manufacturing employment in Barbados, 35 percent in Haiti, 25 percent in the Dominican Republic and 11 percent in Mexico.

In addition to direct employment, assembly operations do create jobs in supplier industries (backward linkages). Moreover, assembly operations also support jobs in the economy at large (macroeconomic effects) as assembly workers spend their income in the consumption of goods and services. However, forward linkages (e.g., jobs associated with the domestic distribution of assembled products) are weak or almost nonexistent in the Caribbean Basin. This could improve if some assembly output were permitted to be sold in the domestic market, as is the case in Mexico.

Assembly operations in Mexico and the Caribbean Basin tend to be concentrated in a few industrial sectors. The electrical machinery and transportation equipment sectors have accounted for about 75 percent of total U.S. 807.00 imports from Mexico since 1983; over the same period, 80 percent of all U.S. 807.00 imports from the Caribbean Basin were assembled apparel items. In most cases, the domestic content of these products (i.e., value-added in the host country) is very small. There is some evidence that assembly operations have fostered industrialization and developed sufficient backward linkages so that some products formerly imported under item 807.00 are able to meet rule-of-origin requirements and enter the U.S. duty-free under GSP or CBI. Overall, however, assembly firms remain primarily enclave operations, and the need still exists to diversify and develop alternatives to the heavy reliance on assembly activities. It is not clear whether smaller countries in the region with limited natural resources and factor endowments can do much to alter this situation.

In Mexico and the Caribbean Basin (as in most developing countries), workers in assembly operations are primarily women, especially young women. Often, these young women represent new entrants into the labor force. In some cases, this might offer new opportunities to supplement family income. In other cases, however, this might accentuate rather than ameliorate the problems of unemployment.[57] Traditionally, female labor force participation rates in Latin America have been among the lowest among both developing and developed countries, but have grown rapidly since the 1960s.[58]

The proclivity to hire women may be associated with the types of assembly operations in the Caribbean Basin (i.e., apparel and electronics) that traditionally tend to employ large numbers of women worldwide.[59] This situation may change in the future if assembly operations expand into other industries. Some evidence of this tendency can be seen in Mexico.

In the 1980s, assembly operations in Mexico and some Caribbean Basin nations have helped to ease a period of economic strain. Pressure to create employment is certain to continue in the immediate future. Labor supply in the region (Mexico included), estimated at 53 million persons in 1980, is projected to reach 93 million by the year 2000 and 140 million by 2020.

Only under the most optimistic growth scenarios can this expansion rate be matched by increases in labor demand.[60] Most likely, assembly operations will continue to be part of the picture, perhaps in a modified form.

In the United States, viewpoints on the impact of offshore export-oriented assembly operations on domestic employment tend to be extremely polarized. However, recent estimates of the effects of repealing U.S. tariff provisions that have contributed to the movement offshore of certain labor-intensive operations seem to indicate that the effect on total U.S. employment in the directly affected industries may be fairly small as a percentage of total employment in those industries. Repealing offshore assembly provisions in the tariff schedules seems far more likely to affect the composition and distribution of total U.S. employment than its level.

With the exception of the recent USITC study, little attention has been given to the importance of items 806.30 and 807.00 in outsourcing decisions. For certain types of manufactured products that require very labor-intensive operations, the USITC found that the major determinant in locating such operations may well be the availability of a low-wage and trainable workforce and a supporting infrastructure. That is, the tariff benefit that items 806.30 and 807.00 provide may be a marginal consideration in location decisions, and offshore assembly operations might continue even if these tariff benefits were repealed. This could help to explain the recent explosive growth of export-oriented assembly facilities in Mexico and the Caribbean Basin.

NOTES

The views expressed here are solely those of the authors and do not necessarily reflect the position or opinion of the U.S. Department of Labor or the U.S. Government.

1. For a more formal definition of EPZs see, e.g., United Nations Conference on Trade and Development, *Export processing free zones in developing countries: Implications for trade and industrialization policies* (Geneva, 1985), p. 10.

2. For background information on the Mexican *maquiladora* program, see Gregory K. Schoepfle and Jorge F. Perez-Lopez, *U.S. Employment Impact of TSUS 806.30 and 807.00 Provisions and Mexican Maquiladoras: A Survey of Issues and Estimates*, Economic Discussion Paper 29, Bureau of International Labor Affairs, U.S. Department of Labor (Washington, 1988), especially pp. 16–25.

3. Secretaría de Programación y Presupuesto, *Estadística de la Industria Maquiladora de Exportación, 1980–1987* (Mexico, 1988).

4. Secretaría de Programación y Presupuesto.

5. Investment Promotion Council of the Dominican Republic, *Investment Opportunity: Free Zones in the Dominican Republic*, (Santo Domingo, 1988), p. 1.

6. For further information, see Francisco Thoumi, *Economic Policy, Free Zones and Export Assembly Manufacturing in the Dominican Republic*, mimeographed (March 1988).

7. American Embassy, Santo Domingo, unclassified cable 012025, March 1989.

8. Leslie Delatour and Karl Voltaire, *International Sub-Contracting Activities in Haiti*, mimeographed (May 1980), p. III–3.

9. Josh DeWind and David H. Kinley III, *Aiding Migration* (Boulder: Westview, 1988), p. 110.

10. See Thomas K. Morrison, "Case Study of a 'Least Developed Country' Successfully Exporting Manufactures: Haiti," *Inter-American Economic Affairs* 29:1 (Summer 1975) and Francisco E. Thoumi, "Social and Political Obstacles to Economic Development in Haiti," in Paget Henry and Carl Stone, editors, *The Newer Caribbean: Decolonization, Democracy and Development* (Philadelphia: Institute for the Study of Human Issues, 1983).

11. Guillermo Pavez Hermosilla, *Industria de máquila, zonas procesadoras de exportación y empresas multinacionales en Costa Rica y El Salvador*, Programa de Empresas Multinacionales, Documento de Trabajo Número 48 (Ginebra: Oficina Internacional del Trabajo, 1987), pp. 28–29, 39–45.

12. Pavez Hermosilla, p. 32.

13. John F. van Houten, "Assembly Industries in the Caribbean," *Finance and Development*, 10:2 (June 1973), p. 22.

14. Frank Long, *Employment effects of multinational enterprises in export processing zones in the Caribbean*, Multinational Enterprises Program, Working Paper Number 42, (Geneva: International Labour Office, 1986), pp. 50–51.

15. Pavez Hermosilla, pp. 65–67.

16. American Embassy, Tegucigalpa, Honduras, unclassified cable 06435, April 1989.

17. Frank Long, pp. 35–36.

18. Long, pp. 41–42.

19. For more details about these provisions, see U.S. International Trade Commission, *The Use and Economic Impact of TSUS Items 806.30 and 807.00*, USITC Publication 2053 (Washington: January 1988), and earlier reports.

20. Special tabulations of the U.S.-content value and the foreign value-added in TSUS 806.30 and 807.00 U.S. imports are made annually for the U.S. International Trade Commission by the U.S. Department of Commerce's Bureau of the Census. Analysis of item 807.00 imports presented here is based on these special tabulations.

21. At the end of 1987, 28 Caribbean Basin countries (or territories) were eligible for CBI benefits; 22 had been designated as beneficiaries. The CBI beneficiary nations include: six **Central American** republics [Belize, Costa Rica, El Salvador, Guatemala, Honduras, and Panama (removed in 1988)], nine small **Eastern Caribbean** island nations (Barbados, Antigua and Barbuda, British Virgin Islands, Dominica, Grenada, Montserrat, St. Christopher-Nevis, St. Lucia, and St. Vincent and the Grenadines), three moderate-sized **Central Caribbean** island nations (the Dominican Republic, Haiti and Jamaica), and four **Oil Refining** nations (Aruba, the Bahamas, the Netherlands Antilles, and Trinidad and Tobago). Six countries eligible for CBI benefits, but never designated as beneficiaries, include: Anguilla, Cayman Islands, Guyana (designated in late 1988), Nicaragua, Suriname, and Turks and Caicos Islands.

22. For further details, see Office of the United States Trade Representative, *A Guide to the Generalized System of Preferences (GSP)*, (Washington: October 1987), and The U.S. International Trade Commission, *Operation of the Trade Agreements Program, 39th Report, 1987*, USITC Publication 2095 (Washington: July 1988), pp. 5–14.

23. For example, $4.5 billion in Mexican products (based on 1986 import levels) were excluded from GSP duty-free benefits in 1987 and $5.2 billion in 1988 (based on 1987 import levels); this represents about one-third of the total value of U.S. imports from Mexico.

24. For more details, see C.R. Shiells and G.K. Schoepfle, *Trade and Employment Effects of the Caribbean Economic Recovery Act, Fourth Annual Report to the Congress*, U.S. Department of Labor, Bureau of International Labor Affairs, Economic Discussion Paper 30, (Washington: September 1988) and earlier reports.

25. To date, Costa Rica, the Dominican Republic, Haiti, Jamaica, and Trinidad and Tobago have entered into bilateral textile agreements with the United States under the program. In 1987, special access apparel imports from these beneficiaries totaled $79 million. Jamaica accounted for slightly over $53 million of the total; special access imports accounted for slightly over 50 percent of all U.S. textile and apparel 807.00 imports from Jamaica in 1987.

26. For more details on these agreements, see U.S. International Trade Commission, *Operation of the Trade Agreements Program, 39th Report, 1987*, USITC Publication 2095, (Washington: July 1988), pp. 4–36/37 and pp. 5–17/18.

27. For example, 110 five digit TSUS items covering items imported from the Caribbean Basin ($41.4 million in 1987) became MFN duty free in 1987 as part of the staged tariff reductions. In an earlier and unrelated action, as the result of an agreement with the government of Japan, the United States agreed to make certain semiconductors MFN duty-free, beginning March 1985. This action affected $171.1 million in 1985 U.S. imports from the Caribbean Basin, primarily from Barbados ($129.1 million) and El Salvador ($40.2 million).

28. United Nations Conference on Trade and Development, p. 18.

29. For a discussion of gender issues associated with assembly operations in Mexico see, e.g., Maria Patricia Fernandez-Kelly, *For We Are Sold, I and My People: Women and Industry in Mexico's Frontier* (Albany: State University of New York Press, 1983); Ellwyn R. Stoddard, *Máquila: Assembly Plants in Northern Mexico* (El Paso: Texas Western Press, 1987), especially Chapter 5; and Mercedes Pedrero Nieto and Norma Saavedra, *La indústria maquiladora en Mexico*, Programa de Empresas Multinacionales, Documento de Trabajo Número 49 (Ginebra: Oficina Internacional del Trabajo, 1987), pp. 42–47.

30. International Labor Organization and United Nations Centre on Transnational Corporations, *Economic and Social Effects of Multinational Enterprises in Export Processing Zones* (Geneva, 1988), p. 89.

31. The employment estimates are from the Starnberg Institute Database and refer to all activities in EPZs and other offshore manufacturing facilities and therefore may overestimate employment in assembly facilities. Considering that assembly firms tend to be predominant in EPZs and other offshore manufacturing facilities in these countries, they are used in this paper as a proxy for assembly employment. Data are not available for many Caribbean nations known to have assembly operations.

32. Computed from data in International Labour Office, *Economically Active Population, 1950–2025*, vol. 3 (Geneva, 1986), Table 1.

33. Another estimate indicates that *maquiladoras* accounted for ten percent of manufacturing employment in Mexico in the 1980s. See International Labour Organization and United Nations Centre on Transnational Corporations, p. 57.

34. Pedrero Nieto and Saavedra, pp. 82, 17.

35. Pedrero Nieto and Saavedra, pp. 42, 48.

36. Secretaría de Programación y Presupuesto.

37. Monique P. Garrity, "The Assembly Industries in Haiti: Causes and Effects," *Journal of Caribbean Studies* 2:1 (Spring 1981), pp. 31–32.

38. Joseph Grunwald and Kenneth Flamm, *The Global Factory* (Washington: Brookings Institution, 1985), p. 177.

39. Francisco A. de Moya Espinal, *Las zonas francas industriales y las empresas multinacionales: Efectos económicos e impacto sobre el empleo en la República Dominicana*, Programa de Empresas Multinacionales, Documento de Trabajo Número 46, (Ginebra: Oficina Internacional del Trabajo, 1986), p. 23.

40. International Labour Organization and United Nations Centre on Transnational Corporations, p. 75.

41. Moya Espinal, p. 26.

42. American Embassy, Santo Domingo, Dominican Republic.

43. Long, p. 42.

44. Pavez Hermosilla, pp. 34, 36.

45. American Embassy, Tegucigalpa, Honduras.

46. See Inter-American Development Bank, *Economic and Social Progress in Latin America: 1987 Report* (Washington, 1988), p. 75.

47. International Labour Organization and United Nations Centre on Transnational Corporations, p. 57.

48. International Labour Organization and United Nations Centre on Transnational Corporations, p. 56.

49. Moya Espinal, p. 30.

50. International Labour Organization and United Nations Centre on Multinational Enterprises, p. 77.

51. For further details, see Grunwald and Flamm.

52. For more details, see United States International Trade Commission, *The Implications of Foreign Trade Zones for U.S. Industries and For Competitiveness Conditions Between U.S. and Foreign Firms*, USITC Publication 2059 (February 1988).

53. See Schoepfle and Perez-Lopez.

54. U.S. International Trade Commission, *The Use and Economic Impact of TSUS Items 806.30 and 807.00*, Publication 2053, Washington (January 1988). To estimate the upper and lower bound employment effects, the USITC used a labor content of trade approach by translating the component- and assembly-related value of

806.30 and 807.00 imports into U.S. labor equivalents with the help of industry labor-output ratios.

55. See Jose A. Mendez, Tracy Murray and Donald J. Rousslang, "U.S.-Mexico Employment Effects of Repealing the U.S. Offshore Assembly Provision," Mimeographed, (Washington, 1988) and Gerald Godshaw, Corri Pinon-Farah, Marco Pinon-Farah, George Schink and Virendra Singh, *The Implications for the U.S. Economy of Tariff Schedule Item 807 and Mexico's Maquila Program*, [Bala Cynwyd, Pennsylvania: Wharton Econometric Forecasting Associates (WEFA) Group, 1988].

56. For example, see Godshaw, *et. al.*

57. Grunwald and Flamm, pp. 226–227.

58. Inter-American Development Bank, p. 93.

59. International Labour Organization and United Nations Centre on Transnational Corporations, p. 64.

60. Thomas J. Espenshade, "Growing Imbalances Between Labor Supply and Labor Demand in the Caribbean Basin," mimeographed, October 1987, pp. 7–12.

2

Trade Policy Measures as a Means to Reduce Immigration in the 1990s

Stephen Lande and Nellis Crigler

I. IMPLICATIONS OF A CHANGING GLOBAL ORDER

As we enter the 1990s, Mexico and the Caribbean Basin countries, as well as the United States, face major challenges. Within these challenges lie opportunities, but successful exploitation of these will require strategies that take into account the fundamental political and economic realignments now underway.

The apparent opening of the East bloc, Europe's single internal market program and other trends in the global economy raise serious concerns for developing countries. Industrialized countries are increasingly preoccupied with maintaining their own competitiveness. Economic and financial assistance programs to the Eastern bloc countries and perhaps eventually to the Soviet Union itself are competing for limited resources. Already, fiscal 1990 aid levels to the CBI countries have been significantly reduced to allow more assistance to Eastern Europe. The value of duty preferences under CBI and GSP has been eroded by the extension of preferences to Eastern European countries, some of them quite developed. This situation is likely to be exacerbated by a shift in the traditional U.S. national security concerns in the region—although new concerns, such as the drug trade, may replace these. Although efforts are underway to encourage Japan to take on a greater role in this hemisphere, its primary focus is on cultivating trade and investment opportunities with its Asian neighbors.

National security, and not immigration or economic concerns, has been the driving force behind U.S. efforts to foster economic development in the Caribbean Basin. If the thaw in the Cold War is permanent, there will be less motivation for unilateral U.S. action or the expenditure of resources, whether financial or political, on the region. Barring a reversal in progress in U.S.-Soviet relations, conflicts in Central America will increasingly be viewed as isolated and containable, particularly given the waning influence of an aging Fidel Castro.

In addition to this shift in geopolitical focus, the United States faces unprecedented global economic challenges which will tend to shift attention away from Central America and the Caribbean. In 1992, Europe's single internal market will remove the United States from its preeminent position as the world's largest market without internal barriers. If sustained, the dramatic opening of Eastern Europe, including the productive Baltic states of the Soviet Union, will greatly magnify Europe's potential as a competitive producer and source of demand. The disadvantages posed by Western Europe's high wage rates and expensive social policies could be offset by the availability of skilled, low cost East bloc labor, new markets for consumer goods and other products and new sources of supply for raw materials and agricultural products.

On its Pacific flank, the United States is embroiled in an increasingly acrimonious relationship with Japan, and similar problems may emerge with Korea, Taiwan and other fast developing Far East economic powers. Mounting U.S. concerns over Japan's intractable trade surplus and growing foreign investment in the United States appear to have forestalled the idea of a Japan-U.S. Free Trade Agreement or Pacific Rim regional economic bloc to counter the European challenge. An increasing number of observers suggest that Japan and the United States are simply too different to be able to turn competition into cooperation in the near future. More likely, the United States will also be faced with mounting competition from Japan and its fast emerging Far East and Pacific Rim neighbors.

While these challenges have had the initial effect of turning U.S. attention away from this hemisphere, with the exceptions of Canada and Mexico, they strongly suggest that it is in the United States' interest to deepen economic ties with the Western Hemisphere. The U.S.-Canada Free Trade Agreement (FTA) was a first step. However, while there is a huge amount of trade between these two very similar economies, the FTA does not offer either partner competitive advantages similar to those offered to the European Community (EC) by the East Bloc countries.

There is already a consensus among U.S. business, government and members of Congress favoring increased cooperation with Mexico. U.S. business has a significant and growing stake in Mexico, which contributes to political support for a special U.S. relationship with that country. The United States has been the main beneficiary of Mexico's dramatic market opening since the Salinas administration took office. Relaxed foreign investment rules should further increase the U.S. business presence there and the number of cooperative ventures aimed at both the Mexican and U.S. markets. Similarly, Mexican businesses are acquiring stakes in U.S. companies which complement their production lines and offer marketing and financing opportunities.

Recognizing Mexico's potential as a market for U.S. goods and a valuable partner in confronting global competition, the Reagan and Bush administrations have promoted increasingly ambitious bilateral trade and investment agreements. Although it is unclear whether a comprehensive free trade agreement, such as that with Canada, is in the offing in the near-term, it appears that further Mexico-U.S. economic integration is assured. In this paper, we focus on provisions to promote this integration and to enhance the benefits to both countries.

To a lesser extent, the United States is focusing increased attention on South America. National security concerns with Central America have been superseded by the drug issue. Driven by strong domestic political concerns that far outweigh public support for U.S. involvement in Central America, the Bush administration has established a new trade initiative for the Andean countries and is increasing foreign assistance there. These efforts to channel trade and investment to the Andean countries may intensify, especially if a new Peruvian president establishes closer ties with the United States. At the time of this writing, the Andean countries are developing ambitious trade initiatives including a Free Trade Arrangement, expansion of GSP and liberalization of textile and apparel trade.

After many years of sporadic and acrimonious contacts, Brazil and the United States have embarked on regular working level discussions of bilateral trade issues. The election victory of Francisco Collor de Mello over leftist Luiz Antonio "Lula" da Silva bodes well for Brazilian-U.S. ties. Like Brazil, Argentina commands U.S. attention because of its debt. While Argentina continues to flounder, President Menem has won U.S. support for resisting a return to Peronism. The Bush administration is seeking to increase GSP benefits for Argentine and Brazilian exports, as well as Mexican and Andean products. Last year, unfair trade cases involving Brazil and Argentina under Section 301 were concluded without resorting to retaliation. Brazil, Argentina and Uruguay have embarked on an integration scheme which may eventually lead to the creation of an attractive market for U.S. business, should their present economic problems be overcome.

Although the Caribbean Basin region as a whole provides a good market for U.S. exports (it is one of the few regions where the United States has consistently maintained a trade surplus in recent years), other export markets in the hemisphere are much larger. In addition, from a business standpoint, the region is fragmented into very small markets. The lack of sizeable domestic markets requires both foreign and local investors to produce mostly for export, which can act as a disincentive. Exporting requires more effort and poses greater risks than producing for a domestic market. Labor rates must be sufficiently competitive to offset added costs of packing, shipping, tariffs, insurance and other charges. Transportation or production delays can pose a serious problem, and profits can be wiped out by high tariffs, import quotas and other protectionist barriers. Finally, the fact that many U.S. companies have not traditionally focused on exporting may also be a handicap for CBI countries, since they make up the largest pool of potential foreign investors in the region.

For those investors who do produce for export in the Caribbean Basin, labor rates are usually the determining factor. But in many of these countries, labor rates are not as competitive as in Mexico with its added advantages of an attractive domestic market and greater proximity to the United States. Until recently, the region could look forward to becoming more competitive with rising wage rates in the Newly Industrialized Countries (NICs) in the Far East. However, the emergence of the Eastern bloc as a production base, with average hourly wages only two cents higher than in Mexico and a much more developed industrial plant and manpower, has introduced a new factor into the equation.

All these elements demonstrate the need for Central America and the Caribbean to develop strategic new economic relationships with the United States and other trading partners, and perhaps most importantly, with each other. A major challenge facing the region is developing markets capable of attracting increased investment. While the region may benefit from the thaw in East-West relations, it can no longer depend on special U.S. attention. Instead, a strategy should be developed to join with U.S. capital to penetrate global markets, including Mexican and South American markets. U.S. policy makers can facilitate this through measures that we will describe in this paper.

This process must begin with the identification of areas where Caribbean Basin countries have comparative advantages in the global economic order of the 1990s, particularly in the context of North American economic integration, but also with regard to Europe in 1992 and relations with South America. A significant potential advantage for the English speaking Caribbean is preferential trade with the United States (through CBI), Europe (through the African, Caribbean and Pacific States-European Economic Community Convention signed at Lomé, referred to simply as Lomé) and Canada (through CARIBCAN, the Canadian Programs for Commonwealth Caribbean Trade, Investment and Industrial Cooperation, the Canadian equivalent of CBI). The Dominican Republic and Haiti have recently joined Lomé, although the Dominican Republic was excluded from the valuable sugar concession. These preferential trade regimes do not extend to Central America or to Cuba.

The "Caribbean Basin" is in many ways an artificial term, implying a regional unity that exists only as a function of geography—one member, El Salvador, does not even border on the Caribbean Sea. There are few close ties between Spanish-speaking Central America and the Dominican Republic, French-speaking Haiti and the English-speaking Caribbean. Even within these groups integration is difficult. Discounting Nicaragua, the Central American democracies face widely divergent situations, ranging from troubled El Salvador and underdeveloped Honduras to the "Switzerland" of Costa Rica. Its British background and historical disputes with Guatemala prevent Belize from interacting significantly with the rest of Central America. In the Caribbean, countries range from economically diverse Jamaica to tiny islands virtually dependent on tourism or single crops such as sugar or bananas. Added to this mix is the island of Hispaniola, shared by Haiti and the Dominican Republic. Haiti is mired in poverty and political instability while its neighbor, the Dominican Republic, is a regional nontraditional export success with serious social problems. Finally, Cuba and until recently Nicaragua, remains oriented toward the rapidly disintegrating Eastern bloc.

Political and cultural differences have discouraged the development of common approaches to Caribbean Basin trade, except within regional subgroups. This, in turn, acts as a constraint on political influence and market potential. In the past, efforts to form regional blocs in the Caribbean Basin region have had mixed success. Perhaps a greater degree of de facto integration can be achieved by taking a common external approach, i.e., by bringing different relationships with other trading partners—the United States, Canada, Mexico, Europe and South America, into region-wide conformity.

The conditions facing the CBI countries and Mexico are very different, both in terms of U.S. business and policy attention and in terms of their global role. As a large and increasingly competitive economy, Mexico is likely to face more resistance to integration into other regional blocs, especially from Canada and perhaps from CBI and South American countries.

On the other hand, Mexico counts on a high level of U.S. interest and strong U.S. political support. The challenge for Mexico will be to head off attempts to restrict its market access as it becomes more competitive and to assure that market opening agreements with the United States and other countries fit in with its domestic objectives.

CBI trade is not viewed as threatening, but it also does not command strong support in the United States. This allows domestic special interest groups to resist attempts to increase access for such important regional products as apparel. Their opposition is not based on the belief that Caribbean imports will disrupt the U.S. market, but out of fear of establishing precedents. In addition, with an influential and active Washington presence, it is easy for such groups to successfully rally against even relatively minor irritants.

To achieve goals and overcome obstacles in the U.S. political system, Mexico and the Caribbean Basin countries should make outreach efforts beyond the traditional constituencies of the U.S. government, Congressmen in border states and the relatively small number of companies having sizeable foreign investments in their countries. The "sacred cow" of U.S. foreign assistance to Israel and the ease with which monies have been shifted from other countries, including CBI countries, to the Eastern bloc illustrate the political power of organized ethnic groups within the United States. Although still emerging as a political force, the size and growth rate of Hispanic Americans in the United States suggests increasing influence, which should be tapped to support measures beneficial to their homelands.

While U.S. business can be an important source of political support, countries should be cautious about relying too heavily on this approach. U.S. multinational corporations often have more important interests at stake in other parts of the world, including the United States. Therefore, they are reluctant to expend limited political resources on a region that is not of highest priority. Secondly, many may be lukewarm toward or even opposed to preferential measures that they may perceive as potentially discriminating against other regions. (For example, although they are the major beneficiaries of special CBI trade regimes, U.S. apparel manufacturers have opposed more liberal CBI trade if "offset" by reductions in imports from the Far East, which may be the only politically feasible way of achieving such liberalization, given U.S. domestic industry concerns.)

To achieve goals, whether legislative or administrative, regional businesses and governments need to strengthen links on a national and regional basis. For the CBI countries in particular, it is critical to be able to present a united front, develop common positions and take an activist approach toward pursuing their own interests in U.S. political channels.

To conclude this section, both Mexico and the CBI countries would benefit from certain U.S. trade policy moves, such as revision of unfair trade laws or integration into the U.S.-Canada FTA. However, because of the differences facing the two, separate analysis of the approaches are appropriate in terms of U.S. policy options. For example, it may not be as politically feasible, at least in the short term, to consider Mexico's integration into the FTA as it would be for the CARICOM members of the CBI, who already enjoy preferential trade with Canada. Therefore, with certain exceptions, we will treat the Caribbean Basin and Mexico separately.

II. TRADE POLICY OPTIONS

The Caribbean Basin: Strengthening Links with the United States, Canada and Europe

As noted in Part I, many CBI countries enjoy advantages over other developing countries, including Mexico, in that they have preferential trade relationships with the United States, Canada and Europe. In this section, we will analyze: a) enhancement of the U.S. Caribbean Basin Initiative; b) beneficial precedents for CBI countries contained in the U.S.-Canada Free Trade Agreement and potential modifications of the FTA which would help CBI countries, and c) provisions in the Lomé Conventions which could be applicable in a U.S./CBI context.

The United States: Building on CBI. U.S. concerns about instability in Central America and the Caribbean led to the establishment of the Caribbean Basin Initiative, enacted in 1984. The centerpiece of CBI was preferential duty-free treatment for products from the region, with some important exceptions. In addition to the exclusion of textile products, leather goods and other items from the program, a major shortcoming of CBI was its lack of an investment component. Many observers have pointed out that tariff breaks alone were not sufficient to attract significant investment to the region. Measures to attract foreign investment, including an investment tax credit or tax sparing (whereby U.S. corporate profits arising from foreign tax breaks would not be taxed in the United States), were proposed but were not politically feasible in an era of tax reform. Providing an effective investment component to CBI remains a problem, with no solution in sight.

Despite these and other shortcomings, CBI has been effective in promoting nontraditional exports from the region. Exports of such products, including textiles and apparel, increased by 80 percent between 1983–88, according to a U.S. State Department report. However, these trade benefits were offset by losses arising from sharply reduced U.S. sugar import quotas and falling prices for petroleum and coffee. Despite the losses in export revenue in recent years, these primary commodities, bananas and apparel remain the region's top foreign exchange earners. In 1988, for the first time, textiles and apparel displaced petroleum and petroleum products as the major U.S. imports from the region. (The value to the region of both petroleum and textile and apparel imports is significantly overstated since they often contain only a small percentage of regional value-added.)

Legislation to enhance the Caribbean Basin Initiative is likely to be passed by the U.S. Congress in 1990. "CBI II" is intended to address some of the shortcomings in the original program: the 12 year deadline, exclusion of products, and losses arising from the U.S. sugar import program. During Congressional debate in 1989, relatively modest provisions which sought to give some measure of preference to apparel and footwear trade from the region were stripped from the bill. With some exceptions, it is now largely viewed as a noncontroversial technical measure and enjoys bipartisan support. It is unclear whether the Senate will attempt to restore some of the controversial provisions dropped in the House.

Still unresolved is the sugar issue. Although Congress and domestic industry find the provision contained in CBI II acceptable in that it would not raise the level of U.S. imports (it would establish a floor for CBI sugar imports at the potential expense of other suppliers), it is opposed by the administration on the grounds that it is discriminatory and GATT illegal. However, the administration accepted an amendment to the 1990 appropriations for foreign operations which reallocated Panama's quota on a "discriminatory" basis to the Caribbean Basin countries and Bolivia. Events in Panama have made implementation of this provision a moot question, and it remains unclear whether the administration will accept any regional preference for Caribbean Basin sugar trade. The situation has been alleviated recently by a decline in the global supply of sugar and a concurrent price increase, which has allowed for a further expansion of U.S. import quotas beyond the relatively generous floor called for in the legislation. If enacted, CBI II will represent the first time that the United States has extended trade preferences indefinitely. The bill also contains potentially significant technical provisions: products assembled or processed in the region from 100 percent U.S. components or ingredients would be completely duty-free, even if on the exempt list, and even if not meeting the origin requirement. CBI products would gain some measure of protection from U.S. unfair trade laws by not being cumulated with other countries' products in injury determinations in unfair trade cases. In addition, the bill would authorize the administration to revise rules of origin to facilitate access for CBI products. Annex I lists additional provisions which would be helpful to CBI countries if incorporated in CBI II.

Although the process has not concluded, the lessons from the CBI enhancement exercise are twofold: the first is that there is no strong domestic U.S. constituency for CBI. In the apparel sector, U.S. companies are a major beneficiary of increased CBI trade. In its 1989 annual report on CBI, the U.S. International Trade Commission determined that growth in Item 807 and 807A apparel (Chapter 9802 under the Harmonized System), which is assembled from U.S. formed inputs, accounts for a significant percentage of the growth in apparel imports from the region. This implies that many countries are developing apparel sectors almost entirely dependent on U.S. fabric for their supply.

Even though it seems logical that these U.S. companies would champion greater access and duty breaks for CBI apparel trade, they have been unwilling to risk labor problems in the United States by breaking out of the domestic textile/apparel/labor political coalition. In addition, many U.S. textile and apparel companies, as well as importers and retailers, have greater stakes in the Far East, and therefore strongly oppose reductions in quota levels in those countries to offset increases in CBI countries. Yet, the political coalition finds increased CBI trade acceptable only in conjunction with such an offset provision.

Difficulties in improving preferences for CBI apparel illustrate that, in the absence of a strong domestic constituency, it is much easier to achieve meaningful trade liberalization through administrative, rather than legislative means. One way to achieve this might be for countries, either individually, or through regional bodies, to engage the United States in a dialogue with the aim of negotiating a bilateral framework covering U.S.-CBI trade, which could be passed by the U.S. Congress on a "fast track" basis. Support organizations for this type of effort might include CARICOM or the Central American Common Market (CACM), regional private sector organizations such as the Federation of Central American

Private Sector Organizations (FEDEPRICAP) and the Caribbean Association of Industry and Commerce (CAIC). A bilateral negotiation would mean that CBI countries would have to offer concessions in exchange for U.S. concessions, but it would also ensure against the United States being able to unilaterally withdraw or alter benefits. New benefits could enter into force without being submitted to the full legislative process. In addition, liberalization could be incremental in nature and provide for a longer phase-in of CBI country concessions, while U.S. concessions could take effect immediately. CBI countries could gain credit for previous commitments made in order to gain CBI eligibility. Lomé countries, which receive more comprehensive and deeper benefits, have fewer criteria to meet than CBI countries to be designated beneficiaries (see Annex ii).

It may be interesting to explore the possibility of converting CBI into a contractual agreement similar to Lomé. Such an agreement could be considered on a Congressional "fast track", would reinforce the trend of continued liberalization and regular consultation, and, perhaps most importantly, would prevent the United States from taking unilateral action with regard to CBI imports. Potential applications of the trade and nontrade provisions of Lomé to CBI are discussed later.

If the Uruguay Round is concluded as planned at the end of 1990, the U.S. Congress will have to pass implementing legislation enforcing the agreements reached in the Round. This "fast track" legislation could provide a vehicle for a contractual agreement with CBI countries, particularly if such an agreement conformed with the Uruguay Round trade liberalization objectives.

As we have already discussed, trade benefits by themselves are limited without foreign investment and an assertive domestic private sector. A telling illustration of this is the fact that the value of U.S. duties collected on CBI imports is increasing due to the success of the textile and apparel sector, which is exempted from CBI preferences and subject to high duties. Duties collected from CBI countries increased 23.2 percent in 1988, even though the dutiable value of many imports declined due to the greater use of U.S. components.

Attracting investment and strengthening the private sector depends to a large degree on local government policies. In addition, the 1988 U.S. tax reform made it politically unfeasible to provide such incentives as tax breaks for U.S. investment in the region. (This may change if tax initiatives from the Bush administration and Congress make inroads into the "inviolability" of tax reform).

The recently approved aid packages for Poland and Hungary may provide useful models for maximizing resources aimed at the private sector. Over half of the $825 million destined for Poland is directed at private sector development: $240 million in grants to private business, including $25 million to modernize the telephone system; $200 million in U.S. export credits to Polish companies and $10 million for training of Polish managers. For Hungary, $60 million of a total of $86 million will be directed toward creation of an "enterprise fund" providing grants and loans to private businesses and credit unions. Similar programs could be directed at helping CBI private sectors develop and market products for export and facilitate wider networks of inter- and intra-regional business ties. In addition, foreign assistance funds should continue to address infrastructure, transportation and communications problems that act as a disincentive to investment. Perhaps a potential source of funds for private sector development might be U.S. duty collections from the region. With the shift in trade from low-duty imports such as petroleum to high-duty products like apparel, calculated duties from CBI beneficiaries have more than doubled between 1984 and 1988, from $75 million to $158 million. Some of these funds could be returned to the region in the form of private sector development initiatives, at no new cost to the U.S. budget.

Finally, one could return to the possibility of encouraging investment through tax incentives. Some form of capital gains tax deduction for investment in the region would be particularly significant.

The Canada-U.S. Market: Issues of Access and Precedent. A logical first step in further integrating CBI countries into the hemispheric economy would be to grant access to the market created by the U.S.-Canada Free Trade Agreement. In addition, the FTA contains other provisions which could benefit CBI countries, including greater protection from escape clause action, nontariff provisions and a bilateral dispute settlement mechanism to handle unfair trade practice allegations.

Incorporating the FTA's notification, consultation and dispute settlement provisions into the CBI and CARIBCAN would increase the security of trade concessions and help ensure additional liberalization. To incorporate such provisions, CBI and CARIBCAN may have to be converted from unilateral grants to bilateral contractual arrangements modelled after EC-Lomé.

Finally, certain technical provisions in the FTA could be adapted for CBI and CARIBCAN. The FTA escape clause procedure protects preferential imports from being inadvertently sideswiped by temporary import relief measures targeting large suppliers. Some of the other nontariff measures contained in the FTA would provide more favorable treatment than do CBI or CARIBCAN. The CARICOM countries already enjoy a preferential trade relationship with Canada through CARIBCAN, the Canadian equivalent of CBI, and other countries in the region are beneficiaries of Canada's GSP program. The duty-free preferences already being extended by both the United States and Canada to countries in the Caribbean Basin region should make it easier, from a political standpoint, to integrate them into the U.S.-Canada FTA. In addition, CBI countries are not perceived as competitive threats to Canadian and U.S. domestic producers, except in certain sensitive products.

For Central American countries, access to the U.S.-Canada FTA may involve a two step process, with the first step being to gain CARIBCAN benefits. This may be facilitated now that Canada has joined the Organization of American States. A coordinated effort by the CARICOM and Central American countries could help rally support in the United States and Canada for FTA access, since the former group has closer ties with Canada and the latter has greater influence on the United States.

Even without modification of the FTA, certain products from CARIB-CAN and CBI beneficiary countries intended as inputs for products finished in the United States and Canada could gain a competitive advantage by having duty-free access to both countries. This advantage is particularly significant given the fact that duty breaks on imports intended for reexport in the FTA have been significantly reduced for other suppliers. By 1994, duty drawbacks, in bond production and duty-free entry through Free Trade Zones will be eliminated for trade between the United States and Canada. CARICOM countries, (and Central American countries if they gain CARIBCAN benefits) should begin to analyze which products could be applicable as inputs into the FTA market.

a) Rules of Origin. With few exceptions, the net effect of the U.S.-Canada FTA will be to discriminate against third country imports, except where they account for a small percentage of a product finished in the United States or Canada. This weighs against the type of production most beneficial to the region and encouraged by CBI and CARIBCAN—the labor intensive finishing of products for reexport to the North. Therefore, the most significant benefit for Caribbean Basin countries would be a modification of the FTA making imports of CARICOM/CBI origin equivalent to those of U.S. or Canadian origin in the FTA market.

Generally, under the FTA's rules of origin, a product must undergo sufficient processing in either the United States or Canada to change its Harmonized System tariff code to be eligible for FTA duty free treatment. There is often an additional requirement that such goods contain at least 50 percent U.S. or Canadian value-added. Therefore, use of third country inputs threatens FTA eligibility of the final product. This may be of little concern now, but as greater integration of U.S. and Canadian production under the FTA is achieved, these factors could serve as a disincentive to investment in Caribbean Basin countries by companies seeking to target the FTA market.

An argument in favor of such a move is that coproduction with CBI/CARIBCAN countries helps U.S. and Canadian industries to be more competitive against third country products. Therefore, the current FTA regulations, which do not differentiate between coproduced and third country products, are not in the interest of either the United States or Canada, and, in fact, distort the intent of both countries' preferential programs in the Caribbean Basin region. Treating CBI and CARICOM inputs as equivalent to FTA inputs would remove these inconsistencies. If both the United States and Canada accepted such a change, both countries would share the burden of accepting more duty-free imports, as well as the benefits of coproduction by their own industries.

Finally, if CBI inputs were granted treatment equivalent to FTA inputs, CBI products would benefit from other favorable provisions in the FTA. For example, CBI components could count toward government procurement contracts in the United States and Canada.

Modification of the FTA to treat CBI/CARIBCAN inputs as equivalent to FTA inputs could be negotiated between the United States and Canada at any time. The subject could be raised by either side during their periodic consultations. Given the uniqueness and newness of the FTA, each country may be reluctant to offer such a proposal in the short term. However, the United States could propose that Canada begin exploring interim facilitating actions. These could include extending CARIBCAN benefits to Central America to provide for uniform, region wide preferences. The United States and Canada, individually or jointly, could also consider extending precedential provisions in the FTA to CBI/CARIBCAN trading partners prior to tackling rules of origin.

b) Dispute Settlement. Aside from the prospect of duty-free access to the FTA market, the most exciting provision in the FTA from the point of view of CBI countries concerns dispute settlement. Chapter 18 of the FTA establishes institutional provisions for avoiding and settling disputes between parties with respect to the interpretation or application of any element of the Agreement. Each party has ready access to binational panels of experts empowered to resolve disputes and issue authoritative interpretations of the FTA.

In brief, the FTA dispute settlement procedure provides for:

1. mandatory notification of any measure which can affect the agreement;
2. mandatory furnishing of information to the other party on any measure, whether or not it has been the subject of advance notification;
3. consultations at the request of either party, concerning any measure or any other matter affecting the operation of the Agreement, with a view to arriving at a mutually satisfactory resolution;
4. use of dispute settlement procedures should the parties fail to arrive at a mutually satisfactory resolution. These include:
   a. compulsory arbitration, binding on both parties, of disputes arising from the interpretation and application of safeguards provisions;
   b. binding arbitration in all other disputes, and;

c. binational panel recommendations to a binational Commission, which, in turn, is mandated to agree on a resolution of the dispute.

Binational panels are composed of five members: two Canadians, two Americans and a fifth member chosen jointly. Panelists are normally chosen from a roster developed by the Commission. Each party chooses its national members, while the Commission chooses the fifth member.

By contrast, there is no advance notification, consultation or dispute settlement mechanism in the CBI or CARIBCAN. Thus Canada and the United States are free to administer their trade laws against CBI imports or to remove products from CBI or CARIBCAN unilaterally and without prior notification or consultation.

Furthermore, under the U.S. CBI program, countries are required to undertake policy commitments in order to attain beneficiary status, including respect for intellectual property rights, protection of workers rights and commitments relating to treatment of foreign investors. These commitments are often more exacting than those found in the U.S.-Canada Free Trade Agreement, particularly when the relative level of development of CBI countries and the United States is taken into account. The FTA even provides for exceptions in order to preserve "cultural independence." No such exceptions are extended to CBI countries.

Upon unilateral determination that these policy commitments have been violated, the United States can reduce benefits or completely remove a country from CBI eligibility. There is no notification, consultation or dispute settlement procedure for CBI or CARIBCAN beneficiaries, since, despite the CBI commitments described above, CBI and CARIBCAN are viewed as unilateral concessions by the United States and Canada, respectively. However, extension of a dispute settlement procedure to CBI is feasible for the following reasons:

1. Although CBI is viewed as nonreciprocal for GATT purposes, the fact that countries undertook commitments to become eligible implies some reciprocity. Since these commitments remain in effect even if benefits are reduced or eliminated, it seems fair to allow for some form of impartial consideration of disputes.
2. EC-Lomé offers a precedent for negotiations and dispute settlement between industrialized and developing nations.
3. A dispute settlement mechanism would enable donor countries to resist political pressure to reduce benefits. For example, it would enable the United States to counter unreasonable interpretations of CBI eligibility commitments.

Caribbean Basin countries might be willing to expand commitments if the United States and Canada were willing to make CBI/CARIBCAN programs contractual and to allow for impartial dispute settlement procedures. Areas of new or deeper Caribbean Basin commitments could include trade liberalization, access to energy and raw materials, and access in government procurement, services, investment and financial services.

c) Protection from Escape Clause Actions. Under the FTA, Canada and the United States agreed to exempt each other from global actions under GATT Article XIX (safeguards) unless either country is an important contributor to injury caused by a surge of global imports. This means that, to a large extent, U.S. and Canadian imports are no longer threatened by emergency actions aimed at blocking disruptive imports in each other's markets. For example, prior to the FTA, Canada was subject to U.S. escape clause actions on steel and the United States to Canadian action on footwear, even though third countries were the major source of the problem imports.

To provide for greater certainty, the FTA sets forth specific thresholds to guide determinations by domestic tribunals as to whether or not the FTA partner is contributing importantly to any injury. In general, imports below five percent of the total are not to be considered substantial and will therefore be excluded from any safeguard action. Imports equivalent to ten percent or more of global imports would be subject to further examination to determine whether they are an important cause of serious injury. Any dispute arising from imposition of escape clause measures, inclusion of the other party in a global action, or adequacy of compensation would be subject to binding arbitration under the dispute settlement mechanism.

Under CBI, the U.S. president can exempt CBI products from escape clause actions in similar situations. However, he is not required to do so, nor are guidelines provided. Applying the FTA language to CBI would reduce the possibility that U.S. trade restrictions would be levied against fairly traded CBI products. These provisions would be important in establishing a more predictable climate for investors to pursue trade opportunities, secure in the knowledge that their access to the market would not be impaired by capricious actions stemming from domestic complaints in the United States and/or Canada.

d) Nontariff Barriers. There are many FTA provisions aimed specifically at liberalizing nontariff barriers which could be applied to Caribbean countries. One example is FTA barriers to wine and distilled spirit imports arising from measures related to their sale and distribution, particularly in Canada. The FTA addresses specific measures such as listing, pricing and distribution practices, blending requirements and standards and labelling requirements affecting different products. The objective is to provide for equal treatment of Canadian and U.S. products in each other's market over time but does not apply to third countries.

Under the FTA, transparency in the listing for sale of wine and distilled spirits and equal treatment of Canadian and U.S. products (based on normal commercial considerations) are required. Any producer applying for a listing is to be informed promptly of listing decisions, given the reason for any refusal and given the right to appeal such a refusal.

On pricing, the FTA permits additional import costs to be taken into account. Differential charges exceeding this amount are to be reduced over a seven year period and eventually eliminated. The method for calculating this reduced differential is specified in the Agreement. In addition, Canada agreed to eliminate requirements that bulk U.S. spirits be blended with Canadian spirits.

Caribbean countries have been negotiating similar arrangements with Canada to protect rum exports from discriminatory retail pricing. An agreement between Canada and the United States on the one hand and the CBI/CARIBCAN beneficiaries on the other hand would be preferable to the clumsy and time consuming method of separate negotiations, and would give Caribbean Basin countries more leverage.

Useful Models in the EC-ACP Lomé Agreement for a U.S.-Caribbean Basin Agreement. a) Comparative Analysis of Select CBI and Lomé Provisions. The scope of the Lomé agreements between the European Community and the African, Caribbean and Pacific (ACP) states is much broader than that of the Caribbean Basin Initiative. The centerpiece of the Caribbean Basin Initiative is duty-free treatment for a wide range of products and a few nontariff trade measures such as a special access for textiles and apparel assembled from U.S. inputs. If enacted, CBI II would add limited protection from U.S. trade remedy laws to these concessions. Nontrade elements of the Caribbean Basin Initiative are relatively minor and include tax deductions for U.S. companies holding business conventions in the Caribbean and access to low interest funds held in Puerto Rico under Section 936.

Unlike CBI, Lomé contains important nontrade provisions, including: a global aid program with mutually agreed upon criteria; financial support for commodity earnings shortfalls under STABEX and SYSMIN (in Lomé, the mechanism for the stabilization of export earning and the special financial facility for mining products, respectively); effective investment promotion measures and an institutional structure ranging from the ministerial to the technical level in government that embraces business, labor, cultural and educational leaders from the private sector. Finally, while CBI is a unilateral grant from the United States, Lomé represents a full fledged negotiation between the European Community and the ACP countries.

b) Trade Provisions in Lomé and in CBI. The basic trade provisions of Lomé and CBI are duty preferences. While eligible CBI products are duty-free, some items remain subject to small duties under Lomé. Important products such as textiles and apparel, footwear and petroleum remain ineligible for CBI duty-free treatment, at least under the terms of the initial CBI program (if CBI II is enacted as passed by the House of Representatives in 1989, leather products other than footwear will gain a 50 percent duty reduction).

In the area of nontariff barriers pertaining to nonagricultural products, there are significant differences between CBI and Lomé. This reflects differences in the way the United States and the EC apply GATT to preferential trade relations and the way they administer trade laws.

The European Community does not perceive any inconsistency between its preferential relationship with Lomé countries and GATT rules requiring most favored nation (MFN) treatment. Thus the EC did not seek a GATT waiver for Lomé, and claimed that the arrangement was in conformity with GATT. The United States did seek such a waiver for CBI and therefore operates under its terms. Since the waiver does not provide for special access for sugar, the United States insists on a nonpreferential approach to CBI imports while the EC freely maintains special preferences for Lomé sugar.

The European Community relies more heavily than the United States on informal arrangements for dealing with trade problems. While Lomé negotiations focus on consultation and agreement, Caribbean Basin countries would benefit more from limited derogation of U.S. trade laws.

Under U.S. trade remedy law, many trade actions are only taken if imports cause injury to U.S. producers. In assessing whether imports are causing injury, the United States International Trade Commission cumulates imports from all sources involved in the complaint. Although they account for only a fraction of the U.S. market, imports from CBI beneficiaries can be cumulated with disruptive imports from large suppliers, and thus, be subject to the resulting import restriction.

Import relief in "escape clause" cases is provided against increasing quantities of fairly traded imports entering at low prices which are judged to be causing serious injury to U.S. production. CBI contains a provision under which CBI imports are not cumulated with other countries' imports and are not subject to import relief remedies unless they are, by themselves, a cause of serious injury in escape clause cases. CBI II has a similar provision applicable to unfairly traded goods.

Under Lomé, EC authorities are asked to take into account the effect of import restrictions on ACP imports and not to take action against these imports if at all possible. In a safeguard action, the European Community is required to monitor ACP imports before taking action, provide advance warning of restrictions and impose only jointly agreed upon import relief measures. The EC Commission is requested to allow time to ACP members to request special treatment and to respond to any such requests within six months.

An exception is provided for actions requiring immediate decisions. Even in these cases, however, safeguard measures are confined to steps which would be the least disruptive to trade between the contracting parties and the least damaging to ACP product export potentials. When new products are brought under control, the EC undertakes to ensure that ACP exports continue to enjoy an equivalent margin of preference in relation to third country products benefiting from the MFN clause.

There are no similar requirements under U.S. law, although the administration often tries to take CBI interests into account. However, without a specific requirement to do so, other priorities can easily overtake interest in assisting the Caribbean Basin countries.

Given the automatic nature of U.S. unfair trade laws covering dumping and countervailing duty proceedings, we do not believe that it would be possible to exempt CBI imports completely from their applicability. However, the U.S.-Canada Free Trade Agreement provides for special judicial procedures under which a binational panel decides whether a U.S. law was correctly applied to Canadian imports. A similar procedure could be developed for the CBI.

Although CBI beneficiaries are not seriously threatened by unilateral U.S. action under Section 301 at the present time, they are exposed to unilateral U.S. retaliation under other procedures. CBI benefits could be removed or limited in cases where beneficiary countries are found to be in violation of designation criteria. In contrast, there does not appear to be a way to cancel eligibility or reduce benefits to a country under Lomé. For this reason, we would suggest that the notification and consultation procedures in Lomé be analyzed, along with those contained in the U.S.-Canada FTA, as a substitute for the unilateral procedures under U.S. trade law and under CBI.

c) Agricultural Trade. Both the United States and the EC apply quantitative import restrictions against imports of selected agricultural products. In the United States, no exception is provided for CBI products. Any preferential treatment must be consistent with the nondiscriminatory provisions of GATT except where the GATT waiver permits such derogations. Thus, the administration has opposed special treatment for CBI sugar despite Congressional willingness to enact such legislation.

In contrast, Lomé requires the EC to provide more favorable treatment to ACP agricultural imports than to MFN imports from third countries. Lomé also includes special protocols for ACP sugar, rum and bananas. For sugar, consultations are required on implementation of guaranteed access for ACP sugar, guaranteed prices and delivery shortfalls. A joint resolution on sugar adopted by the EC-ACP Joint Assembly in 1987 calls for the Commission to reallocate sugar only to states signatory to the protocol. Lomé IV provides for the continuation of special treatment for the region in the context of the creation of a single European market in 1992, although the specific mechanisms for such special treatment are not described. The United States would claim that such special treatment violates GATT.

The United States would be unlikely to agree to special product protocols like those in Lomé since they would violate GATT, particularly Article I or the most-favored nation clause. Besides, there is no need for a special protocol for rum or bananas in the United States since the United States maintains no quantitative limitations on these products and provides duty-free treatment for bananas and rum under MFN and CBI respectively.

Nevertheless Lomé agricultural consultations covering a wide range of issues could provide a useful model for U.S.-CBI negotiations. Such consultations have addressed and resolved the following issues:

1. Customs classification problems on ACP yam exports, due to confusion arising from classification of manioc under the same tariff heading.
2. A request for special tariff treatment for ACP molasses.
3. An ACP clarification request as to whether reduction in the levy on sorghum from Spain would also apply to ACP countries.
4. An ACP complaint about competition from other suppliers in tropical timber.

The Lomé agreement also provides for consultations concerning EC and ACP positions in international trade forums, particularly commodity negotiations. Thus, the European Community and ACP states attempt to develop common positions for the Uruguay Round. Such positions have been developed in the coffee and cocoa arrangements. ACP states must also be notified and given an opportunity to consult if the EC plans to extend trade benefits to other countries which could have a negative impact on the ACP state (such consultations could have particular relevance as trade relations deepen with the East Bloc). No such cooperation or consultation between CBI beneficiaries and the United States is provided for and that which does take place is sporadic and ad hoc.

d) Rules of Origin. CBI II would bring the U.S. rules of origin more in conformity to the Lomé model. For the moment, U.S. and EC rules of origin for products produced with third country inputs are quite different. Both systems bestow automatic origin on products wholly grown, produced or manufactured in one or more of the beneficiary countries. However, Lomé bestows origin on most products where processing in ACP countries results in a change in tariff classification. There are special lists providing for exceptions, i.e., processes that do not confer origin even if they lead to a new tariff classification and those where origin is conferred even though tariff classification is not changed. The result is increased certainty as to whether or not a product will be eligible for duty-free treatment.

In addition, Lomé permits a derogation from the ordinary rules of origin for infant industries. ACP countries can request such dispensation to allow new production to gradually attain the required local content. In such cases, the EC agrees to a derogation for a specified period of time, usually three years and no greater than five years. The United States does not provide for any similar dispensation under CBI. However, a negotiated agreement could include such provisions.

It appears that rules of origin have been significantly liberalized under Lomé IV. Infant industry derogations are easier to obtain and more foreign input is allowed.

Aside from not providing derogation for new industries, the U.S. system is much more subjective. Changes in tariff classification do not confer origin. For any product containing third country inputs to attain CBI origin, Customs must determine whether two conditions have been met. First, the product must be substantially transformed, meaning that the final product must be a "new and different" article of commerce from the foreign materials used in its manufacture. In addition, at least 35 percent of the cost or value of the product must be attributable to direct cost of processing in CBI countries. U.S.-origin materials may be counted toward 15 percent of the 35 percent requirement. Materials from Puerto Rico and the Virgin Islands may count toward the full 35 percent requirement.

As we have discussed, provisions like those in the U.S.-Canada FTA would be much closer to the more liberal and certain provisions under Lomé. Both the FTA and Lomé provide a comprehensive listing of manufacturing processes which confer origin. If a procedure is not listed, then a change in tariff classification becomes the controlling factor.

e) Textile and Apparel Trade. The United States does not provide duty-free treatment for products under the Multifiber Arrangement, although partial duty-free entry is granted to apparel produced from U.S. origin materials. In this case, duties are levied only on the non-U.S. value-added.

Textile imports enter the United States without quantitative restrictions unless they are subject to unilateral or negotiated limits under the Multifiber Arrangement. Furthermore, the United States claims that, where limitations are imposed on CBI countries, they are likely to be more generous. The United States provides particularly generous quotas for imports of apparel and made-up goods produced from materials knitted or woven and cut in the United States under a guaranteed access program. However, such treatment has only been extended to countries that enter into agreements restricting other imports in the category, particularly those assembled from Far East inputs.

The EC provides almost unlimited duty-free treatment for ACP textile imports under both GSP and Lomé, although it reserves the right to cap the total amount of imports entitled to duty-free entry. It also provides quota free entry for imports produced from EC origin materials. The EC has few quantitative limitations against textile imports from ACP countries although importation is very small and far less than U.S. imports from the same countries.

The CBI II provisions reported out of the House Ways and Means Committee in 1989 would have provided for U.S. duty-free treatment of imports under the GAL program and for a 50 percent reduction in duties for imports subject to other quota limitations. However, these provisions were later stripped from the House bill and their future is uncertain. The expedited rules for Congressional votes on negotiated agreements would make it easier to achieve some form of special treatment for CBI textiles.

f) NonTrade Provisions. Lomé is much more comprehensive that CBI in its coverage of nontrade issues. In fact, the only nontrade issues in CBI are the tax incentive for U.S. business conventions held in CBI countries and access to low interest Section 936 funds on deposit in Puerto Rico for countries that sign Tax Information Exchange Agreements.

The most significant nontrade provisions in Lomé potentially applicable to a U.S.-Caribbean Basin arrangement could be those relating to foreign investment promotion. Lomé III devoted a chapter to the development and promotion of private investment in the ACP countries by both parties. Commitments included joint undertakings to accord investors fair and equitable treatment, maintenance of a predictable and safe investment climate and consideration of the negotiation of bilateral agreements toward this end. The Article 193 Committee was also instructed to explore setting up joint insurance and guarantee systems and to study measures to facilitate and expand private capital flows to the ACP states.

Another group of significant Lomé provisions establishes institutional relationships on many levels between the government and private sectors in the ACP states and the EC. The government relationship ranges from Ministerial level contacts to a number of subsidiary groups charged with administering the agreement and negotiating modifications and extensions. A special parliamentary assembly of elected representatives from ACP and EC countries plays a significant role in mobilizing public support for EC initiatives towards Lomé. Committees under the Economic and Social Council consist of representatives of many private sector entities in the EC and ACP states, including chambers of commerce and other business, labor, cultural, scientific, agricultural and educational groups.

We do not believe that there would be sufficient support either in the United States or in CBI countries for the development of a multilateral aid program similar to that under Lomé. CBI countries will not be willing to give up bilateral aid programs in favor of a multilateral approach. For its part, the United States is not in a position to commit significant new funding, especially at levels approaching the approximately $9 billion of aid allocated by the EC during the five years of Lomé III and possibly more than $12 billion planned for the first five years of Lomé IV. In addition, the

United States opposes commodity export earnings stabilization schemes and therefore would be unlikely to agree to STABEX and SYSMIN type arrangements.

However, an agreement between CBI beneficiaries and the United States could provide for the negotiation of criteria to serve as a guide for bilateral aid programs. The Lomé agreement focuses on such diverse areas as promotion of ACP agriculture through extension services; assistance in modernizing internal and external transport and communication networks; and promotion of ACP policies which enhance human resources, increase creative capacities and promote cultural identity.

In agriculture, the Technical Center for Agriculture and Rural Cooperation (TCA) follows a comprehensive approach encompassing research and development, disease control, storage, production, secondary and tertiary back-up activities, drought and desertification control, training and investment and credit facilities.

Positive achievements have also been made by the Centre for the Development of Industry (CDI). In 1987, an initiative was launched for the Centre to become more intensively involved in mobilizing ACP countries' private sectors in economic development, as called for in Lomé III. The work focused on small- and medium-sized enterprises seeking to expand or initiate manufacturing activities in beneficiary countries. Policy adjustment measures related to these efforts included privatization and market liberalization.

Finally, the nontrade consultation provisions under Lomé are very helpful to beneficiary countries. For example, environmental consultations provided a forum for producers of ACP phosphate and phosphate products producers to make their views known with respect to an EC directive to combat cadmium pollution. Such consultations also provided for a special derogation from noise abatement rules for older aircraft, which prevented a disruption in air freight shipments to and from ACP countries. Conversely, when new noise abatement levels were applied in Miami, no consultation with CBI beneficiary countries occurred because it was not required. Finally, while it is not possible for individual Lomé members to keep current with and respond to all proposed changes to EC law, the consultation mechanism allows them to be informed of modifications affecting them and gives them an opportunity to negotiate with Commission officials.

g) Benefits and Pitfalls of the Lomé Approach. The Lomé type approach does present several pitfalls. First, it is conceivable that the United States would ask for reciprocal concessions which the region would not be willing to provide. Given the parliamentary process in many Caribbean countries, agreements with the United States might simply languish in legislative bodies or give rise to anti-U.S. sentiments. Finally, if CBI II is passed as expected, CBI will become permanent. Linking CBI to the whims of negotiators could threaten the permanence and concessions already in place.

However, the advantages of the approach definitely outweigh the disadvantages. The momentum generated by negotiation of such an agreement, combined with potential beneficiaries' concern that they not be excluded, should assure necessary approval by beneficiary nations. In addition, as we mention below, a bilateral agreement should not threaten the permanent trade provisions of CBI. Existing CBI trade benefits would be taken as given, with further discussion revolving around improvements to CBI and the addition of nontrade measures. Fast track congressional approval would provide an opportunity to gain greater trade concessions on sensitive products. Finally, such negotiations would have the advantage of keeping CBI on center stage, an important factor in today's rapidly changing world.

h) Procedures and Political Steps Involved in Developing a Lomé Type Arrangement. The time is ripe to begin new initiatives for the CBI region. We have described the reasons why the United States should be interested in pursuing closer hemispheric economic ties. President Bush gave the go ahead for exploring new approaches to CBI in a 17 November 1989 directive calling on the entire Cabinet to "examine all avenues at our disposal to ensure that the [CBI] program achieves its goals." His only caveat was that these efforts should not entail additional budgetary outlays. Establishing a contractual preferential trade relationship with closer cooperation in the nontrade area should not give rise to additional costs.

In the 1988 Trade Act, the administration was granted tariff and nontariff negotiating authority for bilateral agreements until 31 May 1993. Agreements so reached are subject to "fast track" congressional approval, usually after close consultation with the Congress. Under the "fast track," Congress must vote on the agreement within a specific time limit and amendments and parliamentary delaying tactics are not permitted. Without the use of such "fast track" authority, it seems unlikely that the administration would have been able to gain approval of such a sweeping measure as the U.S.-Canada FTA without numerous restrictive amendments being added by Congress.

Mexico: Integration and Industrialization

Many of the measures discussed with regard to the Caribbean Basin countries—extension of the U.S.-Canada FTA and negotiation of a Lomé type agreement—would also apply to Mexico. However, as a larger and more competitive economy, Mexico may face greater political obstacles and would be pressed to grant greater concessions in exchange. Conversely, Mexico might be able to achieve otherwise ambitious goals due to the strong political support it enjoys in the United States. Although the

U.S. policy focus has shifted to the Eastern Bloc in recent months, U.S. officials and businessmen are already convinced that a closer Mexico-U.S. economic partnership would be beneficial to both countries.

The recent fundamental liberalization of the Mexican economy, including the virtual opening of import markets, will make it easier for Mexico than for CBI countries to adhere to GATT requirements for reciprocity. Nevertheless, it is likely that, in an agreement with the United States, Mexico would be allowed more time to phase in its concessions.

In the long-term, it is possible that some kind of comprehensive North American Free Trade Agreement will be put into place which would include Mexico and the Caribbean Basin countries. We have analyzed the possibility of a negotiated agreement between the United States and CBI countries which would treat the latter in a preferential manner. Most observers believe that 1991 will be the year in which the Salinas administration will decide whether to pursue some form of comprehensive arrangement with the United States.

Even if the decision is made not to pursue a comprehensive free trade area, bilateral economic integration will continue to evolve much more quickly than was anticipated years ago. Since a preferential agreement has already been exhaustively analyzed, we will focus on steps the United States and Mexico could take in the near term to introduce more certainty into trade with the United States and maximize the benefits of such trade to the Mexican economy.

Mexico and the United States could discuss these ideas in the context of 1) the current bilateral Understanding, 2) bilateral and multilateral aspects of the Uruguay Round and 3) informal exploratory sessions.

Precedents in EC-Lomé for U.S.-Mexican Relations. As described in the CBI section, the European Community and its former colonies in Africa, the Caribbean and the Pacific recently concluded the fourth renewal of the Lomé arrangement. The original EC-Yaounde arrangement contained unilateral preferences for member countries in the EC market similar and in some way more comprehensive and deeper than those provided under the U.S. Caribbean Basin Initiative. Because of its level of development, Mexico will be precluded from gaining such extensive unilateral trade benefits as those extended under Lomé or the CBI, or from gaining substantial protection from U.S. unfair trade practice laws. In addition, Mexico may be unwilling to make commitments that the United States would ask for in exchange for an ambitious agreement.

Nevertheless, Lomé does provide useful precedents for U.S.-Mexican relations, particularly the terms of notification and consultation mechanisms. Of potential interest are arrangements that: guarantee fair and equitable treatment for investors; establish official links between private sectors; require consultations prior to taking positions in multilateral economic forums; require consultations on the impact of health, safety, environmental and other nontrade matters affecting beneficiary countries; and provide for agreement by both parties to take into account the effect of trade actions on the other countries' exports, GATT concessions and special protocols on sensitive products. In addition, Lomé calls for institutional structures ranging from Ministerial meetings and legislators' conferences to technical bodies focusing on specific issues and joint promotional efforts in trade and investment.

Many of these issues are being discussed in the context of the bilateral Framework and the more recent Understanding already in existence between the United States and Mexico. However, while Lomé is largely a one-way gift from the EC to former African, Caribbean and Pacific colonies, total or nearly total reciprocity will be expected from Mexico by the United States.

Increasing Access for Mexican Textile Products in the Uruguay Round. In bilateral trade negotiations, the United States has conditioned special access for Mexican apparel assembled from fabric formed and cut in the United States on restrictions in imports of other apparel, including that produced from components formed in Mexico. Given the predominance of U.S. input in these products (some 98 percent of *maquiladora* apparel is U.S. input) and the low paid and unskilled nature of the labor component, questions are increasingly raised as to the value of this type of production to Mexico in the longer term. It is already in the U.S. interest to allow growth in *maquiladora* imports because of their large percentage of U.S. content, thus Mexico should not have to limit exports of national textile and apparel products in exchange. Exports of Mexican national apparel are often so small that unilateral controls are unnecessary. This is due partly to the fact that the domestic industry is not internationally competitive, and reportedly, to the Mexican government's desire in the past to discourage exports that would limit domestic supplies and increase inflationary pressures. With Mexico's foreign investment liberalization, it is likely that joint ventures between U.S. and Mexican textile mill and apparel companies will increase, improving the competitiveness of Mexican industry through technology transfer, while providing the U.S. industry with new markets as well as a new source of supply. It is also possible that the *maquiladora* industry will begin to use Mexican as well as U.S. components. Access to the U.S. market for products with a greater Mexican component must be assured before such growth will take place. U.S. firms stand to gain from recent changes in Mexican regulations which offer greater opportunities for *maquiladora* products to be sold in Mexico's domestic market and hopefully the United States will respond by granting Mexican products more access in the U.S. market.

The U.S. textile industry is under great pressure from efforts to terminate the Multifiber Arrangement (MFA) in the Uruguay Round. Termination of the MFA may also be contrary to Mexico's interest at this stage in its development, since the large Far East producers would likely dominate markets to the detriment of other, less competitive suppliers. The ideal situation for Mexico would be expanded import quotas for Mexican products under the MFA, which would encourage productivity increases while protecting market share from Far East competitors.

Mexico's open foreign investment policy may generate U.S. industry support for greater access for Mexican textile products in the U.S. market. There is much discussion of increased integration of all aspects of the U.S. and Mexican textile mill and apparel industries. A large U.S. apparel manufacturer, Haggar Apparel Co., has recently announced plans to cooperate with a Mexican Group, Portefino, S.A., to develop common production facilities in Mexico aimed at the Mexican market. Technology, design, marketing and capital available in both countries permit cooperation in this sector far beyond the current *maquiladora* experiences.

To conclude, Mexico may gain more through generous treatment of its national industry under the bilateral textile agreement while other countries remain subject to strict U.S. quotas, than from elimination of the MFA. In addition, from a political standpoint, Mexican support for the U.S. position in GATT might facilitate U.S. concessions in bilateral trade. U.S. industry is very concerned about a phase out of the MFA. Hence, they may be willing to soften opposition to special access for Mexican national industry in exchange for favorable Mexican commitments in the multilateral negotiations on textiles and apparel.

We should emphasize that if a phase out of the MFA is agreed on, it will only occur through a transitional arrangement expected to last throughout the decade. Mexico should focus on the details of this transition to assure that it receives preferential treatment in the U.S. market during this period.

Using the Generalized System of Preferences to Enhance Trade. GSP expires in July of 1993. As the largest beneficiary, Mexico has an interest in its extension, particularly now that the United States has introduced flexibility into the program specifically to benefit Mexico. In 1989, the United States announced that it was considering the designation of Mexican products previously excluded on grounds of import sensitivity to GSP and was considering the redesignation of products that had been removed from the program because they exceeded competitive need limits and/or were not granted *de minimis* waivers. The recent removal of Mexico from the priority watch list for intellectual property rights violations removed an important impediment to expansion of Mexican GSP benefits. Such action could result in duty-free treatment being extended to hundreds of additional Mexican products.

There are advantages to including GSP extension in the Uruguay Round negotiation. The main advantage is that, as part of a multilateral trade agreement, it would be subject to special "fast track" Congressional approval, which does not permit amendments. In the last renewal of GSP, which was enacted as part of the Trade and Tariff Act of 1984, Congress attached numerous conditions to GSP (market access, treatment of foreign investment, intellectual property rights, etc.), lowered the competitive need limit ceilings, introduced a labor rights condition, and required the President to remove countries from GSP eligibility once they reach a per capita GNP level ($9,304 in 1987). In addition, Congress mandated that the administration undertake a general review of GSP which resulted in competitive need ceilings being halved on about $5 billion worth of developing country products.

Finally, if GSP renewal is not considered as part of the Uruguay Round package, the issue would come up in 1992, a Presidential election year when Congress will be under pressure not to enact liberal trade initiatives.

The United States could include GSP improvement and extension in the package it presents to Congress through an informal bilateral arrangement between the United States and Mexico. This could be done through a Uruguay Round agreement between the United States and Mexico to avoid increasing duties on products of interest to the other country. Both countries would be able to otherwise increase duties under GATT— Mexico by increasing duties to binding level ceilings, and the United States by removing products from GSP. Since the United States could not legally bind GSP rates, both countries could agree to a best efforts commitment to freeze, and if possible, further liberalize mutual tariff benefits.

Since GSP is a unilateral program, the United States would be reluctant to consider modifying it in the context of the Uruguay Round. However, the Tokyo Round provides two useful precedents for such action. First, the Tokyo Round Framework Agreement approved by Congress recognized generalized preferences for developing countries as a permanent derogation from MFN requirements. Secondly, the legislative package included certain technical modifications improving the operation of the U.S. GSP program.

Mexico could also seek other technical improvements to GSP. The substantial transformation requirement was removed from GSP as a result of a Court decision in 1989. However, a provision in CBI enhancement legislation pending in Congress would reinsert the requirement, bringing GSP into conformity with CBI benefits.

Although substantial transformation is required under CBI, the CBI rules of origin have a significant advantage over those in GSP. Under CBI, up to 15 percentage points of the 35 percent local content requirement can be met with U.S. content. If applied to GSP, this would make some Mexican products, such as corn products, eligible for duty-free treatment.

Mexico should request consultations with the United States on this subject before the Senate modifies the GSP program. Perhaps Mexico could convince the United States to allow U.S. content to count towards GSP eligibility at the same time that the substantial transformation requirement is reinserted into GSP. Because of its proximity to the United States and integration with U.S. production, Mexico would benefit from such a change far more than would other GSP beneficiaries.

Modifying the Antidumping Laws. As with other countries, perhaps the major impediment to increased Mexican exports to the United States in many sectors is the U.S. antidumping law. The most recent manifestation of this problem is a new dumping case against Mexican cement exports. Also, high technology *maquiladora* operations may be disrupted by U.S. attempts to tighten rules in the dumping code to address third country circumvention of dumping orders. If successful, this could make Mexican production using third country inputs even more vulnerable to U.S. dumping complaints.

We would suggest that Mexico focus on the current dumping negotiation underway in Geneva, with particular emphasis on circumvention and perhaps one or two other aspects of dumping.

As we mentioned in the Caribbean Basin section, dumping was addressed in the U.S.-Canada Free Trade Agreement through establishment of a binational panel to review dumping and countervailing decisions in each country. In addition to monitoring the Uruguay Round negotiations, Mexico should monitor operation of the U.S.-Canada binational dispute settlement panel to decide whether a similar panel to handle U.S.-Mexican trade complaints would be in Mexico's interest. Such a panel could be proposed as part of a nonpreferential arrangement with the United States.

Expanding Mexican Content in Coproduction Operations. One of the drawbacks of coproduction facilities developed to take advantage of the United States tariff schedule (HTS 9802, formerly TSUSA 806.30 and 807.00) is that the use of Mexican inputs is penalized. The substitution of U.S. components by Mexican components results in full duty as opposed to duty-free entry of the U.S. component unless the new product is eligible for GSP and it fulfills the origin requirements of the program. It is not in the interest of productive U.S.-Mexican relations to maintain a tariff system which discourages the use of Mexican inputs.

Within the rubric of bilateral talks, Mexico could request that the United States consider making Mexican content of imports under the Harmonized Tariff System (HTS) 9802 equivalent as U.S. content and therefore exempted from duty. Duty would only be applied to third country input. A potential objection which could be raised by the United States is that it is difficult to monitor and differentiate Mexican input from third country input. However, this problem could be addressed through a Customs agreement certifying Mexican input, modeled after the certification procedure in GSP.

Maquiladora imports could also benefit from complete duty-free treatment under HTS 9802 as opposed to exempting only the U.S. input. Since almost all of these imports originate from North America and since U.S. inputs predominate, it would be in the interest of the United States and the hemisphere to eliminate such duties in the Uruguay Round without demanding reciprocity.

Eliminating Discrimination Against Mexico in the North American Market Under the U.S.-Canada Free Trade Agreement. There are many aspects of the U.S.-Canada FTA which discriminate against third country imports, even if those imports enjoy duty preferences in one or both FTA markets. Technical modifications in the U.S.-Canada Free Trade Agreement, similar to those suggested for the Caribbean Basin countries, would benefit Mexican exports. In fact, modifications in the FTA may be even more important for Mexico than for CBI countries, given its large participation in major industries such as the auto industry. Failure to modify the FTA rules of origin will encourage the transformation of low value-added assembly into U.S. or Canadian products, rather than increase the use of Mexican labor and inputs.

The most serious problem is the FTA's failure to confer duty-free status on *maquiladora* products, or finished goods with substantial *maquiladora* content, that enter Canada from the United States. Also, modifications in the Automotive Pact do not treat Mexican inputs as North American content for the purposes of the FTA.

As with the Caribbean Basin countries, Mexico should analyze the U.S.-Canada FTA to identify those areas where provisions discriminate against Mexico and where minor modifications would eliminate the discrimination. Given the likely sensitivity to such a proposal by U.S. and especially Canadian labor, Mexico would probably be pressured to offer market opening concessions in exchange. Through study of the FTA market, Mexico can assess whether modifications in the FTA are worth seeking and, if so, what conditions it would be willing to accept in order to achieve access to the FTA market.

ANNEX I
PROVISIONS TO IMPROVE CBI ENHANCEMENT LEGISLATION

Modifications of Trade Remedy Laws

1. The principle of taking trade action against CBI imports only if they themselves cause injury to U.S. producers should apply to escape clause cases as well as to unfair trade cases. Therefore, CBI II should include a provision similar to that contained in the U.S.-Canada Free Trade Agreement which exempts Canada from most escape clause relief if imports from Canada comprise ten percent or less of total U.S. imports of the product in question.

2. Another provision which could be drawn from the U.S.-Canada Free Trade Agreement concerns the duration of import relief under the escape clause. Under the FTA, if imports from Canada are found to be causing serious injury to U.S. industry, the period of time under which they could lose duty-free treatment is limited to a maximum of three years.

3. The original CBI provided that expedited U.S. import relief against perishable products from CBI beneficiary countries could only take the form of tariffs. The 1988 Trade Law allowed quotas to be imposed on perishable products from all sources, including the Caribbean Basin. CBI II should reinstate the special procedures for CBI perishable products and exempt CBI imports from the newer procedure.

4. The Trade and Competitiveness Act of 1988 may preclude the USITC from accounting for U.S. industry profits from coproduction ventures in determining whether imports are causing injury to U.S. producers. Through coproduction, both United States and Caribbean producers benefit from a successful CBI program. Therefore, in cases involving coproduction between U.S. and Caribbean producers, the USITC should be able to consider profits generated by these activities.

Liberalize Rules of Origin

5. Request that USTR negotiate an arrangement with Canada to assure that Caribbean Basin inputs are treated as equivalents to Canadian or U.S. inputs for purposes of the Free Trade Agreement. This would eliminate the current situation whereby CBI imports which undergo only minor processing in the United States cannot enter Canada duty-free and CARICOM imports which enter the United States after minor processing in Canada are ineligible for U.S. duty-free treatment since

in both cases substantial transformation does not occur to bestow FTA origin. It would also begin addressing the problem of how to gain some form of duty-free treatment for Central American exports to Canada beyond GSP.

6. The EC-Lomé practice of bestowing origin on otherwise ineligible beneficiary exports for a limited but specified period should be adopted in order to permit start up operations to develop sufficient local content to be eligible for trade preferences.

Exempted Articles

7. Establish a system for conferring duty preferences to exempted articles where it is demonstrated that such action would not have an adverse effect on U.S. domestic industry. These determinations could be reached through annual reviews conducted by the Office of the U.S. Trade Representative and the United States International Trade Commission (USITC), similar to GSP reviews. As under GSP, only items subject to a petition would be reviewed. One potential guideline for the review would be designate products where major imports come from other regions and domestic production supplied less than a given percentage (20 percent) of consumption. Such products might include most plastic and rubber footwear and athletic leather footwear (joggers), which are mostly produced overseas. Based on experience with the nonrubber footwear agreements in the late 1970's, it should be easy to identify those categories where U.S. production is nonexistent or so small and/or specialized as to not to be effected by CBI imports. This would also ensure that CBI preferences would not encourage runaway industries. Because specific products would not be mentioned in the provision, a groundswell of domestic industry opposition should be avoided.

8. Extend duty-free treatment to those textile and apparel items which are clearly no threat to the U.S. industry, such as hammocks, toy animals, exotic handbags, wall hangings, etc. Some of these products were included in the original GSP in 1974. However, because a stricter definition was applied, they were not included in CBI. There is a precedent for such exceptions for specific products. In the version of CBI II reported out of the House Ways and Means Committee, the domestic industry agreed to accept a list of fabrics in short supply which would be eligible for liberalized trade, even if not of U.S. origin. We believe it would not be difficult for the ITC or the trade to identify these products. Technically they can be included by allowing ten digit designations and basket categories or by breaking them out of the current basket to permit designation.

9. The exclusion of any product from duty-free treatment provided for under the CBERA should be considered from the date of enactment of CBI II, as equivalent to an import relief measure as provided for under Sections 201–203 of U.S. trade law. The duration of the relief (i.e., exclusion from preferences) shall be established at five years, with the President having the authority to eliminate or phase-down the relief, consistent with Section 201–203 provisions. The President could also extend the relief for a period of up to three years, making the term of relief eight years. As in normal escape clause situations, the relief would terminate, i.e., duty-free treatment would be implemented, in no more than eight years.

Expanded Arrangements Beyond CBI II

10. A "Sense of the Congress" provision should recommend that North American economic integration be furthered through exploration of some form of mutually beneficial, GATT consistent Free Trade Arrangement between the United States and the Caribbean Basin.

11. Put Congress on record as being willing to consider an expansion of CBI into a FTA under the fast track which would take into account the CBI countries' stage of economic development (i.e., concessions could be granted immediately by the United States, but phased in for CBI countries). Such an arrangement would benefit the United States, since under the cover of the FTA the United States would receive phased-in preferential as opposed to MFN concessions from the region. This would provide more security for the concessions thereby increasing investor confidence. The period of delayed phase-in has been accepted since the EC-Israel FTA, which provided 22 years to Israel to phase in concessions compared with 12 years for the EC. Such an agreement could be subject to "fast track" Congressional consideration if concluded before 1993, thereby allowing more controversial and wide ranging concessions and rewarding the region for their past and future liberalization.

Sugar

12. We strongly endorse the proposals for minimum guaranteed access levels for sugar in ways consistent with the GATT. Additional provisions could:

   a. Urge the Administration to develop a GATT consistent formula for sugar allocations which would increase the share of Caribbean sugar if a quota program continues in the future.

b. Guarantee an appropriate level of CBI preference if we go to a process of tariffication of agricultural restrictions as a result of the Uruguay Round.

c. Request that the Administration grant to CBI sugar the equivalent favorable treatment on the U.S. market that Lomé sugar receives in the European market. (The EC has not been prevented by the GATT from offering Lomé countries special quota access, which is not available to non-Lomé suppliers.)

ANNEX II
COMMITMENTS UNDERTAKEN BY COUNTRIES
TO BE ELIGIBLE FOR CBI PREFERENCES

Under the terms of the Caribbean Basin Economic Recovery Act of 1983, the President of the United States may not designate a country for CBI trade benefits if the country:

- Is a communist country,
- Fails to meet certain criteria regarding expropriation of U.S. property,
- Does not take adequate steps to cooperate with the United States to prevent narcotic drugs from entering the United States,
- Fails to recognize arbitral awards to U.S. citizens,
- Provides preferential treatment to the products of another developed country which adversely affects trade with the United States,
- Engages in the broadcast of U.S. copyrighted material without the consent of the owner,
- Has not entered into an extradition treaty with the United States.

The President is authorized to waive several of these conditions for reasons of national, economic or security interests.

In addition to these mandatory criteria, there are 11 discretionary criteria that the President is required to take into account in designating a country. These are:

- An expressed desire by the country to be designated,
- Economic conditions in the country,
- The extent to which the country is prepared to provide equitable and reasonable access to its markets and basic commodity resources,
- The degree to which the country follows the accepted rules of international trade,
- The degree to which such a country uses export subsidies, or imposes export performance requirements and local content requirements,
- The degree to which the trade policies of the country as related to other CBI beneficiaries contribute to the revitalization of the region,
- The degree to which a country is undertaking self-help measures to promote its own economic development,
- The degree to which workers in such a country are afforded reasonable working conditions and enjoy the right to organize and bargain collectively
- The extent to which such a country prohibits its nationals from engaging in the broadcast of copyrighted materials belonging to U.S. copyright

owners without their express consent,
- The extent to which such a country protects the intellectual property rights, including patents and trademarks, of foreign nationals,
- The extent to which such a country is prepared to cooperate with the United States in administering the provisions of Title 1 of the CBI legislation.

To qualify for CBI benefits, Caribbean Basin countries must agree to take all necessary actions to comply with or make progress toward complying with these criteria.

ANNEX III
SUMMARY OF TRADE PROVISIONS OF BENEFIT TO MEXICO

1. Review nonpreferential duty reductions under the fourth renewal of the Lomé Arrangement to determine if there are provisions which would be beneficial to Mexico, if applied in a U.S.-Mexican context.

2. Work with the U.S. textile and apparel industry to develop a consensus on improving access for exports from non*maquiladora* Mexican industry.

3. Extend and deepen GSP benefits in the context of the Uruguay Round as a means of rewarding Mexico for its unilateral but nonbound concessions.

4. Continue to make specific improvements in GSP of benefit to Mexico.

5. Modify dumping procedures through GATT negotiations or through the establishment of a dispute settlement procedure for unfair trade practice complaints, modeled after that in the U.S.-Canada FTA.

6. Expand the benefits or HTS chapter 9802.00.60 and 9802.00.80 (formerly TSUS 806.30 and 807.00) to encourage more Mexican content.

7. Request the United States to push for modification of the U.S.-Canada Free Trade Arrangement to eliminate discrimination against Mexican products in the FTA market.

3

The Potential of Trade Expansion as a Generator of Added Employment in the Caribbean Basin

Stuart K. Tucker

I. INTRODUCTION

U.S. relations with the countries in Central America and the Caribbean have been driven in recent years by regional and internal political strife, tremendous obstacles to development and migration. Although analysts continue to debate the primary causes of the recent, large migration of people to the United States, one fact is clear. Many of the migrants were unemployed or underemployed in their country prior to departing for the United States. The existence of a relatively large pool of underemployed workers is an important factor to consider when looking for political and economic solutions to the current problems in Central America and the Caribbean. In Central America, violent political strife feeds upon the presence of a labor force that is growing more rapidly than the economies can handle.

In the early 1980s, the Reagan Administration recognized that economic development was closely tied to political events in what has now become known as "the Caribbean Basin." The Reagan Administration proposed to address the economic problems of the region by aiding the region's exporters through the launch of the Caribbean Basin Initiative (CBI). Early analyses show that the trade expansion effects of the CBI have been small, due to the limited changes in trade restrictions, the existence of many internal development obstacles and the continuation of the most deleterious trade restraints.[1] However, in 1985–88, some countries experienced significant growth of manufactured and other nontraditional exports, particularly apparel exports, which are covered by the Special Access Program, although they still face high tariffs on the order of 20–30 percent. The U.S. Agency for International Development continues to emphasize export promotion in disbursing its development aid to the region in an effort to sustain and widen this thus far small success.

If these export efforts are to have a significant impact on development, political stability and migration in the region, then they must generate employment as well as provide assistance to the trade balances of the region. This paper provides estimates of export-employment linkages for manufacturing exports from Costa Rica, the Dominican Republic, El Salvador, Guatemala, Honduras, Jamaica, Nicaragua and Panama in an effort to assess the potential of trade expansion to generate new jobs in the region. Reasonable trade expansion scenarios are then reviewed and the related employment is compared to expected labor force growth through the year 2000. This paper concludes with a section on the implications for public policy both in the United States and in Central America and the Caribbean.

II. THE PROBLEM

In the past, the U.S. government has conducted surveys to ascertain the investment and employment effects of the Caribbean Basin Initiative. The resulting data can be criticized on several grounds: it provided no indication of causality; the accuracy of the surveys was suspect due to incomplete coverage; the methods allowed for substantial possible double-counting; and the surveys only track gross increases, leaving out the effects of induced disinvestment.[2]

In the ideal world, employment effects could be estimated using up-to-date input-output tables for each of the Caribbean Basin countries. Unfortunately, such information is not generally available.

III. OVERVIEW OF METHODOLOGY

This study draws together data on gross output, value-added, employment and labor compensation in specific manufacturing industries within several countries in the Caribbean Basin. The paper provides job-creation estimates using three methods (see the "Job-Creation Ratios" section for the estimates). The most accurate estimates are those produced by what is called in this paper "Method 3," which is described in this and the next section. "Method 1" and "Method 2" are estimates produced by taking shortcuts at certain points in the process described below for Method 3. Those shortcuts, though more quickly accomplished, produce what should be considered less accurate estimates.

For each manufacturing industry in each country, the author attempted to piece together the data to calculate the following three ratios:

Equation 1. $(GO/X * VA/GO * LC/VA * J/LC) = DJ/X$
Equation 2. $(IGO/X * MLC/IGO * J/MLC) = IJ/X$
Equation 3. $DJ/X + IJ/X = J/X$
where:

GO/X =	the amount of gross industry output needed to yield a given value of exports
VA/GO =	industry average amount of value-added involved in producing a given level of gross output
LC/VA =	industry average spending on labor compensation for a given level of value-added by the industry
J/LC =	$1/(LC/J)$ = the inverse of the average labor compensation per employee in the industry
DJ =	direct employment (in the industry)

IGO/X =   the value of gross output generated in all sectors of the
                economy as a result of an increase in exports in one sector

MLC/IGO =   the average spending on labor compensation for a given
                level of gross output economy-wide

J/MLC =   1/(MLC/J) = the inverse of the average labor compensation
                per employee economy-wide

IJ =   indirect employment (generated in other parts of the econ-
                omy)

J/X =   total direct and indirect export-related employment due to
                a given amount of exports from a specific industry

Thus, the first equation produces the number of direct jobs generated in
the industry due to a given value of export sales, and the second equation
produces the number of indirect jobs (those generated throughout the
rest of the economy due to the effects of expanding production in the
specified industry). The sum, therefore, is the total (economy-wide)
amount of employment that is generated due to an increase in exports by
a specific industry.

The export-related employment data on each industry then can be mul-
tiplied by the change in export value over a given period to produce job-
creation estimates by industry which can then be summed for all manufacturing and averaged to yield an overall manufacturing average ratio
of jobs per export value for a country.

There are, of course, a number of difficulties that are encountered along
the path to produce these calculations. The appendix provides more detail on the methods used at each turn of the journey.

IV. JOB-CREATION RATIOS

Table 1 provides the export-generated employment estimates for manufacturing exports that were calculated under each method described in
the preceding section. Due to data limitations, three of the five countries
could not be included in methods 2 and 3. The estimates apply to 1986 for
Costa Rica and to 1985 for the other countries. However, to be realistic,
these estimates are only ballpark approximations given the assumptions
necessary during their construction. Table 2 provides the industry-
specific estimates for employment creation due to exports by individual
industries of five of the countries. Table 2 shows the wide variation in labor intensity among manufacturing industries. Typically, food-related
manufactures, apparel products and wood products are among the most
labor-intensive. The large difference between the Method 2 and Method 3
estimates for Costa Rica is due to the very high labor intensity of its apparel exports and their predominance in Costa Rican exports.

The estimates in Table 1 are in the same range as job creation estimates published elsewhere. Using a different methodology, Thomas Espenshade produces estimates of the gross domestic investment necessary to generate a new job.[3] Espenshade estimates imply that $1 million (in 1982 dollars) of investment would create about 28 jobs in Caribbean island countries or 53 jobs in Central America. As $1 million of investment in manufacturing is likely to generate less than $1 million of manufacturing exports, Espenshade's job-creation ratios (jobs/$million) relevant to exports would be higher than 28 and 53.

V. MANUFACTURING EXPORT GROWTH PROJECTIONS

Some Caribbean and Central American countries have been able to rapidly increase their manufacturing exports to the United States during 1985–1988. However, these rates are not an appropriate measure of the potential for total manufacturing export growth in the near future. First, the U.S. economy has grown more rapidly than other trade partners. Certainly trade diversion has occurred—these countries have been diverting some of their exports from other customers to the United States. Consequently, the overall growth rate of Caribbean and Central American manufacturing exports to the world has been lower than for exports to the United States.

Second, the 1985–1988 period was a buoyant part of a growth cycle in Caribbean and Central American exports. The world economy was recovering from a sharp recession, and even the debtor countries achieved moderate growth rates. Projections for the next several years indicate that income growth will slow in the United States as well as in other trading partners of the Caribbean and Central American countries.

Third, with regional currencies tied closely to the movement of the U.S. dollar, the region's trade with other parts of the world have benefitted from the depreciation of the U.S. dollar against other industrial country currencies (32 percent from 1985 to 1988) for products where pricing significantly affects importers' decisions. However, the future does not promise similar rates of dollar depreciation.

Fourth, the 1985–1988 export growth rates reflect a certain amount of recapturing of lost time. During 1980–1986, manufacturing production came to a virtual standstill in all of the countries under study here (Table 3). Therefore, the rate of growth of total manufacturing exports from Caribbean and Central American countries to the world will probably be less than the 20–25 percent real growth seen in U.S. imports from Honduras, Costa Rica and the Dominican Republic. The future growth of manufacturing exports is likely to be closer to the 13.5 percent annual real increase of nontraditional exports to the United States from AID-assisted CBI countries during 1983–1988.[4]

TABLE 1

ESTIMATES OF JOBS CREATED DUE TO MANUFACTURING EXPORTS
(jobs per $million)

	Method 1	Method 2	Method 3
Costa Rica	60	60	129
Dominican Republic	108	110	96
El Salvador	31	43	23
Guatemala	49	50	58
Honduras	69	NA	NA
Jamaica	33	NA	NA
Nicaragua	25	NA	NA
Panama	30	30	25

As a lower bound, it seems entirely probable that the region's new emphasis on export-led development will yield export growth greater than experienced in the previous several decades. Despite the clouded international economic climate, they should be able to increase exports faster than they did during the period 1965–1980. The countries of Central America managed to increase their exports during that period by 2.5 to 5 percent per year, except for Costa Rica, which managed to achieve 7 percent annual growth. These averages are low because they include slowly growing agricultural exports.

Focusing more directly on manufacturing, these countries increased their production by 4.5 to 9 percent annually during 1965–1980. It is reasonable to hope that Caribbean and Central American countries can increase their manufactured exports at similar or faster rates during the 1990s. The question is how much of this faster growth might they achieve.

East Asian newly industrialized countries' (NICs) exports during 1965–1980 outperformed other developing countries dramatically. Manufacturing production grew 10 to 19 percent annually. Total exports grew 27 percent for Korea, 19 percent for Taiwan, 10 percent for Hong Kong and 5 percent for Singapore. Unfortunately, the world economic climate is not as favorable now, and it is unlikely to recapture the income and import growth rates of the 1970s. Furthermore, the increase of global competition has reduced the ability of even East Asia to achieve such growth rates in the future. During the 1980s, East Asian export growth was in the 10 to 13 percent range, while manufacturing production increased more slowly.

On the other hand, Latin American industrial production during the 1980s has been much slower than in East Asia, even for high growth industries. During 1983–1987, overall Latin American manufacturing production increased 6.4 percent, while light manufactures increased less

TABLE 2

ESTIMATES OF JOB CREATION DUE TO INDUSTRY EXPORTS
(Method 2)

Producing Industry	Total	Jobs/$mil. Export:				
(ISIC)		Product Description	Costa Rica	Dom. Rep.	El Salv.	Guate.	Pan.
31					43		
311–312		Food Products	69	204		71	39
313		Beverages	22	38		30	14
314		Tobacco Products	19	35		28	10
32					75		
321		Textiles	114	83		71	51
322		Apparel	225	161		49	53
323		Leather and Fur	104	58		72	27
324		Footwear	137	94		74	48
33					114		
331		Wood and Wood Prod.	87	69		76	51
332		Furniture and Fixt.	76	117		99	66
34					26		
341		Paper Products	27	49		34	15
342		Printing and Publ.	51	76		42	20
35					25		
351		Industrial Chem.	31	72		22	21
352		Other Chemical Prod.	50	82		40	21
353		Refined Petroleum	11	4		5	
354		Misc. Petro. & Coal				13	
355		Rubber Prod.	57	100		69	32
356		Plastic Prod.	60	88		64	25
36					32		
361		Pottery, china	116			134	
362		Glass Products	50	112		29	36
369		Other Nonmetal Min.	62	95		40	31
37					49		
371		Iron and Steel		46		43	24
372		Nonferrous Metals		69		40	
38					52		
381		Metal Products	99	47		23	28
382		Nonelect. Machine.	72	48		40	34
383		Elect. Machinery	37	65		25	13
384		Transport Equip.	44			29	24
385		Prof. & Scien. Equip.		45		83	36
39	390	Oth. Mfg. Indust.	207	86	51	25	

Source: Author's calculations. See text for methodology.

than 5 percent, except for paper products which grew at 10.3 percent annually.[5]

Given that Caribbean and Central American country manufactured exports should outperform their Latin American neighbors, 6.5 percent

TABLE 3

MANUFACTURING PRODUCTION, 1980–86
(annual average percent growth)

Dominican Republic	0.4
El Salvador	− 1.1
Guatemala	− 1.6
Honduras	− 2.1
Jamaica	1.1
Nicaragua	0.8
Panama	− 1.4

Source: World Bank, *World Development Report 1988.*

growth is a reasonable low-end estimate. At the high-end, an estimate of 13 percent puts the region in the ranks of the best performing East Asian NICs. A more probable outcome is somewhere in the middle. Nine percent is the highest estimated short-term growth rate in the region for manufacturing value-added according to statistics from the United Nations Industrial Development Organization (UNIDO). For the purposes of this paper, 9 percent growth per year is deemed to be an optimistic, but attainable growth rate during the medium- to long term for at least some of the countries in the region. Though far beyond the realm of the expected, the effects of a 20 percent growth rate—the average annual growth of manufactured exports of East Asian NICs during 1963–1980—are also estimated.[6]

In summary, this paper estimates potential job-creation between 1988 and 2000 for the four scenarios of export growth shown in Table 4.

VI. EMPLOYMENT IMPACT OF MANUFACTURED EXPORT GROWTH

Table 5 provides estimates of 1988–2000 job creation using both Methods 1 and 3 as explained in the methodological section above. Method 1 allows estimation of new employment for eight countries. The Method 3 estimates can be constructed for only five countries, but since they more closely approximate the structure of manufacturing exports that can be expected during the coming years, Method 3 estimates may be more accurate. The largest difference between the two methods is for Costa Rica, where exports are much more labor-intensive (mostly in apparel) than overall manufacturing production, thereby making Method 3 estimates much higher than those of Method 1.

TABLE 4

EXPORT GROWTH RATE SCENARIOS

Scenario	Assume Average Annual Real Growth of Manufactured Exports *(percentage)*
Low	6.5
Medium	9.0
High	13.0
Phenomenal	20.0

VII. RELEVANCE TO LABOR FORCE GROWTH IN THE REGION

The final issue for analysis in this paper is the significance of the net new employment that might be generated by manufactured export growth in the remainder of this century. Table 6 provides data on the size and growth of the labor force in the Caribbean Basin region. The labor force size calculated for 1988 is estimated from a variety of sources (Table 6). These sources provide data on differing years. The author adjusted those figures to portray 1988 by using the estimated average annual rate of labor force growth during 1985–1990 as listed in the International Labour Organization's *Economically Active Population, 1950–2025.* Increases for the rest of the century are then based upon the same publication's estimates for annual growth during 1990–2000.

According to estimates by Espenshade, Central American and Caribbean countries, in the absence of policy changes, will generate labor demand that will fall far short of accommodating these 7 million new workers. His estimates leave a labor surplus growth (the excess of new labor entrants over expected labor demand) between 3.6 and 4.8 million workers for the period 1985–2000.[7] Thus, about half or more of the new workers in the period 1988–2000 will not find work in the absence of policy changes.

Table 7 shows the proportion of labor force increases that will be absorbed by employment created as a result of growth of manufactured exports (again using the four growth scenarios listed in Table 4). As these tables show, the results are quite diverse. Estimated employment growth in Costa Rica is strongest, relative to labor force growth. Yet, even in Costa Rica, the new employment will be relatively small, unless high or phenomenally high manufactured export growth takes place. One reason Costa Rica fares so well in the long run is its relatively slower rate of labor

TABLE 5

JOB-CREATION ESTIMATES, 1988–2000

Assumed Annual Growth of Manufactured Exports (%):	Low 6.5	Medium 9.0	High 13.0	Phenomenal 20.0
Method 1	Resulting Job-Creation ('000s)			
Costa Rica	19	33	68	193
Dominican Republic	53	92	188	534
El Salvador	7	12	24	67
Guatemala	23	39	80	227
Jamaica	8	14	28	79
Nicaragua	4	8	16	44
Panama	7	12	25	72
Total, 8 countries	134	230	472	1342
Method 3				
Costa Rica	42	72	147	418
Dominican Republic	47	82	167	475
El Salvador	5	9	18	50
Guatemala	27	46	94	268
Panama	6	10	21	58
Total, 5 countries	127	218	446	1269

Source: Author's calculations. See text for methodology.

force growth—2.5 percent annually, compared to 3.3 percent for Central America as a whole.

For the other countries, the new jobs represent less than 20 percent of the expected labor force growth, even with a manufactured export growth rate of 13 percent per year. At the more achievable 9 percent annual growth rate (the "Medium" scenario), the jobs represent less than 10 percent of the new entrants to the work force for the Dominican Republic and less than 5 percent for the other countries.

Consequently, in general, the expected new employment generated by manufactured exports will be rather small in comparison to the rapid increases taking place in the labor forces of Central American and Caribbean countries.

Only in Costa Rica, and possibly in the Dominican Republic, can it be said that new manufactured exports will contribute significantly to fulfilling employment needs in the rest of the century—and only if the export growth rate substantially exceeds 13 percent.

VIII. IMPORTANCE OF NONMANUFACTURING

Although these countries are highly dependent upon foreign trade, their exports are dominated by agricultural products, not manufacturing (Table 8). Thus, the structure of output in these economies supports the

TABLE 6

LABOR FORCE PROJECTIONS FOR THE CARIBBEAN BASIN

	Est. 1988 Labor Force	Est. Increase 1988–2000
	(thousands)	
Caribbean Basin	17414	7162
Central America	9192	4408
Costa Rica	952	316
El Salvador	2066	966
Guatemala	2740	1318
Honduras	1458	837
Nicaragua	1172	693
Panama	804	277
Caribbean	8222	2753
Barbados	114	21
Belize	57	21
Dom. Republic	2614	1048
Guyana	291	97
Haiti	2945	893
Jamaica	1083	339
Suriname	125	46
Trinidad & Tobago	482	132
Other Carib.	511	156

Sources: Labor force size estimates are based on: World Bank, *Social Indicators of Development 1988;* CIA, *World Factbook 1988;* ILO, *Yearbook of Labour Statistics* (1987 and 1988 editions). Labor force growth rates are based on: ILO, *Economically Active Population, 1950–2025.*

conclusion above that manufacturing exports will provide only a small portion of the necessary employment.

IX. POLICY IMPLICATIONS

The employment estimates in this paper suggest that the extraordinary growth of manufacturing exports in the region during the mid-1980s has had a relatively small effect upon the labor force in the region. Estimates developed in another paper by the author indicate that growth of manufacturing exports to the United States during the first five years of the Caribbean Basin Initiative (1984–1988) also did not provide much of the needed employment generation.[8] Consequently, the countries in Central America and the Caribbean should not rely upon export-led growth only within the manufacturing sector. A large majority of new employment, even within Costa Rica and the Dominican Republic, must be generated by agricultural exports and by production (manufacturing as well as agricultural) for domestic consumption.

TABLE 7

ESTIMATED JOB-CREATION COMPARED TO EXPECTED LABOR FORCE INCREASES,
1988–2000
(*manufacturing export-related jobs as a percentage of expected labor force increase*)

| | | Growth Scenarios: | | |
	Low	Medium	High	Phenomenal
Method 1				
Costa Rica	6%	11%	22%	61%
Dominican Republic	5	9	18	51
El Salvador	1	1	2	7
Guatemala	2	3	6	17
Jamaica	2	4	8	23
Nicaragua	1	1	2	6
Panama	3	4	9	26
Total, 8 countries	2	4	8	23
Method 3				
Costa Rica	13	23	47	132
Dominican Republic	5	8	16	45
El Salvador	1	1	2	5
Guatemala	2	3	7	20
Panama	2	4	7	21
Total, 5 countries	3	6	11	32

Source: Data in Table 5 as a percentage of the relevant data in Table 6.

With the region's labor force growing at almost 3 percent annually, agricultural exports must grow substantially faster than agricultural production grew in the 1980s, if jobs are to be created at the current level of real earnings. The price and demand outlooks for most traditional agricultural products are relatively bleak in the medium term. There may be some potential to develop niches in some nontraditional agricultural markets, such as in off-season vegetables, exotic fruits and ornamental plants. However, in aggregate, agricultural production is unlikely to expand rapidly enough in the 1990s.

Expanding production for domestic consumption, therefore, cannot be ignored in the development strategies of these countries in the 1990s. Of course, the potential of the domestic market to expand is limited in these very small, open economies. Integration into the world economy is an inevitable course for these countries. Yet, the employment data in this paper suggest that it would be dangerous to pursue export-expansion single-mindedly without addressing the need for internally generated employment.

In short, the pressures of rapidly expanding labor forces may be too much for these countries to handle in the medium term. Migration may be the only economically viable option for some people. Without migration—or dramatic control of population growth—the region's workers

TABLE 8

MANUFACTURED EXPORTS IN GDP

(percentages)

	Exports/GDP 1986	Mfr. Exports/ Tot. Exports 1987	Approx. Mfr. Exp./GDP 1986/87
Costa Rica	31	40	12
Dominican Republic	9	22	2
El Salvador	25	31	8
Guatemala	16	36	6
Honduras	27	12	3
Jamaica	53	66	35
Nicaragua	13	10	1
Panama	34	13	4

Sources: Exports/GDP from IMF, *International Financial Statistics Yearbook,* 1988; Manufactured exports from World Bank, *World Development Report,* 1989.222

will sink further into poverty.

Recommendations. The region will continue to require the help of the external donor community. On the aid front, a broad-based development strategy should be adopted to generate the necessary employment. Domestic expansion must be seen as a complement, rather than a competitor, with export growth.

As for trade policy, industrial country barriers to trade in labor-intensive products should be removed, especially in the apparel, textile, leather and fur, footwear, pottery and wood product industries. Clearly, the labor-intensive products of the region can have a large impact on employment. Currently, the United States maintains significant tariff and nontariff barriers to the trade of some of these labor-intensive products. Furthermore, particularly for apparel trade, the threat of future U.S. trade restrictions hangs like a black cloud over investment decisions. Abolition of the Multi-Fiber Arrangement (which regulates international apparel and textile trade) would be one of the most effective actions that the United States could take to increase employment in the Caribbean Basin. This would remove the uncertainty associated with the current special access program for Caribbean Basin apparel. A reduction of the high U.S. tariffs on textile and apparel products (generally above 20 percent ad valorem) would be even more helpful. Another action of great potential is reduction of U.S. trade-distorting agricultural policies.

Traditional agriculture will remain significant in these economies for awhile. The boom-bust commodity price cycles have disrupted attempts by the region to finance diversification into production of goods with more stable prices. Since the magnitude of these economic problems is so large, the United States should reconsider its recent opposition to commodity agreements and compensatory financing systems.[9]

Although services may provide some of the more highly educated, English-speaking countries with an avenue of development, the track record so far indicates that service investments tend to be highly volatile and most of the region is not very attractive for such investment, except in the controversial area of tourism. Tourism itself appears to have the drawback of requiring large amounts of imports to satisfy the foreign tastes of the clientele. Environmental concerns also limit the full exploitation of the Caribbean beauty by the tourism industry.

The proposed U.S. legislation to expand and extend the Caribbean Basin Initiative contains useful elements to address some of these concerns.[10] Expanded sugar quotas, increased access for apparel and footwear and an extension of the time period for duty-free access are all worthy efforts to improve U.S. policy toward the region. Unfortunately, changes in the sugar program are likely to be ruled illegal by the General Agreement on Tariff and Trade (GATT), and domestic political opposition to increase access for apparel and footwear seems to be insurmountable except in the context of a multilateral accord in Geneva.

However, the role of development assistance will remain pivotal. Through their impact on infrastucture for export, on the overall policy environment and on the sectoral distribution of production, bilateral and multilateral development assistance will remain the major U.S. policy tools available to address the pressing needs of the region. These aid policies should be held accountable for their employment impact.

APPENDIX:
CONSTRUCTION OF THE DATA AND ESTIMATES

This section goes step-by-step through the process used by the author to gather the relevant data used to produce the job estimates in this paper.

The first stage was determining what was feasible under the constraints of available data. The author desired sets of data that would be roughly comparable across countries, readily accessible and cover a reasonably recent year in the 1980s. Therefore, the primary data sources are the U.N. Industrial Development Organization (for value-added and gross output data), the U.N. International Labor Organization (for labor cost and employment data), the U.N. data banks (for international trade) and the International Monetary Fund (for exchange rates). As it happened, most of the required data in each of the categories were found for the year 1985 (though data for 1986 are available in a number of the categories). When parts of the data for Costa Rica were not found in the standard sources, the author (feeling that Costa Rica is an important country to include in this study) obtained roughly comparable data from Costa Rican sources to fill the gaps.

Method 1 (Average Manufacturing Job/Export Ratio). Value-added data for manufacturing industries (by three-digit International Standard Industrial Code) are provided by country in the statistical annex of the UNIDO *Industry and Development: Global Report 1987* (Vienna, 1987). The UNIDO report also provides aggregate average data on manufacturing for wages and salaries, employment and gross output as well. Thus, using this source and export data, it is possible to calculate equations 1 and 2 once average manufacturing GO/X and IGO/X ratios are estimated (such an approach being called "Method 1" in this study).

Method 1, of course, provides only an aggregate estimate of job-creation due to manufacturing exports (i.e., no industry-specific estimates). Furthermore, Method 1 suffers from not taking into account that overall manufacturing production may not have the same labor intensity as manufacturing exports. As it turns out, for some Central American countries, the labor intensities of overall manufacturing are similar to the labor intensities of manufactured exports. However, Costa Rican manufacturing exports are much more labor-intensive than overall manufacturing production, while the reverse pertains to El Salvador. In sum, Method 1 is but a crude approximation only applicable to overall manufacturing.

The only missing data required to calculate job-creation potential using Method 1 are an estimate of GO/X and IGO/X. While on the surface one could assume that an increase in gross output is equal to an increase in export sales, it is true that some gross output in an industry is actually used up in the production of other output, thereby making GO/X greater than one.[11] Input-output data on the Costa Rican economy in the 1970s show that some 17 percent of textile production does not survive to fulfill final demand because it is used in production of other textiles. Other industries use smaller percentages and many industries essentially deliver all production to fulfill final demand. In the absence of input-output tables for each country, the author used a proxy for the aggregate manufacturing GO/X ratio. The figure of 1.0225 is the unweighted mean of the country-specific figures derived for the five countries covered in this study under Method 2.

The IGO/X ratio represents the amount of gross output necessary in other parts of the economy to support the production of the exports from a given industry. In the United States, this ratio is in the ballpark of one-to-one.[12] However, Central American and some Caribbean economies do not have such an articulated service sector nor the degree of differentiation among manufacturing industries. Therefore, one should expect the ratio to be considerably smaller, as a higher proportion of the production is done within the firm rather than subcontracted to others. Again, in the absence of input-output tables for each country, the author used a proxy for the aggregate IGO/X ratio. The figure of 0.5527 is the unweighted mean of the country-specific figures derived for the five countries covered in this study under Method 2.

In the cases of both the average manufacturing GO/X and the IGO/X ratios calculated under Method 2, the variation among the five countries is relatively small (0.5165 to 0.5670). This is because the distribution of manufacturing value-added among the three-digit ISIC industrial categories is similar for Costa Rica, the Dominican Republic, El Salvador, Guatemala and Panama. In effect, the industrial structures of these economies are very similar. Consequently, the author went ahead and used the unweighted means for other countries as well. Thus, job-creation potential is estimated under Method 1 for eight countries: Costa Rica, the Dominican Republic, El Salvador, Guatemala, Honduras, Jamaica, Nicaragua and Panama (see the "Job-Creation Ratios" section below).

Method 2 (Industry Job/Export Ratios and Manufacturing Average). In addition to the limitations previously mentioned for Method 1, there are considerable discrepancies between the wage and salary data in the UNIDO report and the labor compensation data in the International Labour Office's *Yearbook of Labour Statistics.* For this reason and because industry-specific ratios are necessary for more accurate estimates of export-related employment generation, the author chose to use the labor cost and employment data from the ILO and value-added data from UNIDO in Method 2. Because of missing data, the countries that could be covered under this method was reduced to five: Costa Rica, the Dominican Republic, El Salvador, Guatemala and Panama. In the case of Costa Rica, employment and labor compensation data were obtained for 1986 from the Caja Costarricense del Seguro Social and value-added data are for 1986 and from the Banco Central de Costa Rica.

The ILO yearbook provides average labor compensation per employee (in national currency) by industry (according to the three-digit ISIC classification, except for El Salvador, for which the two-digit level was reported). The values were converted into dollars using the annual average market rate as reported in the IMF *International Financial Statistics Yearbook 1988*. Hourly compensation rates were converted to annual rates using average weekly work hours reported in the ILO Yearbook. The ILO yearbook reports employment in each industry as well. From this data, the annual cost of labor in the industry was calculated as well as the average annual compensation per employee. Unfortunately, the ILO yearbook does not report data for 1985 for all countries. The year 1984 is used for the Dominican Republic and 1983 for El Salvador.

Combining this labor cost data with the value-added data in the UNIDO report, the author computed each industry's labor cost as a percentage of value-added (LC/VA in equation 1) and how many jobs are supported within an industry by a given level of spending on labor (J/LC in equation 1). The manufacturing average value-added gross-output ratio (as reported in the UNIDO report) was used for VA/GO in equation 1.

Industry-specific GO/X and IGO/X ratios are based upon input-output data on the Costa Rican economy that appears in an Inter-American Development Bank paper by Jorge Tejada. Tejada took a 1968 input-output table elaborated by Victor Bulmer-Thomas and updated the table to 1975, creating a 41-sector table.[13] Although the data in this input-output table are quite outdated compared to the actual production structure of the Costa Rican economy in 1985, it may provide good approximations of 1985 industry linkages for some other Central American and Caribbean countries, insofar as those countries are "behind" Costa Rica's level of industrial development. Since these countries have similar resource endowments, infrastructure and trading partners, as did Costa Rica in the 1970s, the input-output data are assumed to provide reasonable estimates of 1985 industry linkages.

Tejada's data are used in this paper to calculate Leontief coefficients which are the basis for the GO/X and IGO/X ratios given by industry in Table A1 below.[14]

After deriving the industry-specific direct job-creation multiplier according to equation 1 for each industry in each of the five countries, a weighted average was derived for each element in equation 1 for each country's manufacturing sector as a whole. The weighing was done by

TABLE A1

DIRECT AND INDIRECT OUTPUT RATIOS

Industry (ISIC)	GO/X	IGO/X
311-312	1.0052	1.0150
313	1.0301	0.3229
314	1.0041	0.2944
321	1.1749	0.3200
322	1.0000	0.4800
323	1.1199	0.4000
324	1.0000	0.6000
331	1.1561	0.5400
332	1.0000	0.8100
341	1.0036	0.1120
342	1.0000	0.1680
351	1.0274	0.3100
352	1.0000	0.4700
353	1.0011	0.0510
354	1.0000	0.0760
355-356	1.0112	0.4280
36	1.0007	0.5228
37	1.0615	0.2790
381-382	1.0131	0.1531
383	1.0011	0.3356
384	1.0004	0.1005
385	1.0000	0.2000
390	1.0333	0.3980

value-added in 1985 (1986 for Costa Rica).

For equation 2, which calculates indirect employment-generation, average national labor costs (including agriculture and services as well as manufacturing) are necessary. However, with this data absent, the author chose to use the national average for manufacturing labor costs as a proxy, recognizing that this causes the estimates of indirect job-creation to be somewhat conservative (since labor compensation in manufacturing is higher than economy-wide in economies where agriculture remains significant and high-skilled services are relatively underdeveloped). Of course, most of the interindustry linkages are with manufacturing or skill-intensive services, making this proxy not terribly inappropriate.

Each industry-specific equation 2 contains the MLC/IGO and J/MLC weighted averages for manufacturing derived within Method 2. Combined with the IGO/X ratios in Table A1, the indirect jobs created by production in each industry are calculated. These figures are then averaged according to the value-added weights of each industry to produce the overall manufacturing indirect job-creation figure. The total job-export ratio is the sum of the direct and indirect ratios (see the "Job-Creation Ratios" section below).

Method 3 (Manufacturing Export-Specific Job-Creation Ratio). The overall manufacturing average job-creation figure calculated under Method 2 reflects the manufacturing sector's labor intensity. As was mentioned previously, the manufacturing exports of these countries do not necessarily involve production with the same labor intensity as overall production. Hence, the author took the next step of producing figures that better reflect the labor-intensity of exported production.

The industry-specific calculations in Method 2 are the same as those in Method 3. However, the overall manufacturing average is weighted according to the size of exports to the world from each industry in 1985 (1984 for Guatemala).

The export data are from the U.N. data bank and are classified according to the Standard International Trade Classification (Revision 2). Consequently, exports can be matched only imperfectly to the industry which produced them. Table A2 provides a rundown of how the author matched ISIC to SITC codes.

TABLE A2

PRODUCT CLASSIFICATIONS

Industry Export (ISIC)	Product	(SITC)
313	Beverages	11
314	Tobacco products	12
321	Textiles	26 + 65
322	Apparel	84
323	Leather and fur products	61 + 83
324	Footwear	85
331	Wood and wood products	24 + 63
332	Furniture and fixtures	82
341	Paper and paper products	64
342	Printing and publishing	892
351-352	Chemical products	5 (−58)
353-354	Petroleum products	33
355	Rubber products	62
356	Plastic products	58
36	Nonmetal mineral products	66
371	Iron and Steel	67
372	Nonferrous metals	68
381	Metal products	69 + 81
382	Nonelectrical machinery	71 through 75
383	Electrical machinery	76 through 77
384	Transport equipment	78 through 79
385	Scientific and prof. eqpmt.	87
390	Other mfg. goods	89 (−892)

NOTES

1. For a full assessment of the CBI during its first three years of operation, see Stuart K. Tucker, "Trade Unshackled: Assessing the Value of the Caribbean Basin Initiative" in *Central American Recovery and Development* ed. by William Ascher and Ann Hubbard (Duke University Press, Durham, 1989).

2. See U.S. General Accounting Office, *Caribbean Basin Initiative: Need for More Reliable Data on Business Activity Resulting From the Initiative* (Washington, USGPO, 1986) regarding the earliest survey. A second, more thorough survey has been conducted, though this more recent effort still gauges gross rather than net effects and conveys only a partial picture of the investment and employment situation. See U.S. Department of Commerce, *Caribbean Basin Investment Survey* (Washington, November 1988).

3. Thomas J. Espenshade, "Growing Imbalances Between Labor Supply and Labor Demand in the Caribbean Basin," in *Mexican and Central American Population and U.S. Immigration Policy,* edited by Frank D. Bean, Jurgen Schmandt, and Sidney Weintraub (University of Texas at Austin, 1989), pp. 140–142.

4. James W. Fox, "Is the Caribbean Basin Initiative Working?" (manuscript, October 1989), Table IV.

5. Light manufacturing is defined as ISIC categories 31, 32, 33, 342, 355, 356, and 39. Data from *U.N. Monthly Bulletin of Statistics*, February 1989.

6. James W. Fox, "A Strategy for Export-led Growth in the Caribbean Basin" (manuscript, November 1989), p. 7.

7. See Thomas J. Espenshade, "Growing Imbalances between Labor Supply and Labor Demand in the Caribbean Basin," in *Mexican and Central American Population and U.S. Immigration Policy,* edited by Frank D. Bean, Jurgen Schmandt and Sidney Weintraub (University of Texas at Austin, 1989), p. 150. Espenshade assumes that the most reasonable expectation of labor demand growth is somewhere between his low– and medium growth scenarios. My labor force supply growth estimates rely upon the same ILO source used in Espenshade's paper.

8. See Stuart K. Tucker, "The Caribbean Basin Initiative and Job Creation in the Basin," (paper prepared for the XV International Congress of the Latin American Studies Association, September 1989).

9. Central American countries could lose annual coffee export revenues on the order of the size of annual U.S. aid to the region due to the July 1989 collapse of the International Coffee Agreement.

10. "The Caribbean Basin Economic Recovery Expansion Act of 1989" was introduced as H.R. 1233 and was passed by the House Ways and Means Committee on 20 June 1989 and and was attached to the Budget Reconciliation Act. However, the Senate dropped it from consideration in 1989. The Senate Finance Committee began to review the whole package in late February 1990, but appears unwilling to fight for dramatic changes in the program.

11. For many developing country manufactures, many of the inputs going into gross-output are imported. This is why value-added/gross-output ratios are low for these countries.

12. Lester Davis, "Domestic Employment Generated by U.S. Exports," U.S. Department of Commerce Staff Report (Washington, April 1983).

13. See Jorge Tejada, "Update of the National Accounting Parameters at Efficiency Prices for Costa Rica," (Inter-American Development Bank Papers on Project Analysis No. 15, April 1980). Tejada used a modified RAS procedure to update the input-output table.

14. Leontief coefficients provide the amount of output required for a given amount of output delivered to final demand (thereby incorporating indirect production and use of indirect inputs).

4

Section 936 as a Development Resource in the Caribbean: Suggestions for a More Effective Policy

Ramón E. Daubón

I. BACKGROUND

Section 936 of the U.S. Internal Revenue Code applies to funds generated by certain U.S. corporations in Puerto Rico during their normal productive activities or by secondary financial investment of previously generated revenues. Since 1976, these funds have been given ample exemption privileges from U.S. taxes under section 936 and are repatriated upon payment of an adjustable "toll gate" tax to the government of Puerto Rico. This toll gate tax decreases with the length of time that the funds are kept in secondary investments in Puerto Rico. Because of their tax advantages, such funds are deposited and loaned out for projects at lower than normal interest rates. As of mid-year 1988, the stock of these funds, including bank and other financial deposits and direct investments by the U.S. corporations, amounted to about $15 billion.[1]

Since January 1987, these funds have been allowed to be invested in eligible development projects outside Puerto Rico in selected countries as a financial complement to the U.S. government's Caribbean Basin Initiative (CBI), and purportedly in the context of the Puerto Rican government's twin-plants initiative[2]. It should be noted that the three programs—Section 936, CBI and the twin-plants program—are separate policy measures with distinct histories and rationales. They are often discussed together to exploit their evident complementarities.[3]

Present regulations for the secondary investment of 936 funds require that 15 percent be placed in Puerto Rican non-exempt public corporations, such as the Government Development Bank (GDB). Because of the reluctance of private depositories of 936 funds to invest in Caribbean projects (given the commercial, political and foreign exchange risks discussed below), it has been widely proposed that the GDB make available a portion of its deposits for small to medium-sized development projects in the Caribbean, either as guarantees or as direct credits, and through channels yet undetermined.[4]

Pursuant to regulations issued by the Secretary of the Treasury of Puerto Rico, the GDB is authorized to make loans outside of the island as long as they benefit Puerto Rico, for example in the context of twin-plant operations.[5]

Simultaneously, a private development CBI Fund is now being established. This fund would be used to directly finance medium and large development projects. Investments in this CBI fund by 936 companies would indeed qualify as eligible investments under 936 regulations as approved by the Government of Puerto Rico and the U.S. Treasury, and would be geared toward financing development loans in eligible CBI countries either directly or through local financial intermediaries.[6]

II. OBSTACLES TO 936 CARIBBEAN INVESTMENTS

Although everyone seems to agree on the desirability of making 936 deposits available for a broad range of Caribbean projects, several obstacles exist.

First, by request of the U.S. Treasury Department, the Congress has stipulated that these funds may be used only in countries that ratify Tax Information Exchange Agreements (TIEA) with the United States. This ratification, which would allow reciprocal access to tax records, has posed delicate political questions in a number of otherwise eligible countries.[7]

Second, the funds are essentially *short-term* financial deposits; owners are entitled to withdraw on short notice. Neither the GDB nor private banks can responsibly enter into long-term financial obligations with such unsecured short-term deposits. This discourages major infrastructure projects and most fixed capital investments, regardless of whether the 936 regulations allow them. However, the export promotion focus of both CBI and the twin-plants concept almost mandate larger industrial capacities and therefore new fixed capital, and these in turn will require added infrastructure in most countries of the region.[8]

Third, the funds *are* bank deposits; they belong to the depositors. The GDB must therefore apply ordinary banking criteria to loan decisions, rather than development banking criteria. Thus, it may only invest the funds in projects where a high probability of success exists. This rules out many new development ventures, especially by rising entrepreneurs without proven records, the very type of local talent that the CBI should aim to develop. Needless to say, these entrepreneurs are also less likely to have the connections and wherewithal to enter into the twin-plant agreements to which the GDB is limited outside of Puerto Rico. Loans by private bank depositories of 936 funds, which also would conceivably be available for "stand alone" projects, would have investment criteria at least as stringent as the GDB's.[9]

Fourth, in addition to the credit risk inherent in any loan, 936 lenders are faced with a foreign exchange risk. Exchange rate instability in situations of high import dependence—as is increasingly a factor in the Caribbean under the CBI—can be an insurmountable problem. Foreign banks will thus be reluctant to lend dollars for operations that generate revenue in local currencies; therefore 936 credits will be limited essentially to use only in export operations. There is also the risk that hard currency reserves may not be available at all in the borrowing country at the time of payment, even if conversion back to U.S. dollars were to be theoretically guaranteed. It is important to note that, as foreign currency payments typically flow through central banks, this affects even export-only operations that involve transactions in hard currencies. In addition, banks will be reluctant to lend dollars to countries which already have high dollar debts. In the case of the two largest 936 depositories, Chase and Citibank, these debts are often owed to these very banks.

Finally, the difference in interest rates between 936 funds and normal Eurodollar sources ultimately amounts to only one or two percentage points less after commissions and handling fees. This is significant, but it will not make or break a project. Therefore, the limitations and extra procedural requirements imposed by 936 sources may justify going to other sources in the first place when such other sources are available.

Thus, 936 credits are actually only available to borrowers who can provide guarantees (and hence have access to other sources); the credits are more available for non-native enterprises; and 936 funds are basically able to be used for short-term applications, not for the capital investment requirements of the expanding businesses that the CBI aims to promote. Moreover, the focus of the 936-CBI-twin plants composite is exports, given the small size of local markets. Yet export operations typically require a scale larger than local infrastructures are used to—or often capable of—accommodating. For example, a $2 million cardboard container factory promoted in Dominica (a small operation by CBI standards) will use up about 25 percent of the country's electrical capacity.[10] But investments to expand infrastructure, typically long-term ventures, are more difficult to establish with the short to medium-term 936 deposits. Therefore, it should not be expected that 936 funds, given present circumstances, will become a substantial source of credit for development in the Caribbean, even of the export-oriented development that the CBI promotes.[11]

Much of the 936 investment that is occurring in CBI countries is in the form of direct investment by the 936 companies themselves, in twin (*complementary* is a better term) operations of their own Puerto Rican plants.[12] Vertically integrated with their Puerto Rican counterparts, these investments allow 936 funds to be invested overseas to provide a low operating cost structure in the CBI country and a complementary tax-favored profit structure in Puerto Rico. These investments create jobs in the CBI country and are therefore desirable. Yet, as they are not tied to the local economies to a substantial degree (the larger shares of the inputs they buy and the outputs they sell are outside the CBI country), and are not a source of entrepreneurial experience for local businesses, the impact of these 936 investments as an engine of development is limited.

III. FOSTERING CARIBBEAN DEVELOPMENT

The relevant issue here should certainly be whether or not such a structure of investment will foster Caribbean development. But neither CBI, 936 nor the twin-plants program directly addresses this issue.

The Puerto Rican twin-plants initiative was devised as a way to continue to promote Puerto Rican industry, after its wage structure became uncompetitive, by also allowing U.S. investors parallel access to lower wage CBI labor markets. The measure was devised primarily in Puerto Rico's interest, however, and does not fully elaborate on what happens at the other end of the twin arrangements.[13]

The CBI, meanwhile, was devised as a means to promote economic and, consequentially, political stability in the Caribbean Basin. While its focus is clearly stable economic growth in the region, its conceptualization was based on wage employment rather than on local business promotion, and on the growth of sales to the United States rather than on the growth of local markets and an increase in transactions within the region. Thus, while the CBI is geared toward the development of employment and incomes, it works within a framework that conceives of the region as an extension of the U.S. economy. While this notion might be appropriate in a development strategy for a depressed region of the United States, or even for Puerto Rico, it fails to acknowledge the Caribbean's limited access to U.S. markets—access subject to political winds in Congress which are far beyond the Caribbean's control—and its restricted labor mobility to the United States. Neither its businesses nor its governments have free access to U.S. capital markets to accommodate the infrastructure needs of rapid growth. The Caribbean is simply not a region of the U.S. economy like Appalachia, or even Puerto Rico, might be and cannot be treated as such.[14]

Finally, section 936 was first devised as a financial agent for Puerto Rico's development, and since January 1987—and primarily at the initiative of the government of Puerto Rico—as a financial resource of the CBI. Until then, the measure had been instrumental in attracting substantial investment to the Puerto Rican economy and in creating a substantive base of employment on the island.[15] Nevertheless, in times of fiscal austerity in the United States, the measure was being questioned in Congress and by the U.S. Treasury as a drain of tax revenues.[16] The Puerto Rican government and other parties recognized that it was in their own self-interest to extend some of the benefits of 936 to the other countries in the region. The regulated use of 936 deposits for investments in selected CBI countries was thus defended as a shot in the arm for the CBI, which since its inception had not generated the expected level of economic activity. The debate at that time centered on giving financial "teeth" to the CBI as it was, and not on whether the exclusive focus on exports should be questioned and expanded to promote the development of local markets. It appears, certainly, that not enough thought was originally given to the concrete ways in which 936 was to contribute to Caribbean development.[17] Funds are simply not as accessible as initial plans anticipated.

Twin-plants have had a degree of success in promoting investments in selected countries, but financing is typically procured elsewhere and not under 936 regulations. The most successful examples of twin-plants development have been the Dominican Republic, a recent signatory to TIEA, and Costa Rica, which had not yet signed the agreement as of this writing.

Consider, then, that small development projects are thought to involve higher risk and are therefore unattractive to private depositories of 936 funds. These small projects are likely to be financed only by the GDB, if at all. Consider also that the GDB is limited by statute to financing only twin-plant projects. Therefore, we must concern ourselves with these issues: does the CBI, in fact, promote development and stability in the Caribbean?, and does the availability of 936 funds through twin-plant investments serve to further this goal of the CBI?

Demonstrably, the CBI has had little effect to date in promoting self-sustaining economic growth and development in the Caribbean Basin. In fact, it is not even clear that the model it promotes, that of export-induced growth financed with foreign capital investment in non-traditional industries, has by itself promoted self-sustained development in other economies as open as the Caribbean's. This can be said even after factoring out extraneous events such as war, debt and commodity price fluctuations.

The comparatively small and unconnected Caribbean Basin economies would appear to be especially vulnerable to the failure of this development model. The formation of strong local and regional markets, in the absence of *guaranteed* external ones,[18] would mandate a greater level of transactions between the various countries. Yet the trade connections fostered by the model favor multiple direct bilateral lines with the ultimate market—the United States—at the expense of intra-regional transactions. Moreover, the present limiting of 936 funds to signatories of Tax Information Exchange Agreements precludes using—and hence strengthening—the regional organizations, because their charters forbid any member's exclusion from any of their programs.[19] While acknowledging that efforts at Caribbean economic integration have been made for decades with only minimal success, it is nonetheless clear that this bilateral emphasis in fact *discourages* the integration of the local markets.

Puerto Rico's own case helps to illustrate the limits of this model. It embodies the ideal conditions for this paradigm: no foreign exchange risks, the political umbrella of a U.S. possession, unhindered access to U.S. markets for its products and to U.S. capital markets for industrial fixed-capital and public infrastructure investments, and freedom for its surplus labor—inevitably displaced by the transformations inherent in the industrialization model—to migrate to the United States. Puerto Rico was quite successful in applying this export-induced growth model.[20] Yet, while a quarter of its population migrated between 1945 and 1965 (largely in the labor ages), its unemployment rates stubbornly remained above ten percent. To this date, Puerto Rico depends largely on external capital and has traditionally found it difficult to promote local entrepreneurship.[21] By focusing so sharply on outside investors, this strategy seemed to breed more salaried managers than homespun investors.

In the CBI countries, which have economic structures resembling those previously found in Puerto Rico but which have few of Puerto Rico's stated advantages, it will be harder to succeed. Moreover, to the extent that the present model *does* succeed, one may question the extent of its contribution to sustained self-propelled growth. Inasmuch as this development strategy draws factors of production away from internal markets or from the developing entrepreneurial class, it will hinder such growth. To the extent that it builds bilateral trade channels with the United States *at the expense of* transactions within the region, it makes that growth even more unlikely.

IV. LABOR FORCE AND MIGRATORY IMPLICATIONS

The experience of Puerto Rico is most illustrative in the behavior of its labor force. Between 1950 and 1960, the best years of Puerto Rican industrial growth, over 600,000 Puerto Ricans outmigrated, almost 25 percent of its population. The rest of the Caribbean should be no different. While unhindered access to the United States is not available to Caribbean migrants, the incentives to migrate are likely to be similar.[22]

The reorientation of factors of production—especially agriculture— toward the export markets, the easy availability of imported manufactures, the rising expectations of living standards, the streamlining of marketing and services and the consequent breakdown of traditional channels all militate against traditional sources of employment and income. The inevitable result is the displacement of traditional labor. This pattern is common throughout the Third World.

These workers gravitate towards the centers of economic activity, typically the urban areas, in search for work. Contrary to popular belief, though, the search is not necessarily for jobs in the expanding modern sectors. At least as many workers are searching for self-employment in the interstices of these sectors, in the marginal economy.

Contrary also to popular belief, these marginal sectors are not always languishing. They are typically very active and provide not just a support economy for their own populations, but are intricately tied to the expanding modern sectors.[23] In the marginal sectors, the modern sector finds a ready source of labor, plus unregulated support services in areas such as maintenance and custodial services, transportation, food services and other low-skill occupations. Although the low-skill sectors are believed to embody uniform deprivation, there actually exists a stratified income scale with some openness and mobility within this marginal economy. Its lower end conforms to the common vision of Third World urban squalor, but its high end overlaps the lower levels of the modern sectors and pushes into their middle class.

Mobility in this sector is severely restricted, however. Ideally, it is a source of occupations likely to attract innovative workers from the traditional sectors: those resisting the rigidity of factory work. But mobility through small businesses is limited by the availability of training in entrepreneurial skills and of credit for operating funds and capital expansions. Investment in human and financial capital is therefore sorely needed.

Workers in these sectors who are unable to penetrate the credit barriers are likely to look for opportunities elsewhere. Factory work is an option, but not the only (or necessarily even the preferred) one. While migration has *always* been a fact of Caribbean life, the advent of satellite television has exposed migrants to a larger world outside. They are now likely to migrate farther and in greater numbers than ever before. As migrant beachheads become established in U.S. cities, the transition and adaptation becomes that much easier for individuals, and the flow increases.

It would seem, though, that those who do manage to get established as entrepreneurs in the marginal sectors would be *least* likely to migrate. In fact, it would appear that these microentrepreneurs would have less incentive to migrate than industrial wage workers with similar incomes. The latter do not have the same sort of stake in their home turf that the entrepreneurs do, and in the enclave of the factory,[24] they would appear to be more removed from their home environment and more in contact with the world outside. In this scenario, factory workers would have in fact begun the migration already, and thus the actual physical move would represent to them a smaller step than to someone coming from the traditional or marginal sectors. Finally, the factory workers would be more likely to have established contact with previous migrants employed in similar industries in the United States or Canada, and more likely to realize that their same work there would fetch a multiple of their present wages.

Clearly, then, a policy to facilitate the development of the informal sectors by providing credit and technical/managerial assistance to small entrepreneurs would serve to energize a potentially dynamic segment of the economy, and to retain at home some of the more creative members of this emerging business class.

The present policy of encouraging investment only in new export industries promotes wage labor at the expense of self-starting entrepreneurs, and places that labor in a position where it is perhaps more exposed to incentives to migrate. This, of course, will deprive the country of the contribution of this work force after it has learned its industrial skills. Ideally, these workers could be involved instead in new local businesses.

In summary, present CBI policy disrupts traditional production and displaces labor, but production technologies in the export sectors offer only limited new opportunities for these workers. Those who are not employed in growth export sectors are forced to find other options. But in an environment that does not foster the growth of local markets because new investment is geared to producing for export, often with necessarily imported inputs, those other options are limited. The answer, often, is to seek to migrate. Moreover, it seems that even those who do obtain jobs in the export sectors may themselves be more likely to migrate than others who manage to achieve similar income levels as entrepreneurs in the marginal sectors.

By promoting one type of development and excluding another, the policies of the CBI thus foment outmigration. And if 936 were more effective in promoting the goals of the CBI, as presently formulated, it would further contribute to this outmigration.

V. AN ALTERNATIVE APPROACH

It should be emphasized, nonetheless, that the Caribbean needs outside investment. It needs the injections of capital that the CBI could bring and it needs the training grounds for its technical managers. It also needs export products to sell in markets that will generate the foreign exchange it must have for its infrastructure and its technology. Section 936 should be a part of this, and the active efforts of Puerto Rico's Economic Development Administration (FOMENTO) to promote it should continue.

But the Caribbean also needs a complement of investments to develop its internal markets and its entrepreneurial capacity, and hence its ability to generate its own future investment. (Given the small size of its individual markets, the Caribbean also needs to develop mechanisms to integrate these markets.) Such investments, though small in comparison to those for export industries, are not materializing now because:

1. the internal economies are not generating the needed surplus of savings,
2. the internal markets are not growing fast enough,
3. the internal financial systems are not geared toward small producers, and
4. the preferred treatment for export industries also draws internal financial resources away from production aimed at local and regional markets.

What is being done now in export promotion should continue, but it cannot, by itself, be the motor of Caribbean development. It *will* generate employment, savings and purchasing power, but it *will not* contribute sig-

·nificantly to domestic investment or to the creation of larger markets within the Caribbean.

The engine for stable development in the region must come at this stage from another source. It is therefore proposed that this source lies in the traditional small producers who are already there. Independent small producers are the backbone of the developed economies; they are no less crucial in the emerging ones. They are a source of future entrepreneurial talent, and they know their products and their markets. Most of all, they have a vested stake in the success of their ventures—a stake which increases as local markets develop. These producers should be the target of CBI overtures and the beneficiaries of some of the financing that the 936 program may make available.

Clearly, no program generated and administered from Puerto Rico can pretend to be accessible to individual microentrepreneurs. The program can deal with them only in groups, hence the need to foster the development of organizations of small producers and merchants or of community-based intermediaries that can deal in turn with individual firms. The activities financed through these arrangements can thus be individual small enterprises or larger operations run as cooperatives. In both instances, there is ample experience from which to draw.

In fact, a number of U.S.-sponsored programs have operated for years in the Caribbean, promoting small businesses or cooperative ventures of small producers. The World Bank, the Inter-American Development Bank and the U.S. Agency for International Development (USAID) have all supported such programs, either directly or through nongovernmental organizations, which have typically been American. The Inter-American Foundation (IAF), an autonomous U.S. government agency, has over the years compiled an impressive record of support for such programs throughout Latin America, with particular success in the Caribbean Basin. The benefit of this experience should be readily available.

Heretofore, these programs have been experimental in nature, and consequentially, their coverage has been limited. With access to 936 funds, however, a substantial portion of the credit needs of these marginal sectors would be covered. Moreover, addressing the needs of these sectors has typically been seen as a holding action while the growth of the modern sectors allowed their eventual absorption of the surplus labor force. I propose that these sectors of small and cooperative businesses be seen instead as equal motors of development, seeding grounds for new entrepreneurial talent and builders of the local markets. Since these sectors typically encompass both users and suppliers of products for local and regional consumption, they will foster the growth of transactions from the region and its commercial integration.

The capital requirements for the development of these sectors are likely to be considerably less than those for the development of the export sectors. And it should be added that loans to these sectors are not unacceptable credit risks; a number of such loan programs at the institutions cited above have proven commercially solvent.

In some selected cases, it is feasible that small local producers could operate in a cooperative export market venture, possibly under a twin-plant arrangement with a Puerto Rican counterpart. A number of export products, typically agricultural or agro-industrial, are now offered by small producers but are exported by marketing intermediaries who are sometimes large producers themselves. With proper credit, technical support and managerial assistance in connecting with the export markets, these small producers could sell their product themselves.[25]

To achieve this development of small and cooperative enterprises for local and export markets, assistance to these sectors should be made available following the general rationale and priorities expressed in HR 4943, the Caribbean Regional Development Act of 1988".[26]

Specifically, the financial resources for these programs would be made available from 936 deposits by the GDB of Puerto Rico. This may require modification of the regulations governing the GDB. Guarantees for these deposits could be provided in equal proportion by the GDB, Overseas Private Investment Corporation (OPIC), USAID and the depositor companies themselves.[27] The guarantees should also cover the foreign exchange risks, as most of these businesses will operate exclusively in local currencies.

The loan fund would be deposited at the GDB, which would act as administrator, and serviced through a newly created loan window. The Inter-American Foundation, which has ample experience with community-based loan programs, could oversee the application of the guidelines in HR 4943 in the regular conduct of its field programs in the region. Grants from the IAF to deserving community-based projects for training and technical assistance could be conceived as complementary to the loans from the fund.

Alternatively, the fund could be invested in secure obligations and set aside as guarantees for loans made by private 936 depository banks to Caribbean borrowers, following the same guidelines as above.

In either case, use of the fund would be regulated by a board composed of the guarantor entities plus the IAF and a rotating representation of Caribbean community-based organizations. Loans or guarantees from the fund would be made available to local development loan institutions, typically community-based organizations, which already exist in the different countries. Applications would be made to the fund through the usual channels for these intermediaries. Direct loans from the fund could also be made for larger projects involving cooperative ventures.

Thus modified, the application of section 936 would become a force militating for the development—not just the growth—of the local Caribbean economies, their integration into a viable regional market, the nurturing of a class of small businesses from which the future entrepreneurial drive of the region will emerge, and an effective alternative to the emigration of some of the most dynamic elements of Caribbean societies. These are all stated goals of the CBI; these mechanisms might be the way finally to achieve them.

APPENDIX:
PERSONS INTERVIEWED FOR THIS REPORT

Carlos Burns, Senior Vice President for Corporate and Municipal Finance, Drexel Burnham Lambert, San Juan, Puerto Rico

Heidi Calero, Esq., Executive Vice President for Corporate and Municipal Finance, Drexel Burnham Lambert, San Juan, Puerto Rico

Luisa Cerar, Director, Washington Office, Puerto Rico Economic Development Administration (FOMENTO)

Vanessa Clark, Assistant Counsel, Subcommittee on Oversight, Committee on Ways and Means, US House of Representatives

Antonio J. Colorado, Administrator, Puerto Rico Economic Development Administration (FOMENTO)

George Dalley, Counsel and Staff Director to Cong. Charles Rangel, Committee on Ways and Means, Subcommittee on Oversight

Eduardo Fernandez, Associate Director, Office of the Commissioner for Financial Institutions, Government of Puerto Rico

Angel Franco-Abarca, Second Vice President, Chase Manhattan Bank, San Juan, Puerto Rico

Marcia Fusilli, Legislative Assistant to Cong. Frank Guarini, Committee on Ways and Means, Subcommittee on Trade

Winston Gooden, Director, Jamaica National Investment Promotion Ltd., San Juan, Puerto Rico

Peter Holmes, Consultant for Legislative Affairs, Puerto Rico USA Foundation, Washington, DC

Hector Jimenez-Juarbe, Esq., Executive Vice President, Puerto Rico Manufacturers Association

Victor Johnson, Staff Director, Subcommittee on Western Hemisphere Affairs, Foreign Affairs Committee, US House of Representatives

Atherton Martin, The Development GAP, Washington, DC

Emilio Pantojas, Proyecto Caribeño de Justicia y Paz, San Juan, Puerto Rico

Jack R. Shah, Group Head, Citicorp Investment Bank, San Juan, Puerto Rico

Arthur Simonetti, Legislative Assistant to Cong. Richard Schulze, Committee on Ways and Means

Susan Spika, Special Assistant, Private Sector Office, US Agency for International Development, Washington, DC

John Stewart Jr., PhD., Economic Consultant, Puerto Rico Economic Development Administration

Gordon Studebaker, Director, Caribbean Basin Initiative Information Center, US Dept. of Commerce, Washington, DC

Lawrence Theriot, President L. Theriot Association and former Director, Caribbean Basin Initiatives Information Center, US Dept. of Commerce, Washington, DC

Jose J. Villamil, Economist, Estudios Técnicos, Inc., San Juan, Puerto Rico

Aaron Williams, Director, Private Sector Office, US Agency for International Development, Washington, DC

NOTES

Although the views expressed here are solely those of the author, the National Puerto Rican Coalition generously contributed to the understanding of this issue of such importance to Puerto Rico and to suggest ways in which the mechanism in question could be made more effective in addressing the social and economic development needs of the Caribbean Basin. A note of acknowledgement is due to the many persons who gave of their time during interviews and in reviewing previous drafts of this report. Special recognition is due in this last regard to the productive collaboration of FOMENTO Administrator Antonio J. Colorado and to Prof. Sidney Weintraub of the University of Texas at Austin for his insightful comments and suggestions.

1. See *The San Juan Star,* Inside Business Section, 2 October, 1988, pp. B1-B2. For a detailed explanation of the 936 measure see David L. Brumbaugh, *The Possessions Tax Credit (IRC Section 936): Background and Issues*, Congressional Research Service, Library of Congress, 11 March 1988.

2. Under this policy, the government of Puerto Rico offers low-cost financing for investment in Caribbean countries in plants which complement a Puerto Rican plant in terms of vertical integration of the two production processes. This presumably allows the investor to take advantage of the Caribbean country's lower labor costs for these parts of the process which are more labor intensive, and of Puerto Rico's higher technology levels for those parts of the proces that require it. See: *Puerto Rico's Caribbean Development Program*, Puerto Rico Economic Development Administration (undated), San Juan, Puerto Rico.

3. For a complete background of Puerto Rico's Caribbean Development Program in the context of Section 936, see Commonwealth of Puerto Rico, Economic Development Administration, *Puerto Rico's Caribbean Development Program, A Progress Report to the Ways and Means Committee, U.S. House of Representatives*, 15 September 1988; and *An Update on Puerto Rico's Caribbean Development Program*, February 1989.

4. See the "Statement of Emilio Pantojas, Proyecto Caribeño de Justicia y Paz," and the supportive ensuing dialogue with Antonio J. Colorado, Administrator for Economic Development, Commonwealth of Puerto Rico in *Hearings Before the Subcommittees on International Economic Policy and Trade and on Western Hemisphere Affairs of the Committee on Foreign Affairs, House of Representatives, 6–7 February 1988*, US Government Printing Office, Washington, DC, 1988, pp. 14–18.

5. Private banks, on the other hand, can make loans for "stand alone" projects, as long as the projects are not found to discourage job creation in Puerto Rico. See Puerto Rico Economic Development Administration (EDA/CDP 3/88), *CBI/936 Guidelines*.

6. Carlos Burns of Drexel Burnham, which jointly with First Boston Corp. would underwrite the fund (contingent upon approval by the Puerto Rico Commissioner of Financial Institutions and the US Treasury Department, in process), explained it as a system for credit enhancement of otherwise credit-worthy customers using guarantees by the GDB, OPIC, and USAID. The fund itself would be capitalized by 936 companies as an eligible investment. Other similar funds are in earlier stages of planning and, as of mid-February 1989, the US Treasury Department

had cleared authorization of guarantees of foreign 936 credits by federal agencies such as OPIC or USAID. Nevertheless, several observers interviewed for this report questioned the attractiveness of such funds to treasurers of 936 companies given the ample availability of alternative and less risky investments.

7. My own sense, shared by many of the persons interviewed for this report, is that the TIEA requirement was Treasury's *quid pro quo* during the 1985–86 negotiations that extended the use of 936 funds to the Caribbean. Treasury argues that 936 is a severe drain of US tax resources; ostensibly, it insisted on the TIEA as the price of giving up its opposition. Once in place, though, the TIEA requirement will serve as a barrier that allegedly compromises far more severely the autonomy of the weaker parties in the agreement—the Caribbean countries. Some observers speculated on whether Treasury's intent was precisely this "wrench in the works" that would keep 936 funds out of the Caribbean and justify a new attack on 936 as inconsequential to Caribbean development. Note also that most twin-plant investments have occurred in the Dominican Republic and Costa Rica, the Dominican Republic having recently signed the agreement, and without the use of 936 funds. The incentive to sign is thus further diminished.

8. The CBI Fund proposed by Drexel Burnham and First Boston addresses this by offering credits of up to ten years. Note that the fund is capitalized with the sale of *shares* to investors. In addition, the government of Puerto Rico provides reduced "toll gate" taxes and eased reinvestment requirements as incentives to 936 funds invested in obligations of five to ten years.

9. Winston Gooden, Director of the Jamaica National Investment Promotion Ltd. in Puerto Rico, told me that, in his opinion, the issue of guarantees for the credits is crucial. Without them, he added, "936 is almost useless."

10. As expressed to me by Jack Shah of Citicorp.

11. Aware of this, the Government of Puerto Rico has actively pursued Caribbean investments with 936 funds, especially in infrastructure and capital assets. A $20 million telecommunications venture with Barbados was approved recently (*Caribbean Business*, 1 Dec. 1988, p.20), as well as a $57.5 million deal in which 936 funds were " . . . an important but not a crucial factor" with Jamaica for the purchase of two Airbus jets for Air Jamaica (*ibid*, 5 January 1989, p.23).

12. Precise figures are hard to come by, but approximately $5 billion of the $15 billion total 936 funds could be held as direct investments. Less than $100 million of that is probably invested outside of Puerto Rico. A mechanism increasingly used for these investments is the "debt equity swap," an eligible 936 investment. Through it, an investor needing local Caribbean currency can purchase discounted dollar loans from creditor US banks and exchange them for local currency with the debtor central bank.

13. See *Puerto Rico's Caribbean Development Program, op. cit.*

14. For an early critique of the concept behind the CBI, see Sidney Weintraub, "A Flawed Model," *Foreign Policy*, No. 47, Summer 1982, pp. 128–133. For a critique from a Caribbean viewpoint, see *The Caribbean Basin Initiative: Caribbean Views. Report of A Congressional Study Mission and Symposium on the CBI, 18–19 Sept. 1987 to*

the Committee on Foreign Affairs, U.S. House of Representatives, U.S. Government Printing Office, Washington, D.C. 1987.

15. An estimated 269,000 jobs of the total employment of 750,00 on the island were directly or indirectly attributable recently to 936 investments. See Robert Nathan Associates, *Section 936 and the Economic Development of Puerto Rico*, prepared for the Puerto Rico-USA Foundation, August 1987. A recent study commissioned by the Puerto Rico Bankers Association (*The Impact of Section 936 on Puerto Rico's Economy and Banking System* by Estudios Tecnicos, Inc., Wharton Econometric Forecasting Associates and Touche-Ross and Co.) found that the repeal of section 936 would have "very significant" negative effects on Puerto Rico's economy, and " . . . non-negligible negative effects on the U.S. economy" (p.2).

16. A White Paper by the Internal Revenue Service, released in October 1988 and obtained for this essay only in draft form, has drawn considerable fire by defenders of 936 as an inaccurate assessment of the cost of the measure to U.S. taxpayers. The fallacy is reportedly Treasury's implicit assumption that the companies would not modify their behavior in the absence of 936 and would not take steps to otherwise protect these revenues, including relocation. Moreover, if these revenues were to be taxed in any event, the Commonwealth of Puerto Rico would have a claim prior to that of the IRS. Private advocacy groups in the United States, meanwhile, concerned about fiscal resources for domestic social programs, downplay the benefits of the measure to the Caribbean and even to Puerto Rico itself. *The Corporate Tax Comeback* (Citizens for Social Justice, Washington, D.C., September 1988) states, " . . . the Puerto Rican tax break has done almost nothing for jobs, while draining revenues from the Treasury into corporate coffers" (p.17). See note 15.

17. Caribbean countries have been quite vocal in their criticism on this point in the past, and continue to be so. See, for instance, "Caribbean Nations, IRS Criticize Tax Incentive Program," *The Journal of Commerce*, 30 December 1988.

18. House Resolution 3101, the *Caribbean Basin Economic Recovery Expansion Act of 1987*, presented by Rep. Gibbons and referred to the Committee on Ways and Means, addresses this need for a stable export market for Caribbean products by expanding the list of eligible items, easing criteria for eligibility, and extending duty-free privileges for 12 years beyond the 12 prescribed in the original CBI legislation. The bill is expected to be reintroduced to the 101st Congress. Asked to comment on these guarantees, a knowledgeable source remarked, "What Congress giveth, Congress taketh away."

19. For a comprehensive critique of this model as it concretely applies to the present situation of the Caribbean, see the various testimonies presented by Caribbean experts in *Hearings Before the Subcommittees on International Economic Policy and Trade and on Western Hemisphere Affairs of the Committee on Foreign Affairs, U.S. House of Representatives, 6–7 February 1988* (U.S. Government Printing Office, Washington D.C. 1988).

20. Much has been written on the history of the Puerto Rican experience of the mid-1940s to mid-1960s; my favorite, nevertheless, remains the eminently readable account by David F. Ross, *The Long Uphill Path* (Talleres Gráficos Interamericanos, San Juan, 1966).

21. The Division of Puerto Rican Industries at Puerto Rico's Economic Development Administration (FOMENTO), the Banco de Desarrollo Económico, and the Cuerpo de Voluntarios al Servicio de Puerto Rico have been valiant attempts at promoting Puerto Rican entrepreneurship at, respectively, the large, medium and small levels. The results in the first two, as testified by persons directly involved, have been disappointing. The latter, though, an effort to recruit unemployed youth as microentrepreneurs, is showing interesting promise after one full year in operation.

22. In spite of restrictions, New York has witnessed a phenomenal growth of its Caribbean communities over the last ten years, especially from the Dominican Republic and Jamaica. Anglophone Caribbeans typically—and increasingly, despite growing restrictions—have Canada and Britain as alternative destinations.

23. The vitality of these sectors, and their inhibition by lack of access to credit and managerial expertise as well as by stifling bureaucracy (often circumvented by large businesses), is vividly explained in the controversial work of Peruvian economist Hernando de Soto *El Otro Sendero (The Other Path,* reviewed in "How to Make Poor Countries Rich," *Fortune,* 16 January 1989, pp.101–104).

24. Free trade zones, increasingly common in some Caribbean countries, are ever more removed from their home economies, often isolated physically to discourage seepage of the restricted output into the local markets.

25. While at the Inter-American Foundation, I was involved in preliminary discussions with representatives of small coffee producers from the Dominican Republic and Costa Rica for a cooperative twin-plant operation with Puerto Rico. Other possibilities discussed at the time included grapefruit producers in Dominica, and producers of exotic tropical fruits (guava, mango, papaya, etc.) in several countries.

26. HR 4943, "to promote equitable and participatory development, national and regional economic integration, and food security and self-reliance in the Caribbean through responsive aid and development policies and programs," was presented by Cong. George W. Crockett and referred to the Committee on Foreign Affairs.

27. The system of guarantees could follow that set for the CBI Fund sponsored by Drexel Burnham and First Boston, discussed above. Note that the users of the guarantees here proposed are not those of the CBI Fund, which is still geared to larger export operations.

5

Incentives and Impediments to U.S. Foreign Direct Investment in the Caribbean: Case Studies of the Dominican Republic and Jamaica

Susan M. Kramer

I. INTRODUCTION

Classical and neoclassical economic theories emphasize the advantages of increased capital flow from industrialized to less-developed countries (LDCs) through foreign investment. Direct foreign investment can increase domestic levels of savings and investment, produce foreign exchange through exports, and increase government revenues by expanding the tax base. It can introduce new technologies and production techniques, which can lead to the creation of backward and forward linkages in the domestic economy, and increased productivity and skill levels in the domestic workforce.

Many of the economies of the Caribbean now encourage foreign direct investment as a way to increase income, exports and employment. U.S. policy encourages U.S. private direct investment in the Caribbean as a way of easing the economic pressure to emigrate from these countries to the United States.

However, there is limited information available to U.S. policymakers on the details of the daily operations of U.S. businesses overseas. Most available information emphasizes macroeconomic considerations rather than the day-to-day impediments U.S. investors must face. The purpose of this study is to examine the microeconomic conditions that encourage or impede foreign direct investment in two important migrant-sending countries of the Caribbean: the Dominican Republic and Jamaica.

II. THE DOMINICAN REPUBLIC

The Dominican Republic (DR) has a population of approximately 6.6 million, and an area of 49,000 square kilometers. It occupies the eastern two-thirds of the island of Hispaniola, discovered and named by Columbus in 1492. The colonial DR was dominated first by Spain and later by France and Haiti. It achieved independence from Haiti in 1844, but truly gained sovereignty in 1865 following a brief reversion to the Spanish Crown. The Dominican Republic achieved representative democracy in 1966 after three decades of dictatorial domination by General Rafael Leonidas Trujillo Molina.

The Dominican constitution establishes executive, legislative and judicial branches of government. The DR is divided into 29 provinces, each with a presidentially appointed governor, and the national district (metropolitan Santo Domingo, the nation's capital), is governed by an elected mayor and municipal council.

There are more than 20 active political parties in the DR. The three major parties are the Dominican Liberation Party (PLD), the Dominican Revolutionary Party (PRD) and the Social Christian Reformist Party (PRSC—formerly the Reformist Party). The PLD is on the left and is headed by former President Juan Bosch (1962–1963). The PRD, whose ideology is slightly left of center, is currently split into the conservative supporters of Jacobo Majluta and the more social democratic supporters of Francisco Peña Gomez. The PRSC, which is slightly to the right of center, is led by incumbent President Joaquin Balaguer.[1]

In 1987, Dominican Gross Domestic Product (GDP) was US $5.25 billion. In that year, real growth of GDP was eight percent, inflation was 22 percent, and unemployment was 35 percent. The Dominican Republic's major industries are light manufacturing, tourism and agriculture. Its leading exports are light manufacturing products, sugar, nickel, coffee, tobacco and cocoa, and its major markets for these products are the United States, Venezuela and Japan. The export growth rate for 1986–1987 was five percent. The DR's principal imports are petroleum, foodstuffs, industrial raw materials and capital equipment. In June 1987, with the peso quoted at DR $9 to US $1, the government abolished the free currency market, closed the exchange banks and set the official exchange rate at DR $6.45 to the U.S dollar. The rate has remained at this level through June 1989.

Dominican Republic: Case Studies

The following case studies examine the investment climate in the Dominican Republic through the operating experiences of individual U.S. firms. Firms A through D are located in export processing zones. Firms E through I are outside of the zones.

FIRM A: *San Isidro Free Zone*

Type of business:	Information services.
Number of Employees:	Not reported.
Wages:	Above minimum wage; productivity incentives.
Size of investment:	US $6 million.
Ownership:	Wholly-owned subsidiary.
Expansion planned:	Not for the DR.

Firm A specializes in data entry. Hard copy in the form of documents is imported, transferred to computer tapes, then exported back to the parent company in the United States. Firm A chose to invest in the Dominican Republic primarily because of labor costs, and chose the San Isidro Free Zone specifically because of its proximity to Santo Domingo, and thus to a supply of semi-skilled labor.

However, the most serious difficulty encountered by Firm A was worker absenteeism. This problem resulted from a lack of worker transportation from Santo Domingo to the free zone. Public transportation is limited, and workers on the second and third shifts could not afford to hire private transport. Firm A solved this problem temporarily by contracting a private bus company to transport workers, a subsidy that will end when the free zone acquires 2,000 workers and the government schedules public service to the zone.

Due to the nature of Firm A's product, the firm has encountered several specific problems; one is the language barrier. Text processed by Firm A is more complicated than simple alpha or numeric data, approximating the technical information similar to that of the medical or legal professions. Firm A's management has found the quality of production to be inferior to that found in the United States.

A second difficulty is erratic electrical service. Firm A relies exclusively on computers, and a constant, uninterrupted electrical flow is crucial to production. After numerous work stoppages and data losses at the beginning of their operations, Firm A now maintains contact with the Corporación de Electricidad and is apprised of impending disruptions. In addition, Firm A has purchased an auxiliary generator, and the free zone has now established a high tension electrical connection to a power main.

Firm A's management also finds that Dominican Customs is disorganized and bureaucratic, needlessly delaying shipments. Customs procedures are ambiguous, passage is sometimes done at the airport, sometimes at the free zone. Nevertheless, Firm A characterizes officials as generally cooperative.

Firm A's management does not anticipate problems as a result of the 1990 Presidential election, and does not believe operations will be affected by a new administration.

FIRM B: San Isidro Free Zone

Type of Business:	Manufacture of electronic equipment.
Number of Employees:	50 total: 2 Haitian, 48 Dominican.
Wages:	Minimum wage.
Size of Investment:	US $250,000.
Ownership:	Wholly owned subsidiary.
Expansion planned:	To 250 employees.

Firm B manufactures electronic components which are shipped directly from the Dominican Republic to U.S. customers. Firm B has been the complementary "twin" to a plant in Puerto Rico since 1981 as part of the twin-plants initiative. It relocated to the DR from operations in Haiti in 1987, and operates under Tariff Schedules of the United States (TSUS) item 806.30.

Firm B located in the San Isidro Free Zone for access to a good supply of labor at low wages. However, due to the scarcity of electronics firms in the

DR, there is a lack of semi-skilled labor in electronics. As a result, Firm B sends new employees to be trained in Puerto Rico. This procedure, however, is cumbersome because it is difficult to obtain the necessary visas from the U.S. Embassy.

Two additional problems faced by Firm B are labor transportation (see Firm A), and the unavailability of replacement parts. The lack of Dominican electronics businesses means no spread industry exists, and usable parts are exceedingly scarce. Where parts are available, production is plagued by inefficiencies attributed to erratic electricity generation, and orders are months behind schedule. Thus, Firm B imports needed parts from the United States or Puerto Rico.

FIRM C: San Isidro Free Zone

Type of Business:	Manufacture of electrical components.
Number of Employees:	60–65; 1 U.S., 59–64 Dominican.
Wages:	Minimum wage with production incentive planned.
Size of Investment:	US $400,000[2]
Ownership:	Wholly owned subsidiary.
Expansion planned:	To 120–150 employees.

Firm C produces and assembles electrical components into finished products to be exported to its parent corporation in the United States. Firm C invested in the DR in 1988 because of unrest in Haiti, where it had operated for 16 years.

In its Dominican operations, Firm C's difficulties have included inadequate electricity service, customs bureaucracy, and the length of time it takes to acquire services. Firm C has now purchased an auxiliary generator to alleviate its electricity generation problems, but government bureaucracy is cited as an ongoing problem. Firm C's move from Haiti to the DR was accomplished in one week, but it took approximately three weeks to acquire services such as telephone connections. Firm A cited a loss of production resulting from the move as its biggest difficulty.

FIRM D: San Cristobal (Itabo) Free Zone

Type of Business:	Manufacture of electrical components.
Number of Employees:	58, all Dominican.
Wages:	Unskilled: slightly above minimum wage. Skilled: competitively high.
Size of Investment:	US $2.7 million.
Ownership:	Wholly owned subsidiary.
Expansion:	From present 60 percent capacity to 100 percent in one year; more expansion in two years.

Firm D manufactures electrical parts for use in major consumer appliances. Firm D is also a Section 936 twin plant that receives all of its raw materials from the United States and exports all of its products to Puerto Rico. At the start of operations, Firm D's biggest concerns were absenteeism, due to a lack of worker transportation, and electricity generation. After strict company regulations governing absenteeism, the plant manager now reports a low rate of 1.6 percent. Use of the auxiliary generator has been cut to approximately once per week.

Firm D's leading concerns at present are the availability of replacement parts and customs inflexibility. At the start of operations, Firm D attempted to purchase needed parts domestically but found that available parts often cost two to three times the price of identical parts in the United States. As a result, Firm D now imports all needed parts.

Product passage through customs takes Firm D's exports an average of two days because customs officials open all boxes and physically count their components. Customs officers can be inflexible when there are typographical errors or slight differences on import packing slips. For example, computers imported as operating equipment are listed as one piece on the packing slip, but arrive in two pieces. Customs officers insist Firm D must pay duties on what they believe is additional equipment. Firm D pays these duties to avoid waiting weeks for the resolution of the matter and use of the disputed item.

Firm D sees Balaguer's government as politically stable, and believes this will not change with a new administration.

FIRM E

Type of Business:	Distribution of pharmaceuticals.
Number of Employees:	45 full time; 7 part time, all Dominicans.
Wages:	Above industry median; benefits; annual and inflation increases.
Size of Investment:	US $3 million including fixed assets.
Ownership:	Wholly owned subsidiary.
Expansion planned:	None.

Firm E has operated in the Dominican Republic for 42 years. The firm imports pharmaceutical products from the United States, Central America and Europe to supply the domestic market. Firm E received no incentives on its investment other than a lower rate of import duty on medicine.

Firm E faces erratic utility provision, and its auxiliary electrical generators are in use approximately 45 percent of the time, on average. Firm E pays an extra, nonofficial fee for garbage pickup on a regular basis. Still, Firm E uses its own trucks six times per month to eliminate the buildup of potentially hazardous waste.

According to Firm E's management, customs officials believe that 95 percent of Dominican imports are undervalued, and they check the contents of every box against documentation. The delay on Firm E's imports is currently two to four weeks, which can critically affect the shelf life of Firm E's pharmaceutical products. Management believes this delay is minimal, however, facilitated by customs officers' familiarity with its products.

Firm E also faces bureaucratic difficulties with product registration. Twenty-six months are required to register a product for the first time, and product registration must be renewed every five years.

It is difficult for Firm E to recruit sales representatives, although it offers attractive benefits, such as company cars and sales commission. One reason for this difficulty is that Firm E requires sales representatives to speak English, and competition for English-speaking Dominican labor is high. In addition, Firm E pays wages in pesos, which makes the company less attractive than those who pay in dollars.[3] Nevertheless, once employees are hired, turnover is low, at an average rate of five to seven years.

Firm E encounters a number of problems with product sales. Thirty-five to 40 percent of the Dominican pharmaceutical business is comprised of government contracts, and payment on these contracts can be erratic. Information also suggests that pharmaceuticals imported from Venezuela are sold illegally in the Dominican market at 75 to 80 percent price reductions. These sales limitations are the reason that Firm E has restricted expansion in the Dominican Republic.

FIRM F

Type of Business:	Distribution of petroleum products.
Number of Employees:	87; 86 Dominican, 1 U.S.
Wages:	Above minimum wage; benefits.
Size of Investment:	US $12.5 million.
Ownership:	100 percent owned branch of U.S. parent corporation.
Expansion planned:	US $1 million, to upgrade facilities.

Firm F markets petroleum products to 148 petrol stations in the Dominican Republic. The erratic domestic electricity system has forced each station to maintain its own auxiliary generators, as gasoline is pumped electrically.

Firm F has difficulty in contracting construction firms to upgrade its facilities, because the government currently employs the majority of them. In upgrading existing facilities, Firm F finds frequent cement shortages when it attempts to make purchases through legal channels at a government subsidized price of 16 pesos per bag. It is possible to obtain cement through the black market at a price of 40 pesos per bag. The government cement monopoly may end, however, because the cement company has been sold to private interests.

All crude oil is imported by and purchased from the state refinery; therefore, Firm F's imports consist of lubricants, oils and greases in liquid form. Firm F has conducted operations in the DR for 70 years, and customs officials know the company and its products very well. Invoices are taken at face value—sometimes containers are not opened and checked—by customs officials. Customs clearance takes an average of two weeks on Firm F's products.

Bureaucratic difficulties and delays are not a problem for Firm F. Often the firm's representatives are more familiar with administrative procedures than government officials, who tend to change with administrations.

Dominican labor is found to be reliable and easily trained at more than one task. Turnover and absenteeism rates have been low; however, Firm F's management sees worker motivation waning as the inflation rate decreases their wages in real terms.

The most serious problems confronting Firm F are exchange rate fluctuations which affect profit remittance and profit margin limitations. Profits are limited by government imposed margins, which have remained at the same level since 1976. Fuel distribution companies are allowed a profit of US $0.016 per gallon on gasoline and US $0.007 per gallon on diesel fuel. Thus, most profits accrued are the result of volume rather than price, and Firm F's management is banking on the continuation of annual increases in gasoline demanded, such as those from 1985 to 1987.[4]

FIRM G

Type of Business:	Production of fruits and vegetables.
Number of Employees:	750; 737 Dominican, 3 U.S., 10 other foreign.
Wages:	Above minimum wage.
Size of Investment:	US $30 million; includes fixed assets and agricultural development costs.
Ownership:	Wholly owned subsidiary.
Expansion planned:	To 2000 employees at peak harvest.

Firm G grows tropical fruits and prepares fruit concentrates for export to the United States. Firm G leases agricultural land from the State Sugar Council (CEA) under a 25-year agreement. The firm operates under the Dominican Agro-Investment Law #409, and also benefits from duty-free treatment of U.S. imports under the Caribbean Basin Initiative (CBI).

Firm G has equipped its farms with electrical generators, but still faces problems with support services, because most domestic enterprises cannot afford the expense of auxiliary generators.

Firm G's corporate policy dictates the purchase of local inputs whenever possible, even if this results in marginally higher costs. However, domestically supplied agricultural chemicals can cost double the price of imports, and Firm G has begun to import these needed chemicals.

Firm G has not encountered difficulties in equipment repair and parts replacement because it purchased equipment available through Dominican dealers. However, in 1987, the Dominican Government imposed a 20 percent exchange commission on all importations and is applying duty on vehicles and equipment.[5] Firm G correspondingly reduced the intended level of investment in its Dominican project. The Dominican government's unwillingness to honor prior commitments, and the constant changes in domestic fiscal and monetary policies aimed at achieving short-range goals, are the main reasons that significant expansion is not planned for Firm G's Dominican operations.

Management has found that customs officials tend to overvalue its imports as a way to increase duty payments. In addition, due to the carelessness of customs officers, customs documents frequently become lost or misplaced, or similar obstacles develop.

The most serious concern cited by Firm G's management is labor availability. Firm G maintains over 2,000 names on its payroll; however, average daily work attendance is estimated at only 800 workers. Firm G has found that women are more reliable and perform agricultural tasks at a consistently higher level than men. As a result, Firm G has shifted more of its recruitment efforts toward the female population in the areas surrounding the farms. Firm G has also begun to provide transportation for workers to the farms, but is apprehensive about maintaining enough labor during peak harvest.

Firm G finds that agricultural employment in the DR is deemed less desirable than employment in other sectors, and skilled workers are therefore more difficult to hire and retain. U.S. firms in the export processing zones compete for trained Dominican professionals through competitive wage bidding, which tends to drive wage levels up.

FIRM H

Type of Business:	Production of fruits, vegetables and sugar cane.
Number of Employees:	25,000 at peak harvest, Dominican
Wages:	Above minimum wage; benefits.
Size of Investment:	US $70 million; includes all Dominican holdings.
Ownership:	Wholly owned subsidiary.
Expansion planned:	Yes, into tropical fruits.

Firm H has operated in the Dominican Republic under various owners for over 70 years. The firm is currently producing fresh fruits, vegetables and sugar cane for domestic consumption. It also produces sugar cane for export to the United States and other international markets.

Firm H's sugar production has been hit hard by the U.S. quota reduction and by exchange rate fluctuations. To make a profit, Firm H must produce and sell over 300,000 tons of sugar. However, Firm H was allowed less than 100,000 tons of the Dominican portion of the U.S. sugar quota in 1987, and domestic consumption did not compensate for lost sales. However, Firm H is now expecting profits due to the rising price of sugar, a bad Cuban sugar crop, and the U.S. drought of 1988.[6]

Firm H finds labor to be abundant and reliable. The firm's sugar workers generally remain with the company for 30 to 40 years and are replaced by their sons or other relatives. Firm H's management believes that the high level of wages and the attractive benefit package it offers contribute to employee loyalty.

Firm H's management believes that the burdensome amount of customs paperwork required is due to the age of the system, which was created in the 1960s under U.S. Customs tutelage and never altered. Dominican Customs processes are undergoing computerization, but most of the documentation is still done by hand. Firm H's management also believes that customs difficulties arise because the Minister of Customs and Commerce reports directly to the President and must account for daily revenue surpluses and losses from operations. The goal of every customs employee is to report a surplus, and this can result in questionable import and export valuations.

FIRM I

Type of Business:	Hotel.
Number of Employees:	Approximately 400; 3 U.S., 20–25 other foreign.
Wages:	Above minimum wage; 10 percent service charge additional.
Size of Investment:	US $36 million.
Ownership:	100 percent U.S.
Expansion planned:	None.

Firm I is a leading hotel in the National District. As in most Dominican hotels, Firm I has installed its own auxiliary generator. Irregular garbage collection has forced Firm I to purchase its own truck.

Dominican hotel industry salaries are among the highest in the country. Still, Firm I finds a shortage of skilled administrative workers and, therefore, most of these positions are held by expatriates. However, unskilled labor is abundant due to high wages paid to hotel employees. High wages in this industry are the result of a ten percent service charge on all hotel bills; this money is distributed among hotel employees in addition to their salaries. This means that as room occupancies decrease, wages also decrease.

There are other obstacles peculiar to the hotel industry in the Dominican Republic. As might be expected, many of the workers speak only limited English, which results in customer service problems for non-Spanish speaking tourists. Also, because of worker unfamiliarity with modern facilities and conveniences, Firm I estimates that hotel workers' productivity is about 20 percent of that of their U.S. counterparts. Workers who have never before seen facilities such as a modern kitchen or toilet must be trained in their functions and the etiquette of their use.

Firm I's management believes that there is a lack of Dominican Government spending on tourism promotion in the United States. The Ministry of Tourism is allowed an annual budget of only US $200,000, and management doubts that amount is actually spent. Tourists from the United States comprise only five to ten percent of Dominican tourist arrivals, and most of these trips are business related, or are by Dominicans holding U.S. passports. European tourists far outnumber those from the United States, despite the greater traveling distance.

Firm I finds the rules of the investment game to be unstable —what is legal today may not be tomorrow. Firm I's management also perceives the absence of a well thought out government strategy to sustain the budget in the long term. According to Firm I's management, "The economy is like a crooked leg that won't support the weight of the body." Management believes the economy will not change a great deal regardless of who wins the 1990 election.

III. JAMAICA

Jamaica, the largest English-speaking island in the Caribbean, has an area of 11,000 square kilometers and a population of approximately 2.4 million. Under Spanish domination, Jamaica was a colonial possession until conquered by the British in 1655. Great Britain formally gained possession of the island in 1670 under the Treaty of Madrid, and Jamaica remained a British colony until 1962, when it became an independent member of the British Commonwealth of Nations.

Jamaica is a constitutional monarchy under which the largely ceremonial Governor General represents the British monarch. Executive authority is vested in the cabinet, led by the Prime Minister. The Prime Minister and members of the Cabinet are selected from a parliament composed of the Senate and the House of Representatives. Jamaica is divided into 13 parishes, which are governed with limited authority by elected parish councils, and the Metropolitan Municipal Administration in Kingston.

There are three active political parties in Jamaica. The People's National Party (PNP) and the Jamaican Labor Party (JLP) far outdistance the communist Worker's Party of Jamaica (WPJ) in popular support. Since 1944, the PNP and JLP have alternated in power every other election, with each party winning twice in succession.

Founded in 1938 by Norman Washington Manley, the ideology of the People's National Party is based on social democratic principles, including greater state ownership and government intervention in the economy. PNP backing is based largely on the support of the National Workers Union (NWU). Michael Manley, Norman Manley's son, holds an important leadership position in the PNP; in 1989, he was elected prime minister with 56.7 percent of the popular vote and 44 seats in the House of Representatives.[7]

The Jamaican Labor Party is the party of the center-right, and its ideology is based on acceptance of a free enterprise system. The JLP, founded in 1943 by Alexander Bustamante out of the labor base of the Bustamante Industrial Tradesmen Union (BITU), was in power from 1980 to 1989 under Edward Seaga.

The Workers Party of Jamaica (WPJ) espouses a Marxist-Leninist ideology. The party is now headed by Trevor Monroe, who is also the president of the University and Allied Workers Union (UAWU).

Jamaican political support has traditionally depended more on patronage and union membership than on the ideological positions of the parties. The two strongest unions, the National Workers Union (NWU) and the Bustamante Industrial Tradesmen Union (BITU) are closely connected to the major parties—the NWU to the PNP, and the BITU to the JLP. The unions' party ties have contributed to the political violence that has surrounded Jamaican elections since the mid-1960s, as have Jamaican gang operations, which are particularly strong in Kingston.

Jamaica's post-war economic development is characterized by alternate swings between promotion and repression of public and private sector activities, corresponding to shifts in power between the JLP and the PNP.

In 1987, domestic price inflation declined to 11 percent from 24 percent in FY 1985–86, and unemployment was down by three percent to about 20 percent of the total workforce.[8] GDP in 1986 was US $2 billion and grew by an estimated four to five percent in 1987.[9] Jamaica's major industries are tourism, bauxite and light manufacturing. The country's principal exports are alumina and bauxite, sugar, clothing, citrus fruits, rum and cocoa. Its primary markets are the United States, the United Kingdom and Venezuela. Exports of nontraditional items accounted for approximately 26 percent of total exports in 1987.[10] This is the result of rapid growth in the garment industry. Jamaica's main imports are petroleum, machinery, transport and electrical equipment, food and fertilizer.

Jamaica began 1988 with an outstanding external debt of US $3.5 billion. Despite this, the outlook was positive for Jamaica's economy, based on a slow but continued economic recovery. But in September, the devastating effects of Hurricane Gilbert represented a temporary setback. The governor of the Central Bank estimated exports for FY 1988 at US $800 million, with imports of US $1.9 billion.[11]

Jamaica: Case Studies

The following case studies examine the investment climate in Jamaica, both within and outside of free zones, through the operating experiences of individual U.S. firms. Firms J through L are in the Jamaican free zones.

FIRM J: *Garmex Free Zone*
Type of Business:	Apparel manufacture.
Number of Employees:	1100; 8 U.S.
Wages:	Above minimum wage.
Size of Investment:	Not reported.
Ownership:	Wholly owned subsidiary.
Expansion planned:	Yes, increased square footage.

Firm J sews together garment pieces that are imported from the United States and the Far East. All of the garments produced by Firm J are exported to the United States by ship. Firm J operates under TSUS item 807.

According to Firm J's management, domestically produced parts for machinery often cost three to four times more than U.S. imports; therefore, replacement parts for equipment are imported. Under free zone status, Firm J may import all parts duty free.

According to the firm's management, the entrance of many Asian firms to Jamaican export processing resulted in the expansion of the Kingston free zone without simultaneous expansion of support systems surrounding the zone.

Firm J encounters a water shortage approximately once per month, although garbage collection and electricity supply are now cited as adequate.

Jamaican customs poses few problems because Firm J's imports clear Jamaican customs at point of entry, and are accompanied to the free zone by Firm J's broker and a customs official. However, Firm J encounters customs bureaucracy in obtaining export documentation. Documentation is required for all products exported and entails obtaining signatures from three or four different government agencies.

In addition, documentation for goods transfer between the Garmex Free Zone and Firm J's sister company in the Kingston Free Zone must be obtained from the Deputy Prime Minister and the Minister of Trade. At the start of operations it took approximately four months to transfer such goods; however, it now only takes between one and three weeks.

An additional problem faced by Firm J is the extra cost of security measures to stop illegal shipments of drugs smuggled into Firm J's containers. These measures include special procedures in the loading of shipping containers and careful monitoring of the containers until they are on board a ship. Firm J's management estimates extra security costs at approximately US $1000 per week.

Firm J finds unskilled labor to be abundant in the Kingston area, and applicants are solicited only through word-of-mouth. According to Firm J's management, a garment consulting firm has been hired to train free zone garment workers. This program is funded 70 percent by the Jamaican government and 30 percent by the contracting firm. Administrative workers hired from the government program are found to be dependable and productive.

Skilled labor is more difficult to obtain, especially for managerial positions. Firm J's management believes that a lack of worker motivation and increased labor militancy are the causes of high absenteeism and low productivity, its main concerns with its Jamaican operation. The firm's management estimates annual turnover at 30 percent and absenteeism at 12 percent, with a higher figure on Mondays. The firm's estimates put Jamaican labor productivity at 80 percent of that of U.S. labor. Labor unrest and militancy have increased over the past two years, resulting in small strikes in the Kingston Free Zone. The large labor concentrations in the free zone are believed to contribute to labor unrest, and according to Firm J's management, free zone companies are reducing employment as a result.

FIRM K: Montego Bay Free Zone

Type of Business:	Apparel manufacture.
Number of Employees:	269; 1 U.S., 3 other foreign.
Wages:	Above minimum wage.
Size of Investment:	US $1.5–2 million.
Ownership:	Wholly owned subsidiary.
Expansion planned:	28,000 sq. ft. to be added this year.

Firm K imports apparel pieces from the United States to be sewn into finished garments and exported back to the United States. Firm K had little difficulty in obtaining factory space, but finds factory rental to be expensive in the free zone. Garbage collection is infrequent and the electricity supply is constantly interrupted. Firm K estimates blackouts and brownouts at least two to three times per week.

Replacement parts and repairs for Firm K's equipment are generally not available in Jamaica, or are drastically overpriced. As a result, Firm K imports all needed parts from the United States, and brings in parent company employees to repair its equipment.

Firm K's management characterizes customs officials as exceptionally helpful because of their familiarity with the firm's management and products. Although Firm K's imports clear customs in Kingston and must be transported overland to Montego Bay, they are usually delivered to the Montego Bay Free Zone within four days of entry. According to Firm K's management, the shipment of illegal drugs with the product has not been a problem because shipments between Kingston and Montego Bay are accompanied by a guard.

Firm K finds a shortage of skilled labor and trains workers internally for technical and management level positions. Unskilled labor is available, however, and the firm has hired some employees through the government funded Human Employment and Resource Training (HEART) program.[12] Nevertheless, Firm K cites the Jamaican labor situation as the major problem for its Jamaican operations. Labor is volatile and unpredictable, and absenteeism and tardiness are great problems. Firm K's management believes that Jamaicans learn very quickly if they want to, but the majority of the workers do not. Firm K has been forced to modify training and employee procedures which have been successfully implemented in Firm K's sister plants in other Latin American countries.

In addition, the Jamaican workers will tell management they understand instructions, whether or not they do. Firm K's management attributes this difficulty to language barriers between management's English usage and the worker's Jamaican patois.

Firm K received funding for its Jamaican operations from commercial banks in the United States. The firm's management also received helpful investment-related assistance from the government investment promotion agencies, Jamaican National Investment Promotion (JNIP) and Jamaican National Export Corporation (JNEC), now unified in Jamaican Promotions Limited (JAMPRO).

Firm K's parent company believes that Firm K's business environment will not change as a result of the election of Michael Manley.

FIRM L: Kingston Free Zone

Type of Business:	Candy manufacture.
Number of Employees:	14–20; 2 U.S.
Wages:	Not reported.
Size of Investment:	US $1 million.
Ownership:	Wholly owned subsidiary.
Expansion planned:	None.

Firm L manufactures pure sugar stick candy for export to the United States. Firm L chose to invest in Jamaica because the island does not have a sugar refinery and white sugar can be purchased at the world price of US $0.15 per pound.[13] If Firm L had been producing in the United States, it would be forced to pay US $0.34 per pound.

Replacement parts for Firm L's equipment must be imported because they are not available on the island. The only items purchased locally by Firm L are packing boxes for shipment.

Firm L has encountered many problems with Jamaican utility provision. Electricity blackouts are a crucial problem for Firm L because all of its equipment is electrically powered. However, the amount of time and candy lost due to blackouts did not justify the expense of an auxiliary generator (US $40,000–50,000) to Firm L's parent company. This strategy has paid off in the long term; in the past year, Firm L has experienced only five or six blackouts. Production is still plagued with three to four daily power surges, however, which stop production and burn out equipment motors. Firm L's management believes that these power surges are the result of a lack of preparation for the massive increase in electricity demand in the expanded Kingston Free Zone.

In addition, many of the buildings in the free zone were built without water lines. Only a few direct lines are connected to the free zone, and water pressure is inadequate for manufacturing processes. Firm L has alleviated its own problems by purchasing water tanks which are filled overnight for the next day's production.

The firm's management believes that incompetence and negligence of government officials contributes to the poor quality of utility services. For example, Firm L did not receive a water bill for a full year after beginning operations. In addition, the firm has been inspected by health officials only once in the five years it has operated in the Kingston Free Zone.[14]

Firm L employs a customs broker to handle its customs paperwork, and does not have problems with imports and exports. The firm has not adopted drug-related security measures because its shipping containers are loaded within the factory by a few dependable employees. Nevertheless, the potential for security problems does exist because Firm L cannot control the containers once they leave the free zone. According to Firm L's management, corruption at Jamaican ports may result in the placement of contraband in shipments.

Firm L has encountered problems with U.S. customs practices, particularly since the implementation of the U.S. zero tolerance policy. U.S. customs regularly searches import container contents; this process is called "stripping." The costs of container stripping are paid by the manufacturer, charged whether or not contraband is found. Therefore, Firm L tries to import to the smaller U.S. ports where stripping is done only on a proportion of imported containers.

Firm L does not encounter difficulties in hiring, and turnover and absenteeism rates are low due to the limited number of workers it employs. Trainability is good because Firm L's management works alongside its employees. However, Firm L also cites language difficulties between management and the Jamaican employees.

Management believes that the labor force available in Kingston is among the lowest quality of the Jamaican labor force. According to the firm's management, the majority of these workers are illiterate and uneducated, and do not understand productivity issues. Workers believe that the government has a responsibility for their livelihoods.

The Kingston Free Zone labor force is not organized; however, according to Firm L's management, the JLP is pressuring the free zone businesses to hire its supporters so that when the free zone comes under union control, the JLP will have an advantage. Firm L cites transactions with the Jamaican government as a serious obstacle to conducting business in Jamaica. Government agencies do not coordinate their efforts, and government workers are inefficient and careless.

Firm L's management received investment information and assistance from JNIP and JNEC, but has found that the JNIP does not have much influence in resolving investment obstacles after the original investment.

FIRM M
Type of Business:	Distribution of photocopy equipment
Number of Employees:	68; all Jamaican.
Wages:	Above minimum wage.
Size of Investment:	Not reported.
Ownership:	Wholly owned subsidiary.
Expansion planned:	Yes.

Firm M imports photocopiers and related equipment from the United States to supply the domestic market. The greatest portion of Firm M's business is equipment servicing. Firm M has operated in Jamaica since 1967 and finds that utility services have vastly improved since the start of its Jamaican operations.

Firm M does not encounter difficulties in hiring unskilled labor. Jamaicans consider employment with Firm M a good opportunity, and Firm M finds few problems in absenteeism and the work ethic of its employees. In addition, Firm M trains and employs many workers under the government funded HEART program. Firm M also finds little difficulty in hiring administrative staff. Technical and managerial level workers are more difficult to obtain, however, and Firm M usually hires at this level through employment agencies. Firm M's employees are not union organized.

Firm M's management finds that access to the foreign exchange auction can take as long as three months. Once allowed to bid, the firm's offer may be negated because one form is not complete. Firm M's requests for U.S. dollars through the auction are usually accommodated, however, because it has operated in Jamaica for many years and is well-known by government officials.

Firm M does not export, but has encountered long delays in customs clearance of imports. The average length of time for Firm M's import clearance is three to four weeks, but customs can delay clearance up to six months. Firm M's management believes the main cause of delays is container stripping for which J $800 is charged per container, whether or not it is physically searched. The customs delay of imports and access to foreign exchange are Firm M's two major concerns with its Jamaican investment.

FIRM N
Type of Business:	Information services/data conversion.
Number of Employees:	222; all Jamaican.

Wages:	Above minimum wage.
Size of Investment:	Not reported.
Ownership:	Wholly owned subsidiary.
Expansion planned:	Yes; new technology.

Firm N specializes in data entry, importing documents from its parent corporation in the United States and exporting magnetic tapes. Turn-around time on Firm N's products is critical, and most of Firm N's exports are shipped via air freight due to the lack of a Jamaican teleport, and to the high cost of satellite telephone connections.[15] Either of these methods would allow electronic transmission of the product directly from Firm N's operations to the United States.

As data conversion depends on computers, a constant uninterrupted supply of electricity is crucial to Firm N's productivity. Firm N's management finds that electrical service is good, but still includes brownouts. Therefore, Firm N has purchased a full electrical standby system, and has resorted to making backup copies of the computer tapes every half hour. This reduces productivity and increases costs.

Firm N wanted to locate in the Kingston Free Zone but located outside because the zone appeared less well equipped for a data conversion operation than for manufacturing. Management also feared possible labor unrest and violence in the 1989 election. Firm N's management believes that the concentration of labor in the free zone makes it an ideal location for such political unrest and violence to develop.

Firm N does not use unskilled labor in its Jamaican operations and has no trouble recruiting skilled workers through newspaper advertisements. With each ad, the firm's management estimates it receives 5,000 applicants. There is difficulty in finding mid-level managers, but Firm N finds that its best managers are productive keyers who have risen through the ranks of the organization.

Nevertheless, Firm N finds productivity is affected by worker attitudes. Keyers do not understand the urgency of rush work or the importance of deadlines. According to Firm N's management, rush work and overtime pay in any particular week will produce greater absenteeism in the following week. Firm N tried to run a third shift, but Jamaicans could not get used to working during the night and would often sleep on the job.

Firm N encountered difficulties in language differences at the start of its Jamaican operations, and found that workers often said they understood when in fact they did not. Firm N has now resolved this problem by sending operators to New York for a one-month training period. Although obtaining U.S. visas for this program has been difficult, it is becoming easier because none of the Jamaicans has stayed in the United States illegally.

Access to foreign exchange is not a problem for the firm because profits are realized in the United States. Firm N's parent company also pays the firm's Jamaican bills. The exchange rate aids Firm N's Jamaican operations because keyers are paid according to the number of keystrokes typed. The cost of 1,000 keystrokes is now worth approximately US $0.85, compared to US $1.50 at the start of operations.

Firm N receives duty-free treatment on all parts and equipment imported from the United States, and on product exports to the United States under CBI incentives. The firm does not encounter export problems related to illegal drug shipment because the packaging of tapes and documents is not conducive to the smuggling of contraband. A problem Firm N does experience in export operations is transportation. Sea transport is too lengthy to meet Firm N's deadlines, and air transport is costly. Air transport is now used, but the firm's management is looking forward to the construction of a teleport which will make telecommunications easier and less expensive than present transmission by telephone.

The biggest problem faced by Firm N in its Jamaican operations is the inconsistent application of government rules and customs policies. Customs procedures are not uniformly applied by all customs officials, and there is an undue amount of paperwork required on duty-free imports.

Firm N's management believes that business will not change with Michael Manley's election, unless Manley begins to espouse anti-American rhetoric.

FIRM O

Type of Business:	Production of sugar and ethanol.
Number of Employees:	800; 1 U.S., 3 other foreign.
Wages:	Not reported.
Size of Investment:	US $20 million.
Ownership:	Wholly owned subsidiary.
Expansion planned:	Yes.

Firm O produces raw sugar for international export, for the domestic market, and to supply its own ethanol factory. Firm O purchases 35 percent of its sugar from 600 private local firms and imports wine alcohol from Europe for ethanol production. Firm O is the largest private investor in the Caribbean under CBI legislation. However, Firm O's CBI eligibility is now in dispute in the U.S. Congress (see discussion on page 22).

Firm O finds electricity service adequate. The auxiliary generator is now used only during emergency blackouts, although production is still plagued by blackouts and by power surges. Firm O finds water quality to be poor, requiring heavy treatment to operate the firm's boilers.

Replacement parts for Firm O's equipment are usually unavailable in Jamaica, and where available, are greatly overpriced. Firm O therefore imports many of its parts directly from the manufacturers.

Firm O reports that Jamaicans believe farming to be low-level work, and that the unskilled labor employed at the sugar farm is of poor quality. Management level employees for the plantation are difficult to obtain for the same reason. Firm O thus employs three expatriates to manage the sugar plantation.

At the ethanol plant, Firm O employs all Jamaican nationals. According to management, however, Jamaican middle managers lack the initiative to make even minor decisions and therefore require constant supervision. Labor at the ethanol plant is non-union, and although labor at the sugar plantation includes supporters of both major parties, the firm's management maintains good labor relations.

Firm O finds Jamaican Customs to be a major cause of difficulties with its operations, as customs officials exercise little personal initiative. As a result, shipments are often held up because of minor problems, such as typographical errors on invoices. Firm O minimizes these problems by employing one full time management level person to handle import and export paperwork. Shipments normally take two to three days to clear customs, which management believes is as quick as anything that clears Jamaican Customs. Delays of up to four months have occurred, however, on items not normally shipped by the firm. Because ethanol is shipped in large bulk containers, Firm O has not felt the need to implement drug-related export security measures.

Firm O's management finds access to foreign exchange through the currency auction to be a problem. The reserve of Jamaican dollars which must be held to obtain access to U.S. dollars through the auction hurts Firm O's cash flow. A more significant problem is the length of time Firm O's parent corporation and its U.S. suppliers must wait to be paid in U.S. dollars. The normal delay for accessing foreign exchange runs about eight weeks, although a recent payment took Firm O approximately six months to obtain. According to Firm O's management, if the Jamaican Central Bank does not possess the amount of U.S. dollars requested, or does not want to release those dollars, there will invariably be an inaccuracy or omission in the requesting firm's paperwork.

Firm O's management also cites a lack of access to working capital at reasonable interest rates as a major investment impediment. Although the ethanol plant was internally funded through Firm O's parent corporation, U.S. commercial banks disapprove of Firm O's Jamaican exposure. Firm O must borrow working capital at high interest rates on the local capital market for its sugar plantation. According to management, the Jamaican market is lending at nominal interest rates between 14 percent and 18 percent annually (Trafalgar Bank and Agricultural Development Bank, respectively).

Firm O's management believes that Manley's election will not affect Firm O's operation, except perhaps in terms of commercial financing.

Firm O's management believes that its relations with the government may even improve under the Manley administration, if the firm is used politically as an example of private foreign investment which was initiated under a market-dominated administration, and is now flourishing under a social democratic administration.

The Dispute over Firm O's CBI Eligibility. Firm O's ethanol factory qualified for duty-free treatment under CBI legislation in 1984, and is the largest private U.S. investment under this legislation. However, in March 1985, Senator Robert Dole (R) of Kansas introduced a bill that would eliminate Firm O's production from qualification under the CBI. A similar bill was introduced in the House by Representative Jim Leach (R) of Iowa and Representative Richard J. Durbin (D) of Illinois.

The result of these bills was an amendment attached to the Tax Reform Act of 1986 which put the feedstock requirement in ethanol produced under the CBI to 30 percent in 1987, 60 percent in 1988, and finally, to 75 percent by the end of 1989.[16] However, due to the structure of sugar production in Jamaica, Firm O maintains that there is not enough feedstock produced in Jamaica which is available for ethanol production.[17] Indeed Petrojam, the government's dehydration plant, was forced to halt production in 1988 because it was unprofitable to meet the new CBI requirements. Firm O was able to continue ethanol production under a two-year grandfather clause.

Firm O has challenged the amendment and has been upheld by U.S. Customs, but as of January 1989, the matter had not been settled. The feasibility of the amendment is under study by the International Trade Commission and the United States General Accounting Office.

Firm O's management believes the increase in value added requirements for ethanol was a result of successful lobbying on the part of the Renewable Fuels Association and the National Corn Growers Association, in conjunction with the Archer Daniels Midland Corporation, which manufactures approximately 75 percent of the ethanol produced in the United States.

FIRM P

Type of Business:	Agricultural production.
Number of Employees:	235; 3 U.S.
Wages:	Above minimum wage.
Size of Investment:	Not reported.
Ownership:	49 percent private U.S.; 51 percent Jamaican government.
Expansion planned:	Yes, after the elections.

Firm P began its Jamaican investment with the intention of producing rice for export, as well as to supply the domestic market. The first study for this effort was conducted in conjunction with the U.S. Department of

Agriculture. Firm P found, however, that the area of the north coast that was deemed most suitable for rice production in Jamaica was not productive, and that it is less expensive to import rice. Firm P now mills imported rice for domestic consumption and has begun to produce tropical fruits on the southern coast for export to the United States and the United Kingdom.

Firm P has its own nursery for production of plant seedlings, but imports all of its chemicals, equipment and replacement equipment parts from the United States. Firm P is allowed duty-free importation on all equipment for the rice mill, but not on farm equipment. Firm P received a seven year tax holiday from the Jamaican government, and also benefits from duty-free U.S. entry of its products. The firm leases its land from the Jamaican government.

Firm P finds utility service to be erratic, and electricity service is interrupted several times per week. This is a problem for the rice mill because it does not possess an auxiliary generator. The problem is a minor one on the farm, however, because electricity is not crucial to farming operations.

Firm P encounters no significant problems in hiring unskilled agricultural workers from the areas surrounding both the mill and the farm. Because agricultural work requires a low level of training, Firm P has found trainability to be good; however, only Firm P's supervisory staff operates its heavy equipment. Firm P finds obtaining managerial staff is more difficult than obtaining technical and administrative workers. Its need for the latter is limited.

Firm P invested in Jamaica when the exchange rate was approximately J$2.00 to US $1.00 and finds that the devaluation of the Jamaican dollar has helped its investment. While the original investment was funded internally, Firm P has obtained credit for equipment and production loans through commercial sources and through the Agricultural Development Bank. Firm P reports no problems in gaining access to the exchange auction, due to partial government ownership. Nevertheless, it takes two to three months on average for the firm to obtain foreign currency.

Firm P ships by both sea and air. A full-time worker is employed to handle customs requirements. Nevertheless, Firm P finds that the time and paperwork required to meet customs regulations and the problems associated with customs procedures have become an increasing burden. Imports now take an average of one week to clear customs.

Firm P's management has begun spending increasing amounts of time and money to combat illegal drug shipment with the export of its products. Firm P's farm exports are now doublechecked—once at the farm by Firm P's employees and once at the port by drug enforcement staff. Often containers are completely unloaded at the port, which results in a dangerous delay for Firm P's perishable products.

FIRM Q

Type of Business:	Agricultural manufacture.
Number of Employees:	200 at peak harvest; 1 U.S.
Wages:	Not reported.
Size of Investment:	US $3.5 million.
Ownership:	99 percent private U.S.; 1 percent private Jamaican.
Expansion planned:	Yes, barring more problems.

Firm Q produces fruits and vegetables to supply the domestic market. As of July 1988, Firm Q had established contracts with 22 of the major hotels on the island, under which Firm Q will provide a variety of products for one year. Nevertheless, Firm Q wants to expand production to supply the United Kingdom and Caribbean Community (CARICOM) markets. A better exchange rate and greater demand for tropical fruits and vegetables in the United Kingdom, and the absence of duties throughout the CARICOM countries make these markets more desirable than the U.S. market.

Firm Q, established as a fruit farm in conjunction with the Jamaican government, was to form a small farmer system under which the farmers would eventually produce and market agricultural products individually. However, according to Firm Q's management, the domestic agricultural distribution network is so fragmented and disorganized that farmers are able to charge extremely high prices for their products. As a result, farmers have been producing one crop and living off its income for the rest of the year. They are not accustomed to constant work throughout the year, which is expected under their agreement with Firm Q. As a result, the farmers tried to coerce Firm Q into paying them a weekly salary. At this point, very little was being produced for market and, upon investigation, Firm Q found that the employees had been selling the product themselves. According to the firm's estimates, this accounted for 75 percent of the 1987 crop.

There are no formal ownership requirements on agribusiness in Jamaica; however, Firm Q's management believes that the Jamaican government is not favorably disposed toward wholly owned foreign agribusiness enterprises. Management believes that the firm would have encountered fewer problems if it had at least half Jamaican ownership. In support of this belief, the firm's management cites the fact that it took six months to obtain formal approval for the enterprise from the Bank of Jamaica. In addition, Firm Q leases its land from a private Jamaican landowner, and management believes that the firm is charged a higher rent simply because it is U.S.-owned.

Firm Q's farms are equipped with water and electricity facilities; therefore, the firm does not encounter problems with utility provision. Firm Q originally imported all of its equipment from either the United States or Israel and now finds that replacement parts are not available on the island and must be imported. Local equipment repair is a major problem. According to the firm's management, it takes an average of two to three weeks for a repair person to even inspect broken equipment. The actual repairs may take from one to two months.

Firm Q imports all of its planting and packaging materials from the United States and has encountered many difficulties with Jamaican Customs procedures. All imports must be facilitated by a customs broker which, according to Firm Q's management, is an expensive process because brokers and agents require a percentage of the value of the imported goods in return for their services. Customs clearance on imports takes an average of ten days—a major inconvenience for Firm Q on equipment parts, and a critical delay on imports of perishable plant seedlings. Firm Q has tried to minimize its difficulties in importing and exporting by employing one person whose sole responsibility is to handle customs transactions.

Firm Q exports via sea and air and, according to the firm's management, the cost of shipping by sea now approaches that of air freight because Jamaican shipping is controlled by an oligopoly. Shipping via air freight is expensive and requires enough volume to fill a DC-9 (30,000 lbs.).

Firm Q has hired a reformed smuggler to oversee all export operations, from the packaging of the products to the actual loading of Firm Q's containers onto transport. Therefore, the firm does not incur problems in contraband shipment beyond the additional expense of employing this person. Nevertheless, the firm's management believes the added expense is necessary to combat the growing problem.

Access to foreign exchange has been difficult for Firm Q, in spite of a transfer pricing system that allows profits to be realized outside of Jamaica. According to the firm's management, access to smaller amounts (US $10,000–15,000) over a one-month period is not a great problem, but for larger amounts, such as US $200,000, access becomes very difficult. Also, to acquire foreign exchange, firms are required to hold a reserve of Jamaican dollars equal to the amount requested in the auction. According to Firm Q's management, these reserves become inaccessible indefinitely because the auction process takes so long. Thus, as a precaution against the possible devaluation of the Jamaican dollar, Firm Q does not keep large accounts receivables or cash reserves.

Firm Q originally received 100 percent duty-free import of supplies and equipment, and by the time the company had invested over US $1.5 million in the Jamaican operations the government gradually began to reduce its duty free incentives. Firm Q no longer receives any such incentives.

Firm Q's investment had been financed by its parent company; however, the company now refuses to invest more funds in Jamaican operations. Therefore, Firm Q will be forced to turn to the local capital markets for working funds at high interest rates.

Firm Q has encountered serious problems in obtaining mid-level managers for its Jamaican operations. According to management, persons employed as management trainees tend to acquire the poor work ethic exemplified by unskilled agricultural labor, and therefore they remain permanent trainees. As a result, Firm Q finds it hires four times the number needed in the hopes that one employee will become an effective mid-level manager. Firm Q's management believes that low Jamaican wages are misleading to investors: if it takes four Jamaicans to do the normal job of one person, it would be more productive to locate in the United States.

Firm Q has also encountered many labor problems stemming from the attitude of the workers. According to management, Jamaicans do not view farming as a good occupation because the hours are long and the work is physically exhausting. Therefore, laborers work just long enough to be able to support themselves until the next week. According to Firm Q's management, unskilled labor availability depends on the location of operations. Due to urban migration, there is a critical lack of available unskilled workers for its farms. Firm Q foresees production problems at its banana operation on the north coast, as available labor is not sufficient for the peak harvest season. The labor in that parish is controlled by its Parliament member who, according to the firm's management, will not allow extra labor to be brought in from surrounding parishes.

Labor militancy has also been a serious problem for Firm Q's Jamaican operations. In approximately one hour, according to the firm's management, one militant leader can induce all workers on the farm to strike. Firm Q has found that firing such a leader, or any of the farm employees, can prompt all other employees to strike. Firm Q cites labor's attitude as one of its main problems in its Jamaican investment. Firm Q's other major concern is employee theft; this has destroyed Firm Q's profits.

IV. INCENTIVES AND IMPEDIMENTS

While each of the 17 firms interviewed for this report have experienced a unique set of circumstances, these case studies present many of the incentives and impediments the firms cited to U.S. investment in the Dominican Republic and Jamaica. The following table lists the incentives and impediments described in all of the firm interviews. As noted earlier, investments in the Dominican Republic are represented by letters A through I, and those in Jamaica are represented by letters J through Q. All

TABLE 1

Incentives	Investors	
	Dominican Republic	Jamaica
Low-wage labor supply	*ABCD*FHI	*JKL*MP
Labor trainability	FH	*JL*MP
Domestic fiscal incentives	*ABCD*	*J*NP
Domestic government funding	*	P
Domestic investment assistance	*	*KL*
Exchange rate devaluation	*	NP
U.S. government funding	*	*K*
U.S. fiscal incentives	*	*JK*
Caribbean Basin Initiative	*ABCD*GH	NOP
Political stability	*A*DH	*
Production location	*AB*D	*J*N

Impediments	Investors	
	Dominican Republic	Jamaica
Labor motivation	*	*JKL*NOQ
Labor productivity	*A*GI	*JK*NOQ
Worker absenteeism	*AB*DG	*JK*NQ
Lack of skilled labor	*B*EGI	*JK*OP
Lack of technical and administrative labor	*B*EFG	*JK*MOQ
Domestic customs regulations and procedures	*AC*DGH	*J*MNOPQ
Domestic government bureaucracy/regulations	*BC*EHI	*JL*NPQ
Access to foreign exchange through the auction (Jamaica)	*	MOPQ
Lack of spread industry	*BC*DG	*JK*OQ
Unavailability/cost of replacement parts	*B*DF	*JKL*OPQ
Erratic utility service:		
electricity	*ABCD*EFGHI	*JKL*MP
water	*	LOQ
Language barriers	*A*I	*KL*N
Political instability	EG	*JKL*Q
Labor strikes	*	*JL*Q
Labor militancy/unrest	*	*JKL*MNQ
Expected election-related violence	*	*JKL*MNQ
Drug-related problems	*	*JL*P

*not reported as incentives or impediments

free zone firms (Dominican: A through D, Jamaican: J through L) are shown in italics.

Labor Incentives

In both the Dominican Republic and Jamaica, the incentive cited by most U.S. investors both within and outside of export processing zones is an abundant supply of unskilled, inexpensive labor. Labor trainability was also cited as a incentive by four firms in Jamaica, but only by two firms in the DR.

A significant difference, in terms of labor, between the Dominican and Jamaican investment climates is the existence of government-sponsored worker training programs. In Jamaica, programs such as the Human Employment and Resource Training Program (HEART) acclimate unskilled labor to a business environment and teach basic skills. The HEART program finances the development of specialized training academies and places trainees into private sector positions. This program was specifically referred to by two U.S. firms that cited labor trainability as an investment incentive.[18] This labor incentive could be enhanced in the Dominican Republic through the same type of government-sponsored training programs (perhaps in conjunction with the private sector).

Nevertheless, six of the Jamaican firms acknowledged that labor motivation was a key impediment to their Jamaican operations. The reasons for the poor worker motivation described by firm representatives include absenteeism, illiteracy, the inability to understand productivity goals and a lack of personal initiative.

These difficulties suggest that future government training programs may improve Jamaica's investment climate by including training at higher skill levels, and by focusing on the development of a positive work ethic at all levels. The implementation of the latter recommendation is difficult at best, but because worker motivation was seen as an impediment by a majority of firms, further study in this area would be helpful.

The unavailability of skilled labor in all areas was a significant drawback to eight of the U.S. firms interviewed, almost evenly split between zone and non-zone firms. However, this is a feature characteristic of small, underdeveloped economies, and may change with increasing development. It is important to realize, however, that as a labor force matures, wages rise along with skill levels, and the very resource cited by the investors as the major attraction to Caribbean investment may become less of an incentive to foreign investors.

Fiscal Incentives

Duty-free entry into the United States of products assembled under CBI legislation was cited as an incentive by a majority of the investors interviewed. However, the CBI excludes some of the two countries' most competitive exports. In the DR, items such as textiles, apparel and shoes, are excluded; in Jamaica, apparel and sugar are excluded. More inclusive U.S. legislation that provides investors with greater incentives to produce and export items in which these countries have a comparative advantage could enhance the prospects for U.S. direct investment in the Caribbean.

Domestic tax and duty concessions were cited as incentives by seven of the U.S. firm representatives interviewed. However, in the Dominican Republic, these concessions were considered incentives only by the firms in export processing zones (EPZs). This incentive might increase foreign investment significantly if future Dominican policy were broadened to include a larger range of industries.

In Jamaica, domestic fiscal incentives were cited as incentives by only one zone firm. While this implies that Jamaican fiscal incentives are not focused specifically on firms producing in EPZs, the fact that they were considered incentives by only three of eight firms indicates that they are not widespread. However, tax and duty concessions in Jamaica are part of a sophisticated system that is used to provide revenue for national insurance and worker training, among other programs. This structure is not easily reorganized to permit exemptions for foreign investors.

Impediments: Electricity Generation

The investment impediment common to all U.S. investments in this study was erratic electricity supply. Although most of the firms interviewed have purchased generators, future investors will unquestionably weigh the cost of electricity generation against the size of their proposed capital investment.

The electricity generation problem is being addressed by the Dominican government. A loan of US $105 million was approved by the World Bank at the end of 1988 for the completion of three new generation plants, and for the upgrade and repair of existing transmission facilities. There have also been discussions between the Bank and the Dominican government concerning a major infrastructural program to be implemented over the next ten years.[19]

In Jamaica, many of the representatives interviewed stated that electricity generation has improved over the last five years. Continued government efforts to refine electric generation and transmission facilities will, nevertheless, enhance the investment climate in Jamaica.

Customs and Government Bureaucracy

Domestic customs procedures and government bureaucracy were cited as obstacles to investment by 15 of 18 U.S. firm representatives interviewed. Specifically cited by all of the EPZ firms in the Dominican Republic, difficulties in these areas seem to be more prevalent in the zones than outside. Complaints center around inefficiencies in government agencies, which often result in the delay of authorizations for product registration and export, and in the unpredictable application of rules and regulations governing business.

Bureaucratic difficulties are faced not only by the U.S. firms in the Dominican Republic, but appear to be evident throughout the business community. The most common complaints described by the firm representatives concerned the myriad of forms and applications to be completed and the time required to obtain authorizing signatures from numerous government agencies. The creation of one specific agency to handle investor applications, authorizations and approvals could significantly reduce these difficulties by consolidating required documentation and agency approvals. Such an agency would further enhance the Dominican investment climate, within and outside of EPZs, were it also relatively free from the highly politicized environment that appears to characterize the business community's relations with official agencies.

Improvements in Dominican customs procedures should involve the effective modernization of the system and the standardization of regulations throughout the country to avoid selective interpretation by customs officials. The Dominican Republic does not possess a merit civil service system; however, customs employment might be made part of a permanent civil service, thereby avoiding employee turnover with each new administration or minister.

Investor difficulties with Jamaican customs procedures and government bureaucracy concerned documentation, the number of agency approvals required, and the inconsistent application of regulations. The Jamaican government has taken steps to alleviate these problems through the creation of JAMPRO (Jamaican Promotions Limited), an organization designed to promote domestic and foreign investment, increase exports and expand industrialization in specific sectors. The creation of this agency is illustrative of efforts to consolidate and simplify the bureaucracy surrounding investment regulations. Two of the U.S. firms in Jamaica reported that JAMPRO's efforts in this respect were indeed helpful. Future policy, aimed at allowing JAMPRO greater authority and official influence after the initial investment, would further ease bureaucratic difficulties. Similar government efforts to consolidate and simplify Jamaican customs procedures, and to reduce regulations and paperwork requirements for import and export operations, might significantly reduce investor difficulties in this area.

Spread Industry

A lack of domestic spread industry and replacement parts were investment disincentives cited by five firms in the DR and six firms in Jamaica. In both countries, it seems that this is a major problem for firms in EPZ manufacturing. However, a lack of backward linkages is not a surprising feature of an underdeveloped island economy. The development of many such industrial linkages may not be appropriate in a small economy that has limited opportunities to develop economies of scale, or to competitively produce the intermediate goods used as industrial inputs.

In addition, the protective import substitution and pricing policies in both countries appears to have distorted both the availability and cost of domestically produced parts and supplies. The domestic parts and supplies that are available are very expensive relative to those produced in the industrialized countries. Thus, imports of these goods are less expensive for the firms, despite transportation and duty costs. To reduce or eliminate domestic industrial protection programs would be a questionable move, however, because the apparent economic cost of substitution programs may be outweighed by employment or other benefits arising from the existence of the domestic industry. In addition, there is no way to insure the development of competitive industry to replace that which may be destroyed by the elimination of protections.

Impediments Unique to Jamaican Investment

Additional impediments cited by a majority of U.S. investors in Jamaica were expected election-related violence (which turned out to be modest), labor militancy and unrest. Historically, labor strikes and violence tend to emerge in Jamaica during election years. According to the firm representatives interviewed, strikes and violence are exacerbated by close ties between the political parties and the major labor unions.

Although only three of the firms interviewed specifically cited drug-related problems as impediments to their Jamaican operations, many of the firm representatives observed that the problem is increasingly translated into higher costs for all export operations. Evergreen Shipping Lines, previously one of the major shipping operations out of Jamaica, has cut back on its Jamaican operations after being fined US $30 million by U.S. Customs for unknowingly transporting contraband into the United States.[20] As a result, exporters now face the problem of limited shipping facilities and schedules as well as higher shipping costs. Additional security measures, such as employing guards, also increase shipping expenses.

Zero-tolerance guidelines implemented by U.S. Customs penalize apparently legitimate export operations for their failure to continually monitor their shipments. This is a difficult task for operations that are located far from the ports or that cannot afford to have an employee accompany the goods from factory to port. Additional security measures undertaken by U.S. firms that ship products into the United States may be negated since exporters generally have little physical control over shipping containers after they have been deposited at the dock. The Jamaican Exporters' Association (JEA) stated that "drugs are predominately loaded on to containers after storage at the port."[21]

The JEA is urging the government to set up a special security zone at the Kingston docks so that sealed containers can be properly guarded.

Strict customs enforcement at Jamaican ports, combined with efforts to streamline port operations, could also help to alleviate the problem.

V. CONCLUSIONS

The 17 investments studied in this report represent a cross-section of U.S. investment in agriculture, manufacturing and services in the Dominican Republic and Jamaica. It is difficult to draw comprehensive conclusions about U.S. investment in the Caribbean from the experiences of 17 firms. However, these experiences provide valuable information about the day-to-day investment climates in the Dominican Republic and Jamaica.

In both countries, the most significant incentives to investment cited by the representatives of these companies were an abundant supply of cheap labor, CBI trade and domestic fiscal incentives. The most commonly cited impediments were inadequate electricity provision and domestic customs procedures.

Dominican and Jamaican government efforts to encourage future foreign direct investment should include the development or extension of labor training programs, streamlining of customs and governmental procedures, and improvements in utilities provision—specifically for electricity generation. The broadening of domestic fiscal incentives might attract more foreign investment, but at a cost. In Jamaica, policy should also focus on attempts to alleviate illegal drug shipment.

In promoting economic development in the Caribbean through U.S. direct investment, the most prominent policy implication for the United States is the expansion and liberalization of investment incentive programs such as the CBI. In addition, on-site measures to control the exportation of drugs without impeding investors from developing legitimate export operations in Jamaica would be valuable.

NOTES

1. Balaguer was first appointed president by Trujillo in 1961, but was elected by popular vote in 1966, 1970, 1974 and 1986. This makes him the longest governing president in Dominican democratic history.

2. This figure was obtained from the United States Department of Commerce, Bureau for Latin America and the Caribbean, 1988.

3. This may change as the imposition of the exchange auction makes it more difficult and expensive for those firms to legally acquire dollars.

4. According to Firm F's management, Dominican demand for gasoline increased by 15 percent in 1985, 20 percent in 1986 and 25 percent in 1987.

5. Under Dominican Law #409, the importation of vehicles and equipment related to Firm G's operations should be duty-free.

6. According to one government official, Dominican sugar prices rose by 100 percent in one month.

7. Economist Intelligence Unit. *Country Report No. 1: Jamaica, Belize, Bahamas, Bermuda.* (London: Economist Intelligence Unit Limited, 1989), p. 10.

8. Economist Intelligence Unit, *Country Report No. 1*, p. 5.

9. U.S. Department of State, Bureau of Economics. *Investment Climate Statement: Jamaica.* (Washington, D.C.: U.S. Department of State, 1988), p. 4.

10. U.S. Department of State, *Investment Climate Statement: Jamaica*, p. 5.

11. Economist Intelligence Unit. *Country Report No. 1*, p. 15.

12. The Human Employment and Resource Training Program (HEART) finances the development of specialized training academies and places trainees into private sector positions.

13. Firm L also considered investing in the Dominican Republic, but the Dominican government required the use of domestic sugar at the Dominican State Sugar Council's (CEA) price, which is also above the world price.

14. Firm L is required to obtain annual food-handling permits for all of its employees. This process entails physical checks, such as blood tests and chest x-rays. Firm L obtained employee health permits for the first year of operations, and found the process to be a bureaucratic nightmare.

15. AT & T and the Jamaican government have been negotiating such an agreement, although it has not been formally announced.

16. Feedstock includes sugar, sugar cane, molasses, corn, or other products from which ethanol can be manufactured.

17. In Jamaica, all sugar is sold to the government and proceeds are divided 60–40 percent between the farmers and producers. The Jamaican production target is 250,000 tons of which 220,000 tons is now being produced.

18. The additional firms that cited trainability as favorable described other reasons for their statements. In one of these firms, management works directly alongside the 14 full-time employees. In the other firm, management states that the low skill level required of its 235 employees contributed to good trainability.

19. Economist Intelligence Unit. *Country Report Number 3: Cuba, Dominican Republic, Haiti, Puerto Rico.* (London: Economist Intelligence Unit Limited, 1988), p. 4.

20. According to a JAMPRO staff member in New York, the original fine levied by U.S. Customs was US $66 million and was reduced to US $30 million on appeal.

21. Economist Intelligence Unit, *Country Report No. 1*, p. 15.

6

Trade Policy and Export Activity in the Mexican Manufacturing Sector

María de Lourdes de la Fuente Deschamps

I. INTRODUCTION

Beginning in 1940 and for more than 40 years, trade policy in Mexico encouraged import substitution in the industrial sector to modernize an until-then mainly rural economy. As a result of that policy, from the 1940s until the beginning of the 1970s, the share of industry in national production grew substantially and constantly at the expense of the agricultural sector. Since then, and faced with the exhaustion of that development model, Mexico has been confronted by the alternative of opening its borders to international competition or maintaining the prevailing system at an ever-greater social cost. Although there were considerable efforts at opening trade in 1971–72 and in 1977–78, various circumstances caused the postponement of basic structural reforms until the beginning of the de la Madrid Administration.

A program of severe macroeconomic stabilization was introduced, beginning in 1983, with a significant reduction in the aggregate demand. At the same time, structural reform tending to liberalize foreign trade was initiated. By 1984, the total number of import categories subject to prior permission was reduced. At the same time, the tariff structure was modified and the average tax was lowered. However, the effective protection structure in Mexico remained practically unchanged. Primary products still had low protective taxes while capital goods continued to enjoy high levels of effective protection. Since July 1985, trade policy has maintained a continual process of liberalizing foreign trade.

In this context, the rapid flow of productive resources to the export sector will play a fundamental role in the attainment of the main developmental goal of the country. It is especially important to analyze the impact of the principal export-promoting measures on the sum and the composition of these aggregates. Also requiring study are the productive processes that are more favored by variations in the terms of trade between the import-substitution sector and the export sector. Thus, we must determine how the assigning of economic resources has been modified as a result of the recent structural changes in trade policy.

Two types of results were obtained in this study: (1) a set of descriptors indicating the recent development and the sectoral composition of exports and other pertinent variables (number employed, real wages, person-hours worked and real value of production); and (2) a collection of analytic results, in the form of statistical models that will allow us to predict the behavior of exports if the process of trade liberalization continues in Mexico in the next few years.

In the first section of this working paper, available evidence about the effect of the opening of trade on the behavior of a sample of Mexican enterprises is presented. Two exercises are carried out: (1) a comparison of the development of the principal aggregates—production, number employed, real wages, person-hours worked—in the group of exporters and in that of non-exporters at the level of the nine divisions that make it up, and (2) a statistical test to determine whether there is a significant difference in the mean growth of the level of fixed assets, number employed and the capital-labor ratio during the period 1984–1987. The results for the group of exporters and of non-exporters are compared.

The second section comments on the estimation of a behavioral model of export supply during the period 1984–1987. An exercise simulates the impact of changes in world income and internal protectionism on Mexican exports.

In the third section, I present a group of analytical results for predicting the behavior of exports if trade liberalization in Mexico is continued in the next few years. A PROBIT model of qualitative selection is used to estimate the probability that a manufacturing industry will transfer resources from the import-substitution sector to the export sector, given its structure and the restrictions it faces.

Finally, the principal conclusions of the study are presented along with four appendices that contain useful information for further interpretation of the results.

II. THE IMPACT OF THE OPENING OF TRADE ON MEXICO'S EXPORT SECTOR

In this section, the impact of the opening of trade on the financial behavior of the Mexican export sector is analyzed. In the first part, based on a sample of enterprises from the Monthly Industrial Survey of the National Institute of Statistics, Ministry of Planning and Budget, a group of exporters is compared with a group of non-exporters for the January–June 1985 period, prior to the invigoration of the process of opening trade and during the most recent period available (January 1987–March 1989) in terms of the development of production, number employed, real wages and person-hours worked. This analysis applies to the aggregate manufacturing industry and to the nine large divisions that compose it.

In the second part, statistical hypotheses tests are carried out in relation to differences in the yearly averages of capital formation and employment for the period 1984–1987. This analysis is based on information obtained by enterprise in an opinion survey of the 500 most important firms—in terms of annual sales—in Mexico.

Development of Exporting and Non-Exporting Enterprises Before and After the Opening of Trade

Table 1 shows the development of real production, number employed, real wages per person employed, and person-hours worked from January 1987 to March 1989, grouped in two categories, exporters and non-exporters. The exporters are those that export more than 40 percent of their production and are included in the sample of the Monthly Industrial Survey. The base for the index numbers shown for each of the variables is January–June 1985 = 100. This period was chosen as it is the semester immediately prior to the principal steps for opening trade. It is interesting to note that, in all of the categories (except real wages) the index values for the exporters are greater than those of the non-exporters.

Note also that the value of production, number employed and person-hours worked grew 30.5, 2.1 and 0.3 percent, respectively (see Table 1) for exporters (until March 1989); for the non-exporters, these decreased −5.9, −13.2 and −16.4 percent, respectively. As for the development of real wages, it is interesting to note that, while for the exporters this variable had a total growth of 3.7 percent, for the non-exporters, it remained practically constant (its total growth during the period was only 0.3 percent. This not-so-marked difference in the development of real wages—in relation to the other variables studied—for exporters and non-exporters might be because the real wage level for the exporters is greater than for the non-exporters, which might have permitted the latter to grant nominal increases to similar salaries.

Tests of Hypotheses Related to the Growth of Assets, Number Employed and the Capital-Work Ratio in Exporters and Non-Exporters

For the purpose of testing statistically whether there is a significant difference in the behavior of exporters and non-exporters, a sample of 211 exporters and 202 non-exporters was compiled, based on data for the 1984–1987 period in several issues of *Expansion*. The results are presented in Appendix A.

Appendix A shows that the mean of total assets, number employed and the capital-labor ratio is greater for exporters than for non-exporters in the sample. The results indicate that, during the period of the opening of trade, both exporters and non-exporters have increased their production capacity in relation to the period prior to liberalization; however, employment has not increased during these years (except for non-exporters in 1987).

The results also indicate that the opening of trade has favored investment and the creation of jobs in the export sector of the economy relative to the non-export sector. Also, production processes have become more capital-intensive during the period. This is perhaps a reflection of the

TABLE 1

COMPARISON OF EXPORTING AND NONEXPORTING BUSINESSES
IN THE MANUFACTURING INDUSTRY
BEFORE AND AFTER THE OPENING OF TRADE

Prior to Jan.–June 1985	After	Value of Production		Personnel Employed		Real Wages per Person		Person-Hrs Worked	
		Exp.	Nonexp.	Exp.	Nonexp.	Exp.	Nonexp.	Exp.	Nonexp.
100.0	1987 J	104.4	84.1	103.4	90.4	90.9	93.5	127.6	108.2
100.0	F	106.5	82.4	103.8	91.1	88.9	91.1	122.9	105.9
100.0	M	123.1	92.2	104.8	91.8	95.0	88.5	131.3	111.4
100.0	A	128.7	86.1	105.2	91.8	95.2	93.7	128.0	105.7
100.0	M	122.4	94.7	105.5	92.4	90.4	94.3	130.4	110.4
100.0	J	123.4	94.7	106.0	92.8	93.3	89.4	133.5	113.4
100.0	J	125.5	91.0	107.2	92.4	93.2	90.4	135.8	112.5
100.0	A	103.4	97.4	106.6	92.0	92.4	95.1	133.7	113.4
100.0	S	118.2	90.4	106.9	92.0	89.0	94.8	133.5	112.4
100.0	O	122.8	93.8	108.5	93.7	96.4	96.4	136.9	116.3
100.0	N	112.0	102.2	106.5	92.6	97.8	97.1	131.3	111.4

100.0	D	119.6	84.3	105.8	91.2	121.3	121.4	131.2	109.7
100.0	1988 J	120.5	75.7	106.8	90.4	90.9	100.0	134.7	109.4
100.0	F	124.9	87.7	106.7	90.3	89.7	99.4	131.5	109.4
100.0	M	129.0	96.7	107.1	90.9	94.4	97.4	133.2	111.4
100.0	A	119.8	98.4	108.8	91.4	90.0	94.4	132.1	111.8
100.0	M	121.6	101.1	108.2	91.4	90.8	96.9	133.3	113.0
100.0	J	122.8	103.8	107.9	91.5	90.5	96.7	135.2	115.9
100.0	J	114.4	86.5	100.8	84.8	90.4	91.3	101.7	83.9
100.0	A	128.2	106.8	101.4	85.1	92.4	89.2	104.6	86.0
100.0	S	121.3	88.6	100.9	84.8	93.0	90.6	101.1	84.0
100.0	O	131.2	95.6	101.4	85.3	92.3	90.6	102.1	84.8
100.0	N	133.4	99.3	101.7	85.2	95.2	99.1	103.3	85.0
100.0	D	115.8	87.4	100.9	84.1	128.2	126.3	93.3	79.3
100.0	1989 J	126.3	95.3	110.5	85.5	84.7	93.9	100.9	84.3
100.0	F	130.1	94.7	101.1	86.7	93.6	93.7	98.7	85.5
100.0	M	130.5	94.1	102.1	86.8	103.7	100.2	100.3	83.6

Source: Monthly Industrial Survey, INEGI, SPP.

heavy importation of capital goods (especially in 1987 and, although it is not included in the sample, 1988).

In terms of job creation, it is important to note that, by 1987 increases were noted in this variable that could mark a tendency toward recovery of such an important indicator. It will be vitally important to reach employment rates compatible with the large expansion in the work force. If the opening of trade contributes to the closing of the gap between these two variables, it will have contributed significantly to the success of one of the principal objectives of economic policy in this stage of Mexican development.

III. SPECIFICATION AND ESTIMATION OF EXPORT SUPPLY BY SECTOR

In this section, an economic model of behavior for export supply by manufacturing activity is specified (from sectors 11 to 59 of the SII classification of National Accounts). In addition, this section contains econometric estimations of said models based on monthly data for the 1984–1987 period. Finally, a simulation captures the effect on export activity in Mexico of the principal variables in several scenarios. The differential impact on Mexican manufacturing industries of the level of U.S. economic activity and the degree of the opening of trade in Mexico is of special interest.

Export Behavior by Manufacturing Sector

The behavior of exports is modeled on a supply function of total exports that takes into account the following considerations.

First, small economy and price taking on international markets are assumed. This implies an infinite elasticity of export demand.

In addition, it is assumed that the process of export supply does not present an instantaneous adjustment; therefore, a time lag between desired exports and exports observed is incorporated—by means of lags in the dependant variable.

On the other hand, variables of scale are included (the level of disposable income in the United States as a proxy variable for the level of economic activity of Mexico's principal trading partners) and variables corresponding to relative prices of exports (I include the ratio of prices of goods exported between the United States and Mexico and the real exchange rate as later defined).

The impact of effective import protection on exports is also considered. This measures the protection to value-added, that is, to the value of the final product minus the value of the intermediate inputs. It is expected that with greater effective protection, the incentive to participate in the foreign market will be diminished and, as a result, exports will be lower.

Finally, because exports show highly seasonal behavior—due to the monthly periodicity of the data—dummy variables are introduced that capture this effect.

The econometric specifications of the model are presented in Appendix B.

Estimation of Export Supply by Manufacturing Sector

In Appendix C, the results of the estimation of export supply for manufacturing sectors is presented according to the specifications in the preceding section.

In general terms, the variables show the expected signs; that is, the real change rate has a positive sign, which indicates that when there is an increase in the opportunity cost of production for the internal market instead of for the external market, a greater volume will be exported. Foreign income has a positive impact on Mexican imports as increases in the level of this variable bring about a greater demand for goods, both domestic and imported. Effective protection has—with limited exceptions—a negative sign, for, as effective protection increases, fewer incentives to export are generated. The relationship of external price to internal price has a positive sign. This indicates that better exchange terms—a higher level of this variable—favor export activity. Finally, there is no expected *a priori* sign for the lags in exports and for seasonal dummies, as said sign will depend on the particular conditions of each sector.

Simulation of the Impact of Changes in World Income and Internal Protectionism on Mexican Exports

This section takes advantage of the principal results of the estimation of export supply in the different manufacturing sectors to simulate the effect on exports, by branch, of two of the principal variables included in the analysis. The differential impact of changes in the level of world income on said industries—captured as substitutes in this study through personal disposable income in the United States—and of variations in the degree of trade opening in Mexico—measured in this work by means of effective protection on manufacturing exports—are especially interesting.

For this, I examined four scenarios relating to the development of world income and internal protectionism. These scenarios were defined in the following manner:

Scenario A: High growth in world income (5 percent)
Considerable decrease in protectionism (-20 percent)

> *Scenario B:* High growth in world income (5 percent)
> Considerable increase in protectionism (20 percent)
> *Scenario C:* Decrease in world income (-1 percent)
> Considerable decrease in protectionism (-20 percent)
> *Scenario D:* Decrease in world income (-1 percent)
> Considerable increase in protectionism (20 percent)

The exercise supposes no interaction between income and protectionism and, in addition, the choice of changes in the variables is somewhat arbitrary. Nevertheless, it illustrates the great dispersion of the effects of changes in these two variables on the different industries. For example, in Scenario A, the impact (in percentage) on the growth of exports goes from -3.3 percent in Sector 55 (electrical equipment and apparatus) to a growth greater than 100 percent in Sector 18 (animal feed). Of course, these results are due to the different income and protection elasticities in both sectors. In turn, these differences in elasticities reflect very diverse economic conditions in both sectors.

Another interesting case appears from the analysis of scenario B, where increases in the level of protectionism, even with high rates of world income growth, lead such sectors as 18 (animal feed) to decrease exports more than 100 percent, while the other sectors maintain healthy growth greater than 8 percent (such as Sector 13, wheat milling; 44, cement; 53, home appliances and 55, electrical equipment and apparatus). These results reflect differences in the respective elasticities, a product of policies and behavioral restrictions observed in the sample period.

In Scenario C (low income growth and decrease in protection), it is interesting to note that exports of some sectors, such as 13, wheat milling; 15, coffee grinding; 27, clothing; 44, cement; 45, non-metallic mineral products; 53, home appliances; 55, electrical equipment and apparatus; and 57, bodies, motors and parts, are very sensitive to changes in world income and present decreases in this scenario, in spite of the opening of trade.

Finally, in Scenario D ("the worst of all possible worlds," with a decrease in income and an increase in internal protection), the decreases in exports in seven sectors exceed 30 percent, and in 19 of them, they exceed 10 percent.

These results are only four from a great number of possible scenarios—especially if we include possible values of the remaining explanatory variables—but they capture the broad responses to exogenous changes of the same magnitude. This is important because generalized policies affect production processes in differing degrees. In this sense, it would be a useful exercise to try to detect the manufacturing industries with greatest export potential. This is especially true if export activity generates new employment or leads to transfers of labor from the informal sector to the modern sector of the economy.

IV. ESTIMATION OF THE PROBABILITY OF MANUFACTURING INDUSTRIES PARTICIPATING IN EXPORT ACTIVITIES

This section seeks to forecast expert behavior if the trade liberalization process in Mexico continues for the next few years. For this, I have used a qualitative choice model—the PROBIT model—to estimate the probability of a manufacturing industry's transferring resources from the import-substitution to the export sector. The specifications of this model are presented in Appendix D.

Estimation of the PROBIT Model

In this section, I present the results of estimation of the PROBIT model specified in Appendix D and describe the data and the variables used.

Data and Variables. The sample consists of observations of 43 of the 49 sectors of manufacturing activity (two digits in the classification corresponding to the National Accounts of Mexico). The sectors omitted correspond to those omitted in the analysis of export supply (see Section III).

The year 1987 was chosen for the analysis as it is the most recent one for which information on all of the selected variables is available (unfortunately there are no data on nominal and effective protection by sector for 1988).

The variables contained in vector X (see Appendix D) represent structural characteristics, conditions of trade policy and relative prices that the various manufacturing sectors present. These were chosen based on both theoretical considerations and availability of information. The variables selected are described below:

> $X1$: Intermediate imports as a percentage of GNP. This variable is used as a proxy variable for the degree of international technological integration of the branch.
> $X2$: Capital imports as a percentage of GNP. This variable is an indicator of the flow of technology incorporated in assets originating abroad.
> $X3$: Direct foreign investment as a percentage of GNP. This variable measures differences in the capital structure and tries to capture diverse systems of organization and administration of the enterprises in a specific sector.
> $X4$: Nominal protection in percentage terms. This variable reflects the degree of tariff protection in relation to the value of the production in a branch.
> $X5$: Effective protection in percentage terms. In contrast to nominal protection, this variable measures the tariff protection in terms of the value added of a sector, that is, in terms of the value of production minus the value of intermediate inputs used in the production process.

X6: Relative world prices of the sector. This variable is measured as the foreign price (in this study, I use the producer price index for the corresponding sector in the United States as an approximation of this variable) divided by the domestic price (the producer price index in Mexico of the sector) in the various industries. In order to create a correspondence of the sectors in the Mexican and U.S. classification, a breakdown by type of good was considered.

X7: Dummy variable of division 7 (basic metal industries).

Y: Variable associated with the participation index. This variable takes the value one if the value of exports as a percentage of GNP exceeds the mean (10.6 percent) of the group of manufacturing sectors and takes the value zero otherwise. This variable is the dependent variable (DP) in the probability model (see also Appendix D).

Results Obtained. Table 2 contains the principal results of the estimation of the PROBIT models of export participation. In it, the specifications of the estimated models as well as the statistics that permit the testing of the significance of the parameters and the generosity of the adjustment are presented.

Due to the nature of the sample, the strategy consisted in first estimating individual PROBIT models, which permitted measuring the isolated impact of each of the explanatory variables on export participation index. Then a model that included all the explanatory variables was used to predict the probability of export participation of each sector, based on its particular characteristics.

The results for the first group of models (equations 1 to 6 in Table 2) indicate that variables $X1$ to $X6$ are significant to the 90 percent level of confidence. In addition, the signs of the coefficients are the expected ones; that is, intermediate imports, capital imports, direct foreign investment and relative prices have a positive sign, and both nominal and effective protection have negative signs. The value of the estimated coefficients does not have a concrete interpretation, as it depends on the units of measurement of the corresponding variables.

Equation 7 contains the estimated values in the model that contains all variables. Note that the T-Student statistics are very low; nevertheless, to the extent that the adjustment is good, it allows us to make dependable forecasts of the probabilities of participation in exports.

The industries with the highest probability of exporting, generally, are those that have large intermediate imports as a proportion of their production (in the case of Sector 56, close to 85 percent), considerable importation of capital goods, a high influx of direct foreign investment, favorable relative prices and lower-than-average effective protection (except in Sector 46). For their part, the industries with lower probabilities of exporting, generally, are characterized by low or moderate importation of intermediate and capital goods, insignificant direct foreign investment and,

TABLE 2

PRINCIPAL RESULTS OF THE ESTIMATION OF THE
PROBIT MODELS OF EXPORT PARTICIPATION

Model	Variables	Natural Log
1.	$-0.893 + 0.0237\,X1$ $(-2.93)\quad(1.87)$	-20.189
2.	$-1.146 + 0.212\,X2$ $(-3.43)\quad(2.49)$	-17.708
3.	$-1.019 + 0.0155\,X3$ $(-3.06)\quad(1.77)$	-18.239
4.	$-1.579 - 0.014\,X4 + 0.257\,X2$ $(-3.06)\quad(-2.23)\quad(2.63)$	-16.789
5.	$-1.392 - 0.00789\,X5 + 0.244\,X2$ $(-3.226)\quad(-2.186)\quad(2.591)$	-16.582
6.	$-8.854 + 45.881\,X6 + 0.379\,X2 + 6.75\,X7$ $(-2.61)\quad(2.34)\quad(2.42)\quad(1.28)$	-11.323
7.	$-1.308 - 0.0485\,X1 + 0.265\,X2 + 0.0107\,X3$ $(-0.70)\quad(-1.37)\quad(1.74)\quad(1.06)$ $0.00653\,X5 + 0.606\,X6 + 4.107\,X7$ $(-1.09)\quad(0.050)\quad(0.596)$	-17.063

Note: The values in parentheses represent the T-Student statistics and the variables considered are:
   X1: Intermediate imports as a percentage of the GNP
   X2: Capital imports as a percentage of GNP
   X3: Direct foreign investment as a percentage of GNP
   X4: Nominal protection in percentage terms
   X5: Effective protection in percentage terms
   X6: External price within internal price of the branch
   X7: Indicator of division 7 (Basic Metal Industries)

in the case of Sector 24, the highest effective protection of the entire sample.

The results presented in this section are useful for detecting the impact of variables subject to modification by means of economic policies that affect export activities in the Mexican export sector. To the extent that policy favors non-petroleum exports in Mexico, it will succeed in accomplishing one of the principal objectives of the development plan initiated in mid-1985. If it permits the creation of permanent, well-paying jobs for a broad cross-section of the population, Mexico will be able to look to a lasting solution to one of the most complex problems it now faces.

V. CONCLUSIONS

The following conclusions are drawn from the investigation carried out for this study.

1. The indices of production value, of number employed and of person-hours worked in exporting enterprises (those that export more than 40 percent of their production) exhibit significantly higher growth than those of non-exporters beginning in July 1985, the month when the opening of trade in Mexico began in earnest. Real wages, nevertheless, have shown similar growth rates in the two types of enterprise. This means that the new stage of export promotion—and virtual abandonment of the import-substitution plan in Mexico—may bring with it rates of economic growth corresponding to the levels of employment and may use installed capacity required to reach greater levels of social welfare in Mexico.

2. In addition, the analysis of the differences in each enterprise between total assets, number employed and the capital-labor ratio indicates that the opening of trade has favored investment and the creation of jobs in the export sector of the economy relative to the non-export sector. At the same time, production processes have become more capital-intensive during the period studied, with a concurrent improvement in labor productivity. This perhaps reflects the heavy importation of capital goods that has been observed in recent years.

3. In terms of job creation, it is important to note that, by 1987, increases in this variable were observed, which might have marked a tendency toward recovery. This reversal will be fundamental in reaching employment growth rates compatible with strong expansion of the work force in Mexico.

4. In relation to the estimation of export supply functions, the adjustments obtained were, in general, very satisfactory. It was confirmed that variables such as the real exchange rate, external income, protection—both nominal and effective—and relative prices have significant impacts on the level of imports per manufacturing sector. If economic policy is handled properly—especially trade policy and market conditions—it could signify high growth rates of said exports in the future.

5. However, there exists considerable dispersion of the effects of said policies and restrictions on the behavior of industries. This is important, as some generalized policies could affect to different degrees—and, on not a few occasions, in opposite directions—the various productive processes.

6. With favorable external growth and moderate protective tariffs, the growth of exports is likely to increase considerably in the great majority of the industries analyzed. This is especially useful, as it has been shown that export activity creates greater employment and transfers a certain

type of labor from the informal sector of the economy to the modern sector.

7. In relation to the estimation of models of qualitative choice to obtain the probability that a manufacturing industry would transfer resources to the export sector, the results were satisfactory. In particular, they indicate that the industries with the highest probability of exporting are, in general, those that have high imports of intermediate and capital goods, a high flow of direct foreign investment, favorable relative prices and moderately low effective protection. On the other hand, the industries with lower export probabilities are characterized in general terms by few imports of intermediate goods and capital, insignificant direct foreign investment and high rates of effective protection.

8. The results obtained from this work will be useful if they aid the makers of economic policy in detecting the manufacturing sectors with highest export potential. To the extent that said policies favor non-petroleum exports in Mexico and there is a concomitant increase in the levels of production and the creation of jobs in Mexico, the prospects for meeting the principal objectives of the development plan begun in 1985 will improve.

APPENDIX A

TABLE A

DIFFERENCES OF ANNUAL MEANS FOR TOTAL ASSETS, NUMBER EMPLOYED
AND THE CAPITAL-LABOR RATIO BY TYPE OF ENTERPRISE

Type of Enterprise	Total Assets	Number Employed	Capital-Labor Ratio
Exporters			
1984	M = 18099	M = 1227.6	M = 14.4
	S = 37882.6	S = 1985.6	S = 15.6
1985	M = 31328.5	M = 1279.7	M = 24.2
	S = 66010.4	S = 2141.7	S = 26.9
	T = 2.52*	T = 0.26	T = 4.58*
1986	M = 68959.8	M = 1304.3	M = 47.6
	S = 157600.3	S = 2953.6	S = 55.5
	T = 3.13*	T = 0.24	T = 6.55*
1987	M = 172720.7	M = 1346.0	M = 127.8
	S = 344531.5	S = 1992.9	S = 160.9
	T = 4.11*	T = 0.15	T = 7.07*
Nonexporters			
1984	M = 3988.0	M = 514.1	M = 8.7
	S = 6270.4	S = 641.2	S = 9.5
1985	M = 6530.6	M = 576.8	M = 14.3
	S = 10231.2	S = 782.3	S = 16.3
	T = 3.01*	T = 0.88	T = 4.23*
1986	M = 10451.3	M = 450.1	M = 24.0
	S = 29096.2	S = 751.8	S = 31.4
	T = 2.25*	T = 0.61	T = 5.35*
1987	M = 39678.4	M = 775.2	M = 86.7
	S = 54006.4	S = 920.0	S = 148.8
	T = 4.99*	T = 3.46*	T = 4.31*

M = Sample median

S = Sample standard deviation

T = Test statistic to prove the difference between the median for the corresponding year and the preceding year

*Indicates the test has a 95 percent significance

APPENDIX B
ECONOMETRIC SPECIFICATION OF THE EXPORT-SUPPLY MODEL

In the econometric specification of the export-supply model, all of the variables are expressed as logarithms (with the exception of effective protection). This type of specification carries with it the advantage that the coefficients represent the respective elasticities. Thus, the model to be estimated can be expressed in the following fashion:

$$Log\ X = \beta 1\ Log\ TCR + \beta 2\ Log\ IPDEU + \beta 3\ PE + \beta 4\ Log\ P^*/P$$
$$+ \beta 5\ Log\ X\ (-1) + \ldots + \beta 16\ Log\ X\ (-12) + \beta 17D1 + \ldots +$$
$$\beta 28\ D12 + u.$$

Where:

Log X represents the logarithm of the exports for the corresponding sector measured in dollars;

Log TCR represents the logarithm of the real exchange rate measured as the ratio between the nominal exchange rate deflated by the consumer price index and the world exchange rate (baskets per dollar) deflated by the IMF foreign price index (133 countries), base 1984 = 100;

Log IPDEU represents the logarithm of personal disposable income in the United States, base 1984;

PE represents the effective protection (as percentage) of the corresponding sector;

Log P*/P represents the logarithm of the ratio between the producer price index in the United States and the producer price index in Mexico for the corresponding sector base 1984 = 100;

Log X(-t) represents the logarithm of the branch deferred t months.

D1 to D12 represent the dummy variables corresponding to the 12 months of the year with seasonal effect; and

u represents the stochastic error of the model.

In addition, we assume that the *u* error in the model is a normally distributed variable with a mean $E(u) = 0$ and matrix of variances-covariances $E = r^2I$; that is, the errors are homoscedastic and independent.

All of the data are monthly for the period January 1984–December 1987. In this work, export supply functions for Sectors 11 to 59 are estimated, with the exception of Sector 14 (nixtamal milling), 25 (thread and cloth made from hard fibers), and 59 (other manufacturing industries), as it was not possible to obtain indicators of foreign prices compatible with the corresponding domestic prices of these sectors.

APPENDIX C

TABLE C1

ESTIMATION OF EXPORT SUPPLY BY BRANCH OF ACTIVITY

Branch	Equation
11	$LX = 1.72 \, LTCR + 0.32 \, LP^*/P - 0.001 \, PE + 0.085 \, LX(-3)$ $\quad\;\; (4.12) \qquad\quad (3.1) \qquad\quad (-0.20) \qquad (0.58)$ $\quad + 0.33 \, LX(-4) - 0.511 \, FEB$ $\quad\;\; (-2.6) \qquad\quad (-2.14)$
12	$LX = 0.713 \, LIPDEU - 0.005 \, PE + 0.645 \, LX(-1) + 0.42 \, MAR$ $\quad\;\; (6.32) \qquad\qquad (-4.46) \qquad (11.61) \qquad\quad (5.84)$ $\quad + 0.260 \, APR - 0.15 \, NOV - 0.207 \, JUL + 0.245 \, FEB$ $\quad\;\; (3.14) \qquad (-2.12) \qquad (-2.95) \qquad (2.98)$
13	$LX = 0.148 \, LP^*/P + 1.69 \, LIPDEU - 0.284 \, DIC - 0.284 \, JUN$ $\quad\;\; (3.26) \qquad\qquad (261.19) \qquad\quad (-2.06) \qquad (-2.08)$
15	$LX = 0.244 \, LP^*/P + 1.14 \, LIPDEU + 0.416 \, LX(-3)$ $\quad\;\; (3.63) \qquad\qquad (5.10) \qquad\qquad (3.62)$ $\quad + 0.337 \, FEB + 0.357 \, MAR - 0.205 \, JUL - 0.487 \, OCT$ $\quad\;\; (2.0) \qquad\quad (2.0) \qquad\qquad (-1.38) \qquad (-3.21)$ $\quad + 0.421 \, DIC$ $\quad\;\; (2.79)$
16	$LX = 1.19 \, LP^*/P + 2.17 \, LIPDEU - 0.011 \, PE$ $\quad\;\; (3.42) \qquad\quad (-0.5) \qquad\qquad (9.6)$ $\quad - 0.254 \, LX(-12) - 2.92 \, JUL - 2.06 \, OCT$ $\quad\;\; (-1.92) \qquad\qquad (-3.39) \quad\; (-2.68)$
17	$LX = 2.13 \, LTCR - 0.021 \, PE - 8.84 \, D17$ $\quad\;\; (39.27) \qquad (-2.72) \quad\; (-15.55)$
18	$LX = 0.35 \, LP^*/P + 1.05 \, LIPDEU - 0.056 \, PE + 0.25 \, LX(-1)$ $\quad\;\; (0.94) \qquad\quad (5.58) \qquad\qquad (-3.48) \qquad (2.12)$ $\quad - 0.290 \, LX(-4) - 2.71 \, FEB$ $\quad\;\; (-2.51) \qquad\qquad (-4.08)$
19	$LX = 0.721 \, LIPDEU - 0.001 \, PE + 0.662 \, LX(-1) + 0.476 \, SEP$ $\quad\;\; (4.0) \qquad\qquad (-0.56) \qquad (8.08) \qquad\quad (4.51)$ $\quad + 0.56 \, OCT + 0.57 \, NOV + 0.42 \, DIC$ $\quad\;\; (5.77) \qquad\quad (5.59) \qquad\quad (3.77)$
20	$LX = 0.096 \, LP^*/P + 1.9 \, LIPDEU - 0.007 \, PE = 0.0335 \, JAN$ $\quad\;\; (2.59) \qquad\quad (118.3) \qquad\quad (-2.71) \qquad (-4.91)$ $\quad - 0.266 \, FEB + 0.22 \, OCT - 0.237 \, DIC$ $\quad\;\; (-3.91) \qquad (3.25) \qquad\quad (-3.47)$
21	$LX = 0.298 \, LP^*/P + 0.967 \, LIPDEU - 0.008 \, PE$ $\quad\;\; (2.86) \qquad\qquad (4.73) \qquad\qquad (-2.27)$ $\quad + 0.484 \, LX(-1) - 0.212 \, MAR - 0.218 \, NOV - 0.319 \, DEC$ $\quad\;\; (4.45) \qquad\qquad (-1.93) \qquad (-1.98) \qquad (-2.86)$
22	$LX = 0.624 \, LP^*/P + 1.76 \, LIPDEU - 0.008 \, PE - 0.221 \, LX(-3)$ $\quad\;\; (3.77) \qquad\qquad (9.27) \qquad\qquad (-0.63) \qquad (-1.81)$ $\quad - 0.584 \, FEB$ $\quad\;\; (-1.92)$
23	$LX = 1.33 \, LIPDEU - 0.003 \, PE + 0.211 \, LX(-1) - 1.14 \, FEB$ $\quad\;\; (5.61) \qquad\qquad (-0.14) \qquad (1.83) \qquad\quad (-1.98)$ $\quad + 1.40 \, JUN + 2.03 \, JUL - 1.41 \, NOV$ $\quad\;\; (2.5) \qquad\quad (3.47) \qquad\quad (-2.52)$

continued

TABLE C1—*continued*

Branch	Equation
24	$LX = 0.628$ LIPDEU $+ 0.159$ LP*/P $- 0.0005$ PE $\quad$ (2.86) $\qquad$ (2.78) $\qquad$ (-2.04) $\quad + 0.353$ LX$(-1) + 0.34$ LX(-2) $\qquad$ (2.48) $\qquad$ (2.54)
26	$LX = 1.682$ LIPDEU $+ 0.575$ LP*/P $- 0.022$ PE $- 0.269$ NOV $\qquad$ (64.79) $\qquad$ (12.01) $\qquad$ (-5.26) $\quad$ (-2.1)
27	$LX = 0.74$ LIPDEU $+ 0.584$ LP*/P $+ 0.002$ PE $\qquad$ (5.21) $\qquad$ (4.0) $\qquad$ (0.27) $\quad + 0.264$ LX$(-2) - 0.213$ LX(-3) $\qquad$ (1.78) $\qquad$ (-1.39)
28	$LX = 0.74$ LIPDEU $+ 0.263$ LP*/P $- 0.002$ PE $+ 0.38$ LX(-2) $\qquad$ (1.93) $\qquad$ (2.06) $\qquad$ (-0.4) $\qquad$ (2.51) $\quad + 0.206$ LX$(-3) + 0.432$ JAN $\qquad$ (1.35) $\qquad$ (2.52)
29	$LX = 0.51$ LIPDEU $+ 0.179$ LP*/P $- 0.0006$ PE $+ 0.70$ LX(-1) $\qquad$ (3.38) $\qquad$ (2.75) $\qquad$ (-2.07) $\qquad$ (7.9) $\quad - 0.197$ FEB $+ 0.30$ APR $\qquad$ (-1.82) $\qquad$ (2.81)
30	$LX = 1.057$ LIPDEU $+ 0.144$ LP*/P $- 0.012$ PE $+ 0.599$ LTCR $\qquad$ (4.08) $\qquad$ (3.02) $\qquad$ (-2.24) $\quad$ (-2.43) $\quad + 0.335$ LX$(-1) - 0.146$ NOV $\qquad$ (2.47) $\qquad$ (-2.40)
31	$LX = 0.97$ LIPDEU $+ 0.321$ LP*/P $- 0.002$ PE $\qquad$ (3.95) $\qquad$ (3.62) $\qquad$ (-1.50) $\quad + 0.755$ LX$(-1) - 0.257$ LX$(-4) - 0.492$ FEB $- 0.314$ JUN $\qquad$ (6.87) $\qquad$ (-2.89) $\qquad$ (-3.80) $\qquad$ (-2.90)
32	$LX = 1.87$ LIPDEU $+ 0.001$ PE $+ 0.302$ OCT $\qquad$ (63.6) $\qquad$ (0.18) $\qquad$ (2.48)
33	$LX = 0.541$ LIPDEU $- 0.002$ PE $+ 0.277$ LX(-1) $\qquad$ (1.74) $\qquad$ (-1.51) $\quad$ (2.10) $\quad + 0.488$ LX$(-2) - 0.294$ MAY $+ 0.307$ OCT $\qquad$ (3.66) $\qquad$ (-1.66) $\qquad$ (1.73)
34	$LX = 0.880$ LIPDEU $- 0.002$ PE $+ 0.570$ LX(-1) $\qquad$ (2.95) $\qquad$ (-1.35) $\quad$ (3.90) $\quad - 0.401$ NOV $\qquad$ (-2.87)
35	$LX = 1.145$ LIPDEU $- 0.001$ PE $+ 0.473$ LX(-3) $\qquad$ (2.88) $\qquad$ (-0.89) $\quad$ (2.57)
36	$LX = -0.435$ LIPDEU $- 0.024$ PE $+ 0.27$ LX(-2) $\qquad$ $(-.43)$ $\qquad$ (-1.66) $\quad$ (1.98) $\quad + 3.126$ LTCR $\qquad$ (1.78)
37	$LX = 2.034$ LIPDEU $+ 0.463$ LP*/P $- 0.002$ PE $\qquad$ (163.06) $\qquad$ (5.92) $\qquad$ (-2.19) $\quad + 0.283$ MAR $+ 0.312$ APR $\qquad$ (2.42) $\qquad$ (2.66)
38	$LX = 1.056$ LIPDEU $+ 0.10$ LP*/P $- 0.022$ PE $+ 0.35$ LX(-1) $\qquad$ (3.72) $\qquad$ (1.31) $\qquad$ (-1.62) $\quad$ (2.45)

continued

TABLE C1—*continued*

Branch	Equation
39	LX = 1.69 LIPDEU + 0.50 LP*/P − 0.007 PE − 0.40 JAN (277.6) (8.70) (−2.94) (−3.74) + 0.19 JUN + 0.26 JUL + 0.27 AUG (1.77) (2.39) (2.54)
40	LX = 16.63 + 0.35 LP*/P − 0.002 PE + 0.738 LTCR (7.62) (4.67) (−2.61) (3.06) − 0.254 LX(−1) (−1.88)
41	LX = 0.103 LIPDEU − 0.003 PE + 1.586 LX(−1) (0.810) (−3.15) (4.09) 0.368 LX(−3) (2.56)
42	LX = 0.318 LIPDEU − 0.008 PE + 0.062 LP*/P (1.99) (−1.55) (0.86) + 0.850 LX(−1) + 0.34 JAN − 0.21 AUG (10.27) (2.18) (−1.53)
43	LX = 0.91 LIPDEU − .004 PE + 0.168 LP*/P + 0.56 LX(−1) (3.64) (−0.73) (1.60) (4.61)
44	LX = 2.00 LIPDEU + 0.180 LP*/P − 0.0007 PE (203.3) (4.70) (−0.80)
45	LX = 1.23 LIPDEU + 0.11 LP*/P − 0.0001 PE + 0.37 LX(−1) (4.94) (2.20) (−0.08) (2.9) − 0.25 JAN + 0.13 JUL (−2.64) (1.56)
46	LX = 0.49 LIPDEU + 0.0152 LP*/P − 0.010 PE + 1.515 LTCR (1.68) (1.32) (−1.52) (2.76) + 0.343 LX(−4) (2.88)
47	LX = 1.44 LIPDEU + 0.056 LP*/P − 0.002 PE + 0.34 LX(−2) (4.92) (1.35) (−0.78) (2.60) − 0.260 FEB (−1.99)
48	LX = 1.13 LIPDEU − 0.002 PE + 0.240 LP*/P (6.17) (−0.66) (4.22) + 0.320 LX(−1) − 0.51 JAN − 0.18 JUN − 0.17 JAN (2.87) (−4.89) (−1.97) (−1.86)
49	LX = 1.73 LIPDEU − .003 PE + 0.44 LP*/P (117.3) (−1.50) (5.32)
50	LX = −18.55 + 3.50 LIPDEU + 0.029 LP*/P − 0.01 PE (−1.78) (2.54) (0.34) (−2.67) + 0.40 LX(−1) + 0.016 OCT − 0.22 NOV (3.07) (2.00) (−2.81)
51	LX = 3.07 LIPDEU + 0.325 LP*/P − 0.017 PE − 1.56 LTCR (10.92) (4.01) (−5.62) (3.37)
52	LX = 2.362 LIPDEU + 0.320 LP*/P − 0.006 PE − 2.122 LTCR (4.96) (2.62) (−4.66) (−3.77) + 0.507 LX(−1) − 0.386 NOV (5.03) (−2.27)

continued

TABLE C1—*continued*

Branch	Equation
53	LX = 1.77 LIPDEU + 0.40 LP*/P − .0001 PE (82.2)　　　　(3.58)　　　　(−0.053) − 0.490 SEP (−2.07)
54	LX = 2.72 LIPDEU − 0.016 PE + 1.080 LP*/P (4.66)　　　　(−4.16)　　(4.40) + 0.473 LX(−1) − 2.76 LTCR (4.08)　　　　(−3.88)
55	LX = 0.94 LIPDEU + .004 PE + 0.217 LP*/P + 0.532 LX(−1) (3.78)　　　　(1.00)　　(2.93)　　　　(4.32) + 0.29 MAR (1.99)
56	LX = 1.25 LIPDEU + 0.792 LP*/P − 0.0009 PE (4.56)　　　　(4.27)　　　　(−0.55) + 0.385 LX(−3) + 0.514 FEB + 0.438 APR + 0.503 JUN (2.86)　　　　(2.15)　　　　(2.08)　　　　(2.39)
57	LX = 0.453 LIPDEU + 0.088 LP*/P + 0.0002 PE (2.03)　　　　(1.26)　　　　(0.050) + 0.80 LX(−1) + 0.625 JAN (8.31)　　　　(3.70)
58	LX = 1.463 LIPDEU − 0.003 PE + 0.288 LX(−1) (4.99)　　　　(−2.40)　　(2.01) − 0.632 OCT (−1.92)

Note: The values in parentheses correspond to the T statistic of the coefficients. The critical value to 95 percent is 1.96.

TABLE C2

STATISTICS OF THE ESTIMATED EQUATIONS

Branch	R^2	R^2 Adjusted	DW	HD	Standard Error
11	.73	.70	—	—	0.39*
12	.90	.87	—	—	0.13*
13	.44	.40	1.92	—	0.26
15	.68	.62	—	0.73	0.28
16	.51	.43	—	−1.6	1.24
17	.86	.86	1.64	—	1.38
18	.67	.63	—	−0.49	1.08
19	.86	.84	—	−1.43	0.18
20	.63	.58	1.86	—	0.13
21	.93	.92	—	−0.18	0.21
22	.52	.45	—	9.81	0.51*
23	.51	.44	—	−0.72	1.06
24	.89	.88	—	−1.3	0.17
26	.84	.83	1.63	—	0.24*
27	.76	.75	—	—	0.30
28	.81	.79	—	—	0.27
29	.91	.90	—	−1.2	0.20
30	.80	.77	—	−0.25	0.11
31	.92	.91	—	−1.28	0.20
32	.22	.18	1.98	—	0.23
33	.56	.51	—	0.65	0.34
34	.43	.37	—	1.20	0.27*
35	.64	.63	2.12	—	0.13
36	.22	.16	1.80	—	1.32
37	.85	.83	1.46	—	0.22*
38	.28	.23	2.05	−0.82	0.39
39	.90	.88	2.06	—	0.20
40	.80	.78	2.12	−1.10	0.16
41	.82	.80		−1.59	0.20*
42	.88	.86	—	−0.24	0.26
43	.63	.61	—	1.51	0.25
44	.70	.68	2.14	—	0.15*
45	.70	.66	—	1.52	0.16
46	.77	.75	2.01	—	0.25
47	.46	.40	2.03	—	0.21
48	.85	.82	—	−0.58	0.17
49	.72	.70	1.44	—	0.28*
50	.92	.91	—	0.87	0.15

continued

TABLE C2—*(continued)*

Branch	R²	R² Adjusted	DW	HD	Standard Error
51	.83	.82	1.70	—	0.24
52	.87	.86	—	−1.49	0.32
53	.46	.42	1.54	—	0.46
54	.92	.91	—	0.97	0.33
55	.78	.76	—	1.72	0.27
56	.89	.88	2.02	—	0.39
57	.81	.79	—	0.48	0.27
58	.43	.39	—	−0.52	0.63

Note: DW represents the Durbin-Watson statistic.

HD represents Durbin's H statistic.

*indicates the equation is corrected coliniarity.

APPENDIX D:
SPECIFICATIONS OF THE PROBIT MODEL

The model used to calculate the probabilities of participation in export activity belongs to the family of qualitative choice models.[1] This type of model associates the dependent variable with two or more possible events. In order to estimate said models, it is necessary to specify behavioral equations that lead to a reduced-form equation for the probability of participation and that is obtained as indicated below.[2]

The PROBIT Model

In order to understand the PROBIT model, let us suppose that there exists an index Z that is determined by the set X of explanatory variables, which can be expressed as:

Z = alpha + β X + u

where alpha and β are unknown parameters, X is a vector of observable variables, and u is the stochastic error term of the model. This index Z is considered a continuous, normally distributed random variable.

This expression poses a different problem from that of the usual econometric model because variable Z is not observable; the only information available concerning Z is that which allows us to discriminate values in two categories, the first associated to large values of Z and the second to small values of the same. PROBIT analysis resolves the problem of how to obtain estimations for alpha and and at the same time obtain information about the index Z.

In the concrete case presented by this study, we are primarily interested in analyzing the behavior of a group of industries in terms of their exports. According to the specific conditions of the industry, it will or will not be capable of exporting. In this case, the index Z will represent an indicator of how favorable the conditions are for the industry to export. It is clear that each industry will have associated with it a different Z value, according to its particular characteristics. Let us assume that the information available refers only to when each industry is exporting and to when it is not. In addition, this Z index has a linear dependency on a vector X of economic characteristics. The PROBIT model will then allow us to obtain estimations, both for the relationship between the variables X and Z and for the independent term of the model.

The relationship that exists between the index Z and the information available is the following. Let *DP* be a dichotomous variable that has the value 1 if the industry exports, and 0 otherwise. Let us suppose also that there exists for each industry a critical value Z^* so that:

$$DP = 1 \quad \text{if } Z > Z^*$$
$$DP = 0 \quad \text{if } Z < Z^*$$

The PROBIT model supposes that the variable Z is distributed normally; therefore, the probability of Z's being less than or equal to Z^* can be calculated directly from the normal accumulated distribution, which associates to a value z the probability of any arbitrary number Z^* being less than or equal to it. The normal standard accumulated function is expressed as:

$$Pi = F(zi) + 1/\sqrt{2\pi} \int_{-\infty}^{zi} \exp(-s^2/2)\, ds$$

where s is a normal random variable with mean zero and variance one. By construction, the variable Pi will be contained in the interval $(0,1)$ and represents the probability that an industry will export, given its characteristics. Since this probability is obtained as the integral from minus infinity to zi, the event will be more probable as the value zi is higher.

To obtain an estimation of the index Z, the inverse of the normal accumulated function is applied, as follows:

$$Zi = F\text{-}1\,(Pi) = \text{alpha} + \beta Xi.$$

The probability that results from the PROBIT model can be interpreted as an estimation of the conditional probability that an industry will export, given its X economic characteristics, which is equivalent to the probability that a standard normal variable will be less than or equal to alpha + βXi.

NOTES

1. R.S. Pindyck and D.L. Rubinfeld, *Econometric Models and Economic Forecasts,* 2nd ed. (New York: McGraw Hill, 1983).

2. Maria de Lourdes de la Fuente, "Determinantes de la participación en la actividad exportadora: un modelo probabilístico," Paper presented at the 19th Meeting of the Sociedad Econometrica, Santiago de Chile, August 1989.

7

Exports and Employment Generation in Mexico: A Sectoral Study

Alejandro Ibarra-Yunez and Chandler Stolp

I. INTRODUCTION

Structural Change, Employment and Public Policy in Mexico

The ability of the Mexican economy to generate employment plays a crucial role not only in shaping the future welfare of Mexico itself, but also in determining the magnitude and patterns of migration we can expect from Mexico to the United States. The history of employment generation in post-World War II Mexico is nothing less than spectacular. Massive movements of people from the countryside to largely urban poles of development, including the U.S.-Mexico border, and exploding birthrates, which by the early 1970s were rivaled only by the poorest developing countries, placed tremendous pressures on the Mexican economy to create employment. In the face of this demographic explosion in urban areas, Mexico was still able to more than quadruple its economically active population from 4.8 million in 1950 to 19.7 million in 1980,[1] while maintaining the open unemployment rate at a fairly constant 5 to 7 percent in the largest urban areas.[2]

One of the greatest engines for employment generation in this period has been the manufacturing sector, which will be the focus of attention in this study. Mexico became a growing producer and consumer of manufactured goods as the economy shifted from a predominately rural and agricultural base to one in which over 60 percent of the population lives in urban areas and turns to manufacturing and services to satisfy consumer needs as well as employment. Among other reasons for selecting the manufacturing sector for special analysis in this study are that:

(1) it has continuously outstripped the performance of the overall economy since the early 1940s;
(2) it has led other sectors in export performance in recent years, achieving more than (U.S.) $1 billion a month since 1986; and,
(3) it offers data that are generally more complete, more easily measurable and more reliable than those available from the agriculture and services.

The significance of these internal adjustments in the Mexican economy extends far beyond Mexico's need to absorb a growing labor force. Increasing global economic interdependencies not only cause these adjustments to have an impact outside Mexico's borders (the long-standing emigration of Mexicans to the United States is only one example of this), but they also are changing the structure of Mexican manufacturing and are placing the country in a new, and perhaps vulnerable, position in the global economy. Outward-looking *maquiladora* manufacturing provides the most obvious example of the structural change from the import sub-stitution orientation of industry that characterized Mexico from the 1950s through the early 1980s. Worldwide economic integration also poses challenges to Mexico. Cooperative economic arrangements such as the United States-Canada Trade Agreement of 1989, the European Economic Community, and speculation of a trading block of Pacific Rim nations all point to the possibility of an economically isolated Mexico, with profound implications for the vulnerability of the economy that go far beyond simplistic notions of foreign ownership of the means of production. The lesson is clear: the ability of Mexico's manufacturing sector to compete internationally will play a far greater role in its future ability to generate employment than it has in the past.

To meet some of these challenges, Mexico has embarked on an explicit policy of export-led development since 1985. It is still premature to draw conclusions on the actual impacts of this policy of *apertura*. However, we believe there are at least two phases in the process of adjustment of the Mexican economy. The first phase, from the promulgation of the National Program for Industrial and Trade Promotion (PRONAFICE) in 1985 through mid-1988, was marked by major policy changes at the top level of government relating to tariff adjustments, exchange rate policy and foreign investment. The second phase, beginning with the inauguration of the Salinas administration in December 1988, has seen *apertura* move from the policy margins to become the centerpiece of the government's strategy for modernization, a strategy designed not only to reorient the economy to external markets, but also to service a domestic market that is expected to grow dramatically in the 1990s. Since the cumulative effects of all these fundamental changes are only beginning to emerge, many of the conclusions we will reach are tentative and suggestive rather than definitive.

Focus of the Study

This study examines the extent to which Mexican manufacturing exports contribute to employment generation and identifies some of the factors that may hinder or enhance this effect. The linkages are complex and economic theory offers a number of competing alternative hypotheses in which to ground statistical models. Whatever the model, the data requirements for an ideal study are daunting. This notwithstanding, the empirical contributions of this study include:

(1) a descriptive and exploratory analysis of several sets of unpublished data from the Banco de México and the Instituto Nacional de Estadísticas, Geografía, e Informática;
(2) an examination of the relative efficiency of manufacturing sectors at the four-digit SIC/CMAP level and its relationship to gross and net export earnings; and,

(3) a variance decomposition analysis of export earnings which suggests that manufacturers were able to effectively exploit export markets as a substitute for recession-plagued domestic markets during the first phase of *apertura*.

The purpose of this report is more in the vein of generating hypotheses than it is of testing them. In the following sections, we lay out some of the perspectives from which economists view trade and employment, especially in the context of economic development in Mexico. We examine a cross section of individual manufacturing sectors of the economy in terms of the factor intensity of export manufacturing and in terms of their relative efficiency. Following this, we estimate a series of conventional labor demand functions over a time series of industries at the two-digit level in an effort to measure the direct effect of exports on the demand for labor in manufacturing. Next we present the variance decomposition analysis of market substitution. We conclude with a summary of our findings and with some policy recommendations.

II. CONCEPTUAL FRAMEWORKS LINKING FOREIGN TRADE AND EMPLOYMENT

Broad Hypotheses

The U.S. National Bureau of Economic Research sponsored a comprehensive study of trade and employment in developing economies in the late 1970s and early 1980s in which the directors laid out three fundamental theoretical perspectives for thinking about the relationship between exports and domestic employment generation. According to the U.S. National Bureau of Economic Research (NBER) study, there are three basic ways in which trade and employment are related:

1) jobs are created by growth in aggregate demand, rather than directly through any effects of trade policy;
2) export promotion policies generate significantly more employment in a developing economy than import substitution policies—as a corollary, labor-intensive industries, according to this view, are expected to generate relatively more employment under export promotion than industries that use less labor;
3) export promotion strategies are not significantly different from import substitution strategies in terms of their ability to generate employment —export promotion may, in fact, conflict with efforts to create jobs.[3]

Each of these hypotheses finds some support in economic theory. Keynesian economics and classical free-trade theory are squarely consistent with the first hypothesis (the latter in the sense that global welfare is maximized through trade). Free-trade theory also supports the second hypothesis and an important corollary to it, namely, that labor-abundant developing countries will export commodities that are more labor intensive in their production. That export industries in developing countries require more labor per unit of capital and per unit of output (and that imports will tend to be capital intensive) also follows from the two-sector Heckscher-Ohlin-Samuelson textbook model of international trade. Significantly enough, the NBER project on trade and employment found general empirical support for this second hypothesis.[4]

Support for the third hypothesis comes from a variety of camps. One of the most intriguing is the structural labor market model developed by John Harris and Michael Todaro that implies that creating employment opportunities can actually lead to greater unemployment.[5] The Harris-Todaro model incorporates rural-to-urban migration as part of a balancing mechanism between relatively high-wage employment in the urban sector and the rural agricultural sector. To the extent that the assumptions hold, the model predicts that an upward shift in the demand for urban labor, such as might be induced by export production, is likely to result in more urban unemployment as rural workers seek urban jobs.

From a policy perspective, the central issues here relate to the choice between outward-looking policies of export promotion on the one hand and inward-looking import substitution policies on the other. The first NBER hypothesis and Keynesian aggregate demand models all suggest that export promotion is not the key policy lever for creating employment, but rather that trade policy has to be subsidiary to macroeconomic policies. Accordingly, employment is more the result of overall economic growth. The second hypothesis, buttressed by Heckscher-Ohlin-Samuelson conceptions of international trade, as well as by the detailed empirical studies sponsored by NBER, are squarely consistent with policies of export promotion as a major vehicle for creating jobs.[6] Others, among them Harris and Todaro, suggest a cautious approach to export promotion, while the last NBER hypothesis and dependency theories all point unambiguously toward import substitution as the favored trade/employment policy.

Relevant Empirical Literature

In the face of these general theories and hypotheses, the development literature seems to have arrived at a consensus in recent years that export-led growth renders larger welfare benefits to developing countries than import substitution growth. The general rationale is that liberal free-trade policies give rise to better price alignments with market conditions, faster and better allocative adjustments, important incentives and spillover effects on capitalization and technology transfers and greater income generation. Protectionist, import substitution policies are increasingly viewed as promoting unnecessary subsidies to inefficiency in production and causing bottlenecks in the flows of capital, technology and foreign exchange resources.

Detailed empirical studies cast some doubt, however, on whether export promotion will be growth and employment generating by definition. While Krueger, Westphal and Balassa see direct and clear linkages between outward-looking trade policies and employment,[7] Berry and Diaz-Alejandro, Lal and Rajapatirana as well as Behar argue that real income and distribution impacts of export promotion can adversely affect the beneficial impacts on employment, or at least that these impacts, along with existing institutional rigidities, must be taken into account in order to maximize the benefits of outward-looking trade policies.[8] Most of the formal theories of the employment impacts of trade, treat exports as an exogenous factor whose effects filter down through the internal economy. Not surprisingly, more detailed empirical analyses indicate that internal conditions play a significant role in determining the way in which trade policy affects employment. Boatler and Behar, for example, argue that developing countries require a minimum level of income and/or a large economic base in order to gain from trade;[9] Chow, Ibarra and economists from the World Bank have provided formal evidence that exports are not purely exogenous variables.[10] To the extent that exports are not exogenous, they are an integral part of economic decision making and depend on the institutional structure of individual sectors, agents and countries. The endogenity of exports also implies that external trade policy must be coordinated with internal macroeconomic policy to maximize its employment and other benefits.

In this paper, we take the issue of the exogenity/endogenity of exports one step further by examining evidence on the extent to which Mexican manufacturers have substituted export production for domestic production in the first phase of *apertura*. This question of market substitution is intimately related to the ability of the economy to generate employment. If increased trade simply shifts production from domestic to international markets, it is clear that little or no additional employment will be generated. In terms of factor markets, exports may serve as a viable substitute for domestic production, sustaining employment in the face of a domestic downturn such as the adjustment period faced by Mexico during the 1980s.

What Do We Mean By Employment?

Just as the linkages between trade policy and employment generation are more complex than simple theories suggest, the very concept of employment turns out to be problematic and elusive, especially in the context of developing countries. To development economists, dealing with unemployment is more than a matter of reducing open unemployment figures, it is embedded in the broader issue of raising real incomes.[11] The employment creation objectives of trade policies, therefore, are consistent with a host of other objectives, such as moving the labor force from lower productivity to higher productivity activities, providing jobs in the already over-populated urban areas, investing in human capital and establishing manufacturing niches in international markets to provide foreign exchange. As a consequence, employment and underemployment, productivity and income distribution have become central issues in the debate concerning alternative trade strategies.[12]

Behar offers some revealing insights on the scale of underutilization of human resources in Mexico. Based on 1976 data from a number of studies and surveys on labor utilization in the three largest cities in Mexico, along with 13 other cities with populations over 100,000, he finds that the open unemployment rate of 7.0 percent balloons to 33.3 percent when disguised unemployment and underemployment are taken into account.[13] Behar's index of the magnitude of the unemployment problem, of course, cannot possibly capture the complexity of the interrelationships that trade and employment policies have with the domestic institutional and economic setting, significant as these are in the final determination of employment outcomes.

One final comment on employment in the context of this study reflects the concern that Harris and Todaro raise with respect to the rural sector and its relationship to the entire economy. Since the 1940s, Mexico has witnessed a dramatic shift from a rural agriculturally based economy to a largely urban, manufacturing and service economy. This not only reflects a fundamental structural change in the way in which labor is deployed and in which society is changed, it also has implications for the patterns of Mexican migration to the United States. Available data make it difficult to discriminate among documented and undocumented Mexican immigrants who are impelled by the lack of opportunities (responding largely to push factors), from those for whom the United States offers a better future (pull factors). Disentangling push factors from pull factors is difficult even at the level of individual motivations, but determining the extent to which urban employment within Mexico is a substitute for emigration to the United States is even more problematic. We recognize the central importance of these issues but we will not explore them in this study.

The Heterogeneity of Mexico's Manufacturing Sector

The error of thinking about the manufacturing sector as a single, homogeneous entity is commonplace. In fact, manufacturing embraces a tremendously diverse spectrum of subsectors, industries and firms. It should not be surprising, therefore, to expect a variety of different, possibly offsetting, impacts on employment of macro-trade policy. Manufacturing industries can be partitioned in any number of revealing ways: export-oriented versus domestically oriented, generally modern versus generally traditional in terms of technology employed, final product versus intermediate product, rural versus urban, high skill versus low-skill, natural-resource based versus value-added based, high labor mobility versus low employee turnover, etc.

Compounding this inter-industry diversity is the fact that the entire manufacturing sector has undergone significant structural change over time, especially since *apertura* in 1985. Firms in Mexico today operate in a completely different environment than they did as recently as five or ten years ago. The meteoric rise of *maquiladora* production comes immediately to mind, but the Mexican automobile industry is an even more specific example of how manufacturing has reoriented itself from the world of protectionist, inward-looking, import substitution. At one time the object of charges of gross inefficiency in dollar terms, the automobile industry is now Mexico's largest exporting four-digit level industry, producing products that are tightly integrated, as substitutes as well as complements, with those of Canadian and U.S. producers. International competition has played an important role in reshaping an industry that many would have considered moribund 15 years ago. Mexican policymakers are keenly aware of the international trend towards penetrating globalized markets such as the North American automobile industry. The experience of the automobile industry will continue to play an important role in shaping the future of Mexico's trade and employment policies.

III. THE CONTEXT OF TRADE POLICY, MANUFACTURING AND EMPLOYMENT IN MEXICO

Gross Domestic Product (GDP) and employment performed relatively well in the 1960s and 1970s (Table 1). Nevertheless, an increasing external imbalance was building up, despite the optimistic expectation of oil exports in the period between 1976–1981. The trade deficit quintupled to $10 billion in 1981 from $2 billion in 1976, leading to net indebtedness that rose from $5.5 billion to $26.5 billion over the same period. Export performance of the manufacturing sector picked up dramatically in the 1980s (not shown in Table 1); non-oil exports as a proportion of manufacturing gross domestic product rose continuously from 11.8 percent in 1980, to 19.3 percent in 1985, to 34.4 percent by 1988.

Until the beginning of *apertura* in 1985, trade policy in Mexico took a back seat to macroeconomic and industrial policy. The stable growth period from 1956--1971, characterized by low inflation and high economic

TABLE 1

MEXICO'S MAIN ECONOMIC INDICATORS

	1966–70 Avg	1971–76 Avg	1976–81 Avg	1982	1984	1986	1987
GDP growth	6.9	6.2	6.9	−.6	3.6	−4.0	1.4
Emp. growth (a)	—	3.2	4.6	−.3	2.3	−1.7	1.0
Unemp. rate	10.0 (b)	10.1	8.7	8.0	8.9	11.7	10.9
Trade Def (c)	−813	−1,972	−5,708	5,942	13,892	5,546	10,409
Net Indebt	322	5,591	26,572	6,370	1,644	3,340	5,371
Debt Srv/Exp	43.9 (d)	145.3 (d)	97.0 (d)	148.3	98.8	73.9	59.6
Debt Srv/GNP	1.6	12.9	10.9	24.2	20.4	14.4	13.0

Notes: a) formal sector b) in 1970 c) end of period in millions of dollars adjusted for yearly avg. free exchange rate d) public sector.

Source: Ciemex-WEFA, "Proyecto Económico de México," with data from Banco de México.

growth rates, witnessed chronic budget and trade balance deficits that had to be tackled by raising tariffs and adjusting effective protection rates, policies that were inconsistent with strategies of overall balanced growth. The Echeverría administration (1971–1976) promoted an economic program that led to a period of debt-subsidizing growth that forced authorities to implement protectionist, non-export promoting strategies in the early 1970s. Ironically, the Echeverría period offered some of the earliest evidence of official recognition of the modern internationalization of the Mexican economy. Under Echeverría, the *maquiladora* industry got off the ground and two significant export-promoting institutions were established: the Instituto Mexicano de Comercio Exterior (IMCE) and the Fondo Mexicano para la Exportación (FOMEX). Major macroeconomic adjustments took place at the beginning of the Lopez Portillo administration (1977–1982), mainly in the areas of reducing the budget deficit and in adjusting the exchange rate. The optimism caused by the oil boom in these early years helped set the stage for policies of trade liberalization. The restructuring of tariffs and import permits was widespread, however, as manufacturing exports declined by 14 percent between 1978 and 1981, mainly to service an expanded domestic market. As the oil shock of 1981 worked its way through the economy, these early attempts at trade liberalization were suspended and even reversed. The de la Madrid administration (1983–1988) took the first and most dramatic steps in stabilizing the disrupted economy that followed the oil crisis of 1982–1983, an event that had exhausted the strategy of economic growth financed through debt.

These historical developments served as a prelude to the *apertura* policies set in motion by the National Program for Industrial and Trade Promotion of 1985. While slowing in the 1960s and 1980s, employment has grown steadily in the postwar period. Recent historical trends in employment reflect the positive effects of manufacturing exports on job creation despite the many crises Mexico faced in the 1980s. Table 2 shows that the pattern of employment generation has relied significantly on the growing, export-oriented manufacturing sector. The tertiary sector includes retail trade, transport, communications, warehousing, government, banking and finance and non-classified employment. Non-classified sometimes includes informal employment.

The growth rate in manufacturing employment began to fall two years before the debt crisis of 1982, even while overall industrial employment (manufacturing plus the construction and electricity industries, but excluding the oil industry) continued to expand (Table 3). Employment growth has been rather slack in the years following the oil crisis, something that may be attributable to the practice of labor hoarding—a slowdown in firing existing workers as well as hiring new workers—in larger firms facing stagnant domestic markets.[14] Some evidence for this can be found by comparing the relative volatility of growth in manufacturing output to the relative stability of employment growth.

Over this same period, labor's share of national income dropped precipitously from 42.8 percent in 1979 to 35.9 percent in 1983, to an estimated 29.8 percent in 1988. This fall in real wages has resulted in a decline in Mexican buying power to 1961 levels. These developments have led to a situation in which labor costs, by our assessment, plummeted to around 10 percent of total manufacturing operating costs by 1987. While contributing to Mexico's attractiveness to foreign investors, current levels of real wages would appear to be unsustainable in the medium run.

IV. MANUFACTURING EXPORT PERFORMANCE

Working with unpublished Banco de México data on exports and imports at the product level, we have mapped trade statistics to production data for manufacturing firms aggregated to the four-digit CMAP level (CMAP is the Mexican standard industrial coding system) for the precrisis year 1980. Although reliable production data at this level of detail are not available for any post-*apertura* year, we can still examine exports and imports for the early *apertura* year 1987. After some minor adjustments, such as eliminating the non-exporting tortilla industry, aggregating some of the smaller subdivisions of the electrical appliance industry, four-digit CMAP aggregation provide us with 49 non-petroleum manufacturing sectors for 1980 and 1987. These sectors, along with the volume of their total and net exports for 1980 and 1987, are listed in Appendix A.

The unpublished production data for 1980 were kindly made available to us by the Instituto Nacional de Estadística, Geografía e Informática

TABLE 2

TOTAL MEXICAN EMPLOYMENT BY SECTOR
(Millions of persons)

Year	Total	Primary	Secondary	Services	Mfg.
1940	5.858	3.831	.746	1.117	.640
1950	8.272	4.824	1.319	1.774	.973
1960	11.332	6.144	2.147	2.959	1.556
1970	12.955	5.104	2.974	4.131	2.169
1980	20.280	5.700	4.670	5.225	2.427
1988 est	21.772	6.100	4.635	n/a	2.409

Source: INEGI (1984), "Cifras Historicas de México," and Ciemex-Wharton, "Perspectiva Económica de México," various numbers.

Note: Sectional employment does not sum to total employment due to the exclusion of informal employment or non-classified employment. In 1988 the service sector reported by Ciemex-Wharton includes non-classified employment and is not comparable with the earlier figures.

(INEGI) and are based on the 1981 industrial census. For our purposes, they provide measures of the total number of employees, capital investment outlays, value of production and value added for each four-digit sector.

Factor Intensity and Exports

These data make it possible to examine how factor intensity and factor complementarily relate to export performance. One of the key issues here relates to the classical free-trade prediction that labor-abundant economies will export labor-intensive commodities. A stumbling block is how to measure capital. Capital can be measured in terms of stock or flow, in terms of some physical measure or value measure, and/or in terms of direct versus total (direct plus indirect) contributions. As desirable as a stock measure of capital would be, the available data often make it necessary for us to impose the assumption that capital investment outlays—a flow measure—are proportional to existing stock. The nature of capital makes it practically impossible to measure at the level for which reliable data are available in Mexico. A common metric for machinery, buildings, and labor-enhancing equipment is hardly possible even in laboratory conditions. Although not an ideal state of affairs, the assumption that flows are proportional to stock is probably less objectionable at the four-digit level of aggregation, where the lumpy dynamics of capital replacement can be expected to cancel out across firms within a sector, than it is at the firm level. Finally, since an up-to-date national input/output table does not exist, it is impossible to separate direct from indirect effects of labor.

If we assume that capital investment outlays are a reasonably adequate

TABLE 3

EMPLOYMENT GROWTH BY SECTOR: 1979–1988

Year	Tot. Emp.	%g	Indust.	%g	Manuf.	%g
1979	19.073	(4.9)	4.3	(9.4)	2.3	(7.5)
1980	20.280	(6.3)	4.7	(8.6)	2.4	(5.5)
1981	21.548	(6.3)	5.1	(9.8)	2.6	(4.8)
1982	21.483	(−.3)	5.0	(−1.9)	2.5	(2.0)
1983	20.995	(−2.3)	4.4	(−11.9)	2.3	(7.1)
1984	21.482	(2.3)	4.6	(4.0)	2.4	(2.1)
1985	21.967	(2.3)	4.8	(3.7)	2.5	(3.2)
1986	21.590	(−1.7)	4.6	(−3.4)	2.4	(3.1)
1987	21.802	(1.0)	4.7	(1.2)	2.4	(1.2)
1988 est	21.772	(−.1)	4.6	(−1.6)	2.4	(0.7)

Notes: Data in millions of persons in the formal sector.

Source: CONAPO and Ciemex-WEFA, various numbers. Industry includes construction
and electricity, but excludes oil.

measure of capital stock and if we define factor intensity in terms of the direct capital-to-labor ratio, our data show that the raw correlation between direct capital-to-labor and export earnings, measured in current 1980 dollars, is a positive and reasonably strong 0.44 for the 49 four-digit manufacturing sectors. This statistic, however, is sensitive to extreme observations. By eliminating 2.5 percent of the observations that most influenced the calculation—the highly protected and subsidized tobacco sector was the greatest outlier—the correlation is 0.63. The more robust Spearman rank correlations for the same data are only around 0.16. While a good case could be made for each of the correlation measures, the robustness of the Spearman correlations make them less sensitive to some of the most dynamic, progressive and capital-intensive sectors, like automobiles. The general conclusion to be drawn flies in the face of classical free-trade theory: Mexico exports commodities which, at least in terms of the direct capital-to-labor measure of factor intensity, tend to utilize more of the relatively scarce capital in proportion to labor.

On the surface, this implies that manufacturing export earnings do not generate as much employment as they might. There is more to the equation, however. In terms of creating jobs, the issue becomes one of determining the extent to which capital substitutes for labor or complements labor. It is, of course, possible to observe aggregate export production taking place in firms with high capital-to-labor ratios, and yet at the same time for capital to be labor-augmenting.[15] To the extent that complementarily holds, it lends support to export policies as means for generating employment.

Unfortunately, the assumption that flows of capital outlays are directly proportional to the more meaningful notion of stocks of capital does not enable us to measure the elasticity of substitution between labor and capital. The elasticity is different for every assumed constant of proportionality. Consequently, we will have to take a more indirect approach in exploring how capital may be labor-augmenting.

One indirect alternative is to compare value added per worker to export performance. The greater the value added per worker for export commodities, the reasoning goes, the greater the demand for workers in labor-rich Mexico. For 1980, the raw Pearson correlation between value added per worker to dollar value of exports is 0.34; eliminating 2.5 percent of the outlying interactions boosts the correlation substantially to 0.43. In terms of value added, exporters tended to do well with labor compared to less export-intensive sectors, and to the extent that qualified labor was available, exporters had every incentive to create more jobs. This all changes, however, when imports are taken into account. The correlation between value added per worker and net exports switches from $+0.34$ to -0.20 (the 2.5 percent trimmed correlation drops even further to -0.43). When imports are factored into the calculation, we find that net exporters tended to be markedly less productive in their use of labor than gross exporters in 1980. The obvious reason for this is that the more heavily export-oriented sectors also tended to be heavy importers. While capital appeared to be labor-augmenting (and, by extension, employment-generating), it was at the expense of net export earnings.

Evidence indicates that this picture changed significantly by the early *apertura* year of 1987. Since production data at the level of detail we are concerned with are nonexistent for 1987, it is impossible to correlate value added per worker in 1987 with gross or net exports. Assuming, however, that value added per worker did not change dramatically over the intervening six years, we are able to correlate value added per worker in 1980 with gross 1987 exports and net 1987 exports. To soften the implications of this assumption, we will substitute Spearman rank correlations for the Pearson product-moment correlations used earlier and will trim 2.5 percent of the outlying interactions.[16] The trimmed Spearman correlation between value added and gross exports jumps from 0.28 in 1980 to 0.46 in 1987. In terms of net exports, the same measure changes from -0.40 in 1980 to -0.18 in 1987. The evidence suggests that the value of labor to the manufacturing sector, and, by extension, its ability to create jobs, rose dramatically over these years. That net exports continue to correlate negatively with value added per worker detracts somewhat from the force of these conclusions, but this correlation is not significant.

Had domestic demand risen during this first phase of *apertura*, the capacity to create jobs would have been larger. This was seen in 1987, for example, when domestic markets began to grow and manufacturing exports reached record levels at the same time that open unemployment figures dropped drastically.

TABLE 4

MAIN MANUFACTURING EXPORT SECTORS IN MEXICO
(exporting more than $100 million USdlls)

1980	1987
Non-ferrous metals (+)	Automobiles (+), *
Canning (+)	Canning (+), *
Automobiles (−)	Basic Chemicals (−)
Basic Chemicals (−)	Non-ferrous metals (+), *
General Machinery/Eqpt. (−)	Iron and steel (+)
Beverages (+)	Office eqpt. and comp. (−)
	Soft fiber weaving (+), *
	General Machinery/Eqpt. (−), *
	Beverages (+)
	Synth. resins and fibers (+)
	Glass (+)
	Paper prods. (−)
	Other Chemicals (0)
	Cements (+)
	Other finished metals (−)
	Other transp. eqpt. (−)
	Special Machinery/Eqpt. (−)
	Sugar (+)

Sectors are listed in decreasing order of export earnings. A " + ", "0", or " − " indicates whether the sector experienced a trade surplus, balance, or deficit, respectively. A "*" denotes sectors that were among the five fastest growing between 1980 and 1987 in terms of exports.

Sources: Own computations based on unpublished information from Banco de México, various years.

Overall, it is undeniable that Mexico underwent a dramatic structural change over the intervening years. The findings that value added per worker correlates rather strongly with export earnings and that export earnings tend to be capital intensive merely suggest that capital complements labor in the production of export products. More detailed micro-level analysis is required in order to come to grips with this important aspect of the employment generation of trade policies.

One final point needs to be made here. To exploit labor-augmenting capital on a large scale requires a trained and educated workforce. If labor is deployed in such a way that this education is not forthcoming, there is little that export promotion can do to have a significant direct impact on job creation.

Export Performance by Sector

The number of four-digit manufacturing sectors contributing over (U.S.)$100 million to exports grew from six to 18 between 1980 and 1987 (Table 4). All six of the main exporters of 1980 remained, significantly enough, among the 18 main exporters in the early *apertura* year of 1987.

The table also indicates whether these large gross exporting sectors experienced a net trade surplus or deficit (denoted by a + or − in the table) and points out the five sectors that grew the fastest in terms of gross export earnings between 1980 and 1987 (denoted by *). With the exception of soft fiber weaving (sector 3212), all of the five fastest growing exporting sectors over this period were large exporters in pre-*apertura* 1980. It is clear from the table that the first phase of *apertura* has led to an explosion in Mexican export activity, even if some of these activities, like basic chemicals and paper products, have negative trade balances.

To complete the picture, Table 5 arrays the sectors that exported less than (U.S.) $5 million in each of the same two years in current dollars. There were ten such sectors in 1980, but this figure shrunk to six in 1987. Three of the sectors appearing in both lists—grain processing, dairy products and edible oils—are expected to be low export performers since they represent basic consumer goods for the poor population.

The before-and-after patterns that emerge from Tables 4 and 5 are not as crisp as one would expect if *apertura* in fact signalled an abrupt structural change that particularly favored labor-intensive sectors or sectors in which capital was extremely labor-augmenting. The clusters of sectors appearing in each of the tables turn out to be highly heterogeneous in terms of value added per worker or in terms of the ratio of capital flows to labor. One preliminary conclusion to be drawn is that generating employment via export promotion requires more disaggregated and detailed study than four-digit aggregation can provide. Another conclusion is that *apertura* is a more gradual process; it takes time for all of the structural changes to make themselves apparent.

Relative Sectoral Efficiency and Export Performance

One basic expectation of open trade policies is that international competition will promote the efficient use of factors of production. The issue has been an important one in public debate in Mexico on the merits of *apertura* as a vehicle for absorbing labor. It is obviously difficult to convince the public of the virtues of *apertura* in the face of the direct unemployment caused by massive plant closings such as were seen with the demise of the inefficient Fundidora Steel Works in Monterrey in 1986.

We already touched on the issue of relative efficiency when we examined the 49 sectors in terms of the value added per worker. A more rigorous alternative approach that takes capital complementarily or substitutability into account would be to estimate a production function and determine which sectors lie above the production surface (and are therefore relatively efficient) and which lie below.

Two problems arise with this approach. First, the nature of the available data would require that we impose the strong assumption that our mea-

TABLE 5

LOWEST EXPORT MANUFACTURING SECTORS IN MEXICO

1980	1987
Other food and kindred prods. (−)	Dairy prods (−)
Dairy prods. (−)	Grain processing (−)
Basic metals (−)	Other metals (−)
Grain processing (0)	Animal feed (0)
Edible oils (−)	Tobacco (+)
Knitted prods. (−)	Edible oils (−)
Metal furniture (−)	
Textile prods. (−)	
Bread prods. (+)	
Domestic accessories (−)	

Sectors are listed in decreasing order of export earnings. A " + ", "0", or " − " indicates whether the sector experienced a trade surplus, balance, or deficit, respectively. A "*" denotes sectors that were among the five fastest growing in terms of exports.

Source: Own computations based on unpublished information from Banco de México, various years.

sure of flows of capital outlays is directly proportional to capital stocks. For technical reasons, this assumption is more critical here than it was with the simple correlations already calculated. Second, a production function would only capture the average relationship among factors of production and outputs across sectors. A study of relative efficiency conceptually requires an "extremal" production function that is defined by only the most efficient observations in the sample. These efficient referents would be used as benchmarks for evaluating the relative efficiency of the remaining sectors.

A recently developed management science technique called "data envelopment analysis" (DEA) provides us with an elegant and unintrusive way, not only for identifying the most efficient sectors, but also for providing indices of relative efficiency for inefficient sectors. DEA is a mathematical programming technique that scores each production unit (here, the individual sectors) on a relative efficiency scale of 0 percent to 100 percent, relative to other sectors in the sample. Unlike more conventional production function approaches, DEA does not require strong assumptions about the relationship between flows of capital and capital stock. This flexibility, however, is purchased at the expense of not being able to generalize about elasticities of substitutions or factor output elasticities.[17]

The lack of 1987 production data for the 49 manufacturing sectors restricts the estimation of a DEA production surface to the pre-*apertura* year of 1980. A broader picture of the relationship between efficiency and export performance is provided by the overall Pearson correlation coefficient. The correlation between the DEA index of relative efficiency and total exports over all sectors in 1980 was 0.22; for 1987, the correlation rose to 0.31.

DEA also has the interesting feature of identifying for each inefficient sector a set of efficient referent sectors that share a similar pattern of factor utilization and output production, but which are 100 percent DEA-efficient. These referents presumably can serve as models for inefficient sectors of how small adjustments in their factor utilization and output goals could lead to increased efficiency. The efficient referents are listed at the top of the diagram in Appendix B. Below them, the inefficient sectors are clustered by shared referent set in order of increasing size of the ratio of capital investment to number of employees.

Two observations follow from the DEA analysis of efficiency. First, there is a clear positive relationship between relative efficiency and export performance, regardless of the causes. Second, this correlation improved significantly from pre-*apertura* 1980 to post-*apertura* 1987. This is consistent with observations that import substitution regimes (such as 1980) cause exports to be essentially residuals of domestic production. Export markets are not integrated into decision making about domestic production. This is one explanation offered for the volatility and variability across sectors of exports under Mexico's pre-1985 import substitution policies. The fact that by 1987 a pattern of exports emerged that was more consistent with meeting the pressures of outside competition points to some salutary structural effects of export promotion.

V. DIRECT IMPACTS OF EXPORTS ON LABOR ABSORPTION

In this section, we take a different tack in examining the force that exports have on employment creation. Although the lack of reliable data makes any theoretically clean analysis difficult, we estimate three single-equation models of labor demand: A Cobb-Douglas specification, a more general Constant Elasticity of Substitution (CES) specification, and an even more flexible Translog specification. In laying out these specifications, "L" stands for the number of workers, "k" the flow of capital outlays ("inversion fija"), "X" the value of exports, "Q" the value of production, and "T" a measure of productivity defined as total manufacturing wages over value added:

COBB-DOUGLAS:
$$\ln(L) = f[\ln(X), \ln(Q), \ln(T)]$$
CONSTANT ELASTICITY OF SUBSTITUTION:
$$\ln(L) = f[\ln(X), \ln(Q), \ln(T), \{\ln(z_i) - \ln(z_j)\}^2]$$
where the last term represents the set of squared pairwise differences of the logarithms of all the inputs

TRANSLOG:
$$\ln(L) = f[\ \ln(X),\ \ln(k/Q),\ \ln(T),\ \{\ln(z_i)*\ln(z_j)\}\ ]$$

Each of these conventional labor demand functions can be derived from a production function conception of the relationship between sectoral outputs, their factors of production, exports and other determinants. A discussion of the mathematical derivation of a labor demand function and all the fairly strong assumptions about efficient markets that it requires is beyond the scope of this study, but can be found in most advanced theoretical economics textbooks.[18] The "T" term has been added to the conventional form of these labor demand functions in order to account for influences on labor demand that may be correlated with adaptation to miscellaneous factors such as labor-augmenting technological change. These models, of course, can only capture the direct effects of exports on employment. To account for direct plus all indirect multiplier effects would require a sophisticated input-output model of the Mexican economy that our data do not permit us to exploit, even if relevant input-output tables existed and even if the underlying assumptions were valid. The distinction between direct and total effects should not be ignored entirely, since some researchers have shown conclusively that the effect of intermediate inputs can give rise to different multipliers and to different rankings of sectoral employment impacts.[19]

Time series data at a two-digit level of aggregation were obtained from Banco de México.[20] The monthly data cover the post-*apertura* period of January 1985 (1985.01) through June 1988 (1988.06) and permit us to examine how the relationship between exports and labor demand evolves over time. Each of the models was corrected for first-order autocorrelation in the error terms across time in estimating the coefficients.

Table 6 summarizes the results in elasticity terms. In all cases, the t-statistics for the export coefficients were statistically significant at 95 percent confidence; the R-squared goodness-of-fit statistics for the sectoral models ranged from 51 percent to 92 percent. In general, however, the estimated elasticities are low, implying that exports have a small direct impact on the demand for labor. According to the Cobb-Douglas model, a 1 percent increase in exports from the food, beverages and tobacco sector will generate a 0.0002 percent increase in direct employment. The three model specifications only agree in sign for the food, beverages and tobacco sector, the basic metals sector and the petrochemicals sector. In the case of petrochemicals, the agreement is in the negative direction: exports tend to reduce the demand for labor. The elasticities for the translog specification vary more across sectors than do estimates from the other models, something that can be expected given the weaker assumptions that translog models impose on output and substitution elasticities. Overall, the CES specification provides the best fits, expected signs of coefficients,

TABLE 6

DIRECT EMPLOYMENT GENERATION OF MEXICAN EXPORTS
IN THE APERTURA PERIOD (1985.01–1988.06)
Export Elasticities of Labor Demand

Sector	CD	Model Specification CES	Translog
Food, Bev., Tob.	.0002	.0031	.0098
Petroleum Der.	−.0001	.0014	−.0572
Petrochemicals	−.0001	−.0021	−.0230
Chemicals	−.0026	.0030	−.0482
Basic Metals	.0135	.00009	.0144
Machinery & Eqpt.	.0021	−.0041	.0081
Other Manufactures	.0167	−.0022	−.0185

Source: Published and unpublished data from the Banco de México (see discussion in text).

and statistical significance.

The conclusions to be drawn from the labor demand regressions lead us in the same direction as those highlighted in other sections of this study, and they also tend to agree with the findings of Balassa, Behar and Levy, each of whom addressed similar questions for different time periods.[21] Levy, using an input-output table, finds employment multipliers to be less than 1.0 in all cases for 1970, implying that exports used 7.7 percent less labor than did imports. Behar finds similar evidence in his analyses of 1970, 1975 and 1980. The total (direct plus indirect) effect of a 100 percent increase in exports on total manufacturing employment according to Behar's 28-sector input-output analysis was only 4.7 percent. Part of the low impact was explained by increases in productivity, and part was explained by decreasing export shares of some sectors, especially food, beverages, and tobacco and petrochemicals. While these findings are more disappointing for Mexico than for other recently industrializing countries like Korea, they may again be due to the fact that the structural changes put into motion by *apertura* have not yet borne fruit.

One final point to make about direct and total multiplier effects of exports is that employment generation is more complicated than simple multipliers or the structure of estimated input-output relations suggest. Other elements, including capacity utilization, the structure of relative prices, and structure of foreign exports play a critical role in determining employment outcomes, especially in an economy undergoing structural change as extensive as Mexico's change. Given the depth of the economic crisis that has befallen Mexico since 1982, it is remarkable that the employment effects of exports have been anything less than disastrous.

VI. EXPORT MARKETS AS A SUBSTITUTE
FOR DOMESTIC MARKETS

This leads us to question the extent to which Mexican manufacturers have exploited export markets as a substitute for declining domestic markets during the first phase of *apertura*. Henry (1970) laid the intellectual foundation for the basic approach we take here.[22] He proposed that increases in domestic demand can be viewed as a proxy for non-price aspects of competition. When price responses are not sufficiently elastic to allocate efficiently, then there may be market substitution between exports and domestic production. To apply this thinking to the context of Mexico, we adopt methods developed by Murray and Behar to first establish that export earnings from 1985.01–1988.06 were driven more by internal quantity, or non-price factors than they were by external price factors. As a second step, we examine the direct pre- and post-*apertura* effects of internal demand on export earnings. In terms of generating employment, we offer evidence that suggests that Mexican manufacturing has undergone a major structural shift since the advent of *apertura*. Manufacturers turned toward export markets, especially after *apertura*, to soften the blow of the post-1982 crisis. By substituting external markets for internal markets in this way, many jobs were saved that would otherwise have been lost in the recession.

The Volatility of Export Earnings

Mexico's export earnings have been uneven across time as well as in their composition by sector. Immediately following World War II, the main exports were agricultural products. In 1970, the five leading exports were sugar, raw cotton, coffee, shrimp, electrical machinery and parts. By 1982, the leading exports had diversified to include secondary products as well; the leading exports were crude oil, shrimp, coffee, machinery and equipment, silver, motors and automobile parts. By 1987, leading exports consisted mainly of manufacturing products: automobile motors, machinery and equipment, automobile parts, electronic equipment, chemicals, as well as tomatoes and non-ferrous metals.

The volatility of exports has expressed itself in unstable earnings across time as well as in shifting ranks and nature of products exported. Behar examined some aspects of sectoral volatility in detail for the pre-*apertura* period 1970–1984 and found little relationship between the stability of manufacturing exports and the growth of exports.[23] As mentioned earlier, this kind of instability in the export portfolio or in export earnings is perfectly consistent with a world shaped by inward-looking import substitution policies in which exports are essentially viewed as a residual of domestic production rather than as an exploitable market in itself.

Following Murray and Behar,[24] we conduct a variance decomposition analysis of export earnings ("E") using the following logic, where "P" and "Q" represent export price and volume indices:

$$E = P * Q$$
$$\ln(E) = \ln(P) \ ¢ \ln(Q)$$

Using one of the elementary rules of probability, this last term can be expressed in variance terms as follows:

$$VAR[\ln(E)] = VAR[\ln(P)] + VAR[\ln(Q)] + 2*COV[\ln(P),\ln(Q)]$$

Since this last expression involves the variance of logarithms, we can think of the variance decomposition as reflecting the trend-corrected variance of export earnings into trend-corrected variances of price and quantity. The underlying reasoning here is that variations in export earnings under an outward-looking export policy would be primarily explained by variations in price (assuming the country is a price-taker), and therefore the $VAR[\ln(P)]$ term would be a larger proportion of $VAR[\ln(E)]$ than would $VAR[\ln(Q)]$. If, on the other hand, internal conditions predominate in determining export earnings, variations in non-price factors (captured by our Q term) would be more important than variations in price in explaining fluctuations in export earnings.

Monthly data on Q and E for the manufacturing sector as a whole from January 1985 to June 1988 were acquired from the Banco de México; information on P for the same period was obtained from the International Monetary Fund.[25] The variance decomposition of these data for the first phase of *apertura* (Table 7) show that quantity dominates price as an explanator of trend-corrected variations in export earnings. This supports the conclusion that internal (non-price), rather than external (price), factors have had a greater hand in determining patterns of export earnings in Mexico.

These findings are consistent with Murray's (1978) study of 24 LDCs and 21 developed countries. The simplistic empirical analysis offered here does not imply that external conditions have been irrelevant in explaining Mexico's *apertura*. It is clear from a broader perspective that international conditions as well as internal conditions have shaped the direction manufacturers have taken in recent years. It does, however, suggest that internal factors such as capacity utilization, institutional rigidities, fragmented markets, etc., play an important role in linking exports to employment generation.

The covariance term sheds additional light on the trade-off between price and quantity variations, relating it to shifts in demand and supply. If Mexico is a price taker and if supply is relatively stable (variations in quantity dominate variations in price), we can expect that fluctuations in the demand schedule will make prices and quantities deviate from trends in

TABLE 7

CONTRIBUTION OF PRICE AND QUANTITY FACTORS
TO EXPORT EARNINGS INSTABILITY: 1985.01–1988–06

V (log E)	.000161
V (log Q)	38.1%
V (log P)	23.8
2 cov (log P, log Q)	+ 38.1

Source: Monetary data from Banco de México and the IMF, *International Financial Statistics,* various numbers.

the same direction. This is analogous to the common textbook diagram in which shifts in demand cause price-quantity pairs to "trace out" the stable supply schedule. A positive covariance is consistent, then, with a picture that suggests that demand conditions, both domestic and international, were a major influence in explaining Mexico's export performance in the period under study.

Pulling these threads together, the simple variance decomposition exercise suggests that internal market conditions, including such things as the decline in domestic demand during the recessionary period of the 1980 (1982–1983, 1986 and 1988), made export markets good substitutes for Mexican manufacturers.

Market Substitution in the First Phase of Apertura

To examine the market substitution hypothesis more directly for the first phase of *apertura,* we would like to estimate a model of exports as a function of productive capacity over monthly data for the pre- and post-*apertura* years. Unfortunately, monthly data on productive capacity simply do not exist. But by using manufacturing value of production as a proxy for productive capacity, and incorporating a one-period autoregressive adjustment, we see (Table 8) that there is a significantly negative relationship between domestic capacity and exports over the entire period January 1981 to June 1988. These results lend additional support to the view that domestic production substituted for exports. When domestic production was growing, as it was before the crisis of 1982, manufacturing exports declined. When domestic production declined as it did in the *apertura* years of January 1985 to June 1988, however, exports increased. Manufacturers took advantage of exports.

This pattern of market substitution contrasts with a historical pattern in which exports were treated as a residual to domestic production and where exports were positively correlated with domestic production. The fact that exports began to take off just as the domestic market was experiencing the worst recession in recent Mexican history marks a historical

TABLE 8

RELATIONSHIP BETWEEN MEXICAN MANUFACTURING EXPORTS
AND MANUFACTURING OUTPUT: MARKET SUBSTITUTION RESULTS

Period	81.01–88.06	85.01–88.06
Intercept	391,452.79 (2.17)	535,592.68 (2.18)
Man. Vol. Prod.	− 13.618 (42.7)	− 11.180 (29.3)
AR(1) adjustment	0.940	0.920
Adj. R sqr.	0.85	0.77
DW	1.49	1.48

Note: t statistics in parentheses.

turning point in Mexican manufacturing. The impact of this on employment generation are significant: underutilized capacity during the crisis has been generally directed outward toward exports rather than inward toward plant closings. All the analysis suggests low, but nevertheless generally positive, direct effects of exports on employment. We expect the unobserved indirect employment effects to be more pronounced during the second phase of *apertura* in the early 1990s, especially as exports continue to grow while the domestic market expands—trends that most experts agree are likely.

VII. CONCLUSIONS AND POLICY IMPLICATIONS

Summary of Empirical Findings

The exploratory empirical work in this study offers findings that are more suggestive than they are conclusive in linking Mexican manufacturing exports to employment generation. Nevertheless, they point to a pattern which is consistent with the hypothesis that policies of *apertura* have created jobs and have softened the employment impact of the post-1982 recession. Contrary to the predictions of classical free-trade theory, Mexican manufacturing exports tend to be more capital intensive in their production than they are labor intensive. To the extent that capital is complementary to labor in export production, we can still expect exports to be labor generating. However, since the available data in this rapidly changing environment do not lend themselves to measuring the elasticity of substitution of capital for labor directly, we turn to indirect measures such as the correlation between value added per worker and export performance. The high correlations suggest that export markets are reasonably effective in generating increased demand for employment.

Since theory suggests that increased international competition has the salutary effect of promoting efficiency in the deployment of production factors, we examined the relative efficiency of manufacturing sectors in pre-*apertura* 1980 in order to identify manufacturing sectors which were better positioned to take advantage of world markets once the economic opening of Mexico took place. Data envelopment analysis of relative efficiency showed that efficient sectors in 1980 tended to be among the very largest exporters in both 1980 and 1987. The long-run implications of this on the sustainability of *apertura* policies, and on the ability of these policies to generate jobs, are obvious.

Direct estimates of exports on labor demand provided evidence that exports may be less employment-generating than the other approaches we took suggested. The estimated export elasticities of the direct demand for labor were low and even negative for some two-digit sectors. This evidence is, however, subject to two significant caveats. First, in order to justify the model specifications, we have to impose a number of strong assumptions about frictionless competitive markets that are difficult to justify. Second, the lack of a detailed and up-to-date input/output table of the Mexican economy only permitted us to examine direct effects of exports on labor demand, rather than the total multiplier effect.

Finally, our analysis of the extent to which export markets have substituted for domestic markets suggests that internal, non-price considerations have played a more important role in explaining export earnings in recent years than they did under the import substitution policies of earlier years. While not definitive, the market substitution analysis supports the conclusion that production for export markets provided a profitable outlet for commodities at a time in which domestic demand was weak.

Mexico faces certain preconditions for it to be able to take advantage of market substitution as a vehicle for creating greater employment opportunities. First, there must be sustainable external demand for the kinds of products Mexico manufactures and exports. Second, investment funds not only have to be available, they have to be properly targeted. Finally, the complementarily of labor and capital in manufacturing exports requires that the training and education of the Mexican labor force keep pace with—and be coordinated with—the fundamental structural changes Mexico faces in the future.

Broad Implications

One of the most compelling conclusions to draw from this study is that the relationships among exports, employment, policies of *apertura* and economic theory are in a state of flux in contemporary Mexico. While *apertura* seems to have punctuated a departure from earlier policies, and while exports seem to have cushioned the effects of recession in recent years, the jury is still out. We prefer to think of *apertura* as emerging in at least two distinct stages. The first phase (1985–1988) has set into motion a number of salutary forces in Mexico's manufacturing sector: job creation, efficient deployment of labor, expanded export base, increased foreign exchange earnings, etc. But the full fruits of *apertura* are not likely to be felt until the mid-1990s or beyond. It is after this second phase of *apertura* that more definitive conclusions can be drawn about the effects of current public policy, particularly as they apply to the urgent need to absorb underutilized labor.

We have to be more modest about the direct impacts that Mexican trade policies may have on migration to the United States. While the Mexican manufacturing sector is undergoing profound structural changes under *apertura*, our empirical findings suggest that the direct employment impacts may be small. The important point to recognize—and one that has been outside the scope of this study—is that these positive, but puny, labor absorption effects will continue to pale beside the enormous draw that employment opportunities offer across the border in the United States. Basic economics tells us that migration to the border and beyond will continue as long as real wages north of the border remain as astronomical as they are in comparison to domestic wages.

This leads to another set of critical issues that this study has regrettably, but consciously, swept aside. Employment and migration involve a host of complex social, political and institutional considerations that cannot at all be captured adequately in the kind of exploratory empirical analysis we have conducted here. Harris and Todaro only mention on some of the more direct links in their conception of rural-to-urban migration. Class structure, ethnicity, regional identities, personal links to the United States, cultural patterns of migration, etc, all play a powerful role in explaining patterns of migration, whether to the United States or to urban poles of development within Mexico. The political dimension only compounds the complexity of the problem. How long, or even whether, policies of *apertura* can be a permanent fixture of Mexican policy is an open question. The political context in which outward-looking policies of *apertura* emerge remain in flux. There is great scope for disagreements that pose a real challenge for consistent decision making. Just because available data are not adequate for exploring these critical dimensions to the larger problem, their importance from a policy perspective should not be diminished.

APPENDIX A
SUMMARY INFORMATION ON MANUFACTURING SECTORS

CMAP	INDUSTRY	TOTAL EXP 80	NET EXP 80	TOTAL EXP 87	NET EXP 87
3111	MEAT PRODS	14.8	− 136.8	34.9	− 117.3
3112	DAIRY PRODS	0.3	− 297.5	0.1	− 171
3113	CANNING	519.3	465.3	749.3	733
3114	GRAIN PROCESSING	0.6	− 9	2	− 5.7
3115	BREAD PRODS	4.4	2.2	10.5	10
3117	EDIBLE OILS	1	− 66.2	5.1	− 69.7
3118	SUGAR	6.8	− 354.6	106.7	104.7
3119	CHOCOLATE	13	10.7	39.1	38
3121	OTHER FOOD	18.3	0	67.5	54.3
3122	ANIMAL FEED	0	− 21	2.3	− 3.1
3130	BEVERAGES	94.7	2.1	293.1	277.4
3140	TOBACCO	5.8	5.7	2.9	2.8
3211	ROPE, HARD FIBERS	10	0.1	16.5	11.4
3212	SOFT FIBER WEAVING	86.5	− 38.2	321.5	216.8
3213	TEXTILES	3.8	− 26.4	35.8	27
3214	KNITTED GOODS	1.2	− 18.3	8.8	4.8
3220	CLOTHING	44.8	− 162.3	91	47.3
3230	LEATHER	6.8	− 0.4	32.6	28
3240	SHOES	28.2	22.5	60.3	59.5
3311	SAWMILLING & CARPENTRY	15.6	− 59.7	67	29
3312	OTHER WOOD PRODS	8.7	3.6	10.7	7.3
3320	NON-METAL FURNITURE	34.9	27.9	56.8	55.1
3410	PAPER PRODS	10.4	− 525.1	186.6	− 358.8
3420	PRINTING	70.9	− 98.8	35.7	− 26.7
3512	BASIC CHEMICALS	313.7	− 839.9	630.4	− 309.3
3513	ARTIFICAL FIBERS	18.1	− 118.2	229	85.1
3521	PHARMACEUTICALS	74.8	− 79.3	62.7	− 71.5
3522	OTHER CHEMICALS	50.4	− 221	171	8.7
3550	RUBBER	8	− 281.5	54.4	− 74.7
3560	PLASTICS	14.6	− 104.4	58.1	− 89.1
3611	CERAMICS	14.2	− 2.3	40.1	34.5
3612	STRUCTURAL PRODS	30.3	− 8.4	33.7	18.7
3620	GLASS PRODS	54.8	− 9.6	209.3	169.1
3691	CEMENT	25.3	− 57.2	163.7	114.8
3710	IRON & STEEL	64	− 2155.5	629.6	1.8
3720	NON-IRON METALS	741.7	138.5	630.2	397.3
3811	MOLDED METALS	0.5	− 99.5	2.3	− 17.4
3813	METAL FURNITURE	1.3	− 7.9	9	2.5
3814	OTH FINSHD METAL PRODS	90.7	− 873.8	150	− 235.7
3821	SPEC MACHINERY/EQPT	53.7	− 1782	124.1	− 505.3
3822	GENL MACHINERY/EQPT	132	− 2896.1	305.2	− 1074.9
3823	OFFICE MACH./COMPUTERS	76.9	− 480.5	465.2	− 223
3831	ELECTRICAL MACHINERY	26.8	− 625.2	25.3	− 160.1
3832	ELECTRONIC EQPT	20.3	− 844.1	30.3	− 230.3
3833	DOMESTIC ACCESSORIES	5.4	− 29.3	57.7	35.3
3841	AUTOMOBILES	382.2	− 2153.1	3215.4	1942.5
3842	OTHER TRANSPORT EQPT	79.9	− 1124.7	137.7	− 352.1
3850	PRECISION INSTRUMENTS	24.1	− 663.3	95.6	− 342.8
3900	ALL OTHER MFG	49.9	− 85.9	68.4	8
			0		0
			0		0

NOTE: Export figures are in millions of current

APPENDIX B
DEA EFFICIENCY AND CLUSTERS OF EFFICIENT REFERENT SETS

CMAP	INDUSTRY	EFFIC.	3611	3823	3140	3720	3122	3710	3841
			DEA-EFFICIENT REFERENTS (in rough order of increasing capital intensity)						
3611	CERAMICS	100%	√						
3823	OFFICE MACH./COMPUTERS	100%		√					
3140	TOBACCO	100%			√				
3720	NON-FERROUS METALS	100%				√			
3122	ANIMAL FEED	100%					√		
3710	IRON & STEEL	100%						√	
3841	AUTOMOBILES	100%							√
3312	OTHER WOOD PRODS	84%	*		*				
3320	NON-METAL FURNITURE	35%	*		*				
3813	METAL FURNITURE	54%	*		*				
3211	ROPE, HARD FIBERS	62%	*		*				
3842	OTHER TRANSPORT EQPT	46%	*		*				
3111	MEAT PRODS	49%	*		*				
3900	ALL OTHER MFG	28%	*		*				
3230	LEATHER	50%	*	*	*				
3550	RUBBER	41%				*	*		
3112	DAIRY PRODS	77%				*	*		
3560	PLASTICS	26%				*	*		
3121	OTHER FOOD	51%				*	*		
3118	SUGAR	25%				*	*		
3691	CEMENT	31%				*	*		
3620	GLASS PRODS	32%				*	*		
3821	SPEC MACHINERY/EQPT	29%			*	*	*		
3117	EDIBLE OILS	87%			*	*	*		
3113	CANNING	32%			*	*	*		
3114	GRAIN PROCESSING	72%					*	*	
3220	CLOTHING	75%			*	*			
3115	BREAD PRODS	53%			*	*			
3240	SHOES	37%			*	*			
3832	ELECTRONIC EQPT	36%			*	*			
3420	PRINTING	27%			*	*			
3822	GENL MACHINERY/EQPT	24%			*	*			
3521	PHARMACEUTICALS	37%			*	*			
3811	MOLDED METALS	18%			*	*			
3831	ELECTRICAL MACHINERY	24%			*	*			
3119	CHOCOLATE	55%		*	*		*		
3214	KNITTED GOODS	29%		*	*		*		
3833	DOMESTIC ACCESSORIES	40%		*	*		*		
3814	OTH FINSHD METAL PRODS	55%					*	*	*
3522	OTHER CHEMICALS	94%					*	*	*
3130	BEVERAGES	87%					*	*	*
3212	SOFT FIBER WEAVING	27%					*	*	*
3213	TEXTILES	65%		*			*		
3850	PRECISION INSTRUMENTS	47%		*			*		
3311	SAWMILLING & CARPENTRY	32%		*			*		
3612	STRUCTURAL PRODS	34%		*			*		
3513	ARTIFICAL FIBERS	62%		*			*		
3410	PAPER PRODS	49%					*		*
3512	BASIC CHEMICALS	74%					*		*

NOTES

1. F. Alba, "Logros y Limitaciones en la Absorbción de la Fuerza de Trabajo en México," *Demografía y Economía*, 18, 1984, pp. 557–580.

2. Jaime Behar, *Trade and Employment in Mexico*, PhD Dissertation, University of Stockholm, Stockholm: Almqvist & Wicksell International, 1988, p. 109.

3. Anne O. Krueger, Hal B. Lary, Terry Monson, and Narongchai Akrasanee, *Trade and Employment in Developing Countries*, 1, (Chicago: The University of Chicago Press, 1981).

4. Krueger, Lary, Monson, and Akrasanee, p. 10.

5. John Harris and Michael Todaro, "Migration, Unemployment and Development: A Two-Sector Analysis," *American Economic Review*, March 1970, pp. 126–142.

6. Other significant studies supporting export policies as a tool for absorbing labor include: G. Feder, "On Exports and Economic Growth," *Journal of Development Economics*, 12, 1983, pp. 59–74; G. Helliner, "Outward Orientation, Import Instability and African Economic Growth," in S. Lall and F. Stewart (eds.), *Theory and Reality in Development*, (London: Macmillan, 1986); M. Michaely, "Exports and Growth: An Empirical Investigation," *Journal of Development Economics*, 4, 1977, pp. 149–153.

7. Krueger, Lary, Monson, and Akrasanee 1–3, 1981–1983; L.E. Westphal, "The Republic of Korea's Experience with Export-Led Industrial Development," *World Development*, 6, 1978, pp. 347–382; B. Balassa, "Export Incentives and Export Performance in Developing Countries: A Comparative Analysis," World Bank Staff Working Papers, No. 248, (Washington, D.C., The World Bank, 1977); B. Balassa, "Exports and Economic Growth: Further Evidence," *Journal of Development Economics*, 5, 1978, pp. 181–189.

8. R.A. Berry, and C. Diaz-Alejandro, "The New Colombian Exports: Possible Effects on the Distribution of Income," in R.A. Berry and R. Soligo, (eds.), *Economic Policy and Income Distribution in Colombia*, (Boulder: Westview Press, 1980); D. Lal and S. Rajapatirana, "Foreign Trade Regimes and Economic Growth in Developing Countries," *Research Observer*, 2(2), 1987, pp. 189–217; Behar, 1988.

9. R.W. Boatler, "Trade Theory Predictions and the Growth of Mexico's Manufactured Exports," *Economic Development and Cultural Change*, 23, 1975, pp. 491–506; and Behar, 1988.

10. P.C.Y. Chow, "Causality Between Export Growth and Industrial Development: Empirical Evidence from the NICs," *Journal of Development Economics*, 26, 1987, pp. 55–63; Alejandro Ibarra, "Causality Between Exports and Industrial Growth: Further Evidence from Mexico," ITESM Working Paper, 1988.

11. David Turnham and Ian Jaeger, *The Employment Problem in Less Developed Countries*, (Paris: OECD, 1970); Michael Todaro, *Economic Development in the Third World*, Third Edition, (New York: Longman, 1985).

12. Widely acknowledged by development economists, these perspectives are clearly laid out in Turnham and Jaeger, and in Behar, 1988.

13. Behar, 1988, pp. 113–114.

14. Behar discusses labor hoarding in his detailed analysis of the manufacturing sector in Monterrey.

15. Santiago Levy finds support for the complementarily of labor with capital in his article "Foreign Trade and its Impact on Employment: The Mexican Case," *Journal of Development Economics*, 10, 1981, pp. 47–65.

16. Spearman correlations are more appropriate here since, by only considering the rank ordering of 1980 value added, they impose less structure on the sample. To the extent that the unobserved figures for value added in 1987 are ordered by sector as they were in 1980, the Spearman correlation will more reliably capture the relationship between exports and value added in 1987.

17. Stolp provides an elementary introduction to the logic of DEA in Chandler Stolp, "A Framework for Evaluating the Efficiency of Health Centers in Nicaragua," in M. Conroy, (ed.), *Profiles in the Revolutionary Public Sector*, (Boulder: Westview Press, 1987). A more technical and comprehensive overview is R. Banker, A. Charnes, W.W. Cooper, J. Swarts, and D.A. Thomas, "An Introduction to DEA with Some of Its Models and Their Uses," *Research in Governmental and Nonprofit Accounting*, 5, 1989, pp. 125–163.

18. Good references include: Eugene Silberberg, *The Structure of Economics: A Mathematical Analysis*, (New York: John Wiley & Sons, 1978); and Henri Theil, *A System-Wide Approach to Microeconomics*, (Chicago: University of Chicago Press, 1980).

19. Levy, pp. 47–65.

20. Sources for L and Q are Banco de México, *Indicadores Económicos*, various numbers; data for X and T are from unpublished Banco de México data.

21. Balassa, 1977; Behar, 1988; and Levy, 1981, pp. 47–65.

22. G.B. Henry, "Domestic Demand Pressure and Short-Run Export Fluctuations," *Yale Economic Essays*, 10, 1970, pp. 43–82.

23. Using Spearman correlations, Behar found no statistical evidence that volatility of exports was related to market concentration, as the literature for other developing countries had suggested. Volatility was, however, strongly correlated with growth in manufacturing output. This implies that the uncertainties surrounding the expansion of Mexico's export base and the penetration of new markets offer a better explanation for the wide variation in export performance than do the oligopolistic practices of firms. See Behar, 1988, pp. 66–70.

24. D. Murray, "Export Earnings Instability: Price, Quantity, Supply, Demand?" *Economic Development and Cultural Change*, 27, 1978, pp. 61–73; and Behar, 1988, pp. 70–73.

25. Banco de México, *Indicadores Económicos*, various numbers; International Monetary Fund, *International Financial Statistics*, various numbers.

8

Mexican Manufactured Exports and U.S. Transnational Corporations

Kurt Unger

I. INTRODUCTION: MEXICAN MANUFACTURED EXPORTS AND U.S. TRANSNATIONAL CORPORATIONS

The Mexican economy's export performance since 1982 has been remarkably successful. Domestic sales and imports fell dramatically after the external debt and internal inflation crises manifested themselves, but surprisingly, this downturn was accompanied by an unexpected rally in exports. This was particularly remarkable given the country's poor trade performance throughout the import substitution industrialization (ISI) period.

In this paper we aim to show that the Mexican subsidiaries of TNCs led the unexpected export response. The response was evident in those industrial sectors previously noted for their inefficiency in international competition. This Mexican trade pattern closely resembles the overall trend in international trade during the last decade, in which intra-industry trade and intra-firm export transactions became the predominant force.

The elements that determine competitive advantage in Mexican trade changed dramatically in the 1980s. TNC decisions regarding Mexican exports was influenced both by strategical determinants arising from global competition as well as by the need for return on sunk investments. Factors, such as the use of economies of scale and of scope and new technologies, even though they varied with the needs of individual industries and firms, may better explain export patterns than most of the conventional factors usually linked to the comparative advantage paradigm.

This paper is divided into four sections. The first section shows the growth of exports from 1976–1988. Trends are noted both by industry and by the 50 or so products representing the bulk of Mexican manufactured exports. The second section briefly discusses the importance that U.S. markets still retain for nonoil exports from Mexico. A third section estimates the participation of TNCs in those exports, particularly exports of firms originated in the United States. A fourth section identifies the two major types of export transactions: intra-firm trading of relatively modern products or their components and transactions between independent parties involving primarily commodities or mature products.

The most dynamic intra-firm exports in the automotive, chemical and computer industries are more affected by strategical factors that affect TNCs than by the more conventional factors of comparative advantage. The final portion of this paper summarizes the implications that this trend will have for future export growth.

II. EXPORT PERFORMANCE OF 1976–1988

In recent years, Mexican manufactured exports have regained the prominence they lost after 1979 when oil prices escalated, placing oil exports ahead of all other products with 75 percent of total export earnings. In 1987 and 1988, manufactured exports again accounted for more than half of total exports with 51.3 percent and 59.9 percent respectively.[1] Since oil prices are likely to remain stagnant in the near future, manufactured products will continue to be the focus of Mexico's export modernizing program. Under this assumption we are justified in centering our attention on manufactured exports in this paper.

Export performance in Mexico can be divided into three distinct periods. The early period (1976–1979) marked a change from the previous ISI bias against exports. The average growth rate of manufactured exports, though still moderate at 8.3 percent, was higher than the percentage growth in the domestic production market. In the period 1979–1981, foreign exchange earnings rose with the proceeds of oil sales, prompting a fast rise in domestic demand, which in turn absorbed the capacity of most domestic industries. Manufactured exports actually declined in 1980 and 1981, as Table 1 indicates. This reflected the preference of Mexican firms for selling in the domestic market.[2]

In 1982, the collapse of the domestic market was accompanied by an upswing in exports that sustained an average growth of 28 percent per year from 1983 through 1987. This sustained growth dropped in 1988 to 10.1 percent, a trend which is likely to continue, as we will demonstrate. The leading manufacturing sectors in the export upswing are automobiles and their components, nonelectrical machinery, steel, oil derivatives and other chemicals. Chemical exports have actually maintained a strong presence in the export market for many years, while the other mentioned industries experienced dramatic rises in exports.

These six sectors represented only 37 percent of manufactured exports in 1975, but climbed to 62.3 percent in 1988. Most of these sectors consist of new-modern industries that are subject to competitive restructuring in international markets and some involve industries reliant on natural resource advantages.

Mexico's most traditional industrial sectors, including food and beverages, textiles and clothing, wood, paper and minerals have all lagged behind in the export drive and have lost shares in the composition of exports, as Table 2 indicates.

When Mexican exports are analyzed for their technological dynamism under United Nations Industrial Development Organization (UNIDO) classification system,[4] new-modern products accounted for 42.4 percent of manufactured exports in 1987, as Table 3 indicates. This reflects an averaged sustained growth rate of 40 percent over the period 1983–1987. Ma-

TABLE 1

EXPORT GROWTH OF MEXICAN MANUFACTURED PRODUCTS
(1982 = 100)

Industries	1980	1981	1982	1983	1984	1985	1986	1987	1988
All Manufactured	-3.5	-1.2	2.3	66.9	28.5	0.2	21.8	22.9	10.1
Food and Beverages	-18.6	-8.1	12.9	3.2	10.5	-5.3	17	41.6	-1.6
Textile and Clothing	-17.7	-9.7	-15.2	32.7	44.8	-21.5	64	57	-2.2
Wood and Wood Products	-28.4	2.0	-11.3	63.1	20	-4.4	11.5	23.2	19.6
Paper and Printing	5.0	-5.9	-2.7	-0.9	30.7	7.1	42.7	53.5	28.5
Oil Derivatives	169.6	27.3	-54.1	211.6	70.1	15.7	-12.1	-18.2	17.9
Petrochemicals	-37.3	1.1	-6.3	29.6	19.2	-29.1	51.7	14.3	107.6
Chemicals	-3.3	17.1	-0.4	49.5	21.9	-4.3	26.4	23.5	11.2
Plastic Products and Rubber	-13.5	7.2	19.7	77.7	48.9	-16.9	61.2	32.9	20.3
Nonmetallic Minerals	-22.3	-2.1	15.8	58.5	39	17	23	11.3	2.5
Steel and Steel Products	-56.1	-9.2	81.7	198.7	20.1	-30.2	86.6	32.8	4.7
Basic Metals	-32.6	-41.2	456.4	56.9	-8.1	-15.3	21.8	24.2	12.7
Metal Products, Machinery, Equip.	8.9	-9.4	-2.3	87.6	32	6.1	32	30.9	7.1
Automobiles	1.1	-4.2	11.2	99.6	40.7	-0.3	29.6	36.8	1.7
Other transport equipment	-75.3	-64.2	-57.1	1337.7	-34.7	15.4	133.8	-6.5	-30.3
Nonelectrical Machinery	6.7	31	-11.5	44.2	14.7	9.9	32.2	30.1	22.5
Electrical Machinery	92.7	-54.4	-14.3	107.4	28.1	33.8	30.7	10.9	15.4
Precision and Professional Equip.	21.7	12.3	-8.4	109	-15.9	48.4	36.8	36.6	16.4
Other Industries	-5.5	2.6	-27.4	110.5	-1.1	22	-33.9	-0.9	30.2

Sources: Banco de México, Informe Anual (1980–1987); INEGI/SHCP/Banco de México, Estadísticas de Comercio Exterior de México, Vol. 9, No. 12, 1989.

TABLE 2

COMPOSITION AND GROWTH OF MANUFACTURED EXPORTS
(percentage)

Industries	Average Growth Rate				Composition	
	1977–79	1980–82	1983–85	1986–88	1975	1988
All Manufactured goods	8.3	−0.8	31.9	18.3	100	100
Food and Beverages	0.1	−4.6	2.8	19	29.8	10.4
Textile and Clothing	−6.1	−14.2	18.7	39.6	11	4.8
Wood and Wood Products	13.2	−12.6	26.2	18.1	1.7	1.3
Paper and Printing	−5.4	−1.2	12.3	41.6	2.6	2.6
Oil Derivates	103.2	47.6	99.1	−4.1	1	3.8
Petrochemicals	738.9	−14.2	6.5	57.9	13.5	11.2
Chemicals	2	4.5	22.4	20.4	0.5	1.2
Plastic Products and Rubber	23	4.5	36.6	38.1	4.1	4.2
Nonmetallic Minerals	12	−2.9	38.2	12.3	3.2	6.1
Steel and Steel Products	26.6	5.5	62.9	41.3	8.1	6.6
Basic Metals	11.1	127.5	11.2	19.6	21.4	36
Metal Products, Machinery and Equipment	13.8	−0.9	41.9	23.4	8.5	22.3
Automobiles	16.9	2.7	46.7	22.7	1.4	0.4
Other Transport Equipment	197.5	−65.5	439.5	32.4	1.1	0.8
Metal Products	23.9	−13.6	27.7	28.7	6	6.9
Nonelectrical machinery	2.3	8.7	22.9	28.2	4.1	4.6
Precision and Prof. Equipment	17.6	8.5	47.2	29.9	0.3	1
Other Industries	5.2	−10.2	43.9	−1.5	1.4	0.7

Sources: Banco de México, *Informe Anual (1980–1987)*; Banco de México, *Estadísticas Históricas—Balanza de Pagos* (Cuaderno 1970–1978); INEGI/SHCP/Banco de México, *Estadísticas del Comercio Exterior de México*, Vol. 11, No. 12.

TABLE 3

PARTICIPATION AND GROWTH OF MEXICAN EXPORTS BY PRODUCT TYPE

Industry	Product Growth Rate			Export Participation		
	1976–78	1979–82	1983–87	1976	1982	1987
New-Modern	22.8	0.1	40.7	25	28	42.4
Mature	10.1	−6.0	31.1	26.8	20.5	23.2
Resource-Based	6.7	3	17.9	48.3	51.5	34.4
Total Manufactured Products	11.2	−0.2	28.1	100	100	100

Sources: Banco de México, *Estadísticas Historicas-Balanza de Pagos* (Cuarderno 1970–78); Banco de México, *Informe Anual (1980–82)*; Banco de México, *Direccion de Investigación Económica*, SIE-BANICO-SECOBI (1983–1987).

ture product industries have also improved their market share since 1982 and in 1987 represented about 23 percent of manufactured exports. Resource-based products, on the other hand, have made a less significant showing. Although they represented about 50 percent of total exports until 1982, resource-based products have experienced a steady reduction in exports share. In 1987, these products represented 34.4 percent of total manufactured exports.

Perhaps the most revealing aspect of this analysis is the extremely high concentration of Mexican exports in a small number of products. This concentration has intensified in recent years. A total of 50 products composed 73.1 percent of manufactured exports in 1988. The top 17 products captured 50 percent of the total, as Table 4 indicates. These products were diverse, including new-modern products such as automotive units and components, computers, plastics; and mature products such as glass, glass-made items and iron-steel products; and resource-based products such as oil derivatives, shrimp, silver and others.

The most important change in export trends from 1982 to 1988 was the increased volume of automobiles, engines, computer-related equipment and oil derivatives, except fuel oil. At the same time, resource-based products like shrimp, silver, processed fruits, vegetables, ammonia, hydrofluoric acid and tequila experienced, at best, modest growth or some decline, although they remained important exports.

A country with highly concentrated export earnings is vulnerable and Mexico's market vulnerability was already evident in 1988. The major export products experienced declines in growth during 1988 for a variety of reasons. This trend encompassed products that early in the 1980s had demonstrated dynamic growth, as shown in Table 5 for automobiles, engines and other products. The export of some of these products will be hindered in the future by the exhaustion of installed capacity in their plants, as in the capacity for engine and parts manufacturing in the automobile industry. They may also be constrained by international demand, as is already evident in certain restrictions and quotas on steel, fibers, etc.

A few other important products face export growth restrictions. Shrimp, silver and polycarboxyl acids were already showing signs of export declines in 1984 or earlier. Some exceptions to these declines are listed in Table 5. These include polyvinyl chloride, computers, electrical wiring, copper bars and photographic equipment.

III. EXPORT DESTINATIONS

The United States is by far the most important trading country for Mexico. It takes about 65 percent of Mexico's exports, a percentage that has declined slightly in recent years with the diversification of Mexico's oil exports. Aside from oil, the U.S. market has become increasingly important to Mexico. The U.S. share of Mexico's nonoil exports rose to 82.4 percent in 1987.[5] For manufactured goods specifically, in 1984 and 1985—the most recent years for which data is available—the United States accounted for

TABLE 4

PRIMARY MEXICAN EXPORT PRODUCTS
1976, 1982 AND 1988
(percentage of total exports)

Products	1976	1982	1988
Primary Product Total	52.7	68.8	73.1
Automobiles	0.6	0.2	8.9
Automobile Engines	3.3	6.3	8.7
Fuel Oil	0.1	5.3	2.9
Autoparts	4.4	3.9	2.8
Frozen Shrimp	15.5	10.9	2.8
Silver Bars	0.0	8.8	2.5
Polyvinyl Chloride	0.2	0.2	2.5
Information Processing Equipment	0.6.0	0.1	2.2
Plastic/Resins	0.0	1.2	2.2
Gasoline	0.2	0.2	1.9
Gas Butane and Propane	0.1	0.8	1.9
Glass and glass products	0.2	0.9	1.8
Iron/Steel Manufactures	0.6	1.3	1.7
Plastics and Resins	1.7	0.8	1.7
Synthetic Fibers	1.8	1.8	1.5
Tubes and Pipes	0.1	0.7	1.5
Polycarboxyl Acids	0.3	0.7	1.5
Machine Parts	0.1	1.3	1.4
Electrical Wires	0.5	0.8	1.4
Raw Iron	0.0	0.1	1.2
Beer	0.9	0.4	1.2
Sugar	0.0	0.2	1.2
Copper Bars	0.4	0.1	0.9
Installation Parts	1.6	2.1	0.9
Dyes and Varnish	0.1	0.4	0.8
Fruits and Vegetables	0.2	3.0	0.8
Photocopying Equipment	3.1	0.3	0.7
Ammonia	0.8	0.5	0.6
Zinc	0.8	0.8	0.6
Wood and Wood Products	0.5	0.4	0.6
Engine Parts	0.0	0.1	0.6
Commercial Vehicles	0.2	0.5	0.6
Manufactures of Electrical Supplies	0.2	0.3	0.6
Hydrofluoric Acid	1.3	1.6	0.5
Orange Juice	0.3	0.6	0.5
Photography Film	0.0	0.3	0.5
Lead	1.1	0.7	0.5
Magnetic Tapes	0.2	0.2	0.5
Ethylene	0.0	0.0	0.5
Tequila	0.1	1.1	0.4
Rubber Tires	0.1	0.1	0.4
Shoes	0.7	0.4	0.4
Copper Tubes and Pipes	0.2	0.2	0.4
Cotton Clothing	1.7	0.6	0.4
Wood Furniture	0.9	0.8	0.4
Silk/Synthetic Fabrics	0.3	0.1	0.4
Frozen Tuna	0.1	0.7	0.4
Coffee	1.2	0.8	0.4

Sources: Banco de México, *Informe Anual (1980–1987)*; Banco de México, *Estadísticas Histor-icas—Balanza de Pagos* (Cuaderno 1970–1978); INEGI/SHCP/Banco de México, *Estadísticas del Comercio Exterior de México*, Vol. 11, No. 12.

TABLE 5

GROWTH OF PRIMARY MEXICAN EXPORT PRODUCTS
(percentages)

Products	1983	1984	1985	1986	1987	1988
Automobiles	60.4	6.2	− 4.5	302.6	137.2	2.4
Automobile Engines	175.4	59.4	3.2	0.8	5.5	0.9
Fuel Oil	17.8	16.8	2.3	32.5	1.9	2.1
Autoparts	33.9	4.7	− 13.1	41.2	12	− 4.8
Frozen Shrimp	4	2.9	− 15.4	1.2	24.2	− 19.6
Silver Bars	41	− 14.3	− 16.4	21.9	9.6	− 23.5
Polyvinyl Chloride	399.4	88.7	− 12	141	23.2	59.9
Information Processing Equipment	497.1	227.9	44.2	27.9	116.4	34.3
Gasoline	10402	76.8	− 47.8	− 46.9	9.8	105.3
Gas Butane and Propane	32.9	12.7	150.9	− 10.2	− 0.3	81.6
Glass and Glass Products	61.9	28	24.4	21	7.1	− 0.7
Iron/Steel Manufactures	322.2	27.8	− 24.4	119.1	11.5	− 19.8
Plastics and Resins	76	67.7	− 14.6	42.8	87.7	9.1
Synthetic Fibers	94	51.2	− 22.4	83.6	38	− 18.2
Tubes and Pipes	194.4	57	− 24.4	− 7.2	104.9	9.7
Polycarboxyl Acids	82.6	19.4	25.7	− 0.1	3.6	5.4
Machinery Parts	109.6	7.9	130	− 3.9	20.4	38.1
Electrical Wire	113.2	20	− 30.8	2.9	215.3	37.4
Raw Iron	107.2	− 1	− 54.9	258.4	32	− 11.4
Beer	− 1.6	33.1	81.3	66.5	87	− 18.8
Sugar	118.2	—	—	181.6	169.7	89.5
Cement	261	78.7	20	35.5	8.2	− 5.6
Copper Bars	42.1	− 63.8	53.8	145	367.8	180.5
Gas/Oil	1127.2	− 55.4	133.2	81.7	− 64.2	− 33.9
Dyes and Varnish	15.5	35.2	21.1	22.1	22.6	10.7
Fruits and Vegetables	− 12	22.2	6.5	− 3	23.2	6.2
Photocopying Equipment	21	36.8	3.1	28.6	105.3	48.3
Ammonia	− 9.4	− 12.5	− 52.3	− 47.5	30.7	240.7
Zinc	509.3	33.1	− 22.8	− 6.1	4.1	34.9
Wood and Wood Products	193.8	9.3	− 16.4	45.5	14.7	4
Engine Parts	45	12.8	3.4	48.1	14.6	− 5.3
Commercial Vehicles	− 0.8	80.4	− 11.1	9.6	− 24.6	287.6
Plastic/Resin Manufactures	45.9	5.2	53.7	58.6	− 2.9	7.1
Electrical Supplies	179.4	27.7	16.4	15.4	51.6	− 7.4
Hydrofluoric Acid	− 6.5	20.9	10.4	3.3	20	− 22.3
Orange Juice	− 2.7	52.6	− 83.3	227.6	106.6	86
Photography Film	386.4	32.1	− 36.1	17.4	41.4	− 3.1
Lead	59.1	13.1	1.4	12	12	12.3
Magnetic Tapes	− 15.8	− 29.4	314.1	140.1	− 39.8	134.6
Ethylene	—	83.3	79	− 16.1	− 92.6	4486
Tequila	10.5	− 1.1	− 3.8	5.7	13.8	9.5
Rubber Tires	641.8	135.8	− 75	129.2	117.5	30.7
Shoes	− 17.8	59.1	− 29	26.7	168.8	14
Copper Tubes and Pipes	196	− 48.8	− 11.3	106.7	96.5	41.5
Cotton Clothing	− 15.3	54.1	− 21.6	− 4.1	164.7	3.3
Wood Furniture	4	30.5	13.1	− 21.6	45.9	10.8
Silk/Synthetic Clothing	273.4	73.6	13.3	57	14	− 12.2
Frozen Tuna	− 74.3	− 92.8	5489.3	509.6	45.2	13.7
Electrical Parts	89.7	35.1	39	− 38.9	4.9	− 7.1
Coffee	49.3	28.9	16.5	− 11	− 40.7	37.6

Sources: Banco de México, *Informe anual (1983–1987)*; INEGI-SHCP-Banco de México, *Estadísticas de Comercio Exterior de México*, Vol. 11, No. 12, 1989.

about 84 percent of exports.

U.S. dominance applies across the board in the manufacturing sectors. · Mexico sells the United States natural resource-based products at a comparative advantage, as well as mature products with a dynamic comparative advantage emanating from well diffused technologies. Mexico also exports some new-modern products and components produced by TNCs that have recently set up plants in Mexico specifically aimed at exporting to the United States and other countries within the region.

The U.S. market is particularly important for exports of resource-based and mature products from Mexico.[6] The new-modern exports are the most diversified products. About two-thirds of these are shipped to the United States, compared to more than 80 percent of the resource-based and mature products, as Table 6 indicates. Among the diverse new products are office machines, computers, plastic materials and resins, films and iron bars. Most of these exports are traded within subsidiaries of the same TNC,[7] as demonstrated later in this text.

TABLE 6

MEXICAN EXPORTS TO THE UNITED STATES*

(percentages of total exports)

Products	1984	1985
New-Modern	66.2	68.8
Mature	78.5	86.1
Resource-Based	83.5	78.2
Total Manufactured Products	84.5	83.6

Sources: Banco de México, *Dirección de Investigación Económica,* SIE-BANXICO-SECOBI (1984–1985).

NOTE: *Figures are the 51 most important products.

Resource-based exports destined for the United States usually involve transactions between independent parties. Shrimp, processed fruits and vegetables, coffee, beer, tequila, wood and wooden furniture, oil derivatives, ammonia, hydrofluoric acid, silver and zinc are all sold to independent firms. Polycarboxyl acids and refined lead products do not have main markets in the United States. Rather, Mexico exports its polycarboxyl acid products primarily to Asia and exports its refined lead products to Belgium, Italy, the Netherlands, Japan and the United States.

The United States is also the primary destination for mature industry products, but in many instances these products are intra-firm traded. Mature products usually include nonelectrical machinery components, wires, lamps and tubes, electrical installation parts, transformers and photographic and cinematographic equipment. Radio and television components are also traded within subsidiaries of the same TNCs, but they are exported from Mexico to subsidiaries in Venezuela, China, India and other countries. Other mature products compete more openly in international markets. These include exports of cement, glass and glass-made items, iron-steel manufactures, toys, sporting goods and some dyes and varnishes.

Several trading operations mark the new-modern product exports.[8] The more technologically dynamic products—automobiles, films, office machinery and computers—are traded between related parties by three different methods that vary according to the destination of the exports. Automobiles and auto parts are mainly exported back to the parent companies in the United States, Germany and Japan. For some auto parts, other subsidiaries in Canada or Latin America may be important, but the major export transactions take place with the country of origin of the TNC.

The export of photographic film involves a different trade strategy. In this scheme, the primary markets are larger Latin American countries, such as Brazil, Argentina, Venezuela, Colombia or Chile, as well as the United States. The leading export firm, Eastman Kodak—whose Mexican subsidiary is Industria Fotográfica Interamericana—set up a Mexican plant to supply their global operations. The scale of operations required for its processing technology determines the need for each plant to serve the markets of several subsidiaries of the same TNC.

Another export strategy involves computers and typewriters.[9] Olivetti, which manufactures typewriters, has adopted the long-term strategy of splitting its product lines among various countries. This way, Olivetti hoped to cushion itself from the pressures of local governments seeking compensation for foreign exchange flows. Mexico was allocated the production of light, nonelectrical typewriters.[10] Other firms exporting these products have used the same strategy. Olympia, International Business Machines (IBM) and Xerox are also exporting nonelectrical typewriters to Europe, the United States and Latin America. In recent years the largest portion of Mexican exports of these products has gone to Western Europe. Germany has received nearly 50 percent, primarily through the export of Olympia products. Exports to Italy and Great Britain are next in rank. The United States, Thailand and Hong Kong also received significant volumes of these Mexican exports.

Computer exports deserve special attention because of their importance, both in export volumes as well as their technological qualities. Computer production (the assembly of integrated circuits and other components) need not be a technologically complex process. Thus, one has to assess more carefully the recent increase in net gains derived from the export of microcomputers. IBM now exports microcomputers from a new plant set up in Mexico to substitute for their more costly operations in

Boca Raton, Florida. From Mexico, IBM's main distribution markets are subsidiaries in the United States, Canada, Japan and Australia. Hewlett Packard is selling to the same countries under a similar strategy. A few other firms like Compubur, a Burroughs affiliate, Wang and Tandem are reacting accordingly, though the scale of their exports is still limited.

We have already identified the type of Mexican exports and the primary countries to which they are sold. We have also considered some types of trading transactions to explain the upsurge of a sophisticated group of exports that are traded less for their comparative advantage than for their ability to meet the needs of TNCs. The following sections offer more insights into the role of TNCs in Mexican trading, as well as the source of their own, distinctive competitive advantages.

IV. THE ROLE OF U.S. TRANSNATIONALS IN MEXICAN EXPORTS

U.S. transnationals play an important role in Mexican manufactured exports. No precise estimates exist on the extent to which these firms trade Mexican manufactured goods, but undoubtedly, foreign firms successfully developed Mexican exports after the domestic market collapse of 1982. The role of these firms should be more carefully analyzed, particularly in light of the role that these companies played in Mexican development during the 1970s and 1980s.[11] In our analysis, we hope to compensate, at least partially, for the limited official sources of sectoral data on these firms.[12]

The fact that foreign enterprises were successful in generating exports after the 1982 collapse is well illustrated by their increased share in nonoil exports, which have boomed in recent years. Nonoil exports from foreign firms enjoyed moderate success from 1981 through 1984, representing less than a 30 percent of total nonoil exports. This total jumped to more than 50 percent after 1986, as Table 7 indicates. Today these firms account for two-thirds of the total private sector exports and may have a much larger share in manufactured exports.[13]

Foreign firms accounted for 37.8 percent of manufactured exports in 1980.[14] In more recent years, however, their share increased significantly, particularly in new-modern products. The subsidiaries of U.S TNCs have led the export drive in these products,[15] as Table 7 also indicates.

U.S. TNCs also lead in the most important export sectors—automobiles and auto parts, computers, typewriters and components and many chemicals, as Table 8 indicates. U.S. TNCs are also active in certain successful markets for products like photocopying equipment, tubes and iron-steel pipes and some electrical devices.[16] In some cases, U.S. TNCs share their export success with other TNCs and some local firms. But Mexican firms mostly concentrate on the more traditional products, par-

TABLE 7

FOREIGN PARTICIPATION IN MEXICAN EXPORTS

(percentages)

Export Type	1981	1983	1984	1985	1986	1987
Nonoil	26.8	22.3	30.1	41.1	52.8	53.4
Private Sector	42.2	33.8	43.5	58.3	65.9	65.1

Sources: Banco de México, *Indicadores del Sector Externo;* INEGI, *Estadísticas de Comercio Exterior de México;* Comisión Nacional de Inversiones Extranjeras, *Informe, 1983–1987.*

ticularly those industries that produce natural resource-based products. These products, with the exception of petrochemicals, have been less dynamic than other products.

In the automotive industry, the U.S. TNCs continue to play the leading role in Mexico, both in exports and domestic production. They maintain this role in spite of the difficulties that many U.S. firms have been facing at home and in most other industrialized countries. The Big Three U.S. auto firms, General Motors, Ford and Chrysler, dominate the most important Mexican exports. They accounted for 96 percent of vehicles exported in 1987 and for about 80 percent of the engines exported in the same year. Volkswagen and Renault account for another 15 percent of exports, but these firms are in the process of pulling out of Mexico.[17] Nissan, on the other hand, has only recently begun to show an export potential in the production of light trucks. These trucks are produced in conjunction with Nissan's Tennessee plant.[18]

The same TNCs lead Mexico's export drive in automobile components, although some of these firms do participate in joint ventures with domestic firms. Ford and General Motors, for example, have entered into joint ventures with Carplastic, Nemak, Vitroflex and Autopartes Condumex. Despite the joint ventures, automobile components declined as a percentage of manufactured exports in 1988 and 1989. This decline resulted from the exhaustion of installed capacity in Mexican plants as well as a declining competitive position of various TNCs.

Most significant chemical exports are produced by the subsidiaries of a handful of large U.S. TNCs. As Table 8 indicates, Celanese, Goodrich, Monsanto, DuPont, Raychem and Eastman Kodak have taken the lead in Mexican chemical production. These firms are producing and exporting plastics, synthetic resins and fibers, film, pigments and even some basic chemicals like hydrofluoric acid.[19] Most of these exports involve intra-firm transactions. At the same time, as Table 8 indicates, domestic firms are also gaining ground in the production of basic petrochemicals like polyvinyl chloride and polycarboxyl acids. These products are traded as com-

TABLE 8

1987 TNC PARTICIPATION IN MODERN INDUSTRY EXPORTS FROM MEXICO

Products and Firms	% Exports	Products and Firms	% Exports
PRODUCTS OF DECLINING EXPORT GROWTH:		General Motors	13.7
Automobiles		Volkswagen de México	12.9
Automobiles seating less than 10		Moto Diesel Mexicana (GM: 40%)	11.3
Chrysler	49.7	Renault	6.8
Ford	29.3	158 other firms	39.3
General Motors	16.9		
Nissan	4	DYNAMIC EXPORT GROWTH PRODUCTS:	
16 other firms	0.1	Chemicals, Textiles, Nonelectrical Machinery, Steel Tubes and Pipes,	
Automobiles: Trucks and Pickups		Electrical Machinery, Professional Equipment and Instruments	
Nissan	95.7	*Chemicals: Plastic Materials and Synthetic Resins: Polyester*	
Dina Camiones	1.9	Celanese Mexicana	53.5
12 other firms	2.4	Fibras Quimicas (Dupont: 40%)	43.4
Automobiles: Car Engines:		13 other firms	3.2
General Motors	39.7	*Chemicals: Polyvinyl Chloride*	
Chrysler	19.3	Policyd (B.F. Goodrich 40%)	49.4
Ford	19.2	Grupo Primex	35
Volkswagen	8.3	Polimeros Mexicanos	11.6
Renault	6.9	32 other firms	4
30 other firms	6.6	*Chemicals: Polystyrene*	
Automobiles: Autoparts and Components		Industrias Resistol (Monsanto: 40%)	62.9
Carplastic (Ford: 40%)	27.1	Productos de Estireno	14.2
Lamosa	15	Polioles	10.5
Volkswagen de México	13.1	Poliestireno y Derivados	10.3
Nissan Mexicana	8.3	23 other firms	2
Chrysler de México	7.8	*Chemicals: Plastic Films and Filaments*	
280 other firms	28.7	Grupo Grafica Nacional	26
Automobiles: Engine Parts		Celulosa y Derivados (B.F. Goodrich: 40%)	24.2
Nemak (Ford: 25%)	16		

Products and Firms	% Exports
Plastiglas	11.5
Celanese Mexicana	9.9
72 other firms	28.5
Chemicals Other Polymer Products	
Pemex	34.6
Raychem Tecnologias	25
Industrias Resistol (Monsanto: 40%)	12.8
Tereftalatos Mexicanos	2.2
Dupont	2.6
154 other firms	16.7
Chemicals: Plastic Flakes and Bands	
Celulosa y Derivados	72.4
Celanese Mexicana	14.1
Consorcio Intermex	13.1
7 other firms	0.4
Chemicals: Other Plastics and Resins	
Magnetico de Mexico	16.4
Auriga Plasticos	10.8
S/DESC.	8.5
Nacional de Resinas	5.4
Plasticos Etka de Mexico	4.7
713 other firms	54.3
Chemicals: Photography Film	
Ind. Fotografica Interamericana (Kodak: 100%)	90.2
S/DESC.	6.5
19 other firms	3.3

Products and Firms	% Exports
Chemicals: Dyes and Varnishes	
Colorants from Vegetables	
Lab. Bioquimex	59.8
Prods. Deshidrata Mex	17.7
Ind. Alcoba	10.2
10 other firms	12.4
Pigments from Titanius Oxide	
Dupont	98
7 other firms	2
Polycarboxyl Acids	
Sintesis Organicas	44.3
Grupo Primex	37.5
Celanese Mexicana	17
6 other firms	1.2
Chemicals: Other Polycarboxyl Acids & Derivatives	
Petrocel (Hercules: 30%)	71
Tereftalatos Mex	27.4
13 other firms	1.6
Chemicals: Hydrofluoric Acid	
Quimica Fluor (Dupont: 33%)	49.4
Nissan Mexicana	30.5
Fluorex	13.7
Ind. Quimicas Mex (Stauffer Chem.: 41%)	6.4
Textiles: Synthetic and Artificial Fibers	
Celanese Mexicana	37.6
Fibras Nacionales de Acrilan	33.4
Celulosa y Derivados (B.F. Goodrich: 40%)	9.8

continued

TABLE 8 CONTINUED

1987 TNC PARTICIPATION IN MODERN INDUSTRY EXPORTS FROM MEXICO

Products and Firms	% Exports	Products and Firms	% Exports
18 other firms	19.3	Hylba	26
Textiles: Cellulose Acetate Yarns		AHMBA	9.4
Celanese Mexicana	87.5	Proc. Aceros Rassini	4.2
Fibras Nacionales de Acrilan	10.7	28 other firms	8.7
2 other firms	1.8	*Electrical Machinery: Electrical Wires*	
Textiles: Discontinued Synthetic Fibers		Conductores Monterrey (U.S. Electrical: 40.7)	43.5
Celulosa y Derivados (B.F. Goodrich: 40%)	92.1	Nacional de Conductores Electricos	15.7
10 other firms	7.9	Industrias Conelec (Phelps Dodge: 40%)	11.5
Nonelectrical Machinery: Computers		Conductores Guadalajara	10.5
IBM de México	70.5	Conductores CM	8.3
Hewlett Packard de México	9.4	67 other firms	10.5
Compubur (Burroughs-Unysis)	6.6	*Electrical Machinery: Electrical Instruments*	
Wang de México	1.6	S/DESC	27.7
187 other firms	8.6	Data General de México	9.1
Typewriters		Amelec	8.4
Olympia de México	43	Emermex	7.7
IBM de México	19.6	Ciudad Electronica de México	4.4
Olivetti Mexicana	19	223 other firms	42.6
Xerox Mexicana	15.3	*Electrical Machinery: Radiotelephonic Equipment Parts*	
8 other firms	3.2	Videotec de México	84.5
Steel Tubes and Pipes, Seamless Tubes		39 other firms	15.5
Turbos de Acero	96.7	*Electrical Machinery: Professional Equipment & Instruments: Photocopying Equipment*	
Precitubo	1.3	Xerox Mexicana	98.4
27 other firms	2	3 other firms	1.6
Steel Tubes and Pipes: (other than seamless)			
PMT (Sumitomo Metal)	51.7		

Source: Dirección General de Asuntos Hacendarios Internacionales, SHCP.

modities in more openly competitive international markets.

The export growth pattern for computers, typewriters and photocopying equipment is similar to the growth pattern in the automotive industry. Although the growth patterns do not necessarily yield the same results year by year, all of these products suffer from an export capacity limited by a shortage of production facilities in Mexico. In the automobile sector, as well as the computer, typewriter and photocopying equipment sectors, the TNCs were prodded into export production by the Mexican government, which demanded compensation for imports. Firms like IBM, Hewlett Packard, Xerox, Olympia and Olivetti[20] are not likely to export much more than is required by the government, particularly since they have positioned themselves as solid competitors in the Mexican domestic market.[21]

Electrical equipment exports are also dominated by TNCs. The most successful export is electrical wire, and more than half of Mexico's electrical wire exports are produced by Conductores Monterrey and Industrias Conelec in joint ventures with U.S. Electrical and Phelps Dodge. Three other domestic firms have the capacity to export, due partly to the competitive edge provided by Mexican copper.

Radio-telephonic equipment parts, also a significant component of Mexican manufactured exports, are manufactured primarily by a single foreign firm, Videotec de México.[22] Tube and steel pipe exports are produced by a handful of TNCs and a few domestic firms. Tubos de Acero, with a minority U.S. ownership, controls most of the seamless tubes exported for oil operations in the United States. Less sophisticated tubing is produced by a domestic firm with some Japanese participation, as well as by several state firms.

Mature or resource-based consumer and intermediate goods exports fall more directly under the control of Mexican-owned industries. The most important products of parastatal industries have suffered from stagnant or negative growth in exports. These include iron-steel bars and other nontube products, copper bars, oil derivatives and basic petrochemicals such as fuel-oil, gasoline, butane gas, propane, gasohol, ammonia and ethylene.

Private domestic producers control many products that are subjected to protectionist trade restrictions or strong competition from independent producers in other industrializing countries. These include shrimp, silver, glass and glass-made products, textile fibers (other than synthetic fibers), beer, sugar, cement, processed fruits and vegetables, orange juice, zinc, lead, tequila, shoes, wooden furniture, tuna fish and coffee.[23]

V. EXPORT TRANSACTIONS: INTRA-FIRM TRADES
AND OTHER EXPORTS

To assess the future export prospects for various Mexican products, it is important to distinguish between the two types of commercial operations producing them. Intra-firm exports obey the overall strategy adopted by the TNCs, which view Mexican exports either as temporary or permanent sources for the conglomerate itself. The export of these products is dependent on conditions elsewhere in the parent firm or the parent firm's other subsidiaries. A case in point is when exports represent the only outlet available to TNCs for making economic use of large, sunk investments that had been made under more optimistic assumptions about the domestic market. These could be considered exports of economic emergency designed to correct past mistakes. Each of these TNC marketing decisions can affect the future growth or sustainability of exports from Mexican subsidiaries.

Independent party transactions, on the other hand, involve a different set of growth assumptions. These considerations may more closely resemble conventional reasoning about the growth of international demand and the comparative efficiency of Mexican exports in the face of international competitors.

To analyze the type of trade corresponding to the major export products thus far discussed, we must rely on information from individual firms. Our primary information source is direct interviews with some of the firms leading the export drive in crucial industries: automobiles, chemicals, electronics, and iron-steel tubes. In this paper we are supplementing information introduced in earlier works.[24]

Although each industry employs a variety of marketing practices, in general, electronics exports are traded intra-firm; the automobile and chemical industries participate in either intra-firm trades or trading with independent parties; steel tubes are exported to independent buyers often involved in large projects that set limits on the use of Mexican tubes.

Automobile exports behave differently, depending on whether the exporters are foreign or domestically owned. Foreign firms use three types of operations. Two involve the large TNC assemblers and the third involves ventures with other foreign firms. For example, engine and automobile exports from Chrysler, Ford and General Motors very clearly show the importance of economies of scale. They also show the importance of economies of plant scope—plants that were originally designed to serve export markets through intra-firm sales. Generally, the U.S. parent company and the Canadian subsidiary are the major destinations of these exports, as Table 9 indicates. Since these exports already utilize most of the installed capacity of their Mexican plants, little room remains for further growth in the medium term.[25] In these cases, additional ex-

TABLE 9

AUTOPARTS EXPORTS BY MAJOR EXPORT FIRMS
(*percentages*)

Firms	Related Exports	Country of Destination
Group 1: Domestic Firms	*Indirect Exports*	
Arbomex	96	U.S. (100)
Bocar	70	U.S. (30), Brazil (30), West Germany (30)
Cifunsa	100	U.S. (100)
Grupo Industrial Ramirez	0	U.S. (100)
Mar-Hino	100	U.S. (100)
Rassini	10	U.S. (95), Canada (5)
Tebo	20	U.S. (50), France (50)
Vehiculos y Componentes	0	Venezuela (90)
Group 2: Foreign Firms	*Exports to Affiliates*	
Bendix Mexicana	0	U.S. (80), Taiwan (10), Korea (10)
Carplastic	100	U.S. (75), Canada (22)
Chrysler—Saltillo	100	U.S. (100)
Ford-Chihuahua	100	U.S. (60), Canada (40)
General Motors—Ramos Arizpe	100	U.S. (100)
Metalsa	100	U.S. (100)
Nemak	88	U.S. (52), Canada (48)
Sector Autopartes Condumex	50	U.S. (100)
Spicer	98	U.S. (100)
Vitroflex	100	U.S., West Germany, Brazil

Source: Kurt Unger, Las Exportaciones Mexicanas Ante La Restructuracion Industrial Internacional. La Evidencia de Las Industrias Quimica y Automotriz, (México: FCE-ECM), 1989, p. 240.

ports could only come from new investment in export-oriented plants, investments that most TNCs have not made in recent years and do not appear likely to make anytime in the foreseeable future. In fact, we have already discussed the stagnating trend of these exports in 1988 and 1989, and demonstrated that this results both from the exhaustion of installed capacity in engine-producing plants as well as the limited demand for vehicle exports, given the short product life cycle left in most of the mature vehicle models assembled for export from Mexico.[26]

A second type of export involves auto parts generated from joint ventures among the same TNC assemblers and large domestic conglomerates that have production advantages gained through their experience in related fields. Such is the case with relatively new plants built to export windshields (Vitroflex), engine heads (Nemak), plastic components (Carplastic), and wiring harnesses (Condumex). Most of these exports are intra-firm sales, although in some cases parts are sold in open markets.[27] In these instances, the Mexican counterparts of these TNCs can be expected to contribute significantly in the form of economies of scope, given the Mexican firms' ability to supply their own basic raw materials, which would be enhanced by these firms' use of installations, training plans and the learning accumulated through experience.

Growth prospects for these exports imply that other sources of parts and components—independent auto parts producers or TNC plants in the process of industrial restructuring within the U.S.-Canadian area—will be displaced. Both TNC trade and industrial strategy and U.S. trade policy will determine the production volume of these components to be allocated to countries that can produce them less expensively. But it may be safe to assume that Mexico's rapid gains of past years are not going to be repeated without competition from the displaced firms.

A third export transaction involves foreign owned automobile parts producers in Mexico that do not belong to the assembly industry. These firms export relatively mature parts and components in which competition and technological change help to reduce production costs. These exports may be sales in open markets or indirect exports in the form of parts that are assembled into larger components, which are then exported by the assembler. This sector's growth seems limited by the nature of mature, highly competitive products.

Domestically owned auto parts exporters present a different case. Their propensity to export is more moderate because they are targeting the domestic market.[28] These firms are occasional or temporary exporters, especially since their products are typically mature, standardized components in the process of being replaced by new products. When they do export, these domestic firms deal primarily with independent buyers in the United States. Some of their exports are indirect—products integrated into larger components.

Table 10 divides chemical exports into two clearly different groups: new/modern/innovative products used in intra-firm trades and commodities traded in open international markets. The commodities are standardized, intermediate inputs subject to cost competition on international markets.[29] Most of the comparative advantage of these products rests on Mexico's natural resources, as in the case of petrochemical commodities, which are in abundant supply and less costly to produce in Mexico.

Other factors also account for the propensity of domestic firms to export commodities. The maturity of their process technology is widely diffused, and the few large conglomerates that are either diversified or well integrated in the domestic supply of basic raw materials enjoy economies of scope. This is probably why firms like PRIMEX, Sintesis Organicas and Resistol will continue to be successful exporters in the future.[30]

TABLE 10

CHEMICAL EXPORTS BY MAJOR EXPORT FIRMS
(percentages)

Products & Firms	Exports to Affiliates	Domestic Integration	Country of Destination
Group II "Commodities"	·		
Polycarboxyl Acids			
Derivados Maleicos	0	high (100)	East Asia
Prom. Ind. Mexicanas—Primex	0	high (75)	China, Indonesia
Sintesis Organicas	0	high (80)	U.S., Taiwan
Hydrofluoric Acid			
Quimica Fluor	80	high (80)	U.S.
Polyvinyl Chloride			
Prom. Ind. Mexicanas—Primex	0	high (80)	Japan
Synthetic Fibers			
Industrias Resistol	4	high (80)	U.S. & L.A.
Group 2: "Modern Products"			
Dyes and Varnish			
Quimica Hoechst de México	90	low (5)	Brazil
Basf Mexicana	70	low (30)	Central America
Plastic Products			
Productos Darex	92	low (40)	Costa Rica
Pharmaceuticals			
Searle de México	100	low (40)	Brazil
Quimica Hoechst de México	100	medium (50)	Latin America
Films			
Ind. Fotografica Interamericana	100	medium (60)	Brazil

Source: Kurt Unger, Las Exportaciones Mexicanas . . . , p. 164.

Some intra-firm chemical exports are much less dependent on natural resource advantages, as Table 10 indicates. In fact, some of these products are only about 40 percent integrated—one half the integration level of other commodities. In these cases, the behavior of exports derives largely from the global strategy of the TNCs that rationalize the production operations of their conglomerates by concentrating each product line in a limited number of plants with regional scope. These products are exported primarily to other Latin American nations, as Table 10 also shows. Specifically, for these exports, the rigidity of plant design forces the conglomerate to produce in volumes too excessive for any single market. This factor explains, for example, the behavior of Eastman Kodak exports, as well as some of the major products exported by Hoechst, Basf and Searle. In each case the TNC distributes its products regionally among its plants, integrating the products in a mutual exchange of exports and imports whose comparative advantage is not always evident.

Today, microcomputers are a successful export from Mexico, but until 1986, IBM and Hewlett Packard's minicomputers dominated this export sector. IBM's minicomputer accounted for 40 percent of sector exports, and Hewlett Packard's minicomputer accounted for 20 percent.[31] By 1988, microcomputers were leading the market. They were produced primarily in a new IBM plant which permitted IBM to increase exports by more than $100 million for a 62.4 percent share of the computer export market in 1987.

Both microcomputer and minicomputers are assembled in Mexico with imported inputs. This assembly process is the special focus of IBM and Hewlett Packard's newer plants. Other firms are more integrated with Mexican domestic materials. Until recently, Unysis-Compubur, IEPRO and Printaform appeared to be increasing their domestic integration.[32] But despite the overwhelming size of the computer giants in Mexico, it is essentially a screwdriver industry based on assembling components and on assembly kits that are almost entirely imported.[33]

Except for Compubur and IEPRO, the domestic content of Mexico's leading computer exports is generally less than 10 percent, as Table 11 shows. IBM's domestic content for both micros and minis is even smaller at 3 percent to 6 percent. Thus, the expansion of IBM's export production facilities in Mexico in 1987 has meant a more than proportional growth in imports, which reduced the domestic content in direct production costs for microcomputers from 24.6 percent in 1986 to 6.5 percent in 1987. For minis the drop was 23.3 percent in 1986 to 17.1 percent in 1987.

In assuming that these export products take advantage of low cost Mexican labor and plant overhead, we can then consider computer exports as standard, mature assembly activities that achieve a good competitive edge in countries like Mexico. But this is not an indication of "high-tech" activities.

The TNC strategy in computers has other international dimensions as well. The microcomputers that IBM exports come from a new Mexican plant authorized in 1985 and completed in late 1986. This plant produces the PC-51 which previously was produced in IBM's Boca Raton, Florida

TABLE 11

DOMESTIC CONTENT IN MAIN FIRMS EXPORTING MACHINES
TO PROCESS INFORMATION
(percentages)

| DOMESTIC CONTENT | IBM de MÉXICO | | | | HEWLETT | COMPUBUR | | DATA GENERAL | | WANG | | IEPRO | |
| | Micros | | Minis | | Minis | | | | | | | | |
	1986	1987	1986	1987	1986	1986	1987	1986	1987	1986	1987	1986	1987
As a Percentage on the Direct Cost	24.6	6.5	23.3	17.1	17.7	39.5	39.6	17.3	18.0	4.8	17.2	50.5	70.0
As a Percentage on the Cost of Raw Materials, Parts and Components	2.5	2.7	6.5	5.9	9.0	37.6	37.6	1.7	3.3	0.7	10.1	59.2	75.5

Source: Dirección de Industria Electronica, Secofi.

plant.[34] This product has a wide range of export destinations in developed nations like the United States, Canada, Japan and Australia, which signifies that IBM's Mexican plant has been told to produce on economies of scale that will satisfy worldwide organizational demand for that particular product line. Future growth of IBM exports from Mexico would require the relocation of another IBM productive activity, a step that IBM has told the Mexican government it cannot easily undertake.[35]

Finally, steel tube exports may represent two additional types of trade. One type involves the export of tubes to the United States, when those tubes can compete effectively against other domestic and foreign suppliers. The second trade transaction involves exports of tubes that are dependent on international sales of large civil works projects that are usually government-funded. Most of the seamless tubes exported for oil operations to the United States are competitive products, even though the firm exploiting the competitive advantage of Mexican labor and energy costs is operating with U.S. capital. Those tubes with less technological sophistication usually involve joint ventures among a firm with Japanese participation and several parastatal firms.

The tubes that are used in large public works projects are interesting in that they frequently become part of larger technology and product packages traded among industrializing countries. One recent example was the package sold to Argentina for the construction of a gas pipeline. The tube exports are dependent on a package sale, which means they are dependent on the design, engineering and installation by several Mexican engineering firms. In the Argentine case, those were Ingenieros Civiles Asociados, Instituto Mexicano del Petroleo and Protexa. The Argentine package also involved a new financing mechanism, compensated trade, as part of the marketing plan.

VI. CONCLUDING REMARKS

The variety of trade transactions described here indicates a need for additional analysis on trade policy utilizing disaggregated schemes. This will be important in future attempts to assess the type of export that Mexico can realistically hope to augment. A thorough assessment of Mexico's trade policy must take into account the conditions relevant to each type of export transaction, not just the macrodeterminants of trade that may be necessary but not by themselves sufficient for international competitiveness. The product-firm approach gives us the information necessary to avoid the risks of simplistic analysis based on the extrapolation of events in the recent past.

We have defined some basic differences between intra-firm traded products and open-market commodity trade. The most interesting and dynamic exports are intra-firm traded, though there have been a few successes in commodity exports. For commodities, the logic of the comparative advantage paradigm still works, to a degree. When competitive pricing is the basis for international sales, the conventional tools for reducing costs are indeed very important. Thus, the rate of exchange, wages, interest rates, transport and energy costs and low-priced, resource-based inputs may play a determining role in the future of these exports. Nevertheless, on the demand side, barriers exist to the increased exports of these products and realistic assessments must take this into account.

For intra-firm trading, important differences exist in product and firm type, not only on the basis of foreign or domestic ownership, but also in the size and position of the Mexican subsidiary within the vertical or horizontal integration strategy that the conglomerate implements.

When all elements of the TNC strategy are considered, our analysis takes us far afield from the conventional comparative advantage paradigm that focuses on labor cost advantages. These exports are best explained by export performance requirements that TNCs use to secure a solid domestic position. Once that position is attained, additional exports beyond bare requirements may not be forthcoming. In fact, we argue that the recent decline in the growth rate of Mexican intra-firm exports is evidence of the exhaustion of the potential provided by installed capacity in several of the larger TNC plants built to respond to government requirements for export performance. For the majority of these firms, additional investments to increase installed capacity are not taking place and do not appear in the short-term plans of these major firms.

The automobile and computer industries, and some sectors of the chemical industry, follow this pattern. For these products, the leading TNCs export very successfully from their Mexican subsidiaries, but these exports are destined either to the parent company, which is usually in the United States, or to other subsidiaries. Past growth trends cannot continue, given the TNCs' internal logic in responding to capacity installation for the conglomerate as a whole—a logic that goes far beyond the competitive virtues of the Mexican subsidiary per se.

The economies of scale and the TNC logic for plant location are among the most important factors affecting exports. TNCs make decisions on plant installations that will best provide the volume needed by the whole conglomerate to operate efficiently. TNCs locate these plants in areas that best allow them to strike a balance between their ability to import and export in certain target areas. Thus, their decisions to build Mexican plants are not based solely on the nation's competitive advantage. In fact, their decisions are based on very complex motivations that demand careful analysis with ever more sophisticated tools.

NOTES

1. Instituto Nacional de Estadística, Geografía Informática, *Estadísticas del Comercio Exterior de México*, vol. 11, no. 12 (1989) p. 13.

2. In 1985 internal demand rallied again, which created an immediate export contraction in nearly all industries. See Table 1.

3. This trend was confirmed during the first seven months of 1989, when the growth rate was 7.1 percent in comparison to the manufactured product exports during January through July 1988. See *Comercio Exterior,* vol. 39, no. 12 (1989) p. 1106.

4. See UNIDO, *World Industry in 1980* (New York: United Nations, 1981). Technological dynamism is adopted there to analyze revealed comparative advantages. Technological dynamism is two-tiered. First, resource-based industries must be separated. Second, nonresource-based industries are divided into new-modern and mature industries in line with the product life cycle theory, which estimates the yearly rate of introduction of new products of each industry. This is Finger's version of the theory.

5. Instituto Nacional de Estadística, Geografía e Informática, *Cuaderno de Información Oportuna*, No. 179. (Mexico City: INEGI, 1988).

6. Our estimates are based on the SITC fractions corresponding to the 51 most important products in those years. For products of lesser importance, the United States is even more important: about 97 percent of these exports go to the United States.

7. Cf. Gerald Helleiner and Real Lavergne, "Intra-firm Trade and Industrial Exports to the United States," *Oxford Bulletin of Economics and Statistics*, vol. 41, no. 4 (1979) p. 307. Recently, intra-firm exports have become more important. In 1977, 71 percent of manufactured imports to the United States from Mexico were intra-firm traded. That percentage may well have increased recently given the dynamic growth of the automobile industry exports. Nevertheless, it is important to distinguish between industries: 96 percent of electrical machinery imports into the United States from Mexico are traded intra-firm, but only 10 percent of textile products were traded in this manner.

8. Omitted from this group are several chemicals and steel products similar to the mature products traded in open markets. Most of them are sold in the United States, including polyvinyl chloride, polystyrene, plastic products, and most of the iron-steel products. Colombia, Argentina and other countries also receive these products.

9. Typewriters have been steadily losing importance among export products, although they still remain within the 70 largest products in 1988. Since 1982, typewriter exports have hovered around $30 million per year. In 1982 and 1983, they were at their peak, (in constant prices), when they represented nearly 1 percent of total manufactured exports.

10. See Rhys Jenkins, *Foreign Firms, Exports of Manufactures and the Mexican Econ-*

omy. Monographs in Development Studies, No. 7, School of Development Studies. (Norwich: University of East Anglia, 1979) p. 165.

11. Writers on all fronts are involved in the debate. At one extreme, the TNC is viewed as the major obstacle to development. Most dependency writers could be included in this group: Dos Santos, Sunkel, Cardoso, and later Fajnyzlber, Evans, Gereffi, Newfarmer, etc. At the other extreme, writers like Baranson, Willander, Johnson and Vernon have argued the benefits of the TNC as the modernizing vehicle for less developed countries. Most writers are middle of the road. Two recent compilations testify to the continuing controversy over this issue. See Theodore Moran (ed.), *Multinational Corporations: The Political Economy of Foreign Direct Investment* (Massachusetts: Lexington Books, 1985); and Alice Techova, Maurice Lévy-Leboyer and Helga Nussbaum (eds.), *Multinational Enterprise in Historical Perspective* (Cambridge, G.B.: Cambridge University Press and Maison des Sciences de'l Homme, 1986). Other references to TNCs and LDCs in the context of globalization can be found in Kurt Unger and Luz Saldaña, *Multinational Corporations, Global Strategies and Technical Change: Implications for Industrializing Countries,* Progress Report to the U.S.-Mexican Studies Center of the University of California at San Diego, June 1989, pp. 1–57.

12. The general lack of information on foreign firms in Mexico may not be due solely to policymakers' cautious definitions of foreign ownership and control. Such a careful approach may well be justified given the uncertain implications still pouring out of the dependency debate. But in the Mexican case, caution has certainly been taken to the extreme, creating speculation that caution has become an excuse for maintaining control over delicate information.

13. For the years in which data can be readily separated for varying manufactured exports, foreign firms have taken on greater significance, particularly for the less traditional goods. In 1975 and 1978, foreign firms accounted for 60 percent to 70 percent of nontraditional manufactured exports (excluding nondurable consumer goods). See Kurt Unger, *Competencia Monopólica y Tecnología en la Industria Mexicana* (Mexico City: El Colegio de México, 1985) pp. 29–30.

14. Cf. Wilson Peres, *Foreign Direct Investment and Industrial Development in Mexico* (Paris: Organization of Economic Cooperation and Development, Development Centre, 1989) p. 66.

15. After all, the bulk of foreign investment comes from the United States, which had a total foreign investment of 65.5 percent in 1987. This was reported by the National Commission on Foreign Investment in its *Informe, 1983–1987.* (Mexico City: Comisión Nacional de Inversiones Extranjeras, 1988) p. 10. Foreign firms' propensity to export may not vary significantly by country of origin, although in certain manufacturing sectors the propensity to export is higher for U.S. subsidiaries operating in Mexico. See, for instance, the comparison with Swedish subsidiaries in Magnus Blomstrom and Richard Lipsey "The Export Performance of Swedish and U.S. Multinationals," National Bureau of Economic Research, Working Paper Series 2081, 1986. When compared to U.S. TNCs, Swedish TNCs supply more of their foreign market with home productions, and they import relatively little from their foreign operations.

16. One indication of the size and power of these firms lies in their U.S. industrial

rankings. See Fortune's 500 largest industrial corporations in *Fortune*, 28 April 1986 pp. 212–214.

17. The most clear-cut case is Renault, which ceased to assemble cars for the domestic market in 1987. Renault had set up an engine plant a few years earlier, which is responsible for the export of engines and engine parts.

18. Nissan's Mexican investment more closely resembles what Kojima characterized as American-style foreign investment aimed at securing a share of a protected domestic market, rather than what he calls the "trade-oriented" model of Japanese investment. See Kijoshi Kojima, *Japanese Direct Foreign Investment: A Model of Multinational Business Operations* (Tokyo: Tuttle Co., 1978) pp. 85–90. In fact, the recent export performance of U.S. and Japanese firms in Mexico reverses Kojima's characterization.

19. These firms are ranked among the top 10 U.S. firms within their own industrial sectors, according to the Fortune 500 list of the largest industrial corporations. See *Fortune*, 28 April 1986.

20. Typewriters are, in fact, a product in decline, as previously stated. At constant prices, typewriter exports have been declining for the last four years. As for the potential growth of computer exports, this issue must be placed in a broader context that takes into account the link between the export goals and the domestic market position that IBM and Hewlett Packard enjoy. It can be argued that exports have played a strategic role in securing a privileged place for these firms in Mexico, which allowed them to erase most of their competitors by responding quickly to exports. Now that they are clearly export leaders, they have no need for this strategy.

21. One indication of this was clearly stated during recent interviews at the Connecticut and New Jersey headquarters of some of these firms.

22. Videotec de México is a wholly owned subsidiary of a large Japanese corporation, although the Mexican subsidiary is reportedly under the control of a U.S. subsidiary. See Victor Kerber and Antonio Ocaranza , "Las maquiladoras japonesas en la relación entre México y Estados Unidos," *Comercio Exterior*, vol. 39, no. 10, (October 1989) p. 838.

23. Cf. Julio Nogues, "Los casos de aranceles compensatorios de Estados Unidos en contra de México," *Estudios Económicos*, vol. 1–2, 1986. He indicates a very high concentration of trade conflict existing between the United States and Mexico in the more domestically based industries.

24. Cf. Kurt Unger, *Las Exportaciones Mexicanas ante la Restructuración Industrial Internacional: La evidencia de las Industrias Química y Automotriz* (Mexico City: Fondo de Cultura Económica and El Colegio de México, 1990); Wilson Peres, *Foreign Direct Investment and Industrial Development in Mexico*, op. cit.; and Kurt Unger and Luz Saldaña, "Las economías de escala y de alcance en las exportaciones mexicanas más dinámicas," *El Trimestre Económico*, vol. 56(2), no. 222 (1989).

25. The argument about the exhaustion of installed capacity best explains the recent drop in engine export performance. For both engines and automobiles, the

prospects for future export expansion are not as bright as they once were. This point was succinctly made in recent interviews with senior officers of TNCs in Detroit. Ford's strategy to source components externally by promoting a world-wide system of competitive specialization involves high risks for the engines plant at Chihuahua. The Ford plant may stay out of the competition if design and other supporting activities cannot be supplied on site when the new model engine is produced in two-to-three years. General Motor's policy favoring increased vertical integration may allow for better use of installed capacity, but the firm must be careful not to expand capacity unless it can guarantee full use of the additional capacity.

26. Automobiles showed only moderate export growth in 1988 and the first part of 1989. This growth was due primarily to Chrysler's exports of its Le Baron, Shadow and Sundance models, which compensated for a reduction in Ford exports. Ford stopped production in its Hermosillo plant, which had exported the Tracer model. The plant is now preparing for a new export model this year.

27. The first three involve Ford's joint ventures with Vitro, Visa and Alfa. Condumex engaged in ventures with General Motors. Condumex exports a significant amount to independent buyers in the United States. See Table 9.

28. Domestic firms frequently request compensatory quotas to exporters from Brazil and similar countries, giving one indication of these firms' domestic market orientation. For an example, see the case of suspension parts in "Recuento Nacional," *Comercio Exterior,* vol 39, no. 10 (October 1989) p. 848.

29. Some commodity exports may take the form of intra-firm trades. Such was the case with Quimica Fluor, which exported to DuPont in the United States (See Table 10). One interviewee told us, however, that these transactions are also subject to price competition on international markets.

30. Resistol is considered a local firm in spite of its association with Monsanto because Resistol controls these exports. Resistol is also linked to other firms in other industrial activities through a conglomerate called DESC. Primex is also a part of the large and diversified conglomerate of Condumex.

31. In 1986, minicomputer exports totaled $78.8 million, nearly three times as much as microcomputer exports. Other important computer exporters included Compubur with 13 percent, Tandem with 6 percent, Data General with 4 percent, and IEPRO with 4 percent. For additional details, see Kurt Unger and Luz Saldaña, "Las economías de escala y de alcance," p. 482.

32. This is the trend according to Wilson Peres, *Foreign Direct Investment and Industrial Development in Mexico,* p. 205.

33. See, for instance, William Cline, *Informatics and Development: Trade and Industrial Policy in Argentina, Brazil and Mexico* (Washington, D.C.: Economics International, Inc., 1987). On the whole, however, it would be unfair to say that the issue of trends in domestic integration has been settled. A conclusive assessment may be premature, but existing evidence does not support Peres' optimism, when he said, ". . . in comparison with an export-import ratio of one-to-one with which Compubur operates, Apple and H. Packard (having opted for the 100 percent for-

eign ownership) are required to have a three-to-one ratio. Such a restriction is far from being irrelevant, as is shown by the impossibility of fulfilling it on the part of Apple, an enterprise which gave up making micros in Mexico in late 1987." (p. 187). Meeting the target is another matter. IBM's agreement involving a two-to-one ratio of exports to imports, for instance, has not yet been attained. This situation resembles that of the automobile industry throughout the 1970s, when firms delayed each year in fulfilling promises to compensate imports with exports. If the domestic market regained growth, imports would continue to exceed exports. On the other hand, IBM's bargaining power has clearly grown as a result of Apple's shutdown. IBM's power is also enhanced because of "the magnitude of the capacity which a firm of world importance such as IBM has installed (100,000 machines in a market in which at the time of approval absorbed at the very most 30,000 or 40,000) leading to a situation of almost total control over the market." (Cline, p. 186).

34. The replacement of the Boca Raton plant is itself another issue for corporate strategy research. Only two years before IBM decided to move its operations to Mexico, the plant was used as an example of the success of new managerial approaches, particularly the "smaller-entrepreneur" approach to decentralized management in large firms. See Leslie Wayne, "Los Nuevos Empresarios," *FACETAS*, vol 67, no. 1 (1985) p. 8.

35. During our visit to IBM's Connecticut headquarters, we received a more realistic vision of the limited role the Mexican operation plays within the firm's global strategy. We were left with the impression that IBM had already done its share of the restructuring demanded in its Mexican operation and that little more should be expected from them in the next few years.

9

Crisis, Adjustment and Employment in the Manufacturing Industry of Jalisco

Carlos Alba Vega and Bryan Roberts

I. INTRODUCTION

In this paper, we examine the effect of the economic recession that began in Mexico in 1982 on the structure of employment in Jalisco whose capital, Guadalajara, is Mexico's second largest city and third most important manufacturing center. We pay special attention to changes in the demand for labor between sectors of manufacturing industry and between the so-called formal and informal sectors of the economy.[1]

Up to the late 1970s, Jalisco, like the rest of Mexico, had an impressive record of expanding its non-agricultural labor force while generating increases in the real wage.[2] This occurred despite very high rates of increase in the urban economically active population due to rural-urban migration and high rates of natural increase. Guadalajara, in particular, grew rapidly through absorbing labor in medium- and small-scale enterprises in manufacturing, commerce and other services.[3] Despite the capacity of its urban sector to absorb labor, Jalisco had an important role in international migration, supplying in 1973 an estimated 26 percent of Mexican migration to the United States.[4] The majority of these migrants were, however, temporary. Until the 1980s, the characteristic pattern of permanent migration in Jalisco was rural-urban migration directed mainly towards Guadalajara. As a consequence, the rural population of Jalisco and that of the other states of the western region of Mexico grew very slowly, gaining their livelihoods mainly from rain-fed agriculture on small plots of land, complemented by non-agricultural activities, including domestic out-working and temporary migration.

In the 1980s, Jalisco changed its economic growth model. It became one of the leading regions of Mexico to adopt an export-oriented manufacturing strategy to overcome the exhausting of import-substituting industrialization as a source of economic growth and employment generation. This economic restructuring is likely, however, to change the demand for labor since many of the new export-oriented enterprises are technologically sophisticated and require skilled workers.

This restructuring coincides with a weakening of some of the traditional sources of labor absorption. Economic stagnation in many rural areas is intensifying the rural exodus.[5] Furthermore, there has been a deterioration in the terms of exchange between agricultural and industrial products, reducing the incentives for the more traditional agricultural and livestock production. Imports of cheap manufactures from Asia negatively affect small-scale manufacturing and out-working in garments and shoes, much of which has been located in the small towns and villages of the region. Competition from imports and a depressed domestic market are also likely to affect urban employment, particularly in the labor-intensive industries that cater to the internal market, such as textiles, garments and shoes. Temporary international migration is likely to be less of a safety valve than in the past, so that Jalisco may require special attention to counteract the negative employment effects of the closing of the United States labor market.[6]

In the following sections, we examine the employment consequences of this economic restructuring, paying particular attention to the manufacturing sector. Though this sector is not the major source of urban employment, it is an important one in Jalisco. The trajectory of Jalisco's manufacturing sector in the 1980s gives some indication of both the possibilities and the obstacles faced by the Mexican economy in the 1990s, particularly in absorbing productively the continuing high rates of increase in its economically active population. The data we use comes from a variety of sources, though our principal source is an industrial survey carried out in 1989, which we will compare with one based on the same sampling procedures, and using many of the same questions, carried out in 1982.[7] We will complement this information with official statistics, the results of other employment studies of the region, and interviews that we conducted with entrepreneurs in different sectors of manufacturing industry and with officials of industrial associations.

II. THE INDUSTRIAL STRUCTURE BY THE END OF THE 1970S

In this section, we briefly describe the industrial structure of Jalisco in the late 1970s, locating it within Mexico's overall pattern of industrial development. This pattern of development followed the import-substitution pattern common to Latin America between the 1940s and the 1970s, in which a preliminary phase of basic goods industries (food, drink, textiles, shoes and garments) was replaced by one in which growth began to concentrate in intermediate, capital and durable consumer goods—though the development of these industries was relatively slow. Mexico's main industrial regions—Mexico City, Monterrey and Guadalajara—occupied different roles within this overall pattern of development. Guadalajara remained a center of basic goods production for the regional and national market, so that by 1980, 56.8 percent of the value of production was in basic goods, compared with 27.3 percent for Monterrey and 32.8 percent for Mexico City. In contrast, Monterrey concentrated on intermediate goods production which, in that year, made up 49.1 percent of the product and Mexico City showed a diversified industrial structure with consumer durables, intermediate and capital goods sharing employment with basic goods industries.[8]

Guadalajara's role in Mexico's industrial structure has been based on the links between the city and its region. This region—the west of Mexico—is densely populated, well-communicated to Guadalajara, and contains important areas of commercial agriculture. The trade flows within the region created a demand for basic industrial products which were supplied by small- and medium-scale enterprises, almost all of which were family enterprises. With very few exceptions, local industrial enterprises in Guadalajara were family-owned.

High rates of population growth, combined with extensive commercialization of the rural economy, generated considerable population mobility. Migration to the United States began in the last years of the nineteenth century, and the accumulation of contacts, especially with California, ensured that labor migration from Jalisco to the United States continued into the twentieth century. The major shift in population was, however, to Guadalajara, which increased its predominance in the region from 16 percent of Jalisco's population in 1940 to 58 percent in 1980.

The contrast with Monterrey is a sharp one. Monterrey's immediate hinterland was sparsely populated, and agriculture and livestock raising relatively poor. Instead of growing on the basis of regional commerce, as did Guadalajara, Monterrey developed as a commercial entry port for the United States and on the basis of its relation with extractive industry.[9] Large-scale enterprises in engineering, metal production, glass and beer production formed complexes that were integrated vertically and served national and international markets. Though these enterprises were also family-owned, marital alliances created an informal corporate structure very different from the individual family enterprises of Guadalajara.

The differences in industrial structure between the major cities had employment consequences. Guadalajara had the most manufacturing employment in small-scale enterprises of the three major Mexican cities, and the most self-employment. In a 1976 official survey of the extent of informal employment in Mexico, Guadalajara showed the highest informal jobs (41.5 percent) of the three cities.[10]

The importance of the small- and medium-scale enterprise in Guadalajara resulted in flexible and dynamic labor markets. The skilled labor supply to large enterprises in sectors such as footwear was trained in small informal workshops.[11] Subcontracting was extensive, with large enterprises subcontracting to workshops, and these workshops contracting out to domestic workers.[12] Wage rates for workers with comparable qualifications were similar between large-scale and small-scale enterprise sectors, and movement between these sectors was common. Workers made trade-offs between the security and welfare protection of the large-scale enterprise, and the high piece-work rates that skilled workers could earn in the workshop sector.

The attraction of Guadalajara as a supplier of skilled and unskilled labor, together with its geographical location, was cited in 1963 by large-scale entrepreneurs as a reason for preferred location in the city.[13] In the 1960s, various modern intermediate, capital and durable consumer goods industries, such as Motorola, Siemens, International Business Machines, Ciba-Geigy and Kodak, located in the city.[14] Many of these were foreign-owned, and most were controlled by extra-regional capital from Mexico City and Monterrey.

III. THE IMPACT OF THE CRISIS ON EMPLOYMENT

Beginning in 1981, Mexico entered a severe recession linked to the external debt and the fall in oil prices. The impact of the recession on employment was immediate, so that between December 1981 and December 1982, there was a drop of more than 60,000 registered workers in the manufacturing industry.[15] Official figures cited by the Economic Commission for Latin America and the Caribbean (ECLAC) indicate that Mexico suffered the most drastic restructuring of employment of any Latin American country.[16] Between 1980 and 1987, the informal urban sector in Mexico increased from 24.2 percent of the total non-agricultural employed population to 33 percent. Public employment increased slightly from 21.8 percent to 25.5 percent, reflecting the nationalization of the banks in 1982. In contrast, employment in large-scale private enterprises declined from 29.1 percent of the total to 21.6 percent, and in small-scale private enterprises from 24.9 percent to 19.8 percent.[17]   This informalization of the urban labor market is produced both by the transfer of workers from the formal to the informal sector as self-employed or family workers, and by the increasing numbers of new entrants to the labor force who begin as informal workers. In Guadalajara, the number of self-employed and unpaid workers increased between 1976 and 1987 from 17.5 percent to 22.7 percent, and this increase was particularly marked among males (See Table 1).

In the manufacturing sector, there was a recuperation of employment in Mexico between 1981 and 1988, as measured by registration with social security. Between December 1981 and December 1987, total registrations of permanent workers rose from 2,248,401 to 2,546,297, an average annual rate of growth of 2.1 percent.[18] In these years, the rate of growth of the economically active population was 3.1 percent.[19] The growth of manufacturing employment differed among the major regions. Jalisco showed the largest annual rate of increase in registered industrial workers (2.8 percent), followed by Nuevo Leon (0.6 percent), with the metropolitan area of Mexico City showing a small average decline (-0.02 percent). The possibility that the Mexico City metropolitan area is de-industrializing is also suggested by the results of the 1985 industrial census. Using this source, Gustavo Garza and Enrique Aguilar show the decline in the number of

TABLE 1

CHANGES IN EMPLOYMENT CATEGORY METROPOLITAN AREA
OF GUADALAJARA: 1976–1987
(percentages)

Work Position	Total	1976 Male	Female	Total	1987 Male	Female
Wage Workers	79.3	78.7	80.4	71.7	71.1	72.8
Employers	3.2	4.2	1.2	5.6	7.7	1.3
Self-employed	13.4	14.0	12.3	15.9	17.0	13.7
Family Worker	4.1	3.1	6.1	6.8	4.1	12.2
TOTAL	100.0	100.0	100.0	100.0	100.0	100.0
(000s)	(932.1)	(628.4)	(304.1)	(638.4)	(417)	(221.3)

Source: Secretaría de Programación y Presupuesto (SPP), *La Ocupación Informal en Areas Urbanas 1976* (México, D.F.: SPP, 1979); Instituto Nacional de Estadística, Geografía y Informática (INEGI), *Encuesta Nacional de Empleo Urbano: Trimestre enero-marzo 1987* (Augascalientes, México: INEGI, 1989).

industrial establishments and in the number of persons employed in Mexico City, arguing that with the recession those working in small-scale enterprises have passed to the informal sector.

Despite the growth of manufacturing employment, there was a shift towards service employment between 1976 and 1987 (See Table 2). Professional and technical service employment grew fastest, but there was also an increase in the proportions of people working in the low-paying services such as commerce and personal services. Particularly notable is the sharp drop in the proportions of males employed in manufacturing, and the increasing proportions of women employed in manufacturing, especially in the 'other' category which includes the new electronics plants. Male employment has grown fastest in the personal services, particularly the repair sector, and also in professional and technical services. Female employment has also grown in professional and technical services, including the health and educational areas. Female employment growth in commerce is pronounced, but there is a marked decline in the proportions of women employed in domestic service.

The growth of registered workers in Jalisco was unevenly distributed among the different industrial sectors. Among the basic goods industries, registered employment grew fastest in the food and drinks industries (5.3 percent annually between December 1981 and December 1986); whereas footwear and garments showed no growth. Intermediate goods industries such as plastics, paper and chemicals showed a growth of 3.5 percent annually in registered employment between the two dates. In sharp contrast, those industries linked to construction and public works (iron and steel, metal products and construction materials) showed a 25 percent annual decline in registered employment. The fastest growing

TABLE 2

CHANGE IN EMPLOYMENT STRUCTURE BY SECTOR METROPOLITAN AREA OF
GUADALAJARA: 1976–1987
(percentages)

	Total	1976 Males	Females	Total	1987 Males	Females
Agriculture	1.1	1.5	0.2	1.1	1.6	0.3
Manufacture	29.4	35.2	18.9	28.9	30.9	24.8
Food	5.1	7.0	1.5	5.8	6.5	4.2
Clothing/						
Shoes	7.7	6.8	9.6	8.0	7.1	9.7
Other	16.6	21.4	7.8	15.2	17.3	10.9
Construction	7.6	11.1	1.0	7.1	9.9	1.4
Electricity	0.2	0.3	0.2	0.5	0.5	0.5
Transport	5.2	6.5	2.6	4.7	6.2	1.6
Commerce	21.4	20.3	23.6	22.1	20.6	25.3
Personal Service	12.9	5.4	26.9	13.7	11.1	18.8
Food/Lodging	3.9	2.2	7.0	5.7	4.1	8.9
Repair	1.8	2.5	0.3	4.4	6.4	0.2
Domestic	7.2	0.5	19.6	3.6	0.6	9.7
Prof & Technical						
Services	10.9	7.7	16.9	13.4	10.2	19.9
Government	4.7	5.2	3.8	4.0	4.1	3.8
Other Services	6.6	6.9	5.9	4.5	4.9	3.5
Total	100.0	100.0	100.0	100.0	100.0	100.0
(000s)	(638.4)	(417.1)	(221.2)	(932.3)	(628.2)	(304.1)

Source: Secretaría de Programación y Presupuesto (SPP), *La Ocupación Informal en Areas
Urbanas 1976* (México, D.F.: SPP, 1979); Instituto Nacional de Estadística, Geografía
y Informática (INEGI), *Encuesta Nacional de Empleo Urbano: Trimestre enero-marzo
1987* (Aguascalientes, México: INEGI, 1989).

sector of industrial employment in Jalisco was the modern capital and
consumer goods industries, such as electronics, domestic appliances and
transport, which recorded a 8.5 percent annual increase in registered
employment.

These statistics suggest that the recession has shifted employment in
two different directions. Population increase and the concentration of
family budgets on foodstuffs to the exclusion of items like clothing,
shoes, or furniture account for the steady growth of employment in the
food industries. On the other hand, there has clearly been an industrial
restructuring resulting in the increasing importance of industries producing sophisticated products often destined for export markets. Two
such firms are Kodak, which has expanded its production from films to
include computer related items, and Siemens, which produces specialized motors.

These changes in the pattern of employment in Jalisco have not resulted in a greater concentration of employment in large-scale enterprises. The data from the industrial census of 1980 indicates that 59.6 percent of Jalisco's employment was in firms of more than 100 workers; by 1985, firms of this size provided 58.3 percent of employment, according to the preliminary results of the economic census of that year.[20] There has been an increase in the number of industrial enterprises between the two industrial censuses, but this increase is negligible (0.5 percent annually compared with a 2.2 percent annual growth in employment). The increase in the number of establishments is accounted for by the metropolitan area of Guadalajara. Outside the metropolitan area, the number of industrial enterprises has declined, and this decline is most pronounced in the small towns of the state.

One result of this trend is that whereas 60.3 percent of industrial establishments were concentrated in Guadalajara in 1980, the city contained 67.3 percent by 1985. The process of concentration is taking place geographically, with industrial employment increasingly locating in Guadalajara.There is, however, a process of dispersion taking place through informalization. Much of this is occurring in the rural areas of Jalisco where the number of registered small-scale manufacturing enterprises has declined sharply, but where domestic out-working is common, and this type of employment has been increasing with the crisis.[21] Even within Guadalajara, there is some evidence of informalization, as the trend for small-scale manufacturing enterprises to register themselves and become formal, evident until 1981, reversed during the crisis.[22]

IV. THE SIGNIFICANCE OF THE CRISIS FOR DIFFERENT TYPES OF INDUSTRY

In this section, we will outline, with the aid of interviews and the 1989 industrial survey, the ways in which different types of industry have been affected by the crisis: small versus large-scale industries, industries oriented to the domestic market and industries oriented to export.

Small-Scale Industry

In interviews, both large- and small-scale entrepreneurs viewed small-scale industry (25 workers or less) as having suffered most during the crisis. Turnover in the small-scale sector has always been high. In 1981, 53 percent of small-scale firms had been in existence for less than 10 years, compared with 19.6 percent of large firms with 100 workers or more. This turnover appears to have increased by 1985 when 530 of the 921 small firms that had been interviewed in 1981 were no longer registered. In Guadalajara, case studies of small enterprises have reported that workers attached to these have experienced a sharper decline in wages than those working for large-scale enterprises.[23]

Factors that our informants cited as reasons for the difficulties facing small-scale enterprise were, first, that suppliers of raw materials had shortened the time required for payment. Also, the cost of these raw materials was rising rapidly with inflation, and small-scale industry was less able to negotiate favorable terms since purchases were small and sporadic. Credit became almost impossible to obtain for small-scale industry, since the small amount of bank or government credit available was given to medium- and large-scale industry.

The types of product in which small-scale industry had specialized—low-quality and low-cost items—were aimed at the low-income market, which suffered a sharp drop in income during the crisis. Furthermore, these products began to face increasing competition from cheap imports from Asia permitted under the General Agreement on Tariffs and Trade (GATT), particularly since Mexico liberalized its tariff structure more rapidly than required by the agreement. Informants in the small towns of Jalisco and in Guadalajara pointed (at times literally) to Asian shoes and garments in local shops that were undercutting the shoes and clothing produced by local workshops and depriving them of contracts with shops and market traders. In the initial results of the 1989 industrial survey, small-scale firms showed the lowest positive attitudes to Mexico's entry into GATT; only five of 21 small-scale firms saw entry as having beneficial results. In contrast, 53 of the 82 large firms stressed the benefits, and only a minority saw entry as having neutral or negative effects.

A further limitation on small-scale industry is its lack of political representation. All enterprises, no matter their size, must belong to the appropriate Industrial Association (for example, the Association of Food Industries, of Shoes, etc.). These associations act as lobbies on behalf of the industry and have the legal right to be consulted by government over industrial policy. The regional associations are integrated nationally through key officers holding posts at both levels. Thus, the president of the Jalisco industrial associations is also vice-president of the national association, CONCAMIN. However, the associations are dominated by large- and medium-scale industrialists who occupy (or whose subordinates occupy) the key administrative posts. In an interview with a leader of small-scale industrialists, it was made clear to us that the small-scale sector felt government policy was dictated by the interests of large-scale industrialists, resulting in the lack of effective credit for small-scale industry, in the lack of government interest in cooperative schemes for small-scale industry, and in a lack of protection in face of the liberalization of the market.

An indication of the problem is apparent in responses to the 1989 survey. Whereas 16 percent of the large-scale industries had received credit from FOGAIN, the fund intended to stimulate small-scale industry, only one of the 21 small-scale industries reported having received such help. This finding must be set against the fact that Jalisco has benefitted more than other industrial states from FOGAIN during 1980–1987, receiving, in 1987, 15.7 percent of the total credits, compared with 8.8 percent for Nuevo Leon and 7.8 percent for the Federal District.[24]

As a result of adverse conditions, many small- and medium-scale industries appear to have informalized, reducing their labor force and relying on family labor. In conversations, small-scale entrepreneurs who had informalized by reducing their labor force and not registering their businesses, cited the need to lower their fiscal obligations, avoid social security payments and have a lower wage bill. Also, production has become more dispersed geographically through domestic out-work. Since the 1970s, the growth of industrial production, through out-work, has been notable in rural areas and small towns of Jalisco. This production has been concentrated in garments, shoes and other leather goods, handcrafts and some lines of foodstuffs such as cheese and sweets. These activities are labor-intensive, and since they are paid by the piece, they do not require immediate supervision. It is likely that this type of outworking system has filled the gap in demand resulting from the closure of the formally registered small-scale enterprises in these sectors.

The Large- and Medium-Scale Industry

The situation for medium- and large-scale enterprises contrasts with that of small-scale industry. The industrialists whom we interviewed and the officers of various industrial associations were relatively optimistic about the prospects for industry. In contrast to the representatives of small-scale entrepreneurs, these informants welcomed Mexico's entry into GATT and saw many advantages and few disadvantages in new legislation that has facilitated foreign investment in industry. There were some exception to this optimism. Those sectors that depended on the domestic market and saw themselves as having few prospects for exporting were more pessimistic. Thus, representatives of the food industry association saw little immediate prospect of expanding production or improving profitability, except in some specialty lines. In the survey, the industrial firms who were least positive about GATT belonged to the food and other basic goods industries, such as shoes and clothing.

The relative success of medium and large-scale industry in overcoming the crisis is based on three different strategies. The first is that of not making new investments, of reducing the on-plant labor force, using subcontracting to meet fluctuations in demand, and seeking cheaper raw materials to mass-produce poor-quality goods. This strategy is most evident in certain sectors of the food industry, in garments, and in shoes. The markets for their products are heavily concentrated in the metropolitan area of Guadalajara and in the region.

The second strategy is that of investing in new technology, raising productivity, and seeking to produce high-quality goods for the higher income sectors of the national market. In the survey, the firms catering to the national market are mainly found in the durable consumer goods sectors and in electrical and electronic products. Industrialists in other sectors have followed this strategy. One produces furniture for the national market and claims that his products are competitive with imports because of the availability of wood, the use of the latest technology and a qualified and relatively inexpensive labor force. Another produces sweaters through computerized technology. These sweaters are sold throughout Mexico and particularly in the dynamic markets of the northern border. Several Guadalajara industrialists have opened factories in the northern border to meet the demand there.

This second strategy overlaps with the third—that of expanding and opening export markets—since firms successful in expanding their share of the national market are also likely to seek to export. The firms that export some of their product (more than 5 percent), but which do not concentrate on exports, are those with the highest concentration of their sales in the national as opposed to the regional market, averaging 60 percent. Firms with no significant exports are, in contrast, mainly concentrated in the metropolitan and regional market.

Compared with 1981, a higher percentage of large industries are engaged in significant amounts of exporting and have increased the percentage of their products exported. Thus, in 1981, 17 percent of firms with more than 500 workers and 3 percent of firms between 50 and 100 workers exported some of their product, compared to 44 percent of firms larger than 500 and 36 percent of firms between 100 and 500 workers in the present survey. Six of the 87 large firms exported the major part of their product, and another six exported more than a quarter of their product. Guadalajara's *maquiladora* plants fall under these high export categories.

Jalisco enterprises, which now export a considerable part of their production, include firms as diverse as the tequila producing firms, a balloon manufacturing firm, a football factory, a plastic container manufacturer, a key manufacturer, and an exporter of agricultural implements.

Another difference from 1981 is in the financial sources for large- and medium-scale industry. In 1981, these industries made reasonably heavy use of bank credit and government loan programs: more than half of the large industries used credit to acquire raw materials, and about a third of them used it to improve technology and expand the plant.[25] By 1989, there was less evidence of credit use, particularly for restructuring purposes. Thus, only 7 percent of firms with more than 100 workers claimed that they had used long-term credit for purchasing machinery and equipment. The exporting industries are the ones continuing to use credit to expand plants and improve technology. The non-exporting industries are heavily reliant on short-term credits (for salaries etc.), but hardly make use of longer-term credits.

Subcontracting and Labor Rotation

During the crisis, subcontracting has continued as a significant element in the production strategies of large-scale firms. The proportion of large enterprises with more than a 100 workers using subcontracting appears to be little different in 1989 than it was in 1981. In 1981, a quarter of large-scale enterprises subcontracted work. This proportion is 30 percent higher among the 87 large firms surveyed in 1989. The pattern of subcontracting is similar between the two periods: in the earlier period, subcontracting was mainly to small-scale industry, followed by family workshops, while at the later date it is mainly to small-scale industry, with domestic outwork and family workshops being cited less frequently (nine cases of such sub-contracting compared to 27 cases involving small-scale industry).

The subcontracting reported in 1989 showed some signs of the diversity of industrial strategies previously mentioned. Most subcontracting is done by firms catering to regional markets. It is in lines such as shoes, clothing, food and metal-working. The expansion of export-oriented manufacture has, however, also created opportunities for local firms to subcontract part of their production process. Four of the large transnational electronic firms subcontract components to a Mexican electronic company, and quality control is maintained by a computer link.[26] Some of the large transnationals, such as Motorola, produce parts for other electronic enterprises in Guadalajara. Three of the 12 firms in the survey that exported more than 25 percent of their products practiced subcontracting. Cases include a supplier of computer cables and peripherals and a motorcycle parts manufacturer.

Rotation of labor in industrial firms in Jalisco was high in 1981. Thus 17.9 percent of the permanent labor force in large-scale industry secured employment in 1981, and 15.3 percent left the firms during the previous year. Rotation among small-scale firms was substantially higher, 42 percent of the workers having been taken on and a similar proportion having left the firm. In 1981, the reasons for this rotation appeared to be the dynamism of the general economy in which even small-scale enterprises had plenty of work and in which workers, especially skilled ones, could obtain higher wages by moving from one firm to another.

In 1989, rotation of the workforce in large firms seems to have increased; 25.9 percent of the labor force of the large firms had been hired in the previous year and 25.6 percent had left their jobs. In contrast, there was very little rotation reported for the 21 small firms, approximately 10 percent of these were hired and none left. However, the number of small firms reporting is too small for this to be a reliable indicator of change. There is also some indication that large firms are using temporary labor more than they did in 1981. In that year, 11.8 percent of labor in large firms was on temporary contract, whereas in 1989, the proportion had increased to 14.4 percent.

It is difficult to be sure of the reasons for the high rotation of labor. Industrialists complained to us about high labor mobility, and from the point of view of the firm, there seemed to be little benefit in having its permanent labor force turn over at the rates reported. A possible explanation lies in the low minimum salaries which declined in real terms by 45 percent from 1976 to 1985.[27]

Workers, especially those with craft skills, may be seeking work in the informal sector which, although depressed in general terms, provides high piece rate incomes for certain categories of worker and entrepreneur. Another possible reason is migration to the border region where demand for industrial labor is high. The *maquiladora* sector has shown, for instance, 20 percent annual increase and in 1988 accounted for 345,000 jobs mainly located in the north.[28] Migration to the United States has been increasing from the urban areas of Mexico, such as Guadalajara.

The picture that we obtain of the changes in the industrial structure of Jalisco is a mixed one. There is clearly a certain dynamism present both in terms of the growth of the industrial product and in terms of the growth of employment. However, there is also evidence of polarization as small and even medium scale enterprises find it difficult to survive, let alone expand. Consequently, the expansion of industrial employment is occurring not only through modern, highly productive enterprises, but also through informalization. It is to this that we now turn.

V. THE SOCIAL CONSEQUENCES OF THE CHANGING PATTERN OF EMPLOYMENT

The recession has produced, we suggest, a certain restructuring of the Mexican economy, polarizing more sharply than previously formal and informal employment.

There is an increasing demand for skilled personnel at all levels, particularly in the expanding branches of industry, and meeting this demand requires an intensive program of vocational, technical and professional education. The modernization of Jalisco's industry, though partial, has led to a greater demand for administrative and technical personnel and an increasing use of outside technical and other services. Thus, in the 1989 survey, over 30 percent of the labor force of large firms was administrative and technical, compared with 22.8 percent of large firms in 1981. The demand for educationally qualified personnel is, then, on the increase. Added to this is the need for skilled manual labor. Our informants in the large-scale sector cited the shortage of skilled labor as one of the major bottlenecks to improving productivity. There is stagnation in those industrial sectors (construction-related and some of the basic goods industries such as textiles and shoes) that traditionally have been users of unskilled and semi-skilled labor.

Jorge Carillo's 1989 study[29] of the re-structuring of the Mexican automobile industry demonstrates how the change in industrial structure with export industrialization alters the character of formal employment. Mexico has increased its automobile production considerably, mainly by increasing exports. This export-oriented industry is located in the border region, and the characteristics of employment there contrast sharply with those in the old car-producing regions of the center of Mexico. Women are a much higher percentage of the northern labor force, being mainly employed in routine assembly tasks, and they are paid about a third less than their male counterparts, even when the job description is the same. Union affiliation is lower in the north, and the unions are more likely to be company ones.

The *maquiladora* labor force has been heavily female (72 percent), with males contributing only 28 percent to the total labor force of 143,918 in 1983.[30] However, there are indications that male employment has been increasing proportionately due to the lack of alternative employment possibilities. By 1987, male labor made up 38 percent of the total *maquiladora* labor force of 325,400.[31] In Patricia Wilson's 1989 study[32] of *maquiladora* plants, the proportion of males ranged from 49 percent in traditional manufacturing plants, to 37 percent in assembly plants and 34 percent in the new, computer controlled production plants.

The changing structure of industry has, then, implications for both the gender composition and the geographical distribution of formal employment. The formal employment opportunities that are growing fastest are ones in which female participation is high. They are concentrated in the border regions and in regions like Guadalajara, which have also attracted recent foreign investment. The stagnation of traditional industry thus means both an absolute decline in formal job opportunities for males and the likelihood that this loss is geographically concentrated in the old centers of this industry, especially Mexico City. In the case of Monterrey, the loss of jobs in heavy manufacturing is partly compensated by the increase in *maquiladora* plants.

Female employment in Mexican manufacturing rose from 21.2 percent to 25.7 percent between 1980 and 1986.[33] This shift in the characteristics of the manufacturing labor force is apparent in Jalisco. Female labor is on the increase, but is mainly concentrated in the modern industrial sector, particularly in the electronics and related sectors. A total of 24.1 percent of the

permanent labor force in the 1989 survey and 25.2 percent of the temporary labor force were female. In the 1981 survey, 12.7 percent of the industrial labor force and 13 percent of labor in large-scale industry was
reported as female.[34]

Even industries that traditionally have not used female labor are now
beginning to use it. An example is the metal-working industry which has
begun to recruit women to manual jobs because, according to our informants in the firms, they help to stabilize the working environment. The
increase in administrative personnel noted above also has led to an increase in the female labor force. Some of the increase in female employment in Guadalajara is informal. In Luisa Gabayet's 1988 study[35] of
women workers in the Guadalajara *maquiladora* plants, the illegal, casual
contracting of workers on a long-term basis was found to be characteristic
of those assembly plants supplying a larger producer. Some were owned
by American multinationals and some by Mexican capital. In those plants
with a more integrated production, the women had proper contracts. In
all the Guadalajara *maquiladora* plants the women were receiving more
than the minimum wage. The other side of the coin to the growth of, and
change in, formal sector employment is informalization—the concentration of job opportunities outside the modern sector in self-employment,
in low-paid employment in personal services and commerce, or in small
workshops where conditions of work are poor, even though income may,
at times, be competitive with that in the formal sector. We can obtain
some information of the significance of informalization by looking at the
results of a pilot survey of informal enterprise in Mexico City carried out
in 1987–1988.[36] This survey took as its population all enterprises (including self-employment) with six or less people. The employment structure
of these enterprises was made up by 8.4 percent owners, 37.4 percent of
employees or unpaid labor, and 54.2 percent of self-employed workers.

Enterprises were asked whether they fulfilled certain requirements:
registration for fiscal purposes, registration with local government, registration with a relevant industrial association, payment of social security
taxes and, where required, registration with the health inspectorate. The
most frequently reported registration was the fiscal one with which just
over half the enterprises claimed they complied. However, only 15 percent
of enterprises legally bound to register with IMSS said that they did so.
Those who did not register complained most frequently not of excessive
regulation—but of ignorance of the law.

The general picture that emerged from the survey was of an employment sector with little economic dynamism and with few links to the formal sector. Only a fraction of enterprises had any appreciable capital. Almost all the enterprises were self-financed, with friends and relatives
being the only other appreciable source of funds, and hardly any had
made any recent investments in the business. Comparing these enter-

prises with their equivalents in the 1983 income and consumption survey, the authors of the report claimed evidence for an investment decline in the intervening period.

Less than one percent of the enterprises used bank or other formal credits. Nor was there any significant evidence of subcontracting. Less than one percent of enterprises reported subcontracting for others. Only 4.3 percent said that they subcontracted to others. Taxes were only 1 percent of expenses, even for the small businesses with employees. Wages, also, were a relatively minor expense, representing 12 percent for businesses with employees. The major expense was raw materials for all classes of enterprise and all branches of activity. Indeed, when reporting on the difficulties they faced, entrepreneurs overwhelmingly stressed competition, lack of customers and the expense of materials. Fewer than 6 percent cited labor or taxes as important.

The levels of income reported bear out a picture of a depressed economic sector. Over 40 percent of both the self-employed and wage earners claimed to earn less than the minimum salary, at a time when the minimum had already declined by approximately 50 percent compared with 1980. Evidence from Guadalajara shows that workers in informal workshops in the shoe and garment trades had the most severe drop in real incomes between 1982 and 1987—from 50 percent to 60 percent—compared with the 45 percent to 55 percent drop experienced by workers in a large-scale shoe factory and the 15 percent in a successfully exporting steel mill.[37] In the Mexico City survey, only among the owners of small enterprises were earnings, on average, more than the minimum salary, and it was among this group that the distribution showed greater spread, with some earning four or more times the minimum.

The nature of household strategies in the face of the crisis provides further insight into the changing balance of formal and informal employment. First, in 1989, households had more of their members in the labor market than in the previous survey. In the Henry Selby re-survey[38] of the city of Oaxaca, the average number of workers per household had increased from 1.4 to 1.85. This increase was most dramatic among the poorest families, resulting in only a modest drop overall in real household income between 1977 and 1987. A similar finding both for income and for the increase in the number of household members working was obtained by Agustin Escobar and Mercedes Gonzalez de la Rocha,[39] as reported in their ongoing study of 100 families first studied in 1982. Unlike the Selby re-survey, the Escobar and Gonzalez de la Rocha sample was not randomly chosen but allowed us to follow the individual changes in labor market strategy. They reported that the largest increases in labor market participation from 1982 to 1985 (the year of their second resurvey of the households), was among adult women (15 years or more) and young men of less than 15 years. This increasing participation is mainly in informal employment. For female heads of households who increased their participation by 20 percent, five of the nine new jobs were concentrated in informal services, one in an informal workshop and three were in formal enterprises.

The Escobar and Gonzalez data indicate that this increasing household participation in the labor market is partly produced by the aggregation of new members: relatives move in and contribute their incomes or a daughter moves back with her children. Extra members only marginally increase household costs but make a considerable contribution to budgets or, as in some of the reported cases, help with domestic chores, thus releasing other members to take on paid work. The impact on overall participation rates in Mexico is, consequently, unclear. There is likely to be an increase in participation in certain categories, particularly adult women, but increases will be offset by the declines that might otherwise be expected from rising levels of educational participation.

The suggestion is that the supply of labor in the urban labor market has, in these last years, become a supply heavily oriented to informal work. The available jobs are likely to concentrate in the service sectors where intense competition and the lowest wages are likely to be found. The tendencies in the formal sector—the reduction in real wages and the feminization of the labor force—reinforce this situation. Male heads of households are decreasingly likely to earn a wage sufficient to maintain the family. In the Mercedes Gonzalez de la Rocha study,[40] male heads of household actually contributed a minority of the income by 1985, creating pressures on other members supplementing household income, including children of school age.

The impact of these trends on the educational levels of poor families is likely to be negative. This would mean an increasing segmentation of the labor market. Poor families are unlikely to educate their children sufficiently to obtain jobs in the best sectors of formal employment. In the Gabayet study, for instance, the best paid and protected female workers had a *minimum* educational level of secondary schooling.

This puts informal employment in a different light when compared to the 1970s. In that period and earlier, it served to help households *"make it"* in the city, permitting mobility to stable formal sector jobs and generating incomes that allowed families to educate their children. In the context of the 1980s, informal employment is more likely to lead to the reproduction of poverty and marginality.

The increase in female employment is marked in the informal sector as well as in the formal sector. During the crisis, categories of women workers, such as married women, have begun to enter the labor market in greater numbers.[41] Women, whether in the formal or the informal sector, earn wages substantially lower than those of men, and their incomes serve to supplement family budgets. Since male real earnings have dropped drastically, the incomes gained by women and by children are now more necessary than ever to ensure a household's economic survival. This creates a paradox. The industrial future of Jalisco requires a more educated and skilled labor force. Yet, the conditions of polarization and segmentation in the labor force create disincentives against schooling and training. It is difficult for families to have children in school when their income is needed to balance the family budget.

VI. CONCLUSION

Though we have focused on the manufacturing sector, there are some general conclusions to be drawn with respect to the prospects for economic and social development. On the positive side, we have noted the relative success of Jalisco in confronting the recession. This is due, we would argue, to the diversification of its economic activities. Commercial agriculture, livestock for consumption, forestry, tourism, and agroindustry have been important sources of employment and of industrial inputs. The state and, particularly, Guadalajara have carved a niche for themselves as locations of export-oriented industries. The proximity to the coast, good communications with the north, an adequate urban infrastructure, and a reputation for having a skilled urban labor force have attracted a variety of multinational companies, particularly in electronics. These changes have recently stimulated the creation of research and development facilities in Guadalajara aimed at product innovation and at improving the production process.

The success of Guadalajara indicates, however, some of the difficulties in the present model of development Mexico is following. Though there is employment creation, there is also what appears to be an increasing segmentation of the labor market. Though there are some opportunities for skilled workers in small-scale enterprises, the major labor market for this class of worker is in modern enterprises wherever they are found—mainly in the north and perhaps the United States. There is the possibility that the rest of Jalisco's urban labor market is becoming increasingly self-contained, with little movement from, for example, the informal sector to the modern sector. The decline in the conditions of work in small-scale enterprises and their increasing volatility mean that this source of skilled training will be less available in future. This situation does not augur well for stimulating the expansion of modern enterprise jobs since it is likely to act as a depressant on educational levels and lead to bottlenecks in the supply of skilled labor.

The impact of this pattern of development on migration patterns is difficult to forecast. There is little reason to think that migration, particularly to the United States, will diminish as a result of the type of economic growth that we have described. Remember that the rate of increase in industrial employment remains substantially below the rate of increase in the economically active population. Urban-to-urban migration, particularly to the northern border, is likely to increase.

If Jalisco is to retain and attract population, it will need, we suspect, to revitalize its small- and medium-scale sector of industrial employment. Part of this revitalization will need to take place outside of the metropolitan area of Guadalajara. To achieve this, a change in bank and government credit policy will be necessary, together with incentives for decentralization and the promotion of cooperation among small- and medium-scale producers, particularly in respect to technical and other services, including information, sales and purchases of inputs. The small- and medium-scale sectors can make an important contribution to exports and to supplying the large-scale modern enterprises, provided that aid is given to improve the technical level of production.

NOTES

1. By informal, we mean the unprotected (by contract and social security) sector of employment which is mainly, but not exclusively found, in small-scale enterprises and among self-employed and unremunerated workers. The informal/informal distinction is a continuum rather than a sharp contrast between types of employment and types of enterprises. Thus, even the largest enterprises will have some unprotected employees. Also, even very small enterprises will often be registered for fiscal purposes even when they do not provide social security for their workers. The applicability of the concept to the Mexican context is discussed in Bryan Roberts, "Employment Structure, Life Cycle and Life Chances: Formal and Informal Sectors in Guadalajara," in *The Informal Economy: Comparative Studies in Advanced and Third World Countries*, eds. Alejandro Portes, Manuel Castells, and Lauren Benton (Baltimore: Johns Hopkins University Press, 1989), pp. 41–59.

2. Carlos Alba, "La Industrialización en Jalisco: Evolución y Perspectivas," in *Cambio Regional, Mercado de Trabajo y Vida Obrera en Jalisco*, ed. Guillermo de la Peña and Agustín Escobar (Guadalajara: El Colegio de Jalisco, 1986), pp. 89–146; Agustín Escobar, *Con el Sudor de tu Frente: Mercado de Trabajo y Clase Obrera en Guadalajara* (Guadalajara: El Colegio de Jalisco, 1986); Roberts (1989); Peter Gregory, *The Myth of Market Failure* (Baltimore: Johns Hopkins University Press, 1986).

3. Carlos Alba, "La Industria de Guadalajara Ante la Crisis," *Revista Encuentro* 3 (1986), pp. 23–49; Patricia Arias and Bryan Roberts, "The City in Permanent Transition: the Consequences of a National System of Industrial Specialization," in *Capital and Labour in the Urbanized World*, ed. J. Walton (Beverly Hills, California: Sage, 1985), pp. 149–175.

4. Jesus Arroyo, *El Abandono Rural* (Guadalajara: Universidad de Guadalajara, 1989), Table 16.

5. Arroyo, *Abandono Rural*, Table 16.

6. Manuel García y Griego, "Emigration as a Safety Valve for Mexico's Labor Market: A Post-IRCA Approximation," in Georges Vernez, ed., *Immigration and International Relations*, Program for Research on Immigration Policy, The Rand Corporation and the Urban Institute, Santa Monica, 1989, pp. 115–134.

7. The 1989 survey is a representative survey of all manufacturing industry in the state of Jalisco. It consists of a stratified sample of large, medium and small-scale enterprises of approximately 1050 cases. We would like to thank the Commission for the study of International Migration and Cooperative Economic Development for the financial support that has helped us to carry out the survey. The present article uses a subset of the responses to the survey—those from large enterprises of over 100 workers. The enterprises in this sub-set employ just over 30,000 workers or approximately 15 percent of the registered industrial workforce of Jalisco.

8. Roberts, 1989.

9. Ignacio Vizcaya Canales, *Los Orígenes de la Industrialización en Monterrey: 1867–*

1920 (Monterrey: Librería Technológica, SA 1971); Mario Cerutti, *Burguesía y Capitalismo en Monterrey: 1859–1910* (México, D.F.: Claves Latinoamericanas, 1983).

10. Secretaría de Programación y Presupuesto (SSP), *La Ocupación Informal en Areas Urbanas 1976* (Mexico, D.F.: SSP, 1979).

11. Agustín Escobar, *Con el Sudor de tu Frente: Mercado de Trabajo y Clase Obrera en Guadalajara* (Guadalajara: El Colegio de Jalisco, 1986).

12. Carlos Alba and Dirk Kruijt, *Los Empresarios y la Industria de Guadalajara* (Guadalajara: El Colegio de Jalisco, 1988).

13. Hugo Soll, "Transfer, Labor, Capital Intensity, and Capital Utilization Rates: a Study of Industry in Guadalajara, Mexico," (Ph.D. Dissertation, University of Texas, 1966).

14. Fernando Gonzalez and Carlos Alba, "Cúpulas Empresariales y Poderes Regionales en Jalisco," *Cuadernos de Difusión Científica 14* (1989), Table 2.

15. Carlos Alba and Dirk Kruijt, *Los Empresarios y la Industria de Guadalajara* (Guadalajara: El Colegio de Jalisco, 1988).

16. Economic Commission for Latin America and the Caribbean (ECLAC), "The Dynamics of Social Deterioration in Latin America and the Caribbean in the 1980s," Reference Document LC/G. 1557. Santiago de Chile: ECLAC, May 1989.

17. ECLAC, 1989.

18. IMSS (Instituto Mexicano de Seguridad Social), *Análisis de Asegurados Permanentes por División y Grupo de Actividad Económica* (México, D.F.: Departamento de Estadística, Jefatura de Planeación Financiera y Programación, 1983–1987).

19. International Labour Office (ILO), *World Labour Report 1989*, (Geneva: ILO, 1989).

20. INEGI (Instituto Nacional de Estadística, Geografía y Informática), *XI Censo Industrial, 1981* (Aguascalientes, México: INEGI, 1988). Also *Censos Económicos 86: Resultados Oportunos del Estado de Jalisco* (Guadalajara: INEGI, 1989).

21. Patricia Arias, "La Pequeña Empresa en el Occidente Rural," *Estudios Sociológicos* 6 (1988): 405–436.

22. Agustín Escobar, "The Rise and Fall of an Urban Labour Market: Economic Crisis and the Fate of Small Workshops in Guadalajara, Mexico," *Bulletin of Latin American Research*, 7, 2 (1988): 183–205.

23. Escobar, The Rise and Fall of Market, 183–205, and Escobar, "The Manufacturing Workshops of Guadalajara and their Labour Force: Crisis and Reorganization (1982–1985)," Texas Papers on Mexico, 88–05, Mexican Center, University of Texas at Austin, 1988.

24. Nacional Financiera, *La Economía Mexicana en Cifras* (México, D.F.: Décima Edición, 1988).

25. Carlos Alba, "La Industrialización en Jalisco: Evolución y Perspectivas," in Guillermo de la Peña and Agustín Escobar, *Cambio Regional, Mercado de Trabajo y Vida Obrera en Jalisco* (Guadalajara: El Colegio de Jalisco, 1986), pp. 89–146.

26. Luisa Gabayet, "Women in Transnational Industry: the Case of the Electronic Industry in Guadalajara, Mexico," Texas Papers on Mexico, Mexican Center, University of Texas at Austin, 1989.

27. Carlos Alba, "La Industria de Guadalajara Ante la Crisis," *Revista Encuentro 3*, 2: 23–49.

28. Bernardo González-Aréchiga and R. Barajas, "Las Maquiladoras: Ajuste Estructural y Desarollo Regional," *Documentos de Trabajo* (Mexico, D.F.: Fundación Friedrich Ebert, 1988).

29. Jorge Carrillo, "The Restructuring of the Automobile Industry of Mexico: Adjustment Policies and Labor Implications," Texas Papers on Mexico 89–07. Mexican Center, University of Texas at Austin, 1989.

30. Jorge Carillo and Alberto Hernández, *Mujeres Fronterizas en la Industria Maquiladora* (Mexico, D.F.: Sep Cultura/Cefnomex, 1985).

31. INEGI (Instituto Nacional de Estadística, Geografía y Informática), *10 Años de Indicadores Económicos y Sociales de México* (Mexico, D.F.: INEGI, 1987).

32. Wilson, Patricia, "The New Maquiladoras: Flexible Production in Low Wage Regions," Texas Papers on Mexico 89–01, Mexican Center, University of Texas at Austin, 1989.

33. Guy Standing, "Global Feminisation Through Flexible Labour," *Labour Market Analysis and Employment Planning*, Working Paper No. 31 (Geneva: International Labour Office, 1989).

34. Departaménto de Programación y Desarrollo del Estado de Jalisco (DEPRODE). *La Situación Industrial de Jalisco, 5 Tomos* (Guadalajara: DEPRODE, 1982).

35. Gabayet, *Women in Industry*.

36. INEGI (Instituto Nacional de Estadística, Geografía y Informática), *Encuesta Piloto sobre el Sector Informal: Documento Metodológico, Presentación de Tabulados y Breve Análisis* (México, D.F.: INEGI/Orstom, 1989).

37. Agustín Escobar and Bryan Roberts, "Urban Stratification, the Middle Classes, and Economic Change in Mexico," Texas Papers on Mexico, 89–04, Mexican Center, University of Texas at Austin, 1989.

38. Henry Selby, A. Murphy, and S. Lorenzen, *Urban Life in Mexico: Coping Strategies of the Poor Majority* (Austin: University of Texas Press, 1990).

39. Agustín Escobar and Mercedes Gonzalez de la Rocha, "Crisis and Adaptation: Households of Guadalajara," Texas Papers on Mexico 88–04, Mexican Center, University of Texas at Austin, 1988.

40. Mercedes Gonzalez de la Rocha, *Los Recursos de la Pobreza: Familias de Bajos Ingresos de Guadalajara* (Guadalajara: El Colegio de Jalisco/CIESAS, 1986).

41. Gonzalez de la Rocha, *Los Recursos*.

10

Privatization, Employment and Migration

William Glade

I. INTRODUCTION

After a few years of flirtation, the Mexican government of President Salinas seems finally to have embraced the policy of privatization. The previous coyness of this and its predecessor administration is widely attributed to several factors, among them the ichnographic status accorded public enterprises by the Mexican intelligentsia and the intimate historical association forged in the railway and petroleum nationalizations in the late 1930s between state intervention and national sovereignty. This association, which was buttressed by an aggressive use of intervention to effect sweeping land reform and to establish a state-owned banking system that in many respects overshadowed the privately owned banks, was subsequently extended in the nationalization of the electricity industry and a concomitant promotion of rural electrification.

All this has given the creation of parastatal firms a strongly populist political resonance. The populist character of this historical association was undoubtedly reinforced further by the quite literal use of the railways as vehicles of revolution, and by the connection between the petroleum nationalization and a bitter labor dispute that ultimately pitted foreign investors against both the labor provisions of the constitution of 1917 and the very authority of the federal courts.

There has been more to it than that, however. Long before the economic leadership of the state was enshrined in the constitution by the *Estado Rector* amendment promulgated during the de la Madrid administration, the state had begun to function as the primordial force in Mexico's economic modernization. The state offered employment to a rising class of professionals (and their politician allies), as well as investment opportunities to the slowly expanding number of national capitalists. An early study, *Industrial Revolution in Mexico* by Sanford Mosk,[1] confirmed what an even earlier student of Mexican development, Frank Tannenbaum, had caught in his interpretive net: namely, the basic compatibility of interventionism, framed by the 1917 Constitution, with the rise of a national bourgeoisie.[2]

II. MEXICAN GOVERNMENT INTERVENTION AND CONTROLS

Three further elements must be kept in mind about the Mexican brand of interventionism to fully appreciate what is involved in dismantling it. First, the distribution of patronage and other material favors through the far-flung apparatus of the state gave the Mexican government an enormous advantage in orchestrating a political equilibrium that was un-rivaled in Latin America for its solidity and longevity. Both direct and indirect intervention were so effectively employed to sustain this equilibrium of interests and regions that other harsher measures, of the sort commonly employed by non-competing regimes elsewhere, were seldom necessary—and never on the scale that has become so depressingly routine in the twentieth century. Thanks to the amplitude of state regulation and the network of public enterprises, the government could use public investment, preferential pricing, state purchasing and regulated relationships to favor almost any group or region that might be needed to shore up the political structure on which the regime historically rested.

Given the damage that political instability has inflicted on most of the Latin American economies in recent decades, the benefits of this mechanism are not to be taken lightly. There can be little doubt that this system of building constituencies enabled the government to establish a stable economic framework that avoided the stop-and-go disturbances that have so plagued policy making elsewhere. In addition, the government could follow macroeconomic policies that created a stable environment in which private decision makers could make the most of the signals being generated by a government-shaped market. For a very lengthy period, fiscal policy was fixed on the aim of promoting a steady rate of growth, and monetary policy was conducive to reasonable price stability, at least by Latin American standards. The external financial situation was also generally manageable. Households, enterprise managers and foreign investors were all encouraged to make the most of their assets, and they evidently did this until the system began to come unglued in the 1970s, due to intersectoral imbalances and other problems that were detectable already in the 1960s.

The cost of this institutional equilibrium, however, was an apparatus of intervention that grew increasingly unwieldy and expensive to maintain. Leaving aside the myriad forms of indirect intervention, one could, at the peak of the period of *rectoria estatal,* or state economic guidance, count well over a thousand state-owned enterprises. These ranged from the huge Petróleos Mexicanos (PEMEX) oil company, steel mills, and the entire commercial banking sector to hotels and restaurants, a nightclub, several chains of movie theatres, soft drink bottlers and a bicycle factory. Ultimately, this sprawling complex of public enterprises lost all coherence, for despite occasional moves to reorganize the parastatal sector to allow for better oversight, public authority was never able to impose real administrative and economic discipline on this organizational leviathan. Operating deficits mounted and were permitted to run on for years, sometimes as a matter of explicit policy, and both internal and external borrowing were pursued by some of the firms as a matter of course.

Between 1977 and 1982, these public enterprises accounted for at least half of the mushrooming Mexican deficit.

In reckoning the costs of the parastatal sector, one must move well beyond the redundant labor force and spiraling payrolls, the materials waste, and other micro-level managerial inefficiencies in production. Since the efficiency of the public and parastatal sector was never, in any comprehensive way, regularly tested and verified, and since enterprises, once started, usually continued to function on the basis of constituencies of their own, government was unable, or unwilling, to exercise the management skill required to shift resources from low-priority activities to new, more productive priorities. At the same time, the widespread reliance on subsidies, overregulation and excessive protection for favored sectors meant that in time the private sector, too, was subject to a growing accumulation of low-priority activities. The stickiness of the resource transfer system that characterized the public and parastatal sectors was mirrored—albeit probably in a less pronounced way—by the private sector in an increasingly politicized and increasingly ratcheted market economy. This economy avoided the constant on-going verification the competitive market is supposed to provide.

Second, the shortcomings of this system of economic management were not obvious at a political level for a very long time. On the contrary, the half-century of aggregate growth that was associated with the Mexican policy mix constituted a world record that strengthened the hand of the political leadership in dealing with those who advocated alternative policies. Indeed, the Mexican experience—and in lesser measure the Brazilian one (to say nothing of the Japanese, Taiwanese and Korean experiences)—argued strongly against any facile acceptance of the kind of market economy prescriptions that have been proffered of late in such an unqualified form. The fortuitous spurt of growth that came with the oil boom of the 1970s rescued the system, for a time, from the critical scrutiny that might have occurred had the OPEC countries not succeeded in running up the price of oil so much and had PEMEX geologists not succeeded in making such extraordinarily rich finds in just this period.

Indeed, during the heyday of this bonanza, which poured both new spending power and new borrowing capacity directly into the public sector, policymakers even toyed with models that would have accentuated the statist features of the Mexican economy even more. Though this current of opinion did not, in the long run, carry the day, it did succeed, before time ran out, in nationalizing the entire commercial banking sector. In addition, in what was quite possibly an even greater policy error, investment rules were upset as exchange controls were imposed and a considerable portion of the value of dollar-denominated bank deposits were confiscated by converting them to pesos at a penalty rate.

By the time the end of the expansion came and the Mexican economy entered the protracted crisis of the 1980s, the global proportions of that crisis probably spared the economic policy mix, for a short while longer, the searching and fundamental critique it had long merited. Given the universality of economic adversity, it took some time to sort out what could be attributed to general conditions that were exogenous to the Mexican system and what circumstances were the product of mistaken Mexican policies.

Third, state economic guidance came to be viewed by the general public as a major assurance of benefits for organized labor and, through an erroneous synecdoche, for the working class as a whole. This belief, too, has contributed to the prevailing policy preference for a prominent role for parastatal companies. While one could cynically argue that this preference has been grounded more on the distribution of economic rent than on conviction, there is no doubt that it very sharply constrained, at least until recently, the development options available to the government. A key feature of the system underscores the point: namely, the strategic position of public (including parastatal) employees—who are, after all, prime beneficiaries of direct intervention—in the constituency structure of the ruling party.

In a recent survey, Peter Accolla has noted the general opposition of organized labor to privatization drives in Latin America, an opposition that has been particularly sharp in Argentina where the Confederación General de Trabajadores (CTG) is strong and closely allied to the Peronist party.[3] In Mexico the situation is not altogether dissimilar. The most notable difference is that the labor-related political party, the PRI, (Partido Revolucionario Institutional) has been in office for over half a century. The chief Mexican labor organization, the Confederación de Trabajadores Mexicanos (CTM), is neither as autonomous nor as strong as the CTG, but it is one of the largest labor centrals in Latin America. Further, of its constituent units, several of the strongest—the teachers union (the largest labor union in Latin America), the public employees union, the oil workers union, the electrical workers union, the railway workers union, the social security workers union, and, since 1982, the bank clerks union—are all ensconced in the public sector, and their rank-and-file are dependent on the vigor of public spending programs for employment prospects. Many are lodged, organizationally speaking, in the labor section of the PRI, but some are key players in the section of the party set up to represent the popular classes. Most notorious is the case of the oil workers union: the union officialdom had at its disposition, until quite recently when the long-time boss was ousted, an ample and well-financed patronage network of its own, supported by funds siphoned off from the coffers of the nationalized petroleum industry. It stretches the imagination to believe, although corroborating evidence is still scant, that the oil workers union was the sole labor organization profiting, as an organization, from its connections into parastatal spending.

In short, as a matter of self-interest, unionized Mexican labor, arrogating to itself the function of speaking for the whole working class, has traditionally operated as a powerful constituency for governmental expansion. In recent years, accordingly, it has operated as a particularly vocal opponent of programs to reform the state sector. Consider, for a moment, the customary elements of policy reform: the reduction of tariffs and other trade controls, the divestiture of state-owned enterprises, the freeing of agricultural prices to vary with changing supply and demand conditions, reduction of the budget deficit, reduction of the consumer demand for imports, the move toward market-determined interest rates to maintain positive real interest rates and thereby ensure the efficient intermediation of savings and investment, braking the rate of growth in the money supply, and eliminating the over-valued exchange rate of the peso. Almost all of these could be seen as having a short-run negative impact on the government and parastatal workers' standard of living, which is to say, on the most sizable and most articulate segment of the organized working class.

In addition, the drive to deregulate and decontrol also reduces the power (and perhaps the informal profits) of those who occupy strategic administrative positions, adding further to the ranks of those who oppose structural readjustment. Fearful of the impact of trade liberalization on Mexico's historically protected manufacturing sector, still other portions of the labor movement (those producing traded goods) have come out against economic restructuring. This is also true of some unions in fields subject to deregulation, such as the trucking industry, where decentralization was initiated only in 1989. These groups have been quite vocal. Much of the intelligentsia—ideologically engaged academics, journalists, commentators, etc.—has, with interventionism as its historic talisman, rushed to the defense of the status quo ante, providing arguments to complement labor's political criticisms with respect to privatization.

For that matter, the business community itself has been divided. All firms, presumably, would have an interest in, say, the improved telecommunications that private investment and management might provide. Many firms, confronting an unprecedented measure of import competition, would have a direct interest in liberalizing national computer policies because of their effects on downstream users. By the same token, most metalworking firms would see the shutdown of a high-cost parastatal siderurgical industry and the free importation of iron and steel as prerequisite to their own ability to withstand foreign competition. But the firms already protected in their production of computers, the sheltered producers of iron and steel, and many other firms—e.g., those subsidized by cheap electric power rates and/or low petroleum prices, those that have enjoyed access to preferential interest rates, low freight charges, and so on, and the host of others who have operated securely behind the scene of a protective trade policy—have been reluctant to push for privatization. Meanwhile, investors, who have had plenty to do in their scramble for survival amidst economic crisis, have shown at best only a mild and somewhat fitful interest in acquiring firms the government might put up for sale. Such firms are often plagued by inefficient management, archaic technology and sweetheart labor contracts.

Even in government, the recognition, as Louis Mark long ago pointed out,[4] that parastatals have traditionally enjoyed favorable access to the international lending institutions, from whom future capital transfers are still anticipated, has tempered the enthusiasm for selling off the chief collateral these lenders have found attractive. Meanwhile, parastatal managers, like managers in private sector companies, have shown notably little enthusiasm for embarking onto the uncertain territory that lies ahead when a change of ownership occurs. Thus, despite the slow-down the crisis occasioned in its expansion and technological up-grading program, the managers of Teléfonos de México, a company in which the government holds 51 percent of the shares but which was private before 1972, could report as late as 1985 that there was no discussion of privatizing the company and that the management was satisfied to remain a mixed enterprise. With at least 150,000 shareholders, Teléfonos de México was, at the time, the most widely traded stock on the Mexican stock exchange, so that it would have been a relatively easy matter to increase its degree of privatization.

III. EMPLOYMENT ANXIETIES

The immediate impact of privatization on employment is largely, but not altogether, a matter for inference. There is, for example, a general impression of overstaffing, which is borne out by international comparisons of employment/output ratios in industries where the technical co-efficients of production are relatively fixed: e.g., petroleum and petrochemicals, iron and steel, electric power, railways, telecommunications. Thanks to its inflated payroll and to union related graft and corruption (e.g., kickbacks on the assignment of noncompetitive contracts), the operating costs of PEMEX take 95 cents of each dollar of sales, far above the industry norm. Similar evidence of overstaffing exists for other branches of production in the parastatal sector.[5] Presumably, a program of economic rectification in these would necessitate laying off redundant workers.

Some privatizations, it is true, have not been associated with major changes in employment levels: such, for example, was the case in the divestiture of the Hotelera Nacional. Similarly, the sale that began in 1984 of some $485 million of corporate shares the government had acquired when it nationalized the commercial banks in September, 1982 involved no significant change in employment in the 339 companies whose stock was involved in the sale. These companies included financial services firms such as insurance companies, stock brokerage companies, venture capital firms, and investment banking operations, along with hotels, department stores, chemical and heavy-equipment manufacturers, and even Mexican affiliates of a number of U.S. companies such as Anderson, Clayton and Company, Deere and Company, Kimberly-Clark, and Union Carbide.

Although the former owners of the nationalized banks were given the first option to purchase the shares owned by their banks, these companies had remained under essentially private, or at least unchanged, management during the interim in which the nationalized banks held the shares—a more than 25 percent interest in a third or so of the cases. The altered ownership period had, in these instances, been too brief to have had any noticeable impact on company payrolls. For different reasons, it would appear, though clear evidence is not at hand, that the seven or so "privatized" firms acquired by the CTM, including the Aeromexico airline company, did not change employment levels much when they were added to the portfolio of some 386 enterprises already owned by the CTM.

On the other hand, the closing in 1986 of the 83-year-old and technologically obsolete Fundidora Monterrey, Latin America's oldest integrated iron and steel mill, represented an extreme form of privatization or marketization. This threw some 8,000 workers out of jobs in the mill itself and brought unemployment to another 4,000 workers in Aceros Planos, an affiliated steel rolling plant. (Founded as a private company in 1903, the Fundidora had become part of the government's SIDERMEX steel conglomerate in the mid-1970s after a series of financial crises had forced government bailouts.) In the same industry and same conglomerate enterprise, the government's Altos Hornos steel mill announced, in 1989, an ambitious program of simulated privatization (i.e., the operation of public enterprises in accordance with commercial performance criteria) that involved a substantial investment to increase production capacity and a reduction in personnel of some 4,500 over the course of the ensuing year.

When Renault shut down the Vehículos Automotores Mexicanos and Renault de México plants it had acquired from the Mexican government, these also represented a net loss of employment. When eight of the 51 sugar mills the government owned as of 1987 were sold in the following year (to two groups of cane growers, two beverage manufacturers, and four other sugar producers who were seeking to enlarge their holdings), there is at least a strong presumption that some paring of the work force occurred, for redundant labor had been a conspicuous feature of the government-owned industry. Still other jobs were lost when the government, in 1988, dissolved eight fishing enterprises that formed part of the parastatal fishing company. Some negative impact on employment also came about with the dissolution of assorted urban development companies and a miscellany of other firms, mostly of small and medium size. It would, therefore, seem reasonable to anticipate a significant shrinkage of the parastatal labor force if other noncompetitive operations were liquidated in the course of subjecting parastatals to the full discipline of the market.

Smaller numbers of workers may well have been discharged with the liquidation or consolidation and merger of the numerous public trust funds, or *fideicomisos*, a type of state enterprise that proliferated to an extraordinary extent in the 1970s. Some of the functionaries in these, as in other shut-down parastatals, may actually have been reabsorbed elsewhere in the bureaucracy, however. Certainly this has been the case when an alleged divestiture has merely transferred operations to other levels of government, a practice the federal government has persisted in including under the privatization rubric. Other factors complicate ascertaining the exact impact of privatization on employment. For example, most of the 23 firms divested in 1983–84 were relatively small, and of the 236 state entities slated for divestment in 1985, only a fraction consisted of actual operating enterprises. The government has had a habit of including nonoperating or paper enterprises in the census of firms subject to privatization.

According to one estimate, the total number of firms put up for *desincorporación* accounted for no more than three percent of the parastatal sector's production in 1983. Small as it is, this percentage may in fact overstate the case, so that even smaller amounts of employment have been touched by the program to streamline the parastatal sector. Exact figures on this, as on so may other aspects, are virtually impossible to come by, for the Mexican privatization program has been nothing if not opaque. Leaving aside the divergent estimates of how many firms the parastatal sector included as of, say, the beginning of the de la Madrid administration, the lack of transparency in the process of implementing privatization has come from several sources: obscurity in the announcements of how many firms have actually been privatized in some recognizable form of that process (as contrasted with relatively frequent announcements of batches of companies that are said to be on the block for sale), a lack of clarity in specifying how much of mixed enterprises will remain in government hands when some shares are sold to the private sector, the fragmentation of procedures for handling privatizations, and conflicting statistics on the process in reports from different official sources. The obfuscation, it is widely believed, has been deliberate—a means of diverting attention from a politically controversial process.

To be sure, there have been a good many cases of clearly identified privatizations besides the instances noted above: e.g., the Garci-Crespo mineral water company and its affiliated enterprises, the large Mexicana de Cobre copper mining concern, the Atenquique paper company (to an international finance corporation, or IFC, group), Mexicana Airlines, Mexicana Acido Sulfúrico, and so on. And in some episodes, most notably the aborted privatization of the Cananea copper mining company, the failure of financing arrangements frustrated completion of a transaction that was clearly intended to be effected (and which in some sources was *reported* as a completed deal). Yet information on employment is seldom available even in these major cases, though in the Cananea case the failure to privatize turned out to be but a prelude to the bankruptcy and closure of the concern—with, presumably, the loss, for the time being, of nearly 4,000 jobs. The closing of the enterprise was a particularly dramatic step, given the high symbolic value of Cananea as the birthplace of the modern Mexican labor movement. The possibility remained that the company, scaled down in its labor commitments, would be reorganized and reopened under private auspices.

The closest thing to an overall employment impact study is the comprehensive sample study by Juan Perez Escamilla, prepared for the Ministry of Finance. In this, Perez Escamilla finds a general tendency for privatization to result in reductions in employment, though the decline has varied considerably from firm to firm, and in some cases there has been an actual gain.[6] As a general rule, moreover, it appears that there has also been a tendency to substitute temporary workers for permanent employees so as to give the firm greater flexibility in adapting to changing economic circumstances. In any case, inconclusive as the record from Mexico is, this seems to confirm that there is indeed a basis for labor's fears that privatization may trim the payroll, at least in the short run.

Given the incompleteness of the Mexican record, the experience of Chile, the Latin American country with the longest record of privatization, is suggestive. At the same time, the implications of the Chilean experience cannot be transferred completely to Mexico, due to the decidedly superior management of the parastatal sector through the Frei administration of the 1970s, and to the exceptional period of politico-economic change that ensued, albeit briefly, with the coming to office of the Marxist Unidad Popular government toward the end of 1970.

Examining the course of Chilean employment over a multi-year period that included both aggressive interventionism and privatizing retrenchment, Jorge Marshall reports that the number of workers in the 36 main public enterprises rose from 138,746 in 1970, the last year they were reasonably well managed, to 164,618 in 1974 at the end of the Allende debacle, during which so many political hangers-on were put on the parastatal payrolls. Some privatization brought the total back down to 123,474 in 1979, though this drop cannot be attributed entirely to privatization. Neither can the 1983 figure of 95,587 which was reached after further privatization.[7] The latter figure reflects the onset of the crisis that hit Latin America in 1982, the 1979 drop reflects not only privatization but also the decline in excess employment that resulted from subjecting all firms, both public and private, to a greater measure of market discipline, thanks to the liberalization program that was enacted in the post-Allende period.

Confirmation of the Marshall findings comes from another set of studies which approach the question from a somewhat different angle. In a comparative study of privatization in Chile (1974–83) and Argentina (1976–81), Rolf Luders and Dominique Hachette found further evidence to confound any simple association between employment and privatization.[8] While in both cases employment declined in the privatized firms, it also declined in firms that had been private all along and, most tellingly, in the state enterprises that remained after divestiture.[9] For Chile, where privatized firms reduced their personnel by 12 percent, private firms cut theirs by 30 percent and public enterprises reduced theirs by 46 percent, due to their being subjected to market constraints. In Argentina, employment in public sector enterprises likewise dropped, at least relative to activity levels; the decrease totalled about 30 percent. But here, too, privatization was not the only factor affecting employment.

At the same time, it must be noted, the aggregates were indicating a general rise in unemployment in much of Latin America, regardless of whether or not privatization had been embraced. It does not appear that, where unemployment was on the rise, privatization as such made a very substantial contribution, even in the short run, to the larger process. Within some countries, moreover, it is possible to find instances in which privatization has served to put employment on a more sustainable footing, and even instances where it served to expand employment at the microeconomic level. What should be said is that in all the cases, even in Chile, where privatization has been pursued more systematically and for a longer period, the *immediate* employment effects of privatization have been overcome by larger employment determining forces.

The comparative figures from different countries suggest that the rectification of economic policy that Chile carried out—which included a comprehensive, if evolving, program of privatization—eventually allowed Chile to achieve employment gains far stronger, and a rate of growth in aggregate output much higher, than did other Latin American countries during the latter half of the 1980s. In the process, debt conversion was facilitated: e.g., the purchase by Security Pacific of a 19 percent share of Chilectra Generación from Corporación de Fomento (CORFO), the government's industrial investment bank; the purchase by Continental Bank of a slightly smaller minority share in the same company and a 31 percent share of a sugar company, Industria Azucarera Nacional (IANSA) that was also being privatized; the purchase by Banker's Trust of one of the newly privatized pension funds. One of the old-line companies that dated back to the pre-World War I nitrate boom, Sociedad Química y Minera de Chile (SOQUIMICH), was able, thanks to privatization, to make a strong comeback through restructuring, technical and organizational modernization, intensive research and aggressive marketing.

It is, perhaps, especially revealing that seven of the most profitable 15 companies in Chile during the first half of 1989 were firms that had undergone privatization. No less revealing is the fact that the efficiently managed parastatal Corporación del Cobre (CODELCO), the giant state enterprise in the copper industry, was able to invest an average of $400 million annually from 1984 to 1989. This allowed CODELCO to keep output on the rise in the face of declining ore grades and ore-crushing problems, with the expectation that production costs could be kept from rising for the next several years. For that matter—and no little irony can be found in the fact—because of the strengthening of the Chilean economy that ensued from the new macroeconomic policy framework, the positive export results, privatization and the success in managing the nation's foreign debt, Chile was the only Latin American country that found itself in a position to mount a major public investment program at the end of the 1980s.

IV. THE COURSE OF MEXICAN PRIVATIZATION

Despite some discussion in the 1970s about the possibilities of privatization and sundry attempts under Echeverriá and Lopez Portillo to reorganize an exuberantly expanding parastatal sector, very little was actually done until the mid-1980s. De la Madrid promised a reform and reduction of the reportedly 1,155 state-owned firms, announcing that 755 would be disposed of in one fashion or another. He began with the return to private ownership (in exchange for indemnification bonds issued for the nationalized banks) of the 339 companies that had been acquired in 1982 as part of the investment portfolio of the banks that were nationalized. These were not counted in the 755 target total. These reprivatized bank holdings included 142 industrial firms, 115 service companies, 13 construction enterprises and, interestingly, 69 nonbanking financial intermediaries.

Periodically, there have been expectations—or hopes—that these financial intermediaries might be allowed to develop as a new private sector banking network, but such has not come to pass. Instead, approximately one-third of the shares of the nationalized banks was put up for sale (though not all to private investors), and from time to time the government has expressed its intention of shaping up banking operations for greater efficiency. Some reorganization of the sector did, in fact, take place in the 1980s, though private commercial banking was never readmitted.

By the end of 1988, when Salinas took office, only 136 of the government's companies had actually been sold (not all to private owners) and 70 (of the 80 once planned) had been merged with other parastatals or transferred to other governmental levels. It was not revealed how many of the 395 companies supposedly marked for liquidation were, in fact, closed down. Although 13 parastatals were reportedly sold soon after Salinas took office, it must be observed that, privatization objectives notwithstanding, the de la Madrid administration also established several dozen new parastatals during its years in office. To put the matter in perspective, the assets of all the 755 parastatals originally identified as candidates for *desincorporación* represented only ten percent of the assets of the parastatal sector, and a fair number of the entities in the program were either paper companies, small trust funds, commissions or advisory boards—not public enterprises in the usual understanding of that term.

Several points must be kept in mind about Mexican privatization. First, as was alluded to earlier, there is a disconcerting ambiguity about the process, from beginning to end. Several "official" tallies have been published regarding the total number of public enterprises before privatization began. These different tallies vary considerably, and there is reason to believe that all of them understate the actual number. No less disconcerting is the unsystematic way the government has reported the progress of privatization since 1982. No precise master list has ever been issued, and the actions actually taken, as contrasted with those announced as to be taken, have never been clearly differentiated from each other. Therefore, the record of what exactly has occurred has largely been left for inference and conjecture. When it comes to the issue of transparency, the Mexican process is 180 degrees removed from the Chilean privatization procedures. This alone would make it impossible to distinguish any direct employment effects of the program, but there is more to it than that.

As elsewhere in Latin America, a variety of forces have been operating in the Mexican labor market. Negative growth rates in 1982 and 1983 were followed by positive growth in 1984 and 1985, albeit at rates much lower than were customary for Mexico before the crisis. The following year brought renewed decline in aggregate output, while in 1987 and 1988 performance was essentially flat. Within this picture, economic liberalization and restructuring were being pushed, with a rapidity that many would have thought impossible, and the labor market experienced considerable change: growth of the informal sector, decline in manufacturing employment and a rise in underemployment. Emigration was also occurring, though the level of this was never exactly established. Under the circumstances, then, there is simply no way to sort out what effects might be attributable to privatization, especially given the studied obscurity with which the government has surrounded the program.

True, there have been verifiable cases of transfer. Some, like the aforementioned VAM and Renault de México, were sold but then were soon shut down as unsalvageable. Others were sold and still continue to operate: for example (to mention only some of the most prominent cases), the Atenquique Mining Company, the Real de Angeles Silver Mining Company, Mexicana de Cobre, Hules Mexicanos and seven other chemical companies, several metalworking companies, four automotive parts manufacturers, two electrical machinery manufacturers, 19 sugar mills, several textile manufacturers and—after two failed attempts to sell it—the Mexicana Airlines (in which, however, the government retained a 40 percent holding). On the other hand, another airline, Aeroméxico, was reported as privatized, but actually a majority of its shares remain in the hands of the central bank and a government-backed airlines union. This makes Aeroméxico, at best, a bogus privatization. In a few cases, such as the joint venture for truck and bus production that General Motors signed in 1984 with Diesel Nacional, the government has relied on foreign participation to rehabilitate its holdings. In other instances, however, such as the Altos Hornos steel mill, the government has taken forthright action on its own to eliminate redundant labor in an effort to raise productivity.

Furthermore, there is simply no reliable information on the extent to which market-oriented efficiency has been instilled into the largest parastatals (simulated privatization), whose share of public sector employment is far larger than that of the firms that have been subjected to some type of privatization. The impact of changes in the operating efficiency of these giants would dwarf all that has happened so far among the firms that have been removed from public ownership, those that have been liquidated, and those that have been consolidated or merged. Neither is there comprehensive information available on what has been happening in the numerous joint ventures that are subsumed under the category of semiprivatization. This version of privatization has long played an important role in the Mexican economy, particularly though not exclusively among the ventures in which the highly regarded Nacional Financiera has invested. There are indications that a fair number of other firms in which the state has an equity interest, such as some of those owned in part by the government's banking institutions, have also benefited from the infusion of private sector capital, management and technology, including private investment of foreign origin.

During November 1989, in fact, Nacional Financiera and Banamex, both leading parastatal financial institutions, concluded agreements with the European Community to promote small and medium-sized joint ventures. These would include both new projects and the expansion or modernization of existing companies. Only a month earlier, the government also announced its intention to sell part of its majority stake in Teléfonos de México, thereby reducing the state's share to a minority interest, and to eliminate the company's monopoly in some service areas. Bids from both Mexican and foreign companies were declared welcome and the government said it might reduce its stake to zero, depending on the attractiveness of the offers received. The employment effects of all these transactions have very probably been mixed but, overall, they are quite likely to move the economy in the direction of a strengthened capacity to generate employment. Yet, as in the Chilean case, the actual employment changes that have been experienced are more properly attributable to restructuring and liberalization, and to macroeconomic swings, than to privatization as such.

V. PRIVATIZATION AND MIGRATION

The inconclusiveness of the information on the employment effects of privatization is heightened by the relative brevity of the Mexican experience with privatization. The context within which companies have left the public sector—in whole or in part—has not been conducive to vigorous expansion, except in those instances in which the output has been directed largely to the export market. The debt overhang and uncertainty over how and when the debt might be resolved has apparently served to restrain the enthusiasm of foreign capital suppliers for adding to investments in Mexico. This is true of investments in both wholly owned subsidiaries and joint ventures with local capital, either public or private, except in the special case of the *maquiladora* firms. And faced with the struggle to remain afloat amidst unaccustomed and difficult circumstances, domestic investors, too, have had all they could do, to manage the firms already in their investment portfolios without seeking out more problematic investment opportunities in the confines of the privatization program. It could be argued, however, that such divestiture as has taken place has at least preserved some jobs without need for continuing subsidy and in that sense has helped to hold workers in Mexico, but either way the numbers involved are but a tiny fraction of the nation's workforce. This being the case, it seems unwarranted to assert that privatization has either fostered or inhibited migration, thus far, in any direct and major way.

From this we need not conclude that privatization is irrelevant to the issue of employment and migration. In at least three ways, it probably contributes to raising employment over the longer run and, therefore, to stemming the tide streaming northward. In the first place, where it has been applied, privatization has strengthened the economic position of companies and, depending on their product, either put them in better shape to withstand import competition or set them up to begin to penetrate export markets. Either way, given the drive to open the economy, privatization turns out to be employment enhancing in the long run. This is the case particularly in industries that have some prospects for exporting, as in many cases the potential size of export demand is much greater than is the potential for growth in the domestic market.

Second, insofar as privatization relieves the fiscal hemorrhaging that has, through crowding out, rendered private sector capital formation so problematic, it contributes to a reactivation of the economy. Hence, privatization helps to foster a resumption of growth in domestic opportunities, particularly in higher productivity resource uses. The striking gains in job creation in Chile during the past several years provide a basis for hope that the open economy model will work even better in Mexico, where the low threshold of transport costs to major export markets serves to broaden the range of potential comparative advantage. Indeed, with savings released from deficit-absorption for private investment purposes, it appears likely that the complements between the factor endowments of Mexico and the United States, combined with low to negligible transport costs, will enable the two to cooperate in building a significant export platform for sales into third country markets.

Lastly, there is the question of alternative uses of public sector funds. When devoted to covering the deficits of capital-intensive operations in the electric power, railway, petroleum, air transport and siderurgical industries, to say nothing of telecommunications, the funds absorbed thereby go to sustain capital-intensive production functions that do relatively little for employment. In contrast, where these funds can be put on a commercial footing—even when retained as public enterprises, or sold off (thereby, as it happens, increasing portfolio choices in the securities market)—the funds once absorbed by these deficits can be put into the ordinary and much needed labor-intensive service functions of the public sector. Here, they have a much greater employment impact. More importantly in the long run, the release of resources from the thralldom of a labyrinthian parastatal sector serves to make them available for more flexible reassignment, through the private sector, as the shifting signals of the market indicate new and more productive alternative uses. For these effects to be realized, however, Mexican privatization would have to be pushed into fields as yet protected by the shibboleths of revolutionary nationalism.

To be sure, exactly the same effect could be achieved by the simulated privatization that requires public enterprises to meet the same performance criteria as market-constrained private firms. In some instances, this effect could also be achieved by the semiprivatization that forms mixed public-private firms and places them under a private management style. The lack of transparency in parastatal operations thus far, however, suggests that this is a weak reed to lean on. Veiled from public scrutiny, as they have traditionally been, the public enterprises have, in the main, been so enmeshed with a web of political compromises that gradual disengagement would appear exceedingly difficult—the more so as the roll back of indirect intervention deprives the government of alternative means of balancing the claims of strategically placed constituencies. It is this residual political function that comes to roost on the parastatal firms that remain after privatization. This, in turn, subjects the nationalized banking system to strong pressures for patterns of resource deployment that are below the optimal from an economic point of view.

Still, to the extent that traded goods are involved and the opening of the economy exposes the public enterprise producers of these to greater competition, and to the extent that the new competitive pressure on all consumers of public sector outputs impels them to demand greater efficiency in the production thereof, then there will be pressure to conform even the companies remaining in government hands to the norms of market-guided performance. It is virtually axiomatic that, to the degree that this is realized, the employment capacity of the Mexican economy will be maximized and the pressures to emigrate reduced.

This is not to say that northward migration will cease. Wage differentials that will be wide long into the foreseeable future, and beyond, will continue to beckon the flow of workers from Mexico. And the persistence of high, if mercifully falling, birth rates will ensure the supply of new jobs in Mexico will fail to match the annual increases in the labor force for years to come. Nevertheless, for all the uncertainties we have reviewed in the course of this discussion, one can reasonably conclude that, ceteris paribus, privatization should make *some* positive contribution to alleviating the pressure to head across the northern border.

NOTES

1. Sanford Mosk, *Industrial Revolution in Mexico* (Berkeley: University of California Press, 1950).

2. The Mexican twist, given Kalecki's hypothesized intermediary regime, could be considered the pioneering Latin American instance, were it not for the fact that the general policy style had been worked out earlier still, albeit far more peacefully and without the agrarian reform dimension, by the Batlle Ordoñez government of Uruguay.

3. Peter Accolla, "Caught in the Middle: a Special Study of Privatization in Latin America and Its Impact on Workers and Their Unions," Washington, D.C.: U.S. Department of Labor, 1988.

4. Louis Mark, Jr., "The Favored Status of the State Entrepreneur in Economic Development Programs," *Economic Development and Cultural Change*, vol. 7 (July 1985), pp. 422–39.

5. The most remarkable overstaffing is probably found in the petroleum industry. According to *Forbes'* 1986 estimate, as of the mid-1980s, the Shell group, the largest of the non-U.S. oil companies, had revenues of $81,791 million and 142,000 employees. The fourth largest foreign oil company, Pemex, had $20,414 million in revenues, but 149,200 employees. By early 1989, in fact, the payroll of Pemex had grown considerably regardless of the doldrums afflicting the industry—170,000 direct employees, according to some reckonings —and more if those working for Pemex contractors are counted.

6. Juan Perez Escamilla, "La venta de empresas del sector público: fundamentos, procedimientos, y resultados". México: Sec. de Hacienda, 1989.

7. Jorge Marshall, "Privatization in Chile," unpublished paper presented at Wilson Center seminar on Privatization in Theory and Practice, Washington, D.C., September 1989.

8. Dominique Hachette, "Aspects of Privatization: the Case of Chile 1974–85," Washington, D.C.: World Bank, International Discussion Paper, April 1988.

9. Dominique Hachette and Rolf Luders, "Privatization in Argentina and Chile: Lessons from a Comparison," Washington, D.C.: World Bank, Internal Discussion Paper, April 1988.

About the Editors and Contributors

Carlos Alba Vega earned his Ph.D. in sociology at the University of Paris in 1987. He was director of regional planning in the State of Jalisco's Department of Planning and Development. Since 1985, he has been the academic secretary of El Colegio de Jalisco, in Guadalajara, and a research fellow of that institute. He is currently a visiting researcher at El Colegio de México. His major publications include: (with D. Kruijt) *Los Empresarios y la Industria de Guadalajara* (1988); and *Historia y Desarrollo Industral de México* (1988).

Nellis Crigler is vice-president of Manchester Trade, Inc. She previously served as assistant director of the Council of the Americas and is coauthor with Stephen Lande of "CBI: The Bermuda Triangle of Trade?" and other articles on international trade issues. She is coeditor of the *American Export Marketer* and serves as the Washington correspondent for *Business Korea* magazine.

Ramón E. Daubón holds a B.A. from the University of Puerto Rico, an M.A. from Pennsylvania State University and a Ph.D. in economics from the University of Pittsburgh. He is the current vice president of the National Puerto Rican Coalition in Washington, D.C. He previously worked for the Inter-American Foundation and American University. He has published widely in professional journals on issues relating to Caribbean development.

María de Lourdes de la Fuente Deschamps is an economist at the Autonomous Technological Institute of México (ITAN). She wrote Chapter 6 while on leave at the Center for Economic Studies at El Colegio de México.

Sergio Díaz-Briquets is with Casals & Associates, a consulting firm in Washington, D.C. He was research director of the Commission for the Study of International Migration and Cooperative Economic Development, created by Congress. Earlier he held appointments with Duquesne University in Pittsburgh and with the Population Reference Bureau in Washington, D.C., and was a program officer with the International Development Research Centre (IDRC) in Ottawa, Canada. Díaz-Briquets has been a consultant to the U.S. Agency for International Development, the World Bank, and other international development agencies. Holder of a Ph.D. from the University of Pennsylvania, Díaz-Briquets is the author of several books on a variety of development-related topics, including *The Health Revolution in Cuba* (1983), and coauthor of *Social Change and Internal Migration* (1977). Most recently he edited *Cuban Internationalism in Sub-Saharan Africa* (1989).

William Glade is currently serving as associate director for Educational and Cultural Affairs at the United States Information Agency (USIA). He is a professor of economics at the University of Texas in Austin. Prior to joining the USIA, he was acting secretary of the Latin American Program of the Woodrow Wilson International Center for Scholars in Washington, D.C., to which he came as senior program associate in 1987. The author of numerous books and articles, Dr. Glade's research has centered on Latin American development and the role of public enterprise in development. He holds a Ph.D. in economics from the University of Texas, where he was director of the Institute of Latin American Studies from 1971 to 1986.

Alejandro Ibarra-Yunez is an associate professor of economics at the Instituto Tecnológico y de Estudios Superiores de Monterrey (ITESM) specializing in international economics, U.S.-Mexico relations, and regional economics. He has been a visiting professor at the LBJ School of Public Affairs at the University of Texas at Austin and is the author of numerous scholarly articles in the areas of trade, finance, and macroeconomic policy. Professor Ibarra studied economics at the University of the Americas and did his graduate work at the University of Michigan. He chaired the Economics Department at ITESM from 1980 to 1987.

Susan M. Kramer received a B.A. in political science from the University of Illinois at Chicago in 1987. She earned an M.P.A. from the Lyndon B. Johnson School of Public Affairs at the University of Texas at Austin in 1989. Ms. Kramer has been a contributing author to two policy research projects, *Immigration and Development in Latin America* and *The Economic Linkages of Tourism in Guerrero, Mexico* (both in press). She is currently a consultant/editor at the LBJ School of Public Affairs.

Stephen Lande, president of Manchester Trade, Inc., focuses on international trade and negotiation. He has participated in many negotiations to liberalize U.S. import barriers on steel, textiles and other products. He formerly served as an assistant U.S. trade representative and chief negotiator and was a foreign service officer in Greece and Luxembourg. He is an adjunct professor of international trade at Georgetown University and has published widely on trade issues.

Jorge F. Pérez-López is director of the Office of International Economic Affairs, Bureau of International Labor Affairs, for the U.S. Department of Labor. He received his Ph.D. in economics from the State University of New York at Albany. He has published widely in professional journals on various aspects of U.S. trade policy.

Bryan Roberts earned his Ph.D. in sociology from the University of Chicago in 1964. He served on the faculty at the University of Manchester, United Kingdom, from 1964 to 1986. In that year he moved to the University of Texas at Austin to take up the C.B. Smith, Sr., Chair in United States-Mexico Relations. His major publications include: *Organizing Strangers* (1973); *Cities of Peasants* (1978); and with Norman Long, *Miners, Peasants and Entrepreneurs* (1985).

Gregory K. Schoepfle is director of Foreign Economic Research in the Bureau of International Labor Affairs at the U.S. Department of Labor in Washington,

D.C. Dr. Schoepfle taught economics at the State University of New York at Stony Brook and at American University. He has published widely in such well-known journals as the *Journal of the American Statistical Association, Annals of Economic and Social Measurement* and *Economic Development and Cultural Change.* He holds a B.A. degree from Oberlin College and an M.S. and Ph.D. from Purdue.

Chandler Stolp is an associate professor at the LBJ School of Public Affairs, University of Texas at Austin, where he specializes in Latin American studies, applied statistics and information management. Much of his work has been in the area of health and information policy in Central America and Mexico. Dr. Stolp completed his undergraduate work in economics and engineering at Stanford University and his graduate work in public policy and social and decision sciences at Carnegie-Mellon University.

Stuart K. Tucker is a fellow at the Overseas Development Council (ODC), working on international trade policy and Latin American development issues. He has written numerous articles on international economic policy, including the linkage between the debt crisis and U.S. exports and jobs, the impact of the U.S. Caribbean Basin Initiative and U.S. agricultural trade policy.˙ He coedited *Growth, Exports, and Jobs in a Changing World Economy: Agenda 1988.* Prior to joining ODC in 1984, he was a research consultant for the Inter-American Development Bank, the Urban Institute and the Roosevelt Center for American Policy Studies.

Kurt Unger received his Ph.D. in economics from Sussex University in the United Kingdom. He is currently a professor at the Center for Economic Studies at El Colegio de México. Dr. Unger was a visiting fellow in 1988–89 at the U.S./Mexican Studies Center at the University of California at San Diego. His book *Industrial Organization and Technology Transfer in Mexican Industry* was published in 1985 and another publication entitled *Mexican Manufacturing Exports and the International Restricting of Industry: Automobiles and Chemicals* is forthcoming.

Sidney Weintraub is Dean Rusk Professor and director of the Program for U.S.-Mexico Policy Studies at the Lyndon B. Johnson School of Public Affairs at the University of Texas at Austin. He is also a Distinguished Visiting Scholar at the Center for Strategic and International Studies (CSIS). As a career diplomat (1949–1975), he was an assistant administrator of the Agency for International Development, Deputy Assistant Secretary of State for international finance and development, chief of the AID mission in Chile under the Alliance for Progress, and chief of commercial policy in the State Department. Dr. Weintraub also has authored numerous books and monographs focusing on Mexico-United States relations, including *Mexican Trade Policy and the North American Community* (1988), *Industrial Strategy and Planning in Mexico and the United States* (Westview, 1986), *Free Trade Between Mexico and the United States?* (1984), and *A Marriage of Convenience: Relations Between Mexico and the United States* (1990). He is co-editor with Luis F. Rubio and Alan D. Jones of *U.S.-Mexican Industrial Integration* (Westview, forthcoming).